The Jour. Francis Asbury

Bishop of the Methodist Episcopal Church

Francis Asbury

APPLEWOOD BOOKS
Bedford, Massachusetts

The Journal of the Rev. Francis Asbury
was originally published in
1821

ISBN: 978-1-4290-1789-3

APPLEWOOD'S
American
Philosophy AND *Religion*
SERIES

Thank you for purchasing an Applewood book. Applewood reprints America's lively classics—books from the past that are still of interest to modern readers. This facsimile was printed using many new technologies together to bring our tradition-bound mission to you. Applewood's facsimile edition of this work may include library stamps, scribbles, and margin notes as they exist in the original book. These interesting historical artifacts celebrate the place the book was read or the person who read the book. In addition to these artifacts, the work may have additional errors that were either in the original, in the digital scans, or introduced as we prepared the book for printing. If you believe the work has such errors, please let us know by writing to us at the address below.

For a free copy of our current print catalog featuring our bestselling books, write to:

APPLEWOOD BOOKS
P.O. Box 365
Bedford, MA 01730

For more complete listings, visit us on the web at:
awb.com

Prepared for publishing by HP

THE

JOURNAL

OF THE

REV. FRANCIS ASBURY,

BISHOP

OF

THE METHODIST EPISCOPAL CHURCH,

FROM

AUGUST 7, 1771, TO DECEMBER 7, 1815

—⁕⁕⁕⁕—

In Three Volumes.

—⁕⁕⁕⁕—

VOL. II,

FROM JULY 15, 1786, TO NOVEMBER 1, 1800

NEW-YORK:

PUBLISHED BY N. BANGS AND T. MASON FOR THE METHODIST
EPISCOPAL CHURCH.

➤➤❖◄◄

Abraham Paul, Printer, 182 Water-Street.

—❀❖❀—

1821.

JOURNAL

REV. FRANCIS ASBURY.

MARYLAND.—Sunday, July 15, 1786. I rest from riding. Preached on " Who hath warned you to flee from the wrath to come ?" I had sweet communion with God in the woods—my soul hath rest in the Lord.

Monday 10. Came to Old Town, and preached on 1 Tim. i. 15. ; and administered the sacrament.

Tuesday 11. I rested to look over some papers and prepare some parchments. Spent nearly a third of the day in prayer, that the Lord would go with me to the springs. O what hath God wrought for brother Jacobs and his wife since I lodged with them four years ago ! I believe from that day the Lord heard our prayers for them.

There has been a remarkable storm of hail at, and about the warm springs, by which great damage has been sustained : some of the hail, it was said, measured seven inches in circumference.

VIRGINIA.—Tuesday 13. I came to Bath ; the water made me sick. I took some pills and drank chicken-broth, and mended. I am ill in body, and dispirited. I am subject to a headach, which prevents my reading or writing much, and have no friends here ; but I desire to trust the Lord with all my concerns. Having no appointments for three weeks to come, I have concluded to stay here awhile ; and I am the more inclined so to do, as I am apprehensive my stomach wants all the healing efficacy of the waters to restore it to its proper tone.

Sunday 16. I had some divine assistance in speaking to the people under the trees, on " Lovers of pleasure more than lovers of God." In the afternoon I enlarged on " Having the form of godliness, but denying the power thereof.

Monday, Tuesday, and Wednesday. Quite weak, and considerably affected by the water.

Thursday 20. I am better. Employed in reading Mr. Harvey, and Brooks's Practice of Physic; more than ordinary in prayer, and spoke in public every other night.

Sunday 30. I spoke plainly and closely in the playhouse on "Oh! wicked man, thou shalt surely die." The people were serious : I cannot get the people to attend preaching except on the Sabbath : this evil is to be remedied only, I presume, by our getting a preach-ing-house, and preaching therein by candle light.

Saturday, August 5. I began to pack up, in hopes of moving on Monday.

Sunday 6. I had a serious, little congregation in the country. Re-turned to town, and preached at four o'clock.

A pleasing thought passed through my mind ; it was this, that I was saved from the remains of sin ; as yet, I have felt no returns thereof. I was solemnly impressed with the account of the death of poor Styor, a German, who dropped down suddenly and died. He was a man of piety, and had a gift to preach ; had a noble spirit, and sound judgment. I have spent twenty-three days at this place of wicked-ness (Bath.) We are trying what can be done towards building a house for worship : we collected something on the Sabbath for that purpose, and it appears the business is entered upon with spirit. My horse was running in the pasture last week, and hurt himself, so that I find him utterly incapable of travelling, and that I am compelled to linger here another week ; this, as it is, I am willing to do, for the sake of the people, the cause of God, and my health ; and I am dis-posed to consider it a providential call, although I should not remain, was my horse able to carry me away. I sent brother B. to my ap-pointments, and directed him when and where to appoint for me. My hopes revive here, and I trust my labour is not all in vain.

Tuesday 15. I preached for the last time during this visit, but the people showed but little affection for the word.

Capon River being full, I crossed in a canoe, and found my horse better. The cut was a deep one, but we applied a piece of bacon to the wound, bound some leather round it, and on Thursday I took my departure from this unhappy place.

Came to my old friend B. Boydstone's. I had the happiness of seeing that tender woman, his wife, who careth for the preachers as for her own soul : full oft hath she refreshed my spirit : her words, looks, and gestures, appear to be heavenly. Here I could make no stay, lest I should miss my appointments in Philadelphia ; and if so, be too late for those made in the Jerseys and New-York.

MARYLAND.—Sunday morning, Rode twenty miles to Pipe-Creek chapel, and preached to a large congregation.

Monday 21. Reached Mr. Gough's, where I spent two days : the weather was very warm ; but for one hundred miles and upwards I have had it sufficiently agreeable.

Came to Abingdon—Our college is still without a cover, and our managers, as I expected, almost out of breath. I made but little stay, but hasted on to Philadelphia, and arrived there on the twenty-sixth, Saturday.

NEW-JERSEY.—Monday 28. I came to Trenton ; and thence proceeded on to Brunswick. I was accidentally, or rather providentially, favoured with a ride in a carriage ; else, I know not how I should have proceeded on my journey. I reached New-York on the thirty-first of August, having travelled three hundred and fifty miles since I left Bath, in Virginia.

NEW-YORK.—I was taken ill, and was confined about eight days, during which time I was variously tried and exercised in mind. I spent some time in looking over my Journals, which I have kept for fifteen years back : some things I corrected, and some I expunged. Perhaps, if they are not published before, they will be after my death, to let my friends, and the world see how I have employed my time in America. I feel the worth of souls, and the weight of the pastoral charge, and that the conscientious discharge of its important duties requires something more than human learning, unwieldy salaries, or clerical titles of D. D. or even *bishop* :—the eyes of all—both preachers and people, will be opened in time.

Saturday, September 17. It was a very solemn season at the ordination of brother Dickens to the eldership. I gave the charge from 1 Tim. iii. 10, 14. In the afternoon I preached to the people from these words, " Pray for us ;" and in the evening from " The world by wisdom knew not God : it pleased God by the foolishness of preaching to save them that believe." I met the society, and opened my mind to them on various subjects.

Tuesday 20. I rose with a sense of God upon my soul.

I have been a little grieved with letters from ———— : but it is in vain to look for more than *man* in the best of men : my witness is on high ; and I shall have respect to my Great Shepherd in all things. After preaching on " The grace of our Lord Jesus Christ, and the love of God," &c. and settling some temporal matters relative to the support of the stationed preachers, I left the city and came to Elizabethtown : at seven o'clock I preached and had much liberty.

NEW JERSEY.—Friday 21. We dined at Amboy, and reached Monmouth at nigh.

Saturday 22. I preached with life and love at Leonard's : the people here appear very lifeless. I have lately been much tried and much blessed.

Tuesday 26. I had many to hear at Potter's church, but the people were insensible and unfeeling.

Wednesday 27. I met with brothers P—s and Budd ; we sailed over the bay to the sea, for the benefit of the air.

Thursday 28. Since this day week we have rode about one hundred and fifty miles over dead sands, and among a dead people, and a long space between meals.

Friday 29. I preached in a close, hot place, and administered the sacrament ; I was almost ready to faint. I feel fatigued and much dispirited. We lodged at Freedom Lucas's, near Batskow, an honest-hearted man. We shall see whether he will continue to be the same simple-hearted Christian he now is, when he gets possession of the estate which, it is said, has fallen to him in England.

New-Jersey.—Sunday, October 1. We had a very large congregation ; to whom I enforced " Look unto me, all ye ends of the earth, and be saved."

Cape-May.—We stopped at the Cape.—I find there is a great dearth of religion in these parts ; and my spirit is clothed in sackcloth before the Lord.

Tuesday 3. At P. Cresey's we had a few cold hearers—the glory is strangely departed.

Thursday 5. There are a few pious souls at Gough's ; but here also there is an evident declension. My soul is under deep exercise on account of the deadness of the people, and my own want of fervour and holiness of heart.

Friday 6. At Morris-River church I was warm and close on " Lord, are there few that be saved ?" The people were attentive to the word.

Sunday 8. At New-England Town we had a small house and large congregation ; I had liberty in preaching on " By grace are ye saved through faith." Thence I proceeded to M—'s, where I had poor times. Next day I felt quite unwell for want of rest, so annoyed were we the night before.

Thursday 12. I was shut up in speaking on 1 Cor. i. 30. At Marfrey's we had many dull, prayerless people. We came to the widow Airs's ; the mother and daughters are serious, and the son thoughtful. The weather is oppressively warm, and I feel weary and faint. I was much shut up at Bethel on 1 Pet. iii. 18. Three times have I been here, and always straitened in spirit.

Saturday 14. Came to Sand-Town: the weather very warm, and the people dull : I administered the sacrament, and rode away to Cooper's ferry, where we left our horses and crossed to the city : (Philadelphia) here I found brother Whatcoat, with whom I took sweet counsel.

PENNSYLVANIA.—Sunday 15. I had some energy in speaking, and at sacrament. In the afternoon it was a feeling time on " The Lord will give grace and glory."

NEW-JERSEY.—Monday 16. Rode to Holly, where I preached on " Come, ye blessed of my Father," &c.—and then at New-Mills on " Suffering affliction with the people of God."

At Burlington I enlarged on, " Neither is there salvation in any other," &c.—these are not a zealous people for religion.

PENNSYLVANIA.—Wednesday 18. We returned to the city of Philadelphia. Next day I preached, and was close and pointed.

Friday 20. I was led to treat on the sufferings of God's people ; as entirely distinct from those they endure in common with other men, and certainly unavoidable by all who are really alive to God. I found it necessary to change some official men ; and to take proper steps in preparing to defray our church debt, which is now £500. I gave them a sermon on " By this shall all men know that ye are my disciples, if ye love one another."

Sunday 22. In the afternoon I left the city, and preached in the evening at Chester.

DELAWARE.—Monday 23. I rode forty-five miles to Dickenson's, in the Delaware State. Preached at Little-Creek, and then rode five miles to Dover, and preached in the court-house. I bless God for peace of mind, and communion with him.

Sunday 29. I had many to hear at Dover, and had power and liberty in speaking on Gal. i. 5.: we also had a good sacramental time. In the afternoon I spoke on the latter part of my text—how and what it was to suffer according to the will of God. Thence to Thomas White's, where I was closely employed.

Sunday, November 5. I preached at Cambridge on " We preach Christ crucified," &c. little light, and less heat. I was blessed in my own soul, and had liberty in preaching at M'Keels's in the afternoon, where there is some revival among the people.

Thursday 9. I rode to Mr. Bartholomew Ennalls's ; the notice was short, and the congregation small ; the word, nevertheless, reached some hearts. I crossed at Vienna, a dead and dark place for religion.

Friday 10. We had more than I expected of hearers at Quantico chapel. Thence I went to Wycomico-River, and lodged at Captain

Conoway's, where we met with a kind reception. I feel the need of being more than ever given up to God. I preached in Curtis's chapel : our love-feast was lively : several holy women spoke of the perfect love of God.

Sunday 12. According to the custom of the place, I preached to accommodate them ; my subject was Joshua xiv. 8.

Monday 13. I had about fifty hearers at Myles's chapel, where I preached a funeral sermon on Ezek. xxxvi. 25.

Tuesday 14. I crossed Pocomoke-River, and had some-enlargement in preaching at Melvin's.

VIRGINIA.—Thursday 16. Rode to Paramore's. The winter comes on apace. I am at times beset with temptation ; but sin is as hateful to me as ever.

Friday 17. The weather was cold and rainy, so that there were but few people at the widow Burton's ; among these there were some who enjoyed, and others panting after, the perfect love of God.

Sunday 19. I rode about twenty miles through the rain to Garrettson chapel, where about fifty whites, and as many blacks met me, to whom I preached with liberty.

Monday 20. I rode about forty-five miles ; and on Tuesday preached at Snow-Hill to about one hundred people. Here I visited some prisoners under sentence of death ; they were sunk down with fear and horror.

DELAWARE.—Friday 24. My soul has peace under sore temptation. I want to live from moment to moment under a sense of God.

Saturday 25. We had a cold, long ride to the sound. On Sunday we had an open house, and the weather was very cold ; but my preaching was not all in vain : I spoke from these words, " I will give them a heart of flesh."

Monday 27. I rode thirty miles to Lewistown, very unwell. I preached at Shankland's, and the people were serious, but I was compelled to cease from speaking by a violent pain in my head, accompanied by a fever.

Tuesday 28. I preached in the court-house at Lewistown, and I trust the word went with some weight ; the congregation was large.

MARYLAND.—I attended a quarterly meeting at William Frazier's, where I rested from travelling two days ; the first day I spoke on "Fight the good fight of faith ;" and on the second, " Look unto me, all ye ends of the earth, and be saved." My soul was blessed, although our meeting was cold ; and our dwelling-house crowded with a dozen preachers, besides others.

Sunday, December 3. Preached at Tuckahoe chapel on "These shall go away into everlasting punishment, but the righteous into life eternal." I spoke again at widow Lyder's at four o'clock.

Monday 4. I rode to the bay-side through snow and hail, and met about one hundred people: this we owe to the revival of religion among them. Our return thence was through heavy roads. I stopped in my way at H. Banning's, whose wife felt conviction under my preaching three years ago.

Tuesday 5. I had a few people at Bolingbrook, and spent the evening with Colonel Burckhead, who wants to know the Lord; he opened his mind to me with great freedom and tenderness. Brother White says that five hundred souls have joined society in this circuit (Talbot) this year; that half that number profess to have found the Lord; and more than one hundred to have obtained sanctification; good news this if true.

At Barratt's chapel there was some move during the course of the quarterly meeting, especially at the love-feast. I rode in the evening to Dover, and preached on " so is every one that layeth up treasure for himself, and is not rich towards God."

Friday 15. We had a heavy ride to queen Anne's chapel. I did not arrive there until near two o'clock. My soul melted for backsliders. I was much led out on Hos. xiv. 14.; and hope it will never be forgotten. We dined, and then rode to Newtown by sunset.

Sunday 17. A day of rest to my soul. I preached, and administered the sacrament in Newtown. They have a comfortable house for worship here, especially in the winter. Came to Worton chapel, and had some life in speaking to a few people.

We waited at the widow Frisby's for a boat to cross the Chesapeake bay; but none was to be had. We rode round the head of Elk River, and crossed the Susquehannah: we came in, after riding that evening in the rain and snow, with the wind in our faces, about twenty miles.

MARYLAND.—Thursday 23. Reached the college; and on Friday went to Baltimore, where I was in great haste to settle the business of the book concern, and of the college.

Saturday 25. We called a meeting of the trustees, formed our constitution, and elected new members. I preached twice on the Sabbath, and ordained Woolman Hickson and Joseph Cromwell to the eldership. I met the trustees and adjusted the accounts. We find we have expended upwards of £2000; we agreed to finish two rooms, and to send for Mr. Heath for our president. On Tuesday I left town, and came to Annapolis about seven o'clock. Finding my appointments were not made, I determined to direct my course towards Alexandria. The Lord has been powerfully at work at Annapolis since I was here last Autumn : twenty or thirty whites and some blacks have been added to the society.

VIRGINIA.—I reached Alexandria, and on Saturday, preached in the court-house on " If we suffer, we shall also reign with him."

January 1, 1787. Preached at brother Moss's on 2 Chron. xv. 12, 13. on the people's entering into covenant with God.

Tuesday 2. We rode near fifty miles on our way to Westmoreland ; next day, by hard riding, we came to Pope's, in Westmoreland ; but I have not been more weary many times in my life.

Saturday & Sunday. Attended the quarterly meeting in the Northern Neck: there were many simple and loving testimonies delivered in the love-feast.

Thursday 11. Rode through the snow to Fairfield. Here a Capt. R. had turned the people out of the barn in which worship was held, and threatened to take brother Paup to jail if he did not show his authority for preaching; after all this vapouring of the valiant Captain, when the affair was brought before the court, Captain R— found it convenient to ask pardon of our brother, although he sat upon the bench in his own cause :—so the matter ended. The Lord is at work in the Neck : more than one hundred have been added to the society since conference, who are a simple, loving, tender people.

We had a good time on Friday the 12th ; I spoke on Acts xxvi. 18. I think God has spoken by me to S—s, a wild man—but the Lord can tame him : O Lord, speak for thyself!

Sunday 14. We had a crowd at the Presbyterian meeting-house in Lancaster, to whom I delivered a very rough discourse : it was a close and searching time, and we had many communicants, both white and coloured.

Tuesday 16. Preached at the church on the love of Christ. I find it hard to the flesh to ride fifteen or twenty miles every day and perform the duties of my station ; especially when indisposed and suffering therefrom the bodily pain incident thereto. Lord, give me patience ! I feel uncommon affection for the people here.

Wednesday 17. I had a crowd of careless sinners at Mrs. Ball's, who is a famous heroine for Christ. A lady came by craft and took her from her own house, and with tears, threats, and entreaties urged her to desist from receiving the preachers, and Methodist preaching ; but all in vain. She had felt the sting of death some years before, and was a most disconsolate soul ; having now found the way, she would not depart therefrom.

Thursday 18. Rode ten miles to the ferry ; but being unable to cross, I returned to Mrs. B.'s : next morning I came away before day, and reached Shackford's.

Saturday 20. Preached at Douglas's—very low in body and spirit.

Sunday 21. & Monday 22. Cold times in religion in this circuit, (Gloucester) compared with the great times we have had in Lancaster.

Tuesday 23. Came off early, and preached in Yorktown to some well-behaved women. Dined with Mr. Mitchell, and went on to dear brother Weldon's, whose heart and hands were open.

Wednesday 24. According to appointment, I attended at Williamsburg. I had about five from the country, and about fifteen hearers from the town, besides a few blacks and children. I spoke with freedom on " They made light of it." I returned through the rain, but hope to receive no harm.

> " He guards our souls, he keeps our breath,
>   Where thickest dangers come :
>   Go, and return; secure from death,
>   Till God commands thee home.

Friday 26. We waited four hours in the rain before we could cross the ferry at Old Jamestown ; it was two hours after night when we came to brother Morings.

Tuesday 30. We held a quarterly meeting at Craney Island ; the weather prevented many from attending. I was blessed in the company of the preachers.

Wednesday 31. I enlarged on " What shall the end be of them who obey not the Gospel of God ?" I observed to them that the Gospel had once been taken away from them ; and that they ought to lay it seriously to heart, lest it should be the case again. We had some quickening in the sacrament and at the love-feast. Thence I went through Portsmouth, and preached on " Ye are now returned to the Shepherd and Bishop of your souls."

Saturday, February 3. Visited my old friend Fullford : he is feeble in body, and not much at ease in his worldly possessions, yet happy in God.

Brother Poythress frightened me with the idea of the Great Swamp, the east end of the Dismal ; but I could not consent to ride sixty miles round ; so we ventured through, and neither we nor our horses received any injury.—Praise the Lord !—Our passing unharmed through such dangers and unhealthy weather, feelingly assures me that I am kept by the immediate interposition of His providence

I preached in the new chapel.—I hope not in vain. I am now sur-
rounded with waters, and hideous swamps, near the head of Pasquotank-River.

NORTH CAROLINA.—Thursday 9. Came on, wet and unwell to
Proby's.

Went on to Nixonton, where I had many to hear, and was blessed in
my own soul, and, I think, spoke to the cases of some of my audience.

Friday 10. I had a long ride of nearly fifty miles to Gates county.
We stopped at one Newby's, one of the society of Friends, who en-
tertained us kindly. We reached sister Gibson's, cold and weary.
The poor flesh complains, but my soul enjoys peace and sweetness.

Sunday 11. We had a large congregation, and an open time at
Knotty-Pine chapel.—Here we have a little revival.

Tuesday 13. I had about sixty people at Wicocon: I spoke as I
felt on Jer. xiii. 11. I mourned over the people and left them.

I came to Hardy's, where I spoke with some light on Matt. xxii. 5.
I unhappily ran a splinter into my leg which has alarmed me.

I found we had to go twelve miles by water, and send the horses
another way. O what a world of swamps, and rivers, and islands,
we live in here! I met brother B— and A— ; two devoted young
men ; the former, a native of Maryland ; the latter of Virginia. At
the desire of several of the brethren I preached at Washington,
where many collected in the court-house, whom I addressed on my
favourite text, 1 Tim. i. 15. Three miles on the water, and riding
three more on roads under the water, (such is the inundated state of
the country,) made our jaunt unpleasant.

Thursday 22. We set off for Newbern. Stopped at Kemps-
Ferry, kept by Curtis, where we were kindly entertained, *gratis*. I
feel heaviness through labour and temptation, yet I am given up
to God.

Friday 23. I arrived at Newbern. I felt the power of death as I
journeyed along. We rode round the town, and could get no certain
information about preaching, brother Cole being absent. We were
at last taken in at Mr. Lathrop's. The place and people were in
such a state, that I judged, by my own feelings, it would be as well to
leave them just as I found them—and so I did.

Tuesday 27. It was rather a dry time at the love-feast and sacrament. There was some life and melting while I enforced " Look
unto me, and be ye saved, all ye ends of the earth." We then rode
to H——'s on Island Creek. I went alone into the woods, and had
sweet converse with God. At night we were poorly provided against
the weather ; the house was unfinished ; and, to make matters worse,

a horse kicked the door open, and I took a cold, and had the toothach, with a high fever.

Thursday, March 1. I had more hearers, and they were more attentive than I expected : I trust it was a profitable time. Rode to brother Johnson's—without the labour of slaves he manages to have abundance for man and beast.

Tuesday 6. My horse is stiff, and almost foundered, and there is an appearance of a swelling on his head. I have always had hard struggles to get to Charleston—Lord, give me patience, and bear me up !

Wednesday 7. Crossed the main fork of Black-River, and came through a wild country to Colonel R——'s : the Colonel's wife is a tender, devoted woman.

Thursday and Friday 8, 9. Directed our course to the south : crossed Cape Fear, and reached Drowning-Creek. Rested a day at W——'s, a kind people, but without religion.

SOUTH CAROLINA.—Sunday 11. Preached at Robinson's new court-house. Rode in the evening to M—'s. Crossed Little Pee-Dee ; stopped at S—'s ; ate a morsel, and came on to Buck Swamp.

Thursday 15. Preached at the new church at S—'s : here I heard that Doctor Coke was in Charleston. Proceeded thence to the widow Port's, where I had much ado to prevail on brother H. to stay.

We rode nearly fifty miles to get to Georgetown. Here the scene was greatly changed : almost the whole town came together to hear the word of the Lord.

We arrived in Charleston, and met Doctor Coke. Here we have already a spacious house prepared for us ; and the congregations are crowded and solemn.

Sunday 25. I enlarged on, " I had rather be a door-keeper in the house of God, than to dwell in the tents of wickedness ;" at night again on Isai. xlv. 22. We held our conference in this city.

Tuesday 27. We exchanged sentiments on matters freely.

Wednesday 28. The Doctor treated on the qualifications and duties of a deacon.

Thursday 29. Our conference ended.

Friday 30. I left the city, and rode thirty miles, although my horse had been injured by over-feeding. Next day I rode forty miles through the rain, and begged a lodging with Doctor W.

Sunday, April 1. We came to Santee Ferry, and there was such an overflowing of water in our route that we had to swim upon our horses several times : my horse performed so well that I was not wet much higher than my knees : that day we rode thirty miles, and the next day fifty miles, and came to Moore's. Here we met with brother R. Swift, who had been near death, but then was recovering : we advised him to go with us for his life. The people here begin to feel, and yield to the power of truth.

Wednesday 4. At Camden I preached on " They made light of it :" thence we rode on to quarterly meeting, where I met with a multitude of people who were desperately wicked—but God hath wrought among them : we had little rest by day or night.

Friday 6. Rode forty miles to preaching at Jackson's ; and then to brother Pace's.

Saturday 7, and Sunday 8. Attended Anson quarterly meeting, in North Carolina : the Doctor preached on the love of Christ, and I on " the grace of God that bringeth salvation ;" sacrament followed.

From Saturday to Saturday, I have rode about three hundred miles, and have preached only about half the time : O may the Lord seal and water his own word, that all this toil of man and beast be not in vain.

Tuesday 10. The Doctor and myself preached to a few simple people at W.'s, I hope not in vain. At our next meeting we had many hearers. We have scarcely time to eat or sleep.

NORTH CAROLINA.—Thursday 11. I preached at Salisbury. Afterward rode to Huggins's, where we had many hearers, and a melting among the people.

Good-Friday, 12. I was much led out at Caton's. Thence to M'Knight's chapel, where we found a living people.

Saturday 13. We hasted to C—y church, where we had many people : after riding twenty-two miles, we had another meeting about six o'clock; and about midnight got to bed.

Sunday 15. Rose about six o'clock, and went to Newman's church, where the Doctor and myself both preached : the people were rather wild, and we were unwell. I came to Arnat's about eight o'clock, having rode forty miles : the Doctor went by Dick's ferry, and did not get in until near midnight.

Monday 16. Rode to Jeremiah White's, and on Tuesday about fifty miles to Page Mann's, in Charlotte county, Virginia.

VIRGINIA.—Wednesday 18. Rode to Rough-Creek. On Thursday the 19th, our conference began at William White's. We had much preaching, morning, noon and night; and some souls were converted to God.

REV. FRANCIS ASBURY'S JOURNAL.

Saturday 21. I gave them a discourse on Jer. iii. 15. " And I will give you pastors according to mine heart."

Sunday 22. The Doctor spoke on the qualifications of a deacon ; and I gave them a charge. Some said there were three thousand people to hear : it was a solemn, weighty time.

Monday 23. We called at Hampden and Sidney college, in Prince Edward : the outside has an unwieldy, uncommon appearance, for a seminary of learning ; what the inside is, I know not. The president, Mr. I. Smith, is a discreet man, who conducts himself well. About half past eleven o'clock we reached John Finney's, in Amelia, having rode about sixty miles. I want to live more constantly in the spirit of prayer.

Wednesday 25. Preached at I. A.'s, and then rode to Manchester, where I preached again. The Doctor preached in Richmond.

Thursday 26. Went onwards to the north. We have made it a point to pray in the families where we lodge, whether public or private ; and generally where we stop for refreshment.

Saturday 28. At night the Doctor preached in Alexandria ; and again on the Sabbath morning, to many hearers. We were kindly entertained on Sunday night at S. Turner's, near Bladensburg, Maryland, and on Monday reached Baltimore about noon.

MARYLAND.—We had some warm and close debates in conference ; but all ended in love and peace. After much fatigue and trouble, our conference ended on Monday the sixth of May. We went forward to Perry Hall. Thence we went to Cokesbury ; drew a deed for the conveyance of the property of the college, and settled our temporal matters there.

Wednesday, May 8. Many attended at Elkton, and we were received by the Rudolph family with great respect.

Thursday 9. We attended at Wilmington at noon ; and at Chester, at night.

Friday 10. We reached Philadelphia, where the Doctor preached that, and the following evening. We spent the Sabbath in the city, and on Monday came to Trenton, where we found a lifeless people.

NEW-JERSEY.—Tuesday 14. The Doctor preached with life in the Episcopal church at Elizabethtown, and we had a good time.

NEW-YORK.—Wednesday 15. Arrived in New-York and rested. On Friday, Saturday, Sunday, and Monday, the Doctor preached with great energy and acceptance.

Tuesday 16. After long silence I preached on " For Zion's sake I will not hold my peace, and for Jerusalem's sake I will not rest."

Rode twenty miles on Long-Island, to Hempstead Harbour, and preached with some liberty in the evening. I am now out of the city, and have time to reflect : my soul returns to its rest, and to its labour for souls, in which I can live more by rule.

Thursday 18. I rose very sick—felt solemn and devoted to God. I preached in a paper mill on "If any man will do his will he shall know of the doctrine whether it be of God."

I preached at Moscheto Cove, where many attended notwithstanding the rain : there was a power went with the word.

Saturday 26. Rode to ———— : our friends had procured the Presbyterian church for me. I felt a spirit of life on these words, "Be ready to give an answer to every man that asketh you a reason of the hope that is in you." I called to see my old friend and assistant, James Glaisbrook, who was the first preacher I travelled with upon a regular appointment in England. He is now a Presbyterian minister ; much changed in his outward man, but I believe his sentiments are much the same as when I first knew him. The Lord be with, and bless him !

Sunday 27. I came to Harper's, where we have a little, new house, and about thirty members : I hope, and expect, in a few years, to see a circuit of six weeks formed here, and four or five hundred members in society. The people on this island, who hear the Gospel, are generally poor, and these are the kind I want, and expect to get. I have had great assistance and freedom in speaking.

Monday 28. Came to York—Preached at night on "They that are after the flesh do mind the things of the flesh, and they that are after the Spirit, the things of the Spirit." I found it necessary to stop brother Hickson from going to Nova Sotia : brother C— is married, and I expect brother Jessop will go alone.

Tuesday 29. I delivered a close and awful discourse on "They shall come from the east, and from the west, and from the north, and from the south, and sit down with Abraham, and Isaac, and Jacob," &c. 1. A scriptural view of the kingdom of heaven. 2. The subjects or citizens thereof. 3. Sit down with Abraham, famous for faith ; Isaac for justice, truth, meditation, and walking with God ; and Jacob, mighty in prayer. I was in prayer until near midnight. O Lord make me all life and love ; patience and resignation under the troubles of the church and disappointment of its ministers.

Sunday, June 3. I had a gracious time on 2 Cor. iv. 1, 2, 3, 4. Ordained E. Cooper a deacon. In the afternoon my soul had peace whilst I enlarged on Matt. xviii. 15. to the end.

Tuesday 5. Preached on "No man having put his hand to the plough, and looking back, is fit for the kingdom of heaven." I felt freedom and power in speaking.

Wednesday 6. Met leaders and trustees, and after some explanation, settled matters relative to singing in public worship. I preached at the poor-house on "Whosoever shall call on the name of the Lord shall be saved." My soul has peace. I keep myself busy in visiting the families of the society, or the sick, or meeting class, if some other business does not call me.

Sunday 10. I had some life in preaching on Luke iv. 18. and in the afternoon on "I thank thee, O Father, Lord of heaven and earth because thou hast hid these things from the wise and prudent," &c.

I left the city in great union with the Lord and with the church. My soul is variously exercised: I want the country air, and to live more in the spirit of solitude and of prayer. Came to East-Chester and preached in the shell of the new church on "To-day if ye will hear his voice, harden not your hearts;" the power of God was felt. I came to the widow Bartoe's, where I lay sick fifteen years ago, and was treated with the greatest tenderness; may the Lord reward them all a hundred fold, and convert their souls!

Tuesday 12. I found it the same at New-Rochelle town as in times past: will it always be so?—If there is no change I shall trouble them no more. In the afternoon I rode to C—'s, where I laboured many years ago, and there is some fruit remaining to this day.

Wednesday 13. We had a long and warm ride to North-Castle. Here a multitude were gathered together, to whom I spoke in an orchard on "Him hath God exalted with his right-hand to be a Prince and Saviour, to give repentance unto Israel, and remission of sins." I was quite unwell, *faint yet pursuing.*

Rode to R—'s, of the society of Friends, who received us with great love.

At H—'s a multitude came to hear, whom I exhorted to "Seek the Lord while he might be found."

I was happy in being alone. I poured out my soul to God for the whole work, and the dear people and preachers of my charge. My body is weak—my soul enjoys peace. I have power over all sin, and possess a spirit of prayer and watchfulness: I feel myself dead to all below, and desire to live only for God and souls

Friday 15. I preached to a listening multitude at Peekskill; and was alarming and close on "By grace ye are saved through faith."

I thought there were no people here of spiritual understanding ; but I was informed, to my comfort, that a number of simple-hearted people had formed themselves into a society for prayer : perhaps these will be some of the first-fruits in this place.

Saturday 16. Rode over the mountain, and was gratified with the sight of a remarkable recess for the Americans during the last war : the names of Andre and of Arnold, with which misfortune and treachery are so unhappily and intimately blended, will give celebrity to West-Point, had it been less deserving of notice than its wonderful appearance really makes it. It is commanded by mountains rising behind, and appears to be impregnable : there are blockhouses on the east ; and on the west, stores, barracks, and fortifications. From West-Point we crossed a high mountain, and came to Newburgh.

Sunday 17. In the love-feast, sacrament, and public exercises, we were employed nearly seven hours : there was some life in the love-feast, but the congregation appeared very little moved under preaching.

Monday 18. I presume I had nearly seven hundred hearers at Allen's, to whom I spoke with some power on Luke xi. 13. I baptised several adults, and some children ; and came to W——'s, and baptised others. Thence to Mr. Ellis's, whose wife (a dutch lady) entertained us *like a queen*.

I visited Colonel P——, supposed to be at the point of death : after close examination, I administered the sacrament to him.

NEW-JERSEY.—Wednesday 20. I came to Warwick, where I suppose not less than a thousand people were collected : I was very low both in body and spirit, but felt stirred up at the sight of such a congregation, and was moved and quickened while I enlarged on Gal. i. 4. I baptised some, and administered the sacrament to many communicants.

Thursday 21. A multitude attended at B——'s, in a barn. Here God hath wrought a great work for a poor, blind, ignorant people.

Friday 22. I preached at the stone church, after riding upwards of thirty miles : we then rode until ten o'clock in the night through a heavy rain. I was much tried in body and mind : I had nothing to eat but a little bread and milk, and that made me sick.

Saturday 22. We had a good time at Sweezy's. After administering the sacrament, we had another long ride after night.

Sunday 24. I preached in the woods to nearly a thousand people. I was much oppressed by a cold, and felt very heavy in body and soul. Like Jonah, I went and sat down alone. I had some gracious feelings in the sacrament—others also felt the quickening power of God. I baptised a number of infants and adults, by sprinkling and by immersion—I felt my body quite weary *in*, but my spirit not *of*, the work of God.

Tuesday 26. Preached at W. Wallace's to a dull, contracted people. Since last Monday two weeks, I have rode about three hundred and fifty miles.

PENNSYLVANIA.—Wednesday 27. We had a warm ride through a fertile, pleasant country to Trenton; and on Thursday the 28th to Philadelphia. Here I found T. V. had scattered firebrands, and thrown dirt to bespatter us.

Friday & Saturday 29, 30. Taken up in writing letters, packing up books, and begging for the college.

Sunday, July 1. Preached three times in the city of Philadelphia —On Monday 2. to a few simple-hearted souls at Radnor.

Tuesday 3. We had a flat time at the Valley.

Wednesday 4. We had a few feeling souls at Uchland—afterward went to Coventry Forge.

Saturday 7. I had some energy in preaching to a few people at Morgans-Town.

Sunday 8. Preached at Evans's, Rich-Land—a poor people for religion: I hope, nevertheless, that God will visit them.

Monday 9. Preached at I. Miller's, who has a pious wife.

Friday 13. We rode to Hagerstown; and found it a journey of about fifty miles: we and our horses were weary enough. I was sorry to hear that the people came twice to hear me last year; and the lameness of my horse caused me to disappoint them.

Saturday 14. At five o'clock in the evening the court-house was opened; a few of the great and many of the poor attended, to whom I spoke with divine assistance. I preached again on Sunday at eleven o'clock.

I find T. V. has misrepresented us as having cast off Mr. Wesley, making this a plea for his re-ordination.

VIRGINIA.—Monday 16. Set out for the springs.—In the first place we missed our way; then my baggage horse ran back two miles—I was tried not a little.—O, how sad the reflection, that matters trifling as these should make a person so uneasy. We reached the springs about seven o'clock. I preached the two following days with some satisfaction. By advancing nine pounds, for nails and planks, I engaged brother Eaton to have our chapel covered by the first of August.

MARYLAND.—Friday 20. We had a heavy ride to Old Town : we met with a kind reception ; and had a reviving season in the family.

Saturday 21. Was a day of rest to my soul and body. Preached on Cant. iv. 16.

Sunday 22. We had sacrament attended with some power in the evening.

Tuesday 24. There was to have been great doings at Cumberland, but Mr. B—, a minister, failed coming. I had a good time in Mr. Bell's mill on " Thou art fairer than the sons of men."

We had feeling and weeping at Barratt's—my subject, " I sleep, but my heart waketh," &c. eight or nine verses. I feel a sweetness of spirit, and much of the love of Christ. Came to Cressap's.

Friday 27. Ordained brother Phœbus deacon, and had a serious time.

Sunday 29. At Jones's; all death ! death ! death ! My mind was devoted to God. I administered the sacrament, but could find no openings. Rode to Old Town.—Six years ago I preached in this place, when there was scarcely a soul that knew any thing of God ; now there are sixty in membership, many of whom are happy in the knowledge of the truth. We held a love-feast, and had a quickening time.

Tuesday 31. Rode to the springs (Bath) much tried in spirit. I gave myself to reading and prayer.

Wednesday, August 1. Preached at Bath.

Sunday 5. Preached on Pet. iii. 9. to a large congregation, with but little liberty.

Monday 6. I began my lectures on the Prophecies by Bishop Newton, and had more hearers than I expected. The weather is very warm ; many are sickly ; and continued changes of comers and goers—all this leaves but little opportunity for prayer. I forbear reading on account of my eyes, lest I should not be able to read in public.

Tuesday & Wednesday 7, 8. Had very few to hear, so I gave them up : every thing that is good is in low estimation at this place. I will return to my own studies : if the people are determined to go to hell, I am clear of their blood. My soul is clothed in sackcloth and covered with ashes before the Lord.

Thursday 9. I enjoy some peace.

Friday 10. I feel a calm within, and the want of more life, and more love to God, and more patience with sinners. I read my

Testament. Oh! what a weariness would life be without God, and love, and labour. The two first weeks of my time at Bath have been spent in carrying on the building of the new chapel, reading Newton on the Prophecies, visiting, bathing, &c. My soul has been under great trials, at times, but hitherto the Lord has helped.

Tuesday 21. O, how sweet will labour, and Christian society, and the solitary woods be to me.

Thursday 23. I have been under great exercises, but was divinely assisted in preaching on "The eyes of the Lord are over the righteous," &c.

Sunday 26. I preached on "How beautiful upon the mountains are the feet of him that bringeth good tidings," &c. It was a solemn time—my soul was stayed upon God. We had a melting sacrament and love-feast, and many spoke. The devil is angry, and so are his children : brother Whatcoat spoke at the steps, and it was with difficulty the people kept themselves within decent bounds of respect.

VIRGINIA.—Friday 31. I gave them my farewell address at Bath, and had many hearers.

Saturday, September 1. I set out in the rain, and came to the widow Stroud's, where I met with T. V. who made some acknowledgments for what he had said in the heat of his zeal at Philadelphia and at Bath.

Sunday 2. I attended at a place where every one has liberty to preach ; but it so happened that no one had an appointment there but myself—The Methodists would do well to withdraw from this as a preaching place in their circuit. I had a large congregation at Shepherds-Town, to whom I spoke on Luke iv. 18. I have had some trials and great consolations ; and at times, it is Paradise Regained with me since I left Bath and the wicked there.

MARYLAND.—Friday 7. I had a cold time at Ryster's on "Wo to them that are at ease in Zion." Thence I rode to the new church, where I had not much life. Came to Baltimore. The weather is extremely warm.

Sunday 9. Preached in the morning—my text, "Thou art fairer than the sons of men :" in the afternoon at Mr Otterbine's church : and at night on "They shall come from the east, and from the west, and from the north, and from the south," &c.—large crowds attended : I was straitened in speaking. The following was a week of haste and business. Wednesday I went to Perry-Hall—thence to Cokesbury—fixed the price of board, and the time for opening the college. On Friday I returned to Baltimore. In the midst of business my mind is calm.

Sunday 16. Preached at town and Point. On Monday, the people waited nearly two hours at Evans's before I arrived, owing to my horse being out of the way: I found he had stuck a nail into his foot, so that I had to leave him. Under these discouraging circumstances I was much exercised; nevertheless, I had liberty in speaking, and there was a melting time among the people. Thence I hastened to Hunt's chapel, where I enlarged on " I know you, that you have not the love of God in you."

I rode by I. C—'s gate—an old stand of mine—It is now, in two senses, fallen into decay. The want of religion oftentimes causes the want of economy. Ah! how do the persons and fashions of this world pass away!

Tuesday 18. I found the work of God in a reviving state at G——'s.

Wednesday 19. I had a liberal opening at Wilson's on " whosoever shall call on the name of the Lord shall be saved." Thence I hasted to the Fork church, and preached on Cant. iii. 1—6. I lamented the gayety of the children of Methodists; but yet they do not appear to be so full of enmity against God and his people as other children.

I hasted to Cokesbury, it being the examination: some gentlemen, and some triflers were present. Friday I preached at Joseph Dallam's.

Saturday 22. I preached at Havre de Grace, on Acts ii. 23.

Sunday 23. I had a large congregation at Elk-Town, and some power attended the word. In the evening spoke at Isaac Harshay's.

Monday 24. I had a large, solemn congregation at Wilmington. I feel a persuasion that God will revive his work at this place.

Tuesday 25. I attended at Chester; and next day came to Philadelphia. I had liberty in speaking on Cant. v. 6—10. On Thursday and Friday, I had not freedom as I wished. I was seized with a violent headach, exceeding any thing, as I thought, I had ever felt.

Saturday 29. I felt a little better. My mind was stayed upon God.

Sunday 30. We had a good sacramental occasion. In the afternoon brother Willis preached; and at night I had some enlargement on Ephes. iv. 17, 18, 19.

Wednesday, October 3. I met the people, and explained the nature and design of the college.

Thursday 4. I preached on the primitive design of the church.

Friday 5. We had an uncommon love-feast—a gracious season—much speaking. On Saturday I met class, and on

Sunday 7. There was life in the administration of the sacrament. I felt humbled before the Most High. I trust the Lord will revive his work, and make his power known.

Monday 8. I came to Chester, and preached on "My grace is sufficient for thee."

DELAWARE.—Tuesday 9. I had unusual freedom in speaking at Aaron Mattson's. Thence I pushed on through the rain, and was sorely tempted to complain.

Wednesday 10. I was at Wilmington; and next day came late to Dickinson's.

I visited Duck-Creek Cross-Roads, where we have a comfortable house which cost about two hundred pounds.

Saturday 13 Came to Dover very unwell, and brother I. E. preached in my stead.

Sunday 14. I read prayers, and preached on 2 Tim. iii. 10.; and solemnly set apart Jacob Brush and Ira Ellis, for the office of deacon : I trust it was a profitable time. I spent two days at Thomas White's.

Tuesday 16. I preached the funeral sermon of Joshua Barack ; a faithful, steady man, who had followed the Lord about ten years, my text was, " These all died in the faith."

Thursday 18. I had divine aid in preaching at Millford's : the house was open, and the day was cold.

Friday 19. Came in the evening to Shanklands. Here I found the people in disorder and violence about the election ; some had gone so far as to take up fire arms.

Sunday morning, 21. Before sacrament I preached on Psalm ii. 24, 25. and then in Lewistown, on " God sent not his Son into the world to condemn the world," &c.

Tuesday 23, and Wednesday 24. I had a good time at quarterly meeting, at the Sound church : thence, through a barren sandy country, we came to Evans's church, where we had a good and gracious time, more so than I have felt for some time. From Evans's we rode to the beach, and gratified our curiosity with a sight of the raging, roaring sea.

Wednesday 24. I spoke closely upon the discipline of the church—my subject, " all Scripture is given by inspiration of God.

and is profitable for doctrine," &c. After meeting, we had a very long ride to brother Bowen's.

MARYLAND.—Friday 26. After preaching at Pennall's on "I will give them a heart to know me," &c. I rode in the evening to Downing's.

Saturday 27. Reached Paramore's at night.

Sunday 28. We had a gracious time indeed.

Monday 29. There were life and power among the people in the sacrament and love-feast. I was greatly comforted to find the Lord had greatly blest the labours of brother S——, and that a revival had taken place all around the circuit. In the evening I rode to Burton's, in Virginia. The former inhabitants have gone to the dust.

It seemed as if I was let into heaven, while I enlarged on "Behold what manner of love the Father hath bestowed upon us, that we should be called the sons of God." We have twenty miles, and sometimes more, a day to travel ; but we have fine roads, kind friends, and good entertainment.

Thursday, November 1. The people coming in still after I began, caused me to lengthen out my discourse. Came afterward to Captain Burton's, and spoke with life and consolation.

Friday 2. Was a day of sore exercise of soul, and barren preaching. I visited Mr. R. and administered the sacrament to him. Rested that evening with Mr. Curtis.

Saturday 3. Quarterly meeting. I was close on keeping the feast, and on discipline—some felt the word.

Sunday 4. Preached on "Thou shalt arise and favour Zion." I believe God will make his power known ; and I trust brother Everitt will be made a blessing, as well by strictness of discipline, as by faithful preaching.

Monday 5. I had a few living people at Phœbus's. My soul is given up to God ; but I have felt Satan near : Lord, help, or I perish!

Sunday 11. I had some light in preaching at the Fork chapel. Spent the evening with brother Ennall.

Monday 12. I preached at Hooper's—Thence I rode to Johnson's chapel, and spoke on 2 Tim. 8—12. I had some enlargement.

After riding thirty miles, and preaching twice, we held a watch-night at Todd's.

Sunday 18. We went to church at Cambridge, and heard a sermon. Afterward I spoke to a large congregation at Tucker's on Rom. x. 1—4. : upon the whole it has been a laborious, trying time of late.

Tuesday 20. We rode through excessive rain thirty miles. Our quarterly meeting at Frazier's chapel was large and lively. I had very few to hear at Doctor Allen's, the fiery edge is greatly worn off there.

Thursday 22. We had a feeling time at Bolingbrook ; but it is not here as in months past. Oh how soon does the power of religion decline ! I came to Easton, Talbot county, where we had a watch-night, and the gentry had a ball.

Friday 23. We had a gracious season at the Bay side, where many attended.

Saturday 24. My soul is dejected : O that it was perfectly re-signed to the will of God !

Sunday 25. I stopped at Keet's on my way to Kent Island. Although under a great depression of spirits, I was uncommonly led out whilst I enlarged on " Wo to them that are at ease in Zion," to a large assembly of people.

Monday 26. My mind is still depressed. I called on poor Colonel H. who bears his imprisonment for debt with great forti-tude : I had a good time at Boardley's, notwitstanding two drunken men came in and made some disturbance.

Friday 27. Cold, straitened for time at Tuckahoe—something better at Choptank. I here heard of the conduct of A. C——so ; he is gone from us at last. There were many people at Barrett's chapel during quarterly meeting, but I had little life in speaking.

Monday, December 3. We had a melting time at Queen Annes chapel. I enforced " Because iniquity shall abound, the love of many shall wax cold."

Tuesday 4. At Chestertown, I had but little life on Isai. liii. 1—5.: at night the Lord was with us indeed, while I enforced " Let your moderation be known to all men."

Wednesday 5. After preaching at Worton chapel, we set out to cross the Bay, and were on the water until ten o'clock at night.

Thursday 6. We opened our college, and admitted twenty-five students. I preached on " Trust in the Lord, and do good." On the Sabbath I spoke on " Oh! man of God, there is death in the pot"—and on Monday, " They are the seed of the blessed of the Lord, and their offspring with them." From Cokesbury I came to Baltimore, where I was closely employed, and much in haste about temporal concerns.

Saturday 15. I had a cold ride to Annapolis ; and but few to hear me on Sunday morning. Brother H. attempted to travel with

me, but was soon glad to resign. My soul has been kept in peace,
and for three weeks past, I have enjoyed a most devoted frame of
mind.

Thursday 20. We must now direct our course for Lancaster,
Virginia, through a barren route of sixty miles. This is the only
uncultivated part of Maryland ; and God will surely visit these
people, and bless them in his own time, if they hear his voice.
We crossed Patuxent-River at sunrise : brother James having un-
dertaken to be our guide, led us ten miles out of our way. Bearing near to Port Tobacco, we came to the ferry, crossed about
sunset, and put up at Mrs. H.'s, where we paid eight shillings for
our oats, and six for our fodder—all this exclusive of charge for
lodging, as she said.

Friday 21. Reached Pope's some time in the night. On Saturday I read the apostolical canons, pulished by Johnson—curious
enough : he is a violent churchman, and appears to have little
charity for the Presbyterians, upon whom he is unmercifully
severe. I have been sorely tempted, and at sword's point with
the enemy.

Sunday 23. I had very little life in preaching to a few dead
souls at Pope's ; on Monday, at Hutt's, it was nearly the same both
in preaching and sacrament ; in the evening at brother Cannons,
the Lord powerfully broke into my soul, and the cloud disappeared.
That night while sleeping, I dreamed I was praying for sanctification, and God very sensibly filled me with love, and I waked shouting glory ! glory to God ! my soul was all in a flame. I had never
felt so much of God in my life ; and so I continued : this was on
Christmas day, a great day to me.

I rode to the widow Wollard's, and preached on " For this purpose was the Son of God manifested that he might destroy the
works of the devil." During the five last days, we have rode one
hundred and forty miles. We crossed Wicomoco and came to
G.'s : death prevails here : my spirit was clothed in sackcloth.

Saturday 29, and Sunday 30. Held quarterly meeting at Lancaster meeting-house : there was a large gathering, and some life on
the first day. On Sunday there was much snow, and only about
three hundred people attended. I ordained E. Ellis a deacon.

Tuesday, January 1, 1788. Preached at the widow Ball's on
Psalm xc. 12.

Thursday 3. Crossed the Rappahannock and came to G.'s, but
did not feel free to stay. I went on to Blake's. Came to brother Billups's, in Kingston parish, Gloucester county : here we were

at home, and happy in our religious exercises. During the last
one hundred miles of our journey we have preached very little
for the want of appointments. We left brother Billups's, and, after
riding forty miles, and preaching by the way, we came to Cappaho-
cey-Ferry ; but being unable to cross, we rode on ten miles to
the Widow Roe's.

Tuesday 8. There being a storm of rain and a thaw, we set out
to cross the river at York : we succeeded, but with some difficulty :
I had had some distressing apprehensions of this. I preached at
B——'s ; on " How beautiful upon the mountains are the feet," &c.
We came to James-River ; the ice was in the way, yet we pushed
through safely to the opposite shore, and arrived at Moreing's just
as the quarterly meeting ended ; nevertheless, we too, had a meeting, and the cry of glory ! was heard in great life : God is among
these people. Brother Cox thinks that not less than fourteen hundred, white and black, have been converted in Sussex circuit the
past year ; and brother Easter thinks there are still more in Brunswick circuit. I preached at P.'s in Nansemond circuit : thence
to Cowling's, and preached on Isai. liii. 1—4. We came on to
Sleepy Hole Ferry ; being unable to get our horses over, we walked
five miles to Turner's.

Sunday 13. I had some liberty on Isai. lii. 6, 7, 8.

Monday 14. We continued our meeting nearly four hours, but
had little satisfaction by reason of the extreme cold. There is a
growth in religion here since last year.

We came to Portsmouth, but too late, the ice hindered : however, I preached at three o'clock. Next day it rained, and few
attended ; so that, upon the whole, we had but a low time there.
I preached at N. Wilson's. Here I had an interview with I.
M. : he wants to go into the Old Church. I had a great and good
time at brother Williams's on Isai. xxxv. 3, 4, 5. the power and
love of God were manifested and felt.

NORTH CAROLINA.—Sunday 20. I preached at Col. Jarvis's ; and
on Monday at Saunders's—dull times at both these places.

Tuesday 22. At Coenjock : there is a death here. —— has
been experimenting on extremes—wise doctrine—hard discipline.
I doubt whether it will end well.

I have rode about eighty miles, and preached four times to
about eight hundred people, most of whom were dead and ignorant ; yet I hope God will arise.

Currituck—a pleasant place : I rode along the shore and enjoyed the view of its banks of evergreen.

I preached at Camden court-house with freedom, but the people appeared insensible : after meeting, we rode, hungry and cold,
to brother C———'s.

Thursday 24. We had a violent storm ; so we kept within
doors ; and man and beast were well provided for.

Friday 25. Was an uncommonly cold and windy day ; I nevertheless attempted to preach at Richardson's chapel. In the evening visited W. P.

Saturday 26, and Sunday 27. We had cold weather, and a cold
people at the quarterly meeting at Flatty-Creek chapel. On Sabbath evening I preached at Nixonton.

Monday 28. Rode to Gates's ; and next day preached at Knotty-
Pine chapel : there were but few people, and it was a barren
meeting.

Wednesday 30. Preached on " The grace of God that bringeth salvation hath appeared unto all men." Alas ! for the rich—
they are so soon offended. Rode to Winton, a little town on
Chowan-River ; here I had a dry meeting with a few people in
the court-house. I housed for the night with W———. I seldom mount my horse for a ride of less distance than twenty miles
on ordinary occasions ; and frequently have forty or fifty, in
moving from one circuit to the other : in travelling thus I suffer
much from hunger and cold.

I preached at W———'s, with some liberty.—Our brother
Chastaine stamped to purpose.

Saturday, February 2. At Wicocon I enlarged on Peter's fall.

Sunday 3. I preached on Hebr. vi. 11, 12. I rode that evening
to friend Freeman's, whom I had not visited for five years past : I
found him still an honest Baptist, and we were kindly entertained.

Rode to Ross's in Martin's county. The rise of the waters of
the Roanoak-River had inundated the low-lands more than a mile
from the banks, and made the ferry altogether a wonderful sight.
We came to our lodging about nine o'clock, and found a plain, kind-
hearted host.

I preached a funeral sermon—my text, " The sting of death is
sin." I spoke on the nature of the law—of sin ; its guilt, power,
nature, and punishment,—and the victory through Christ. Does it
not appear that those who live in sin, which is a breach of the law,
wish to abolish the law, seeing they must know the necessary consequence of its violation ?—And if this *postulation* is just, what
saves them from theft, murder, rape ?—self-preservation. Alas !
poor world, is this all thy virtue !

Wednesday 6. Rode twenty miles, and had the ice to break in two swamps. Preached at Lloyd's, near Washington.

Saturday 9. I had a very unfeeling people at Mr. O.'s, to whom I preached with some freedom on Luke iv. 18.—Death! death! death! in the low-lands!

Sunday 10. I had many to hear at S.'s; but it was an uncomfortable time: thence I rode to Cox's on Neuse River, where we had an open time, and there is a prospect of good. We then had to move towards Trent. Our rides are still long—from fifteen to twenty miles a day.

Wednesday 13. We had many dead souls at the quarterly-meeting at Lee's.

Thursday 14. My heart melted for the people: they do not, will not pray; and if they so continue, must be undone.

Friday 15. Came to poor J.'s, where I spoke dreadful things to a lifeless people on Isai. liii.

Saturday 16. We rode to T——'s, an old stand in Duplin county, where I was met by a few souls. We had nought to eat, nor where to lodge short of Colonel C——'s; we pushed for that shelter, and reached there about nine o'clock at night: a poor place for religion it is, but we met with good entertainment.

Sunday 17. I had about five hundred hearers at Samson courthouse, to whom I enlarged on Peter's denial of his Master. 1. He was self-confident. 2. Followed afar off. 3. Mixed with the wicked. 4. Denied his discipleship, and then his Lord.

Tuesday 19. At Fayetteville I was unable to preach. Wednesday we pushed on for the south state, but being unacquainted with the way, we fell ten miles too low: after riding as many in the night, we ended our blunders and our fatigue for that day at S.'s, who used us kindly.

SOUTH CAROLINA.—Thursday 21. We rode twenty miles in the rain through the woods and sands, and had but a poor time at Col. M.'s: thence we descended to the Green Ponds, fifteen miles, where we were very comfortable at C.'s.

Saturday 23. I attended the quarterly-meeting at the Beauty Spot: the weather was cold, but I had great assistance on Isai. xxxv. 1—6.

Sunday 24. I preached on Zech. xi. 12.: we had a gracious, moving time.

Monday 25. We crossed Pee Dee at the Long Bluff, and rode nearly fifty miles to brother Gardener's.

I preached at Black-Creek on Psalm cxlv.: I was much fatigued, and had a high fever; but my soul had peace and was stayed upon God.

Wednesday 27. After preaching at D.'s, I had to ride ten miles out of my way to cross Lynch's Creek. We moved forwards to our worthy friend Rembert's, who entertained us kindly, and supplied us with horses to ride to our appointments at Lenoir's and Moore's, where we had few hearers and dead times. After our meetings at these places we returned to Rembert's, at whose house our quarterly meeting began on Saturday the first of March, which was not without some life: in our love-feast there appeared to be more feeling than speaking.

Monday, March 3. We rode through the snow to Bradford's; and next day had no small difficulty in crossing the swamps in order to get to Santee Ferry: we made it a ride of about fifty miles to H.'s, and did not get in until about nine o'clock at night.

Wednesday 5. I passed Dorchester, where there are the remains of what appears to have once been a considerable town: there are the ruins of an elegant church, and the vestiges of several well built houses. We saw a number of good dwellings, and large plantations on the road leading down Ashley-River. In the evening we reached the city of Charleston, having rode about fifty miles.

Sunday 9. Brother Ellis preached in the morning. In the evening I felt some liberty in enlarging on Rom. x. 1, 2, 3. On Monday my soul and body enjoyed some ease and rest.

Friday 14. Our conference began, and we had a very free, open time. On Saturday night I preached on "I have set watchmen upon thy walls," &c. On the Sabbath, on "The Lord turned and looked on Peter," &c. It was a gracious season, both in the congregation, and in the love-feast. While another was speaking in the morning to a very crowded house, and many outside, a man made a riot at the door; an alarm at once took place; the ladies leaped out at the windows of the church, and a dreadful confusion ensued. Again whilst I was speaking at night, a stone was thrown against the north side of the church; then another on the south; a third came through the pulpit window, and struck near me inside the pulpit. I however continued to speak on—my subject, "How beautiful upon the mountains," &c.

Upon the whole, I have had more liberty to speak in Charleston this visit than I ever had before, and am of opinion that God will work here: but our friends are afraid of the cross.

Monday 17. Preached in the morning, and took my leave of the city: when I reached Mr. Giveham's the congregation had been dispersed about ten minutes.

I preached at R.'s, at L.'s, and at C. C. church, in the Edisto circuit: the people are insensible, and, I fear, are more in love with some of Christ's messengers than with Christ. I now changed my course and went through Orangeburgh by the congarees to Saleuda, and thence up to Broad-River quarterly meeting: we rode till one o'clock on Friday the 21st of March; I believe we have travelled about two hundred miles in five days: dear brother Smith accompanied me. I was so unwell that I had but little satisfaction at the quarterly meeting: my service was burdensome; but the people were lively.

Wednesday 26. We rode from Finch's to Odell's new church, where we had a good time whilst I enlarged on Tit. ii. 14. and administered the Lord's Supper. Thence to Smith's, thirty miles; after preaching we had a night meeting that prevented our getting to bed until about twelve o'clock: we had a comfortable cabin, and were very well entertained.

Thursday 27. I had but little freedom on "The foundation of God standeth sure." Brothers Mason and Major spoke after me. I went alone into the woods, and found my soul profitably solitary in sweet meditation and prayer.

Friday 28. Rode about thirty miles to B.'s: my soul was tried, but it was also comforted in the Lord. I was much led out on Eph. vi. 18. and we were employed till nearly twelve o'clock at night.

Sunday 30. I had some liberty in preaching, but the people began to move about when they were pointedly dealt with. Brothers Mason and Major spoke after me. I found it good to be alone by the solitary stream and silent woods, to study the welfare of Zion, and to pray for her prosperity.

Monday 31. We rode within a mile of Savannah River. The land in general, during our route, is very fine. We were benighted, and moping in the woods, made our journey a long one of about fifty miles.

Tuesday, April 1. We crossed the Savannah at the Forks, and came where I much wanted to be, in Georgia; nevertheless, I fear I shall have but little freedom here.

GEORGIA.—Wednesday, April 2. I rested; and compiled two sections, which I shall recommend to be put into our form of discipline in order to remove from Society, by regular steps, either preachers or people that are disorderly.

Saturday 5. I was led out in preaching at the quarterly meeting on Zech. xii. 10.

Sunday 6. There was a moving on the souls of the people ; and I felt much life on Isai. xlv. 22.

I have been told, that during the last rupture, the Indians butchered nearly one hundred people.

Wednesday 9. Our conference began at the Forks of Broad-River, where six members, and four probationers attended. Brother Major was sick, and could not meet us : soon after, he made his exit to his eternal rest.

Thursday 10, and Friday 11. I felt free, and preached with light and liberty each day. Many that had no religion in Virginia, have found it after their removal into Georgia and South Carolina : here at least the seed sprung up, wherever else it may have been sown. Our little conference was about sixty-one pounds deficient in their quarterage, nearly one third of which was made up to them.

SOUTH CAROLINA.—Sunday 13. I called at a Presbyterian meeting-house, and heard Mr. Hall, the minister, preach a good sermon on Isai. lv. : after meeting we rode to brother Moore's, twenty miles on the Seleuda.

Monday 14. Was almost entirely occupied with writing letters to the north.

Tuesday 15. I had many people at the widow Bowman's. While here we had a most awful storm ; I was afraid the house would come down. We rode in the night to M. Moore's : I was seized with illness on the way, which continued during the night ; next day however, I was able to pursue my journey.

Friday 18. We rode along crooked paths to Kasey's, where we received the afflicting account of the death of dear brother Major, who departed this life last Saturday : he was a witness of holiness, and died in peace and love.

Saturday 19. I preached at Wilson's, with some liberty, on Peter iii. 7.

Sunday 20. I spoke with little enlargement. Our friends here on Tyger River, are much alive to God, and have built a good chapel. We rode to Buffington's in the evening, on Fair-forest Creek, and were kindly entertained.

NORTH CAROLINA.—Tuesday 22. Rode to Rutherford court-house ; and the next day to Burke court-house : it being court time, we went on, and reached brother White's, on Johns-River, about ten o'clock at night : here I found both the saddles broke ; both horses foundered ; and both their backs sore—so we stopped a few days.

I preached on Rev. xxii. 5—8 ; and had liberty in speaking to the people : our souls were blest in a near access to the Lord. Our preachers in the Yadkin circuit have been sick : they have had hard travelling the past winter ; and the work has consequently suffered. I have read D.'s Study of Divinity—the catalogue of books at the end I thought of more value than all the rest of the work.

Sunday 27. I preached at the Globe, on the main branches of Johns-River, where there are a few who fear God : there was some stir, and I hope some good done.

Monday 28. After getting our horses shod, we made a move for Holstein, and entered upon the mountains ; the first of which I called steel, the second stone, and the third iron mountain : they are rough, and difficult to climb. We were spoken to on our way by most awful thunder and lightning, accompanied by heavy rain. We crept for shelter into a little dirty house where the filth might have been taken from the floor with a spade : we felt the want of fire, but could get little wood to make it, and what we gathered was wet. At the head of Watawga we fed, and reached Ward's that night. Coming to the river next day, we hired a young man to swim over for the canoe, in which we crossed, while our horses swam to the other shore. The waters being up we were compelled to travel an old road over the mountains. Night came on— I was ready to faint with a violent headach—the mountain was steep on both sides. I prayed to the Lord for help : presently a profuse sweat broke out upon me, and my fever entirely subsided. About nine o'clock we came to Grear's. After taking a little rest here, we set out next morning for brother Coxe's on Holstein-River. I had trouble enough : our route lay through the woods, and my pack-horse would neither follow, lead, nor drive, so fond was he of stopping to feed on the green herbage. I tried the lead, and he pulled back.—I tied his head up to prevent his grazing ; and he ran back : the weather was excessively warm.—I was much fatigued and my temper not a little tried. I fed at I. Smith's and prayed with the family. Arriving at the river, I was at a loss what to do ; but providentially, a man came along who conducted me across ; this has been an awful journey to me, and this a tiresome

day, and now, after riding seventy-five miles, I have thirty-five
miles more to General Russell's. I rest one day to revive man and
beast.

Friday, May 2. Rode to Washington, where I met brother Tunnell on the way to Mr. C.'s. We have to put up in houses where
we have no opportunity for retirement.

VIRGINIA.—Saturday 3. We came to General Russell's—a most
kind family in deed and in truth.

Sunday 4. Preached on Phil. ii. 5—9. I found it good to get alone
in prayer.

Tuesday 6. I had many to hear at Easley's on Holstein. I was
much wearied with riding a strange horse, having left mine to rest.
It is some grief that I cannot be so much in prayer on the road as
I would be. We had a good time, and a large congregation at K.'s.

TENNESSEE.—The people are in disorder about the old and new
state : two or three men, it is said, have been killed.

At Nelson's I had a less audience than was expected ; the people having been called away on an expedition against the new-
state men : my subject was Hebr. vi. 11, 12. Rode to Owens's, and
met our brethren from Kentucky, where I preached on Psalm cxlv.
17, 18, 19, with some fervour.

Came to Half-Acres and Keywoods where we held conference
three days, and I preached each day. The weather was cold ; the
room without fire, and otherwise uncomfortable, we nevertheless
made out to keep our seats until we had finished the essential parts
of our business.

Thursday 15. We came to General Russell's,—and on Friday to
I. Smith's on the south fork of Holstien-River.

Sunday 18. Rode to a chapel near New River, where I preached
on " How beautiful upon the mountains are the feet," &c. After
eating a morsel, we hasted on our way to F———'s. A twenty miles'
ride through the mountains brought us to our lodgings for the night
at K-———'s, near the Flower Gap.

Monday 19. We rode about fifty miles to S———'s : the weather
was warm in the extreme ; we had rain, thunder, and lightning—
and were weary enough.

Tuesday 20. After riding nearly thirty miles, we came to
M'Knight's chapel in North Carolina ; here I preached on Peter's
denial of Christ. Thence we went to Hill's : after meeting, we
proceeded to the neat and well-improved town of Salem : making
a journey, besides the labours of the day, of nearly forty miles.

I came to the quarterly meeting at C——'s, where I spoke feelingly and pointedly; and the word appeared to have effect.

Thursday 22. Preached at P——'s chapel: we then rode to C——'s, about seven miles from Guilford court-house, where we had a good time.

Friday 23. Was a damp, rainy day, and I was unwell with a slow fever and pain in my head: however I rode to Smith's chapel and preached: and thence to brother Harrison's, on Dan-River, and preached.—In the space of one week we have rode, through rough, mountainous tracts of country, about three hundred miles. Brothers Poythress, Tunnell, and myself have had serious views of things, and mature counsels together.

Sunday 25. Preached, and had a love-feast and sacrament.—I then rode to the widow Dicks's: many were waiting here, and the power of God was felt by some, whilst I enlarged on Isaiah lv. 1, 2, 3.

Monday 26. We had a good time at Martin's—Leaving this, on our way to Stamfield, we were obliged to swim our horses across Dan-River, and losing our road, made it late before we arrived. . Riding thirty miles brought us to Hammon's: here we had a serious, feeling time, whilst I spoke on Isaiah lxi.

Thursday 29. Reached E. T——'s about two o'clock, and gave a short discourse on "Happy is he that hath the God of Jacob for his help." Thence to Pope's, to Hill's, to Long's, and to Jones's chapel: on our way to the latter place we got out of our route when within a mile of the chapel, and did not reach it till two o'clock.

Sunday, June 1. At Clayton's there are a hundred blacks joined in society; and they appear to have real religion among them— here Ethiopia doth stretch out her hand unto the Lord. I suppose there were not less than a thousand souls at preaching.

NORTH CAROLINA.—Monday 2. Preached at Moore's in Northampton—once a poor, dead people, but now revived, and increased from eleven to sixty members.

We had much of the power of God at Clark's: sixty members, among whom are some children, are the subjects of this work.—I feel life among these people—preaching and praying is not labour here: their noise I heed not; I can bear it well when I know that God and Christ dwells in the hearts of the people. Thence I passed through Southampton, where I also beheld the power of God manifested in several lively meetings.

VIRGINIA.—Rode to and rested with Philip Davis. On Saturday I had a feeling, living time on Psalm lxxxv. 9, 10.

Sunday 8. We had a gracious season : it was a memorable day, and my soul was much blessed. After meeting, we hastened to Petersburg, where I preached on 2 Cor. v. 20. Our elders and deacons met for conference : all things were brought on in love. The town folks were remarkably kind and attentive ; the people of God in much love.—The awful circumstance of B. C—'s losing his religion, and lately attempting to pull out R. Swift's eyes, may yet be sanctified to some, and explained by his conduct hereafter.

Friday 13. I preached a pastoral sermon, under a large arbour near the borders of the town, on 1 Tim. iv. 13, 16. with considerable consolation.—Ordained Henry Ogburn and John Baldwin, deacons ; and Edward Morris and Ira Ellis, elders.

Sunday 15. I preached at the Manakintown—then rode to Maxey's.

Monday 16. Rode about fifty miles to brother Agee's in Buckingham county ; and thence to Bedford circuit ; in our route we were compelled to ford the James-River, not without danger : we were hospitably entertained.

Wednesday 18. At night I had some opening whilst I enforced " Whosoever shall call upon the name of the Lord shall be saved."

Heavy rains, bad roads, straying, bewildered in the woods,—through all these I worried to Murphy's : great was the cross under which I spoke on " The grace of God that bringeth salvation," &c. I had a high fever, and was otherwise distressed in body, and ill at ease in mind : I was afraid the medicine I had made use of would be injurious to me in consequence of my getting wet.

Saturday 28. I had considerable liberty, though unwell, at Ayres's new chapel.

Sunday 29. After preaching I went to V———'s, and after trying, had to silence him. O, my God, what awful subjects come before me !

Monday 30. Crossed the high mountains, and came to H———'s in Green-Brier.

Tuesday, July 1. I enlarged on Gal. iii. 22. We then rode to M'Pherson's, a serious family on Sinking-Creek, where I preached with some freedom. After crossing some considerable mountains, and preaching occasionally, on Friday we arrived at the Sweet-Springs : here I preached, and the people were very attentive.

Saturday 5, and Sunday 6. I had large congregations at Rohoboth ; I preached with some satisfaction.

Monday 7. Our troubles began ; it being the day we set out for Clarksburg. Thirty miles brought us to W——'s, on the Great-Levels.

Tuesday 8. Reached M'Neal's, on the Little Levels, where almost the whole settlement came together, with whom I found freedom on Matt. xi. 28, 29, 30. Our brother Phœbus had to answer questions propounded to him until evening.

Wednesday 9. We rode to the Clover-Lick, to a very remote and exposed house : here we found good lodgings for the place. The former tenant had made a small estate by keeping cattle, horses, &c. on the *range*, which is fertile and extensive.

Thursday 10. We had to cross the Alleghany mountain again, at a bad passage. Our course lay over mountains and through valleys, and the mud and mire was such as might scarcely be expected in December. We came to an old, forsaken habitation in Tygers-Valley : here our horses grazed about, while we boiled our meat : midnight brought us up at Jones's, after riding forty, or perhaps, fifty miles. The old man, our host, was kind enough to wake us up at four o'clock in the morning. We journeyed on through devious lonely wilds, where no food might be found, except what grew in the woods, or was carried with us. We met with two women who were going to see their friends, and to attend the quarterly meeting at Clarksburg. Near midnight we stopped at A——'s, who hissed his dogs at us : but the women were determined to get to quarterly meeting, so we went in. Our supper was tea. Brothers Phœbus and Cook took to the woods ; old —— gave up his bed to the women. I lay along the floor on a few deer skins with the fleas. That night our poor horses got no corn ; and next morning they had to swim across the Monongahela : after a twenty miles' ride we came to Clarksburg, and man and beast were so outdone that it took us ten hours to accomplish it. I lodged with Col. Jackson. Our meeting was held in a long close room belonging to the Baptists : our use of the house it seems gave offence. There attended about seven hundred people, to whom I preached with freedom ; and I believe the Lord's power reached the hearts of some. After administering the sacrament, I was well satisfied to take my leave. We rode thirty miles to Father Haymond's, after three o'clock, Sunday afternoon, and made it nearly eleven before we came in ; about midnight we went to rest, and rose at five o'clock next morning. My mind has been severely tried under the great fatigue endured both by myself and my horse. O, how glad should I be of a plain, clean plank to lie on, as preferable to most of the beds ; and where the beds are in a bad state, the floors are worse. The gnats are almost as troublesome here, as the moschetoes in the low-lands of the sea-board. This country will require much work to make it tolerable. The people are, many of them, of the boldest cast of adventurers, and with some the decencies of civilized society are scarcely regarded, two instances of which I myself witnessed. The great landholders who are industrious will soon show the effects of the aristocracy of wealth, by lording it over their poorer neighbours, and by securing to themselves all the offices of profit or honour : on the one hand savage warfare teaches them to be cruel ; and on the other, the preaching of Antinomians poisons them with error in doctrine : good moralists they are not, and good Christians they cannot be, unless they are better taught.

Tuesday 15. I had a lifeless, disorderly people to hear me at Morgantown, to whom I preached on " I will hear what God the Lord will speak." It is matter of grief to behold the excesses, particularly in drinking, which abound here. I preached at a new chapel near Colonel Martin's, and felt much life, love, and power. Rode to the widow R——'s, and refreshed with a morsel to eat : thence to M. Harden's, where, though we had an earth floor, we had good beds and table entertainment.

Friday 18. Rode forty miles to quarterly meeting at Doddridge's ; where we had a melting season.

Sunday 20. From twelve o'clock to-day we rode forty miles—my soul in sweet peace.

Tuesday 22. Our conference began at Union-Town : we felt great peace whilst together ; and our counsels were marked by love and prudence. We had seven members of conference and five probationers. I preached on 1 Peter v. 7.: and brother Whatcoat gave us an excellent discourse on " Oh! man of God, flee these things."

Friday 25. We concluded our conference.

Saturday and Sunday, 26, 27. Attended quarterly meeting.

Monday 28. Came over the mountains along very bad roads. Brother Whatcoat and myself were both sick. We stopped at Simkins's, and were comfortably entertained.

Virginia.—Tuesday 29. Reached Barratt's, where we had a little rest and peace. We had left our horses at Old Town on the other side of the river, but I thought it best to have them brought over, and so it was ; for that night there were two stolen. On

Monday we rested ; on Tuesday rode down to Capon ; and on Wednesday visited Bath. I took lodgings at brother Williams's, was well fixed, and found the waters to be of service to me.

Sunday, August 10. Preached at Bath. I received heavy tidings from the college—both our teachers have left ; one for incompetency, and the other to pursue riches and honours : had they cost us nothing, the mistake we made in employing them might be the less regretted. I have read one volume of Church History, by Mosheim, containing an account of the state of ecclesiastical matters in Germany, and the different churches.

Sunday 17. I attempted to preach at Bath, on the lame and the blind : the discourse was very *lame ;* and it may be, I left my hearers as I found them—*blind.*

I am now closely engaged in reading, writing, and prayer—my soul enjoys much of God. We have great rains, and are obliged to keep close house ; but we have a little of almost every thing to improve the mind—the languages, divinity, grammar, history, and belles-lettres : my great desire is to improve in the best things.

Sunday 24. Preached at Bath on Isaiah lxiii. 1. with little liberty and poor attendance. But we have some stir among the poor people in the country.

Friday 29. We left Bath, and on the Saturday and Sunday following attended a quarterly meeting. I felt enlargement on Peter's case, and also in the love-feast.

Monday, September 1. I enlarged with some freedom on the case of the man who brought the child to our Lord.

Wednesday 3. Rode from I. Hite's to the Blue-Ridge : the weather was warm, and so were the hearts of the people.

Thursday 4. I preached at Leesburg, and was very warm on " Thou wilt arise and favour Zion ;" and the people appeared to be somewhat stirred up. To-day I received a letter from brother Tunnell, informing of the spreading of the work of God in West New-River ; and several parts of North Carolina—Glory be to God, for his great and glorious power !

MARYLAND.—Wednesday 10. Our conference began in Baltimore. I chose not to preach while my mind was clogged by business with so many persons, and on so many subjects.

Sunday 14. I felt considerably moved at our own church in the morning, and in the Dutch Church in the afternoon : the Spirit of the Lord came among the people, and sinners cried aloud for mercy : perhaps not less than twenty souls found the Lord from that time until the Tuesday following.

Monday, Tuesday, and Wednesday, were spent at Cokesbury in examining and arranging the temporal concerns of the college.

PENNSYLVANIA.—Sunday 21. I preached with some satisfaction, morning and evening, in Philadelphia. On Monday our conference began and held until Friday 26.

Saturday 27. We left the city.

NEW-JERSEY.—Sunday 28. Preached with some assistance in Elizabethtown.

NEW-YORK.—Monday 29. Rode to New-York. Next day (Tuesday 30.) our conference began, and continued until Saturday the 4th of October.

NEW-JERSEY.—Sunday October 5, and Monday 6. My soul was uncommonly led out in prayer and preaching—I found it a very gracious season. My return brought me through Elizabethtown, Amboy, Hydestown, Crosswecks, and Burlington.

DELAWARE.—Sunday 12. I was much depressed in spirit whilst in Philadelphia. I left there on Wednesday, and preached at Chester; where I had some energy; and had openings at Wilmington and Duck-Creek, where I also administered the word of life.

Monday 20. Our meeting in Dover was attended with some power. At Milford we had liberty and love. At Johnstown I was very unwell, and was under the necessity of going to bed, but our friends were alive: God is with them of a truth. Preached at Shankland's. My soul enjoys great peace and love. On Sunday I was under bodily affliction, but I went to the court-house and spoke a few words on "Ye will not come to me that ye might have life." We have a house now building, and I hope something will be done here.

Monday was remarkably warm weather, and I was ready to faint whilst I rode to the Sound. We reached Powell's about three o'clock.

Wednesday 22. I was very alarming—seldom, if ever, have I felt more moved. We came away, and rode twenty-five miles, having nothing to eat from eight o'clock in the morning till six at night. My body was weak, but my soul was kept in peace. Knowing the obligations I am under to pay money to several persons to whom the college is indebted, my mind is much exercised, and I feel very heavily the weight of such responsibility. The Lord opened the heart of ——, and I thankfully received the kindness as from God and man.

MARYLAND.—Preached at Bowen's, and I trust the Lord was present; as also at the Lord's supper. We then hasted to the widow Paramore's, about nineteen miles : the people were moved whilst I exhorted them to come boldly to the throne of grace.

On Friday I met with an engaged people at Pernal's, and they appeared tender whilst I enlarged on "My grace is sufficient for thee." After meeting we rode to B.'s, nineteen miles.

VIRGINIA.—Saturday, November 1. Attended a quarterly meeting at Garrettson-chapel—O how changed ! A preacher absent nearly nine weeks from his circuit, failing to give proper notice of the quarterly meeting. Other persuasions are less supine ; and their minister boldly preaches against the freedom of the slaves. Our brother Everett with no less zeal and boldness, cries aloud for liberty—emancipation.

Sunday 2. Brother Whatcoat preached, and I exhorted a little. My soul and body are deeply depressed. We rode fifteen miles that evening, and held meeting again.

Monday 3. Myself and the people were comforted at S.'s : we had a meeting in the evening.

Wednesday 5. I preached at the school-house, on Peter's denial of Christ : it was a time of refreshing—there were few present that did not feel the word. Spoke again in the evening at S—'s to a very unfeeling people.

Friday 7. Preached at the court-house, to many people, with liberty. We have had heavy riding ; dust, heat, and fevers. Our meeting at Downing's almost overcame us with heat and fatigue.

MARYLAND.—At Annamessex quarterly meeting I was at liberty on Rev. iii. 20. Again I preached on "Fear not little flock," &c. most of our members in these parts have freed their slaves.

Wednesday 12. We had a precious season at the line chapel on Rev. "I counsel thee to buy of me gold tried in the fire," &c. After meeting I rode to Broad-Creek. We have travelled little less than two hundred miles a week.

Thursday 13. At quarterly meeting I preached on "Thy teachers shall not be removed into a corner."

Friday 14. My subject was "Is my hand shortened at all that I cannot redeem, or have I no power to deliver ?"—there was some moving on the souls of the people. Rode twelve miles to L—'s, and preached at night on "Search the Scriptures."

DELAWARE.—After preaching at North West Fork, I rode twenty-five miles to quarterly meeting at E—'s : here we had a good time. I preached at Johnson's, Todd's, and at the chapel. I feel myself weak, but the Lord is present.

Friday 21. I felt some power in speaking on Matt. xi. 5, 6. at Mr. K.—'s. We came on to Hooper's, where we had a time of refreshing.

Saturday 22, and Sunday 23. Attended quarterly meeting at William Frazier's : there was some quickening among the people each day.

We crossed Choptank to Bolingbroke—death! death! The second day of our meeting a great power went through the congregation, and a noble shout was heard among the people.

I was much led out at the Bay side. At Doctor Allen's I was greatly comforted after a wet ride of thirty miles.

I preached at Queenstown to a few people, who appear to be far gone in forgetfulness of God.

MARYLAND.—I went to Kent-Island, and found about two hundred and fifty people, among whom were some of the rich and great : we had a good meeting. I then returned to Queenstown, and gave the citizens another *rally;* there were more to hear than before.

Saturday 29. I felt some power in preaching at Boardley's. We had a little move among the people at Choptank. My soul is kept in peace. In times past I have felt some disagreeable impressions on my mind about the college being burnt; now I have heard of an attempt to do it : but I trust the Lord will encamp about the house. We had a very good meeting at Dover, although the weather was very cold.—We had meeting again that night in town—I hope not in vain. Next day I rode to Dudley's church, Queen-Annes ; and thence to Chester-Town, and preached on "Let us have grace whereby we may serve God acceptably, with reverence and godly fear."

Saturday, December 6. I had some freedom in preaching at Still-pond church, on "Simon, Satan hath desired to have you that he might sift you as wheat," &c.

Sunday 7. I preached at the widow Woodland's—was not in a good frame of body or mind. At Georgetown I felt still worse ; and to crown all, I had a long dispute with Mr. B— about ordination and experimental religion.

Monday 8. Rode to Cecil court-house, and had, I trust, a profitable time. We crossed Elk-River to brother Ford's, and had a gracious meeting at his house.

Tuesday 9. We had a damp ride to Cokesbury, and found it was
even as it had been reported to us :—an attempt had been made
to burn the college by putting fire into one of the closets ; but
some of the students made a timely discovery, and it was extinguished. I stayed two days and expended more than £100, and
felt my spirit tried. I put the young men to board in the college.
—We have some promising youths among them for learning, but
they want religion.

I came to Baltimore and found some tokens of the Divine presence, at the quarterly meeting, on Chron. xv. 8. " Thou canst save
by many, or by those that have no might."

Monday 15. Came to Cromwell's and preached with some satisfaction. Thence I hasted to Annapolis, where the Lord was present while I declared " The Lord's hand is not shortened."

Tuesday 16. Rode to Weems's chapel, and preached with fervour on " Oh! Zion that bringeth good tidings," &c. Thence to
Calvert quarterly meeting : the weather was very cold, but there
was some spiritual heat among the people.

Virginia.—Friday 19. Rode thirty miles to Hoe's ferry ; and
thence to Pope's, about thirty miles more : the weather is still
excessively cold.

Sunday 21. I preached to a few tender souls at P—'s, on Isaiah
xxix. " Yet a very little while and Lebanon shall be a fruitful field."

Tuesday 23. Had a few lively people at Woollard's. I read,
write, pray, and ride ; and hope to see much of the power of God
on this journey.

Christmas day. I preached in the open house at Fairfield's, on
Isaiah ix. 6. I felt warm in speaking—but there was an offensive
smell of rum among the people.

Saturday 26. At the Presbyterian church in Lancaster, there was
a divine stir in the congregation. Envy and disputation have been
injurious to the work of God in these parts—O may the Lord yet
help us and revive his work! I found our opposing the doctrine of
final perseverance had given offence : a house of our own will
alone fix us properly.

January 1, 1789. After waiting about two hours, the wind suddenly calmed, and I crossed Rappahannock and came to Cheese-
cake.

We had a comfortable meeting at R. M.'s, in Kingston, thence to
B——'s; and afterward to D——'s, where, although I had an unfeeling audience, I had satisfaction in my own soul.

We came to James-City; where God has wrought a glorious work; as also in New-Kent county in the same circuit: a number of young people have been made the subjects of this grace.

Thursday 8. I had a most agreeable passage, for the season, across James-River.—Arrived at Mooning's about three o'clock, and found a lively people. Christians here appear to stand faithful, but sinners are not brought in.

Friday 9. Was a good day at Ellis's: my soul felt peace, and I was happy to find our old friends standing fast.

Saturday 10. We had a happy meeting at Lane's chapel. I went to the widow Lane's: I felt uneasy; but I found it needful for me to be there.

Sunday 11. Preached on "Kiss the Son," &c. and afterward rode fifteen miles to Moss's. They are a dear people at Lane's chapel: slavery is greatly on the decline among them.

Tuesday 13. An appointment had been made at Mabry's chapel, but the sleet and rain hindered the people from attending; so I preached at brother Theweett's to about six preachers, and as many members.

Wednesday 14. I had about three hundred hearers at the Low-Ground chapel: our brethren shouted whilst I enlarged on Isaiah lxiii. 1. I have felt very solemn for two or three days past, as though God would speak through me to the souls of the people.

Thursday 15. Rode to Moore's—had a dead, dull people—except those few who came from a distance. Crossed Roanoak, and arriving at the place of preaching a little after night, I spoke on "Comfort ye, comfort ye my people," &c.

NORTH CAROLINA.—Saturday & Sunday 17, 18. Preached at Whitaker's chapel, where we had a profitable time: I found God had been working, and that many souls had been awakened.

We came to J——'s: in this neighbourhood the Christians are singularly devoted, but sinners yet stand it out. The Lord has begun to work on Sandy-Creek, in Franklin county, where twenty souls have been lately brought to God.—Came to Bemnet Hills, hungry and unwell. My soul enjoys much of God.

We had a shaking time at H——'s: a sweet love-feast and sacrament. Thence I went to Pope's chapel: I came to G——'s.

Saturday 24. Rode to Kimborough's, twenty miles, where there were many people, and but little engagedness among them. After attending a few appointments on Tuesday 27, I crossed Haw-River, and rode twenty miles to brother Kennon's, in Chatham

county: I had not been in this county for eight years; we had a
meeting at night, but I was strangely shut up.

Thursday 29. Rode to W.'s, wet and water-bound: we found
the poor Antinomian drunk; however, as the rain was great, we
made out to stay.

Friday 30. Rode through the rain to Bowdon's. Deep River
was very high; and we had an awful time in crossing it.

Saturday 31. Came to Fair-Creek, which was nearly swimming
high. Then to Little-River, but we could not cross: we stopped at M'D.'s, and ate our own morsel; afterward we rode down
the river, and was thankful to be housed.

Monday, February 2. I attended an appointment made for another preacher at Mask's, where there were a few serious souls.

Tuesday 3. I stopped on my way at Dr. King's, and took dinner,
and had my horse shod. By some means my appointments have
not been published.

SOUTH CAROLINA.—Came to the Green-Ponds; where there was
an appointment for me; I felt a little comforted. I have rode about
one hundred and forty miles in the last seven days, through a very
disagreeable part of the country to travel in when the waters are
high: I have had various exercises, and have suffered hunger, fatigue, and fever, and have not had a comfortable bed for a week past.

Wednesday 4. I was much moved at the Beauty-Spot, on " Ye
did run well," &c. I found it had been the case here; but ah!
the use of strong liqour.

We rode to R.'s, a long stretch across a deep swamp: we came
in late, and I preached with little liberty. I lodged at —— a poor,
kind man.

Sunday 8. Notwithstanding the rain, we had many to hear at
Flowers's. It was in due season that I was led out here on Peter's
denial of his Master: for there has been a great falling away, particularly by drunkenness: this was not told me till after preaching.

Monday 9. Rode to Rewell's meeting-house: my soul was in
peace, and uncommonly led out in preaching. Thence to Port's,
Long-Ferry, three miles across Pee Dee: the inundation of the
river, occasioned by the rains, has made a mere sea. My mind
has been variously tried and strongly exercised by dejection. Lord,
give me faith and patience!

Tuesday 10. Came, after a ride of forty miles, to Georgetown,
and lectured on Isai. xl. 1—9.

Friday 13. Rode forty-five miles to Wappataw; and next day
arrived in Charleston in sweet peace of soul.

Sunday 15. Preached in the morning with some light. In the afternoon on Matt. xi. 28, 29, 30. I preached again on Tuesday and on Wednesday. My heart was drawn out greatly for these people.

Firday 20. I spoke very pointedly on Rev. iii. 20—22. but the people are of small spiritual understanding. Lord, stir them up! I was closely employed in making my plan, and arranging the papers for conference. I made out a register of all the preachers on the continent who bear the name of Methodists.

Saturday 21. I was very ill with a fever and cholic; and it being rainy, I kept within doors.

Sunday 22. Very rainy, but I had about a hundred blacks, and nearly fifty whites to hear me. I preached also in the afternoon, and at night.

Tuesday 24. I set out for Edisto circuit, journeying up the south side of Ashley-River. Here live the rich and great who have houses in the city and country, and go backward and forward in their splendid chariots: the land, however, with the exception of the rice-fields, is barren, the weather is cold; but my soul has peace, full and flowing peace. After riding thirty-six miles, I was kindly entertained by Mr. Giveham—but there was still something wanting.

Wednesday 25. They were out of bread at P——'s, and we found our own stores of use. We had to send one of our weary horses eight miles to fetch the flour from the mill.

Thursday 26. Rode to Bruten's, and enjoyed uncommon happiness in God. Some time in the night Dr. Coke came in : he had landed in Charleston about three hours after I left the city: next day he and myself both spoke at Ridgell's.

Sunday, March 1. We spent the day at Chester's : we had very few hearers, occasioned, in part, by a black man's preaching not far distant.

Monday 2. I was violently exercised. The Doctor and myself both preached at Puckett's. Thence we set out with a design to reach Treadway's, but were greatly deceived, and went up the road that leads to Ninety-Six; at last we thought we had gone far enough, and stopped at a house twenty-one miles from the place whence we started, and still further from the place we aimed at.

GEORGIA.—Came to Doctor Fuller's, at Beach-Island, and next day arrived in Augusta, Georgia. Riding late two nights past, has much disordered me ; having taken a cold, attended with a fever and pain in the head.

Thursday 5. I obtained a little rest at brother Haines's.

Friday 6. Although it rained, we had a few people at Browns-borough : next day there was some life at Scott's : here they have built us a large chapel.

Sunday 8. Our conference began at Grant's. Here we have a house for public worship; and one also at Merreweather's. On Thursday we appointed a committee to procure 500 acres of land for the establishment of a school in the state of Georgia. Conference being ended, we directed our hasty steps back to Charleston, calling at the several places we attended on our journey hither.

SOUTH CAROLINA.—Sunday 15. We reached the city, having rode two hundred miles in about five days and two hours. Here I received a *bitter pill* from one of my greatest friends—praise the Lord for my trials also—may they all be sanctified!

Tuesday, Wednesday, and Thursday, 17, 18, 19. were spent in conference : it was a time of peace and love. My mind was much hurried with book, and other temporal concerns. We had an unkind attack published against us relative to our slave rules; it was answered to purpose. I had not much doubt who the author of this unworthy work was.

Saturday 21, was spent in preparing to move on Monday next.

Sunday 22. Doctor Coke preached an ordination sermon in the forenoon; and in the afternoon I felt lively in soul whilst I enlarged on Ezek. xxxiii. 5.

Monday 23. We left the city, and rode upwards of forty miles.

Tuesday 24. Crossed Santee, and came to brother Browman's.

Wednesday 25. Preached at Gibson's—then rode to Ramsay's, near Statesburg, sixteen miles.

Thursday 26. I was hurried away to preach a funeral sermon. I have rode about one hundred and fifty miles, and preached three times since I left Charleston, last Monday morning. I am at times tempted to lightness; yet, blessed be God, my soul has sweet communion with him.

Saturday 28. At Bradford's chapel I preached on Hebr. xi. 16, 17. At Rembert's, on Isaiah xl. 1. My soul was blest among the people.

Sunday 29. I was led out in preaching and prayer; the people were melted; and the work of God progresses. I trust the Lord will get himself great glory here.

Monday 30. We rode about fifty miles to Colonel Marshall's : the weather was very warm, and we were hungry and weary.

NORTH CAROLINA.—Wednesday, April 1. The people came together at Jackson's at twelve o'clock; I did not reach there until three—I enlarged a little on Zech. xiii. 12. and was somewhat severe. I rode to Savannah-Creek, and met with an Antinomian people. Reached Threadgill's; having been out twelve hours, and rode nearly forty miles, without food for man or beast.

Friday 3. Preached by the way, and came to Randall's, twenty miles. We have rode three hundred miles in about nine days, and our horses' backs are bruised with their loads. I want more faith, patience, and resignation to the will of God in all things. I wish to send an extra preacher to the Waxsaws, to preach to the Catabaw Indians: they have settled amongst the whites on a tract of country twelve miles square.

Sunday 5. We had a move whilst I was speaking on Isai. xxxiii. 14, 15. some souls were brought to experience peace with God. Here Doctor Coke came up with us: we expect to continue together for some time. We had a long ride to Jones's: I preached there, and continued on to M'Knight's, on the Yadkin.

Friday 11. We opened our conference, and were blessed with peace and union; our brethren from the westward met us, and we had weighty matters for consideration before us.

VIRGINIA.—We left M'Knight's, having about two hundred miles to ride in four days. We had a tedious ride to Almond's, and a blessed season of grace.—Set out from Almond's, and reached Good's.

Saturday 19. We rode thirty-six miles to Petersburg. On Sunday the Doctor preached. I had nothing to say in public. We met the preachers on Saturday and Sunday evenings, and brought our work forward. I had disagreeable feelings while here; there is a spiritual death among the people.—I spoke a little on Monday and on Wednesday.

Thursday 23. We came to Manchester. My exertions, want of rest, and distress of mind, brought on a violent headach; instead of preaching, I found myself under the necessity of going to bed. Doctor Coke had gone over the river to Richmond and preached there.

Friday 24. We rode about fifty miles; and next day reached Fredericksburg, but found no door open. We met with one soul in distress.

Sunday 26. Having no appointment to preach, we pushed on and rode forty-five miles, and lodged in Prince-William county.

Monday 27. Arrived at Leesburg, and opened the conference. We found a little rest comfortable to man, and advantageous to beast.

MARYLAND.—Thursday 30. We crossed Patomac into Maryland. My soul cleaves to God ; but I am again afflicted in my head. Reaching brother Nicholson's, in Montgomery, we were kindly entertained.

Friday, May 1. I felt life in speaking.

Saturday 2. We attended quarterly meeting. Not being permitted to use the chapel, we went into a tobacco-house : many attended—and the young converts shouted aloud.

Sunday 3. Was a great day to saints and sinners : God has wrought wonderfully in brother Pigman's neighbourhood ; fifty or sixty souls have been suddenly and powerfully converted to God.

Came to Baltimore, and had very lively meetings ; multitudes came to hear, and great cries were heard among the people, who continued together until three o'clock in the morning ; many souls professed to be convicted, converted, sanctified.

On reaching Cokesbury, we found that here also God was working among the students. One, however, we expelled. We revised our laws, and settled our temporal concerns.

Tuesday 12. We were detained at Susquehannah-Ferry, so that we were compelled to ride in the night to reach Chester-Town.

We had a blessed work of God on our way, loud shouting was heard in almost every meeting—at sacrament especially, the Lord's power and presence were great indeed.—At Duck-Creek we had a good season.

Saturday 16. Doctor Coke preached in Wilmington.

Sunday 17. The Doctor preached at Chester ; and in Philadelphia in the evening.

Wednesday 20. In the evening the Lord's power came down among the people in the city ; and I hope to hear He is doing great things.

NEW-JERSEY.—Thursday 21. Rode to Burlington in Jersey. In crossing the Delaware we encountered an uncommon storm, but were providentially brought safely over. We were comfortable in our meeting ; but we had a painful interview and explanation with L. H. H. O, my soul, keep near to God !

Friday 22. We rode to Trenton ; and on Saturday 23. opened our conference in great peace. We laboured for a manifestation of the Lord's power, and it was not altogether in vain.

Sunday 24. We had abundance of preaching.

Monday 25. We rode through a heavy rain to Elizabethtown.

and next day reached New-York. I was under great travail of
soul for a revival of religion.

NEW-YORK.—Thursday 28. Our conference began : all things
were conducted in peace and order. Our work opens in New-York
state ; New England *stretcheth out the hand* to our ministry, and I
trust thousands will shortly feel its influence.—My soul shall praise
the Lord. In the midst of haste I find peace within.

Sunday 31. We had a gracious season to preachers and people,
while I opened and applied Isaiah xxv. 6, 7, 8. " And in this mountain shall the Lord of Hosts make unto all people a feast of fat
things ; a feast of wines on the lees ; of fat things full of marrow ;
of wines on the lees well refined."

Friday, June 5. Doctor Coke left us and went on board the
Union for Liverpool. My soul retires into solitude, and to God.
This evening I was enabled to speak alarmingly, and felt my heart
much engaged for about thirty minutes on Isaiah xxix. 17, 18, 19.
the power of God, and a baptising flame came among the people.

I have lately read Whiston's Translation of the Apostolical
Institutions (so called)—Also Cave's Lives of the Apostles and
Fathers.

Sunday 7. Was a good day. I felt inwardly quickened towards
the close of my morning's discourse, and the people were moved;
in the afternoon many were divinely drawn, and my own soul was
humbled and filled with the love of God.—Several souls have been
stirred up this conference : I trust the Lord will claim the people of York for his own.

Tuesday 9. We left the city of New-York, and came to Kingsbridge ; after refreshing ourselves and our horses, we pushed on to
East-Chester.—The appointment for us was to have been made at
D—'s : there came together about two hundred people, among
whom there was a considerable move.

Wednesday 10. My horse was lamed, (by fetters, I suppose) so
that I had to walk part of the way to New-Rochelle : proper
notice of my coming not having been given, I had but one hundred and fifty hearers.—We have a good house here ; a large society ; and several of the old members whom I formed into a
society some years past, are still alive to God.

Thursday 11. My horse continues lame ;—the journey is long,
and the day unfavourable—yet I must go.

I came on to Crum-Pond, and expected to have preached at
Oakley's church, but my appointment was made at P—'s, where

I had but few.   Returned to F——'s ; we had a comfortable time at Oakley's church at seven, o'clock.

We rode four miles, and stopped at K—'s for some refreshment : then hasted on to Peekskill-Hollow, where I found a poor, simple-hearted people, to whom I enforced " Repent, and be converted, that your sins may be blotted out ;" there was a power attended the word.   We rode about twenty miles to brother Jackson's, where brother Cook lay sick : we had heard that he was dead.   I laboured under violent temptation—vast consolation followed. Glory! Glory to God! He bears me up, body and soul. In our way we stepped into a house, exhorted and prayed with the mother and daughter, who appeared thankful for our services.

Sunday 14. Preached at Jackson's, in Dutchess county, to a considerable number of quiet hearers; I hope not in vain.   Brother Cook is low in body ; but his soul is solidly happy in God, who will be glorified in his life or death.   The people here are a still kind of folks ; but God can work in a storm or a calm.

Monday 15. We rode about twenty miles to Dover : the settlers in this neighbourhood are mostly Low Dutch.   It is a day of small things with us ; yet I trust there are a few feeling souls.   We had very alarming meetings at noon and at night.   Thence to Oblongs, where I found a dull people : I exerted myself, sick as I was ; and had I been well, I should have made no little noise.   After meeting we rode to ——, where an Antinomian came, drunk as he was, to tell his experience : he gabbled strangely until I stopped his mouth ; he then left us. Rode to L——s, and preached on " Seek ye first the kingdom of God," &c. the people appeared like rocks ; O that the hammer and fire of God's word and love might come down among them !

Friday 19. I preached in a barn on the North-River : my hearers were chiefly Low Dutch.   Our congregations are small—*the craft is in danger;* we are therefore not to wonder if we meet with opposition.   To begin at the right end of the work, is to go first to the *poor;* these *will,* the rich, *may possibly,* hear the truth : there are among us who have blundered here.   I feel as if I wanted to get across the river ; I am pressed in spirit, and pity our preachers who labour here ; it seems as if I should die amongst this people with exertions and grief.

Sunday 21. Preached at Latin-Town to a poor, dull people ; some, however, appeared to be moved.   At Allen's I was more enlarged, and many wept, and felt the word.   We have had a trying, warm day to ride in, and preach twice.

Monday 22. Rain and business prevented most of the people from attending at Newburg, except a few women. I felt moved while I spoke on Isaiah lxiii. : I hope the Lord will water the word sown.

NEW-JERSEY.—Thursday 25. I was sick. Brother Whatcoat gave them a sermon at Warwick, on the " wages of sin ;" and I gave them a finishing exhortation : I have no desire to see them again until there is some change.

Friday 26. The power of God came down among the people at B.'s, and there was a great melting. After meeting we rode through the heat fifteen miles to Pepper-Cotton.

Saturday 27. Rode to the stone church ; and found stony hearts. The Methodists ought to preach only in their own houses—I have done with the houses of other people : brother Whatcoat bore the cross, and preached for me here. When I see the stupidity of the people, and the contentiousness of their spirit, I pity and grieve over them. I have hard labour in travelling amongst the rocks and kills.

Sunday 28. My body is weak ; my spirits are low ; and I am burdened under the spiritual death of the people : yet, O my soul, praise the Lord ! I spoke a few words with freedom at Sweezey's, to insensible people : we then drove through the heat to Axford's, where I found life and liberty amongst my hearers.

Monday 29. We had a heavy ride to C.'s, where brother W. preached, while some of the audience slept. Thence we came to M'Cullock's. I had no small trial with A. C. who was once a preacher amongst us and disowned. He had, in some instances, fallen short of his quarterage during his ministry, and now insisted on my paying him his deficiencies : I did not conceive that in justice or conscience this was required of me ; nevertheless, to get rid of him, I gave him £14.

PENNSYLVANIA.—Wednesday, July 1. I had a good time at Newman's, near Hunt's ferry. We crossed the ferry on Thursday, about six o'clock, got some refreshment at Inkletown, whence we proceeded to Climer's, where we had a good meeting.

Friday 3. Came to Philadelphia ; here I found enough to do. My soul longs for more religion in this city ; I am distressed for these people : twenty years have we been labouring in Pennsylvania, and there are not one thousand in society : how many of these are truly converted God knows.

Sunday 5. We had a dead time, O that the Almighty would bless and stir up this people !

Rode to Randon, where there were a few feeling souls.

Tuesday 7. It being harvest-home, and short notice, we had few hearers. I love God supremely, and feel myself greatly weaned from earth : I have a glorious victory ; sweetly resting and suffering in Christ. Yesterday I felt so unwell that I could scarcely sit on my horse. My soul was so filled with God, that it appeared as if all sense of pain was suspended by the power of faith. I was so led out in speaking at the Valley church, that all my sufferings were forgotten. I spoke very loud a part of the time ; we had a gracious season.

Wednesday 8. After riding thirty miles, I preached at Rodfong's at night with satisfaction, and souls were brought to God.

Friday 10. I called on Mr. H——, a Dutch Presbyterian minister ; he and his wife were both very kind : I believe they are children of God. I had an interview with Mr. M——, a Lutheran minister, and teacher of languages : he is a childlike, simple-hearted man, and has a considerable knowledge of the arts and sciences. We came to York ; but I felt no desire to preach. I proceeded on to Carlisle : in the morning I was permitted to preach in the church ; but in the evening, this privilege was denied me : it was said, the reason was, because I did not read prayers, which I had forborne to do because of my eyes ; I apprehend the true cause might be found in the pointed manner in which I spoke on " Blessed is he whosoever shall not be offended in me." I went to the court-house and called them to repentance, from " Look unto me, and be ye saved, all ye ends of the earth ;" to the great offence of all who set themselves up for judges, and who declared it was no preaching.

Wednesday 15. Came to Juniata-River ; we were well nigh being lost in the woods, but kind Providence brought us safe in company with brother W—— to I. C——'s, and we lodged there.

Thursday 16. Came to G——'s, nine miles from Bedford, and being informed that the people thereabouts were willing to hear, we yielded to the persuasion of some who desired us to stay and preach.

Friday 17. We rode on to Wells's, a place visited by our preachers : here we had a good night's rest.

Saturday 18. We passed Greensburg, stopping at Hanover Davis's, a man who has had trouble and conviction : his three sons were killed by the Indians ; his wife and two children taken prisoners, and detained from him eighteen months.

Sunday 19. Came to Rowlett's and dined ; thence we set out and

reached Pittsburg, twenty-five miles; I preached in the evening
to a serious audience.   This is a day of very small things : what
can we hope? yet, what can we fear ?   I felt great love to the people ; and hope God will arise to help and bless them.

Monday 20. I preached on Isai. lv. 6, 7. had some zeal: and
the people were very attentive ; but alas! they are far from God,
and too near the savages in situation and manners.   We were not
agreeably stationed at ——, who was continually drunk, and our
only alternative was a tavern.

Tuesday 21. I spoke on " The Son of Man is come to seek and
to save that which was lost :" we were crowded, and I felt more
courage.   The night before, the rude soldiers were talking and
dancing about the door; but now they were quiet and mute ; this,
I judged, might be owing to the interference of the officers, or
magistracy.

Wednesday 22. We left Pittsburg, and came by the Alleghany-
River to Wilson's, who was formerly an elder in the Presbyterian
Church.   Brothers Green, Willis, and Conway, were my compa-
nions on the road.

Thursday 23. We had a number of poor, attentive people at
M'G——'s, the weather was excessively warm, and we were in a
close log-house, without so much as a window to give us air.

Saturday 25. We rode through a heavy rain to Yohogany, to
brother Moore's quarterly meeting.   We had a shout amongst the
people, and I felt much liberty of soul in speaking.   In the love-
feast the Lord manifested his power ; one woman, in particular,
was so wrought upon that she fell to the ground.

We came to Union-Town, where there appeared to be some
melting love among the people.   Now I believe God is about to
work in this place : I expect our circuits are better supplied than
formerly ; many of the people are alive to God ; and there are
openings in many places.   I wrote a letter to Corn-planter, chief
of the Seneca nation of Indians.   I hope God will shortly visit
these outcasts of men, and send messengers to publish the glad
tidings of salvation amongst them.   I have constant consolation,
and do not feel like my former self.

MARYLAND.—Friday 31. I crossed the mountain, and lodged, I
trust for the last time, at S——'s.   Preached at Barratt's, to a
dry, unfaithful people.   The number of candidates for the ministry are many ; from which circumstance I am led to think the
Lord is about greatly to enlarge the borders of Zion.

Monday, August 3. Preached at Cumberland.   It is partly fulfilled—none cared to give us ought to eat. My poor country-woman, who sometimes heard and trembled, was absent this time; in her sickness she cried out, "it is too late"—and rejected prayer. It was a time of refreshing at Old Town, in Maryland ; the Lord is among this people. Brother Willis preached the funeral sermon of Mrs. Sprigg; a blooming, fair woman ; at her own desire she was interred in our burying-ground. She died greatly lamented by her family, to whom her death is one loud call to turn to God. I trust she died in peace.

VIRGINIA.—Friday 7. Came to Bath. I took lodgings with our Virginia friends, Adams and Summers.

Saturday 8. My soul has communion with God, even here. When I behold the conduct of the people who attend the springs, particularly the *gentry*, I am led to thank God that I was not born to riches ; I rather bless God, that I am not in hell, and that I cannot partake of pleasure with sinners. I have read much, and spoke but little since I came here. The water has been powerful in its operation. I have been in great pain, and my studies are interrupted.

August 19. I left Bath ; which was much sooner than I expected.

God was powerfully present at Hendrick's, where there were twelve or fifteen hundred people : many professed to be converted to God—Glory be to his name ! My body enjoys better health ; and blessed be God! my soul is wholly kept above sin: yet I blame myself for not being more watchful unto prayer; and I sometimes use unnecessary words. We made a tour through Berkley circuit, where I had some freedom; and where we found not a little living affection in the congregations.

Sunday 23. We had alarming words at Winchester, from Ezek. xxxiii. 11. I feel the worth of souls, and their disobedience gives me sorrow of heart.—Oh Jehovah ! work for thine own glory !

Saturday 29. Our quarterly meeting began in the woods near Shepherd's-Town : we had about seven hundred people : I felt energy and life in preaching, and power attended the word. Brother Willis spoke, and the Lord wrought powerfully.

Sunday 30. Was a high day—one thousand or fifteen hundred people attended ; sinners began to mock, and many cried aloud ; and so it went. I was wonderfully led out on Psalm cxlv. 8—12 ; and spoke, first and last, nearly three hours. O, how the wicked contradicted and opposed !

Maryland.—Wednesday, September 1. I came to brother Philips's, in Maryland, and had a quickening time. God has preached to the whole family by the death of his daughter, and the fire spreads throughout the whole neighbourhood.

We must needs go through Samaria.—I called at Frederick-Town, and had a number of wild, unfeeling hearers. Thence to Liberty, where the Almighty is working amongst the people. I preached in the day, and again at night—I hope not in vain.

Friday 4. I rode to Seneca—O what hath God wrought for these people ! many precious souls have been brought to the knowledge of salvation.

Monday 7. Preached at Rowle's : here fifty or sixty souls profess to have been brought to God in a few weeks. We had a shout, and a soul converted to God. I preached in the evening at Baltimore, on " Lord, increase our faith."

Tuesday 8. Preached in town and at the Point. The last quarterly meeting was a wonder-working time : fifty or sixty souls, then and there, appeared to be brought to God : people were daily praying from house to house ; some crying for mercy, others rejoicing in God, and not a few, day after day, joining in society for the benefit of a religious fellowship. Praise the Lord, O my soul ! I spent some time in visiting from house to house, and begging for the college. The married men, and the single men ; the married women, and the single women, I met apart, and was comforted. Many of the children of the Methodists are the happy subjects of this glorious revival. We have more members in Baltimore, (town and Point,) than in any city or town on the continent besides.

Sunday 13. I preached three times ; baptised, and administered the sacrament twice ; and ordained A. F—— and W. L—— deacons. I trust it was a profitable time to many.—I took cold, and was much hurt by labour, so that I could hardly move my body.

Monday 14. Came to Daniel Evan's, one of our oldest members, and his house one of our oldest stands ; to this day he has continued to be steadfast.—The Lord has now made bare his arm, and brought in forty or fifty young people, among whom are some of his own children, for whom so many prayers have been offered up to God : the fire of the Lord spreads from house to house, and from heart to heart.

Tuesday 15. I had but few hearers at Hunt's chapel, but the Lord was present, and I am persuaded there was not an unfeeling soul in the house. I spent the evening with one of the great : the

Lord and his own conscience will witness that I did not flatter him. O that his soul were converted to God!

Friday 18. At G——'s we had a solemn time ; the power of the Lord has been displayed here to great purpose.

Sunday 20. Was an alarming time at the Forks church—a number of serious people—no trifling here now : how many dead souls restored from a backsliding state ! and their children converted too.

Monday 21. Rode in the evening to Cokesbury. I found I. Steward had gone to his final rest : he was a pious lad who kept too close to his studies. He praised God to the last, even when he was delirious : it made the students very solemn for a season.

Sunday 27. Preached at Gunpowder chapel in the forenoon, and at Abingdon at three o'clock.

Monday 28. After a long absence I preached at Bush Forest chapel : this was one of the first houses that was built for the Methodists in the state of Maryland ; and one of the first societies was formed here. They had been dead for many years ; of late the Lord has visited this neighbourhood, and I suppose, from report, fifty souls have been converted to God.

I preached at Havre de Grace with divine illumination and authority. Thence I went to ——; I was hardly welcome—perhaps I wrong him ; I shall know when I call again. Called at I. and S. Hersey's, and found the Lord had not departed from these houses ; I hope their children will all come to God.

Wednesday 30. At Wilmington I was warm in spirit. Thence I rode to Philadelphia ; where I gave a short discourse on another man's appointment ; my subject—Jacob's wrestling with God. On Friday night I spoke on " Who may abide the day of his coming?"

Sunday, October 4. We were not without the presence of the Lord at our love-feast and sacrament this day. Brother Willis spoke feelingly in the afternoon.

Monday 5. We had a meeting of the principal members in order to consult about the incorporation of our church.

NEW-JERSEY.—Tuesday 6. After twenty years preaching, they have built a very beautiful meeting-house at Burlington ; but it is low times there in religion. At New-Mills both preachers and people appeared to feel, and the watch-night was attended with some breathings after God.

Thursday 9. We had a poor, dry meeting at Mount-Holly : some were alarmed with fear, lest we should make a noise as we had done in Philadelphia; some dear country friends felt the Lord powerfully, and carried home the flame.

Friday 10. I felt inward strength at Bethel on Isai. lxiii. 12. The power was present, but there is not as much religion amongst them as formerly.

Saturday 11. My ride to Bethel was thirty miles; and thirty miles more brought me to Deerfield; I spoke very alarmingly, and to little purpose at the Methodistico-Presbyterian church.

Sunday 12. At the Glass-House I felt myself, and the Lord made others feel—to purpose, I hope. Thence to Salem, at three o'clock: it was levelling work, storm and thunder, whilst I opened and applied Isai. xxx. 20, 21.

Monday 13. I returned to Philadelphia, where there were five criminals hanged; one of them professed conversion.

Tuesday 15. Was the day of election for representatives; preaching in the evening was to little purpose, on "Arm of the Lord awake." "O Lord, of life! when shall it be."

DELAWARE.—I preached at Wilmington, on the dedication of our new chapel: thus far are we come after more than twenty years' labour in this place.

Thursday 17. I preached at Dickinson's. Here we have a good house built; and a blessed foundation of living stones fixed on the chief corner-stone. After preaching at Severson's and Duck-Creek Cross Roads, we came on Saturday to Dover quarterly meeting; here the congregation was large and serious.

Sunday 20. Preached on "The Lord whom ye seek shall suddenly come to his temple." Ordained W. I. and I. B. elders. We have had encouraging intelligence of an opening in New-England: we shall send Jacob Brush to assist Jesse Lee, who has been some time visiting those parts.

Reached judge White's in the evening, and rested there on Monday.

Tuesday 22. Rode to Millford; where we had a great move and noble shouting. I felt myself very unwell. We had a very comfortable love-feast next morning. I was taken with a sore throat, and brother Whatcoat supplied my lack of service. I was laid up four days; a violent headach and fever attended the inflammation in my throat, with little or no perspiration. I made use of flaxseed tea, and a very great expectoration followed.

Wednesday 30. I came to Lowry's, at the head of Nanticoke.

I still feel much pain, with a fever and hoarseness. I must take blame to myself for riding sometimes in the night and cold evenings without an upper coat : I am growing old ; and I live much in southern climes. I lodged at brother H——'s, who was ill with a bilious and nervous complaint.

Thursday 31. Came to W——, and was kindly entertained.

Friday, November 1. We rode in the rain—it was almost enough to kill healthy men.—After steeping our feet in warm water, we came to brother Downing's. Next day we rode twenty-eight miles to Paramour's ; my rest being interrupted, I rose early, and rode through the cold to the love-feast, where we had great shouting.

Although very weak in body, I rode thirty miles ; a dish of tea, and a biscuit and a half, was all my food till six o'clock in the evening.

Monday 4. I rode forty miles to Magotty-Bay, and preached to a few people. The Antinomians please them and gain them—alas ! for us. O, that the Lord would send an earthquake of his power among them!

Tuesday 5. We had an open time at brother J——'s. The school for the charity boys much occupies my mind : our annual expenditure will amount to £200, and the aid we get is but trifling : the poverty of the people, and the general scarcity of money, is the great source of our difficulties ; the support of our preachers who have families absorbs our collections, so that neither do our elders or the charity school get much. We have the poor, but they have no money ; and the worldly, wicked rich we do not choose to ask.

I have rode about one hundred miles from Sunday morning till Tuesday night ; at the same time very unwell with a cold and influenza, which spreads in almost every family.

Wednesday 6. We had many people at Accomack court-house, and power attended the word whilst brothers E. and W. spoke

Thursday & Friday 7, 8. We held quarterly meeting at Downings ; the first day the Lord was powerfully present, and the people were greatly agitated ; on the second day at the love-feast and sacrament there was a shout, and I believe two hundred souls praised God at one time; my soul was happy among them.

MARYLAND.—Saturday 9. At Annamessex quarterly meeting the Lord was amongst the people on the first day. On Sunday at the love-feast, the young were greatly filled, and the power of the Most High spread throughout ; it appeared as if they would have

continued till night if they had not been in some measure forced
to stop that we might have public worship. I stood near the window and spoke on Isaiah lxiv. 1—5. there was a stir, and several sinners went away. There were very uncommon circumstances of a supernatural kind said to be observed at this meeting.
The *saints of the world*, are dreadfully displeased at this work;
which, after all, is the best evidence that it is of God.

The preachers urged me to preach at Princess Anne; I did so;
and many poor, afflicted people came out; I trust some will be
able to say of Christ, "He is altogether lovely!"

I felt uncommon power in preaching at Thomas Garrettson's—
surely the Lord will work.

At the quarterly meeting I did not speak the first day; the second, I preached on Rom. x. 14, 15. there was a little stir, yet
this is said to be the dullest, or one of the dullest places in the
peninsula.

Thursday 14, was a warm day, and we had a heavy ride to
the Line chapel : there were but few hearers, owing to the great
affliction that prevails. The influenza, and other complaints, carry
off many people ; and it is an awful time.

Friday 15. Came to Broad-Creek chapel, where some of the
wicked had broken the windows. There had been a stir at the
quarterly meeting, and a testimony borne against their revellings,
and it was judged, that on this account the injury was committed
on the house. My throat was sore, and my testimony feeble on
2 Cor. vi. 1. I rode to the head of Nanticoke, where brother
Whatcoat preached a warm sermon.

Saturday 16. Preached at Brown's chapel : the general affliction hindered many from attending ; but we were happy together,
and it was a strengthening, confirming time to many tried souls.

Sunday 17. The people were shouting the praises of God when
I came ; after the noise and fervour had subsided, I preached on
the men of Nineveh's repenting at the preaching of Jonah ; and
the word sunk into some hearts.

Monday 18. We had a noble shout, and the people rejoiced in
the Lord.

Friday 22, being the day of our quarterly meeting fast, we
strove to keep it as well as our feeble bodies would admit.

Saturday and Sunday, 23, 24. There was a shaking among the
people ; some were alarmed; some professed to be justified ; and
others sanctified ; whilst the wicked brought with them much of

the power of Satan. I received some relief for my poor orphans.
For some days past I have been kept in an humble, living, holy,
conquering frame.

Monday 25. Although the north-west wind blew very strong,
we crossed Choptank River and came to Bolingbroke : here we
had loud shouts, and living testimonies from many of our oldest
members, whilst some of our gay young Methodists were mute.
Being a day of public thanksgiving, I rode to Wye, where there is
a good new chapel : the rain hindered, so that we had but few
hearers. Came through the rain to Tuckahoe.

Friday 29. There was a good move at Choptank-Bridge. I
ordained five persons to the office of deacons.

Saturday 30. Preached with some freedom at Dover.

Sunday 31. I preached at Duck-Creek. Stopped, and gave
them a discourse at Middletown ; and spent the evening with a
worthy kind friend. A number of dear old brethren accompanied
me to Cokesbury, where we had an examination of the boys, and
stationed eleven on charity. Thence we hastened on to Baltimore.

Thursday, December 4. Our council was seated, consisting of
the following persons, viz.: Richard Ivey, from Georgia ; R. Ellis,
South Carolina; E. Morris, North Carolina; Phil. Bruce, north
district of Virginia ; James O'Kelly, south district of Virginia ;
L. Green, Ohio ; Nelson Reid, western shore of Maryland ;
J. Everett, eastern shore ; John Dickens, Pennsylvania ; J. O.
Cromwell, Jersey ; and Freeborn Garrettson, New-York : all our
business was done in love and unanimity. The concerns of the
college were well attended to, as also the printing business. We
formed some resolutions relative to economy and union, and others
concerning the funds for the relief of our suffering preachers on
the frontiers. We rose on the eve of Wednesday following.
During our sitting, we had preaching every night ; some few souls
were stirred up, and others converted. The *prudence* of some
had stilled the noisy ardour of our young people ; and it was difficult to rekindle the fire. I collected about £28 for the poor suffering preachers in the west. We spent one day in speaking our
own experiences, and giving an account of the progress and state
of the work of God in our several districts ; a spirit of union per-
vades the whole body ; producing blessed effects and fruits.

Thursday 11. This and the two following days were spent in
writing, and other necessary business. I also preached at town and
Point.

Sunday 14. I delivered some alarming truths at our meeting-house with some life. I preached at the German church in the afternoon ; and in the evening I spoke on " The men of Nineveh shall rise up in judgment against the men of this generation, and condemn it," &c.

Monday 15. To my comfort I found one of Thomas Cromwell's children under deep distress ; when I formerly frequented the house she was a child.

Came on to Annapolis, and found the work rather dead.

Tuesday 16. I preached with more liberty than the evening before.

Wednesday 17. Set out for Herring Bay : it rained, and our ride was heavy. I lodged with William Weem's, once a great zealot for the Old Church.

Thursday 18. We rode to Childs's—it was an awfully stormy, rainy day, and we had no meeting. The Lord has made bare his arm since my last visit here, and souls have been converted and sanctified.

Friday 19. Rode to Gray's : here also the Lord hath wrought powerfully amongst the children.

Virginia.—Saturday 20. Rode through Charles county to Hoe's ferry.—Death ! death ! We had prayer at our lodgings : Mr. H. treated us very kindly.

Sabbath morning 21. I read part of the thirty-third chapter of Ezekiel's prophecy, and gave an exhortation. We then rode twenty-five miles through the snow to Pope's, where I spoke with some liberty. We found ourselves not at home, so we went to our friend S——'s ; my spirit has been wounded not a little. I know not which to pity most, the slaves or their masters. Thence we went on to the widow Hutt's ; I am ill, and have little to do, which makes me worse.

On Christmas eve I made a visit to counsellor Carter ; a very social gentleman, a Baptist. After preaching we had fifteen miles to ride to sister W——'s ; and twenty miles the next morning to Lancaster quarterly meeting.

Sunday 27. Feeling myself unwell, brother Whatcoat preached ; and our public and society meeting occupied six hours and a half. Notwithstanding the rain, we had many to hear, both white and black. I was very sensible that the work of grace was deepened in the souls of the people : several spoke of the pure love of God.

Monday 28. I felt much enlarged in spirit. It seemed to me as if

he Lord was only beginning to work; but the Antinomians oppose.
—Nevertheless, I have growing hopes that the glory of Zion will
shortly appear.

Tuesday 29. After waiting at the ferry about four hours, we
made an attempt to cross in an old boat, with tattered sails, which
gave way near the middle of the river: through mercy we got safe
over. Thence directing our course to Turks-Ferry, a poor old
negro made out to get us across in a little flat: about eight o'clock
we arrived safely at sister D——'s, where we found three of the
preachers waiting for us, preaching having been appointed for the
morrow. We had the presence of God with us in the meeting,
and at the sacrament.

Thursday 31. We had a few attentive people at brother Bellamy's. O Gloucester! Gloucester! when will it be famous for
religion. Finding my appointments not made, we crossed York-
River, and came once more to my dear old friend Welden's.—I was
much indisposed.

January 1, 1790. No appointment for preaching. We are bound
to the south, and shall proceed on as fast as we can.

Saturday 2. We were refreshed in the evening. Next day
(Sabbath) I preached at Chickahominy church once more: sinners, Pharisees, backsliders, hypocrites, and believers, were faithfully warned; and of all these characters there were doubtless a
goodly number in the large congregation which attended. Brother
Bruce went to Brown's, and brother W. and myself to Welden's;
at both these places the Lord was powerfully present in our
meetings.

Monday 4. We crossed James-River, with a fresh wind a-head,
and only two poor blacks, where four ferrymen are necessary.
Two brigs under sail came down full upon us, and we had hard
work to get out of their way. These large ferries are dangerous
and expensive: our ferriages alone have cost us £3 since we left
Annapolis.

Tuesday 5. Rested, and next day preached at brother Morings;
I felt some power among the people; but the glory is measurably
departed; the imprudent haste of the young people to marry un-
believers, and divisions excited by other causes, have done much
injury.

Thursday 7. Was an ameliorating time at Ellis's church. The
next day, at Lane's, I had many people, although it rained; I felt
comfortable in speaking to them.

Saturday 9. Was a cold time in a cold house at brother M——'s

I felt unwell, and much dejected at the situation of the people, whom I found divided about the merits of a certain character, once a preacher among the Methodists, but now disowned, and striving to make a party; this man, and the disputes for and against slavery have been hurtful.

Sunday 10. Came to Jones's church, and was much lifted up in spirit.

Monday 11. I had many to hear at Mabry's.

Tuesday 12. From Mabry's we came to Brunswick quarterly meeting, where there was a considerable quickening, and manifestation of the Lord's power. We had a good meeting at Roanoak chapel; I rejoiced that the society had increased to more than a hundred souls.

I received a letter from the presiding elder of this district, James O'Kelly: he makes heavy complaints of my power, and bids me stop for one year, or he must use his influence against me—power! power! there is not a vote given in a conference in which the presiding elder has not greatly the advantage of me; all the influence I am to gain over a company of young men in a district must be done in three weeks; the greater part of them, perhaps, are seen by me only at conference, whilst the presiding elder has had them with him all the year, and has the greatest opportunity of gaining influence; this advantage may be abused; let the bishops look to it: but who has the power to lay an embargo on me, and to make of none effect the decision of all the conferences of the union?

NORTH CAROLINA.—Friday 15. Crossed Roanoak, and was met by several preachers at sister Pegram's, where the Lord was with us.

Saturday 16. I had a long ride to R: Jones's; we had a good season at the sacrament: several spoke powerfully of the justifying and sanctifying grace of God. A hundred souls have been brought to God: thus the barren wilderness begins to smile. I found it a time to speak from Isai. lii. 1.

We had to ride sixteen miles; and here, O what my spirit felt! It is a day of very small and feeble things, and but little union among the people. I found it needful to enforce that prayer. O Lord, revive thy work! One poor black fell to the ground and praised God.

Tuesday 19. I had some freedom in preaching at B——'s; but I fear there is too much vanity and Antinomian leaven amongst them to permit much good to be done.

Rode to Tomlinson's—but here they had made no appointment.

Merritt's chapel, on New-Hope Creek, Chatham county, I enforced " How shall I give thee up, O Ephraim!"—there was some feeling among them; but they are not a united people.

Thursday 21. I rode to the widow Snipe's, twenty miles; and preached on Isaiah xlv. 22. then crossed Haw-River, and came to ——'s, about two hours in the night, where I found a congregation waiting, to whom I spoke on " I am not ashamed of the Gospel of Christ," &c. the people were tender.

Friday 22. Came to Rainey's, in Orange county, to a quarterly meeting. where seven of our preachers met together; the first day the people were dull; the second, our congregation was large; my subject was, " We will give ourselves to prayer and the ministry of the word." I ordained Thomas Anderson to the office of an elder. We rode through a heavy rain sixteen miles to our friend Burr's; here they have built us a complete house of the heart of oak. Proceeded twelve miles to Rocky-River, and preached at M'Master's chapel; afterward we had a night meeting, and upon the whole I believe we were speaking about four hours, besides nearly two spent in prayer. We came to our friend K—'s, and were kindly entertained. Thence we went to Mr. Bell's, on Deep-River, and were received in the kindest manner; before I left the house, I felt persuaded that that family would come to experience the power of religion.

Tuesday 26. We had to make our way through a dreary path, and rode about fifty miles : we were favoured by only getting a sprinkling of rain, which became very heavy after we were housed Thomas C——'s, about eleven o'clock. Rode to Doctor King's, twenty-five miles, and performed the funeral rites of Captain C—, who was sick when I was here last year. I then prayed for him, and felt as if his sickness was unto death: now, I preached his funeral sermon—my text was, " It is appointed unto men once to die," &c. I felt some enlargement in speaking, and a few people appeared to be moved.

I have read an account of the wonderful revolution in France; may the good of Protestantism and the glory of God be advanced by it!

Since we crossed Roanoke-River, we have passed through Warren, Granville, Wake, Chatham, Orange, Randolph, and Richmond counties, in North Carolina.

After passing Hedge-Cock creek, I preached at Night's chapel on "My grace is sufficient for thee :" there was some quickening, and I was blest. It is no small exercise to ride twenty miles, or more, as we frequently do before twelve o'clock; taking all kinds of food and lodging and weather too, as it comes, whether it be good or bad.

I saw the hand of the Lord in preserving my life and limbs when my horse made an uncommon start and sprung some yards with me, it was with difficulty I kept the saddle.

SOUTH CAROLINA.—We had a severe day's ride; and called at the Beauty-Spot: the beauty here has somewhat faded: the society is disjointed, and in a poor state. We made it a fifty miles' ride, or thereabouts, to Pryor's.

Sunday 31. There were some signs of remaining life seen under preaching, and a little spirit and feeling in the love-feast. I felt great enlargement on "Oh! Ephraim, how shall I give thee up," &c. I found it heavy work.

Monday, February 1. Brother W. preached at the Grove; I. E. and myself spoke after him, and there were gracious signs of tenderness among the people. An elderly Baptist preacher attended, whose heart the Lord touched, and he acknowledged the power of the Most High to be present. We lodged at old friend J——'s, having rode twenty-five miles; we were weary and hungry, having breakfasted on tea at eight o'clock, and taken nothing more till six o'clock at night. Lord, help me to bear all things without murmuring or disputing.

At Flowers's there was a living stir; one soul found peace; and I had freedom in preaching.

After riding fifteen miles to Sweet's meeting-house; on a cold day, we had about a dozen people: of these few, some were drunk, and began to laugh and trifle round the house. After three exhortations and prayers, we came to Port's ferry, and had to cross in the night, and wade the low places.

Came to sister ——, and had a comfortable table spread before us, which, to us, who had rode thirty miles through heavy rain, without eating or drinking, was almost necessary. I think our kind hostess has several of the marks St. Paul gives of a widow *indeed*.

I have lately read Thompson's Seasons, containing upwards of two hundred pages. I find a little wheat and a great deal of chaff; I have read great authors, so called, and wondered where they found their finery of words and phrases; much of this might be pilfered from the "Seasons," without injury to the real merit of the work: and doubtless it has been plucked by literary robbers; and my wonder may cease.

My own soul has peace : but I feel a death amongst the people.
I hope the Lord will come and visit them in power ; if they do not
turn to God, I expect they will be cut off, and that soon.

Saturday 6. Rode to Georgetown ; and on the Sabbath, brother
W——— preached on "In all places where I record my name, I will
come in to thee, and I will bless thee."

Monday 8. I gave them a close and serious address on rightly
lividing the word of truth.

Tuesday 9. Came to Wapataw, and preached on 1 John iv.
16, 17.

Wednesday 10. Came to Charleston. Here I received good
ews from Baltimore and New-York : about two-hundred souls have
een brought to God within a few weeks. I have been closely oc-
upied in writing to Europe, and to different parts of this continent.
Ve feel a little quickening here : brother Whatcoat preaches
very night.

Saturday 13. The preachers are coming in to the conference. I
ave felt fresh springs of desire in my soul for a revival of religion.
) may the work be general ! It is a happy thing to be united as is
ur society ; the happy news of the revival of the work of God flies
om one part of the continent to the other, and all partake of the joy.

Sunday 14. I preached twice. Next day (Monday) our confe-
ence began : our business was conducted in great peace and love.
'he business of the council came before us ; and it was determined
1at the concerns of the college, and the printing, should be left
/itn the council to act decisively upon ; but that no new canons
hould be made, nor the old altered, without the consent of the
onference ; and that whatever was done on this head, should come
1 the shape of advice only. We had some quickening seasons,
nd living meetings : several young people come under awakenings.

Wednesday 17. I preached on " If thou take forth the pre-
ous from the vile, thou shalt be as my mouth:" it was a search-
ig season : several spoke and prayed ; and we had noise enough.
'he evening before an extract of sundry letters from New-York
nd Baltimore was read in the congregation, at which saints
1d sinners were affected. But we have not a sufficient breast-
ork : our friends are too mute and fearful, and many of the out-
)ors people are violent and wicked. I have had a busy, trying
me for about nine days past ; and I have hopes that some hun-
reds in this city will be converted by this time next year. Our
)nference resolved on establishing Sunday-schools for poor chil-
en, white and black.

Friday 19. We rode to Edisto : at Gueham's I preached on the " Great salvation :" there appeared to be attention, and some were affected.

Saturday 20. Was a dry time at Lynder's. Brother Whatcoat preached—I was very unwell with a headach.

Sunday 21. We had a better season at Cattle-Creek, on Mal. iii. 1. May God arise to help these people, and revive and work mightily for and amongst them !

Monday 22. We had a heavy ride to B.'s : it was still more so when we came to preaching. Poor souls ! the Antinomian leaven brings forth death here : some appeared hardened, others, nevertheless, appeared a little melted—may God help these people ! I was unwell—could eat but little. I was not at home—I felt as if God had departed from this house, and was miserable until I left it.

Tuesday 23. We rode to R——'s. Here we found people of another spirit. We had a large congregation—but very blind, deaf, and dumb. O Lord ! can these dry bones live ? I spoke very close, but to little purpose. May the Lord help, and stand by the poor preachers who labour on this side Edisto !

Wednesday 24. At Chester's, and next day at P——'s there was a small stir. Some here have been awakened, but they lean to Calvinism, and the love of strong drink carries almost all away : my spirit was bowed down amongst them. I spoke a little, and so did brother Whatcoat. We appointed a night meeting ; there came only two men, and they were drunk.

Friday 26. There came about a dozen people to hear us at Treadwell's, to whom brother Whatcoat preached on the " works of the flesh," and the " fruits of the Spirit."

After riding thirty miles through heavy sands, we came to Doctor Fuller's. I am strongly inclined to think I am done with this road and people ; they pass for Christians—a prophet of strong drink might suit them. I was clear in not receiving any thing without paying for it.

Saturday 27. Rode to Campbell-Town, and stopped at brother G——'s. Since Friday, the 19th, we have rode about one hundred and sixty miles.

I have been under various trials and exercises, and have some dejected hours : this also shall tend to my humiliation, and work for my good.

Sunday 28. I preached on 1 Tim. i. 15. I had a very still and unfeeling congregation. The inhabitants of this little town (Campbell-Town) seem to be sober and industrious ; but even here I found some drunkards.

GEORGIA.—Monday, March 1. We crossed at Augusta, in Georgia, and rode to S. C. church. I had some enlargement on Luke iv. 18, 19. Thence we proceeded to Brier-Creek.

Tuesday 2. I preached in an old church, near Waynesborough; at Wyche's, in the evening ; and next day at Golphin's, Old Town—the house was open, and the day cold.

Thursday 4. I preached with liberty in a new church, near Fan's bridge. We have been exercised in public night and day ; frequently we have not more than six hours' sleep ; our horses are weary, and the houses are so crowded, that at night our rest is much disturbed. Jesus is not always in our dwellings ; and where He is not a pole cabin is not very agreeable : provisions for man and horse we have plenty of. Our journeys are about thirty miles, day by day ; but under all these trials I enjoy peace and patience, and have much of the love of God.

Sunday 7. We had a crowded congregation at H.'s ; brother W. attempted to preach, but soon concluded. We lodged with brother S——, above the forks of Ogeeche. My mind has been much tried under so much bodily fatigue.

I went to view four hundred acres of land, and found it not suitably situated for a seminary of learning. Came to S——'s—a cold place, and cold congregation there.

Wednesday 10. Our conference began at Grant's. We had preaching every day, and there were some quickenings amongst the people. Our business was conducted in peace and unanimity. The deficiencies of the preachers, who receive a salary of sixty-four dollars per annum, from this conference, amounted to seventy-four pounds for the last year.

Thursday 11. We had a rainy day, yet a full house, and a living love-feast ; some souls were converted ; and others professed sanctification. I had some opening in speaking from Ezek. ii. 7. We have a prospect of obtaining a hundred acres of land for every £100 we can raise and pay, for the support of Wesley and Whitfield school. On Monday we rode out to view three hundred acres of land offered for the above purpose. My soul has been much tried since conference began : I must strive to keep from rising too high, or sinking too low.

Tuesday 16. We set out on our journey, and came to the new chapel at Bibb's Cross Roads ; I preached with some life and liberty, and ordained brother Bennet Maxey to the office of deacon. I

spent the evening at brother Herbert's, where lie interred the
remains of dear brother Major. I was told that a poor sinner was
struck with conviction at his grave, and thought he heard the voice
of God calling him to repentance. I was also told of a woman who
sent for brother Andrew to preach her funeral while living; she
was blest under the word, and died in peace.

SOUTH CAROLINA.—Wednesday 17. We were kindly entertained
at P. C——'s ; and next day, after riding twenty-two miles to
P——'s, we had an evening meeting, and were happy with a few
living souls. The Presbyterians are very kind, giving us freely
whatever is needful for man and horse. I have great consolations, and severe trials.

Friday 19. We had some stir, especially amongst the young people, at the widow Bowman's on Reedy-River.

Saturday 20. Rode to M——'s ; and finding brother Ellis was to
be at C——'s, we hasted to see him, and rode twenty miles, crossing Ennoree-River, near the *slaughter ground,* where a battle
was fought in the last war.

Sunday 21. Preached to a quiet people, and had a small stir.
We had a meeting in the evening at brother Smith's.

Monday 22. I feel myself unwell with a sick and nervous headach, which returns once a month, and sometimes oftener. We have
travelled about six hundred miles in about three weeks, besides
the time taken up in conference. Thou, Lord, wilt have mercy,
and save both man and beast. I expect Providence brought us
this way, to pity and to help the people. Dear brother and sister
S—— are unspeakably kind.

NORTH CAROLINA.—Friday 26. Rode about twenty-two miles;
stopped at Col. Graham's, dripping wet with rain ; he received us,
poor strangers, with great kindness, and treated us hospitably.
We had awful thunder, wind, and rain. I was still unwell with a
complaint that terminated the life of my grandfather Asbury, whose
name I bear ; perhaps it will also be my end. We were weather
bound until Monday morning, the 29th of March : for several days
I have been very sick and serious ; I have been enabled to look
into eternity with some pleasure. I could give up the church, the
college, and schools ; nevertheless, there was one drawback—what
will my enemies and mistaken friends say ? why, that he hath
offended the Lord, and He hath taken him away. In the afternoon
I felt somewhat better. Brother Whatcoat preached a most excellent sermon on " The kingdom of God is not in word but in
power"—not in sentiments or forms, but in the convincing, con-

verting, regenerating, sanctifying, power of God. I am making close application to my Bible ; reading the Prophets at my leisure whilst on my journey, I met with a pious Baptist—Glory to God for what religion there is still to be found amongst all sects and denominations of people !

Wednesday 31. Rode to Gilbert-Town, and preached at H——'s with some freedom, but was very unwell in the afternoon.

Thursday, April 1. Rode about fifty miles through Rutherford and Burke counties : it is a day of small things here.

Crossed Catawba-River at Greenlee's ford, and came to our good friend White's on John's River about eight o'clock at night. When I set off in the morning, it seemed as if I should faint by the way, I was so ill with a mixed internal complaint to which I am subject. We arrived in the very nick of time, Friday being a very rainy day, and there being no necessity, that day, to ride. I feel happy in the prospect of death and rest ; yet am I willing to labour and to suffer the Lord's leisure.

Saturday 3. Quarterly meeting began. Brother W— and myself both preached, and there was a reviving among both white and black ; and I trust some souls were blessed.

Sunday 4. Was a serious day—none were admitted to our private meeting but members : many spoke, and most felt the power of God. We then hasted to the Globe chapel, where the people met, but had not patience to wait : we had a rough road, and John's River to cross twenty times. I was desired to preach sister B——'s funeral. She was formerly a Presbyterian ; then a Methodist ; and last of all a Christian ; and there is good hope that she died in the Lord :—I was resolved to fulfil her desire, and preached on 1 Cor. xv. 56, 57. to about eight souls.

Monday 5. We made an early move. After worming the stream for awhile, we took through the Laurel Hill, and had to scale the mountains, which in some places were rising like the roof of a house. We came to the head of Watauga-River—a most neglected place. Here the people have had their corn destroyed by frost, and many of them have moved away. It was thus we found it in Tyger's Valley. We passed by W————'s, a poor lodging, and slept at the Beaver-Dam in a cabin without a cover, except what a few boards supplied : we had very heavy thunder and lightning, and most hideous yelling of wolves around—with rain, which is frequent in the mountains.

TENNESSEE.—Tuesday 5. We were compelled to ride through the rain, and crossed the Stone Mountain :—those who wish to

know how rough it is may tread in our path. What made it worse
to me was, that while I was looking to see what was become of
our guide, I was carried off with full force against a tree that
hung across the road some distance from the ground, and my head
received a very great jar, which, however, was lessened by my
having on a hat that was strong in the crown. We came on to the
dismal place called Roan's Creek, which was pretty full. Here
we took a good breakfast on our tea, bacon, and bread. Reaching
Watauga, we had to swim our horses, and ourselves to cross in a
canoe ; up the Iron Mountain we ascended, where we had many a
seat to rest, and many a weary step to climb. At length we came
to Greer's, and halted for the night.

Wednesday 6. We reached Nelson's chapel about one o'clock,
after riding about eighteen miles. Now it is that we must prepare
for danger in going through the wilderness. I received a faithful
letter from brother Poythress in Kentucky, encouraging me to
come. This letter I think well deserving of publication. I found
the poor preachers indifferently clad, with emaciated bodies, and
subject to hard fare ; yet I hope they are rich in faith.

Friday 8. After receiving great kindness from dear sister Nelson, we came on to brother Bull's, who wrought for us, *gratis*,
what we wanted in shoeing our horses. Thence we went on to
brother Gott's, and to brother P———'s ; and thence, groping
through the woods, to brother Easley's ; depending on the fidelity
of the Kentucky people, hastening them, and being unwilling they
should wait a moment for me. We crossed Holstein at Smith's
ferry, and rode thirty miles to Amie's, where we were well entertained for our money.—Coming along, I complained that the people would take no pay for their food or services—that complaint
has ceased. Very unwell as I was we pushed down Holstein to the
last house ; here we had no hope of company from the eastern or
western side. We turned out our horses to graze, and they strayed
off—so here we are anchored indeed.

The unsettled state of my stomach and bowels makes labour and
life a burthen. We are now in a house in which a man was killed
by the savages ; and O, poor creatures ! they are but one remove
from savages themselves. I consider myself in danger ; but my God
will keep me whilst thousands pray for me.

Sunday 11. My soul is humbled before God, waiting to see the
solution of this dark providence. The man of the house is gone
after some horses supposed to be stolen by Indians. I have
been near fainting ; but my soul is revived again, and my bodily

strength is somewhat renewed. If these difficulties, which appear to impede my path, are designed to prevent my going to Kentucky, I hope to know shortly. I spent the Sabbath at Robert Beans's. In the evening, a company of eleven came to go forward. Our horses were not to be found without a great sum.

Monday morning 12. We loaded brother Anderson's little horse with my great bags, and two pair smaller; four saddles, with blankets and provender. We then set out and walked ten miles, and our horses were brought to us, and those who brought them were pleased to take what we pleased to give. Brother A—— sought the Lord by fasting and prayer, and had a strong impression that it was the will of God that I should not go with that company.

Tuesday 13. We came back to A——'s,—a poor sinner. He was highly offended that we prayed so loud in his house. He is a distiller of whiskey, and boasts of gaining £300 per annum by the brewing of his poison. We talked very plainly; and I told him that it was of necessity, and not of choice, we were there—that I feared the face of no man. He said, he did not desire me to trouble myself about his soul.—Perhaps the greatest offence was given by my speaking against distilling and slave-holding.

Having now been upon expenses from Friday until this day, for four horses and three men, I judged it high time to move.

Thursday 15. We rode fifty miles; and next day preached at Owens's.

Saturday 17. We rode on with great violence, which made me feel very serious.

Sunday 18. Brother W. preached at General Russell's, on the birth, character, and office of John the Baptist.

Monday 19. I resolved on taking a *proper* dose of Tartar-emetic: this has wrought me well, and I hope for better health.

From December 14, 1789, to April 20, 1790, we compute to have travelled two thousand five hundred and seventy-eight miles. Hitherto hath the Lord helped. Glory! glory to our God!

VIRGINIA.—We had a good prayer-meeting at General Russell's. This family is lavish in attentions and kindness: I was nursed as an only child by the good man and woman of the house, and indeed by all the family.—God Almighty bless them and reward them!

Thursday 22. We had a lively prayer-meeting at Keywood's—Come, Lord, like thunder, and break in upon these dear young people!

Friday 23. We had a very lively prayer-meeting and exhortation. We trust the Lord will do something for these people before we leave the rich Holstein-Valley : I feel for their state—they are settled, and dwindling. I have been happy in my own soul, and have gained bodily strength. Two weeks are now spent, one in waiting on the Kentucky business, and one, illness has prevented my improving, except that it has furnished time to publish my appointments on Clinch and Nolachucky.

Saturday 24. Many attended a prayer-meeting at M'Henry's, but there was little life.

Sunday 25. Preached at General Russell's on Ezek. xxxiii. 11. I saw, I felt, I knew that some of my congregation were touched.

Monday 26. We rode through the *poor* Valley, calling on F——, who had been sick and frightened with convictions and the fear of death ; we prayed, fed our horses, and rode on to Clinch-River.

Tuesday 27. We had a house well crowded, but there was but little stir among them. I felt for these dear souls, and judged that Providence was about to open a way for a circuit to be formed here in Russel county, for one preacher.

Wednesday 28. I preached at brother B——'s, a frontier house, and a *station*. In time past, a person was killed here by the Indians. The people showed their zeal in purchasing two magazines and several hymn-books. Some say, nothing but whiskey will bring money ; but I proved the contrary, and I give them credit. We have had cold weather, and severe frosts for two nights past.

We had a dreary ride down to the Ford of Clinch, through a solitary plain : many attended at L——'s.

We rode down to Blackmore's station : here the people have been *forted* on the north side of Clinch. Poor Blackmore has had a son and daughter killed by the Indians. They are of opinion here, that the Cherokees were the authors of this mischief : I also received an account of two families having been killed, and of one female that was taken prisoner, and afterward retaken by the neighbours and brought back.

Friday 30. Crossed Clinch about two miles below the fort. In passing along I saw the precipice from which Blackmore's unhappy son leaped into the river after receiving the stroke of a tomahawk in his head ; I suppose, by the measure of my eye, it must be between fifty and sixty feet descent ; his companion was shot dead upon the spot—this happened on the 6th of April, 1789.

We came a dreary road over rocks, ridges, hills, stones, and streams, along a blind, tortuous path, to Mockason Gap and Creek ; thence to Smith's ferry across the north branch of Holstein. Here

I found some lies had been told on me ; feeling myself innocent,
I was not moved.

Saturday, May 1. Rested. Next day (Sabbath) I preached to
a hardened people.

Monday 3. I preached at brother Payne's, and had some
encouragement among our Maryland people. Sabbath night, I
dreamed the guard from Kentucky came for me ; and mentioned it
to brother W——. In the morning I retired to a small stream,
for meditation and prayer, and whilst there saw two men come
over the hills : I felt a presumption that they were Kentucky men,
and so they proved to be ; they were Peter Massie and John Clark,
who were coming for me, with the intelligence that they had left
eight men below : after reading the letters, and asking counsel of
God, I consented to go with them.

Tuesday 4. We prepared ourselves and horses for our journey,
and the next day came once more to Amie's.

Thursday 6. Came to Crabbe's, at the lower end of the Valley,
and were occupied in collecting our company.

Friday 7. We formed the whole of our company at the Valley
station ; besides brother W——t and myself, we were sixteen
men, having thirteen guns only. We moved on very swiftly, considering the roughness of the way, travelling, by my computation,
thirty-five miles to-day. Next day we reached Rich-Land Creek,
and encamped on the road about nine o'clock at night, having
made, by computation, forty-five miles.

Kentucky.—Sunday 9. We travelled about fifty miles ; and
next day forty-five miles, and reached Madison court-house, passing
the branches of Rock-Castle River : on our journey we saw the
rock whence the river derives its name ; it is amazing, and curious,
with appearances the most artificial I have ever seen—it is not
unlike an old church or castle in Europe. We stopped at M——'s,
whose wife, now a tender, gracious soul, was taken prisoner by
the Indians during the last war, and carried to Detroit.

Tuesday 11. Crossed Kentucky-River. I was strangely outdone for want of sleep, having been greatly deprived of it in my
journey through the wilderness ; which is like being at sea, in
some respects, and in others worse. Our way is over mountains,
steep hills, deep rivers, and muddy creeks ; a thick growth of
reeds for miles together ; and no inhabitants but wild beasts and
savage men. Sometimes, before I was aware, my ideas would be
leading me to be looking out ahead for a fence ; and I would, without reflection, try to recollect the houses we should have lodged

at in the wilderness. I slept about an hour the first night, and about two the last: we ate no regular meal; our bread grew short, and I was much spent.

I saw the graves of the slain—twenty-four in one camp. I learn that they had set no guard, and that they were up late, playing at cards. A poor woman of the company had dreamed three times that the Indians had surprised and killed them all; she urged her husband to entreat the people to set a guard, but they only abused him, and cursed him for his pains. As the poor woman was relating her last dream the Indians came upon the camp; she and her husband sprung away, one east, the other west, and escaped. She afterward came back, and witnessed the carnage. These poor sinners appeared to be ripe for destruction. I received an account of the death of another wicked wretch who was shot through the heart, although he had vaunted, with horrid oaths, that no Creek Indian could kill him. These are some of the melancholy accidents to which the country is subject for the present; as to the land, it is the richest body of fertile soil I have ever beheld.

Wednesday 12. I preached for the first time at R——'s, on Jer. l. 4, 5. and the Lord was with me.

Thursday 13. Being court time, I preached in a dwelling-house, at Lexington, and not without some feeling. The Methodists do but little here—others lead the way. After dinner I rode about five miles in company with poor C—— W——. Ah! how many times have I eaten at this man's table, in New-York—and now, he is without property and without grace. When about to part, I asked him if he loved God: his soul was in his eyes; he burst into tears, and could scarcely speak—" he did not love God, but he desired it." Our conference was held at brother Masterson's, a very comfortable house, and kind people. We went through our business in great love and harmony. I ordained Wilson Lee, Thomas Williamson, and Barnabas M'Henry, elders. We had preaching noon and night, and souls were converted, and the fallen restored. My soul has been blest among these people, and I am exceedingly pleased with them. I would not, for the worth of all the place, have been prevented in this visit, having no doubt but that it will be for the good of the present and rising generation. It is true, such exertions of mind and body are trying; but I am supported under it:—if souls are saved, it is enough.' Brother Poythress is much alive to God. We fixed a plan for a school, and called it *Bethel;* and obtained a subscription of upwards of £300, in land and money, towards its establishment.

Monday 17. Rode to Coleman's chapel, about ten miles from Lexington, and preached to an unengaged people. We thence rode to I. Lewis's, on the bend of Kentucky-River. Lewis is an old acquaintance, from Leesburg, Virginia; I was pleased to find that heaven and religion were not lost sight of in this family. Brother Lewis offered me one hundred acres of land for *Bethel*, on a good spot for building materials.

We rode through mire and rain twenty-one miles to Francis Clark's, near Danville, where we had a numerous congregation.

Saturday 22. We had a noble shout at Brown's, and four souls professed to be converted to God. Reached the Crab-Orchard, and lodged under a tree, very feverish and unwell—a poor beginning this.

Monday 24. We set out on our return through the wilderness with a large and helpless company; we had about fifty people, twenty of whom were armed, and five of whom might have stood fire. To preserve order and harmony, we had articles drawn up for, and signed by our company, and I arranged the people for travelling according to the regulations agreed upon. Some disaffected gentlemen, who would neither sign nor come under discipline, had yet the impudence to murmur when left behind. The first night we lodged some miles beyond the Hazelpatch. The next day we discovered signs of Indians, and some thought they heard voices; we therefore thought it best to travel on, and did not encamp until three o'clock, halting on the east side of Cumberland-River. We had gnats enough. We had an alarm, but it turned out to be a false alarm. A young gentleman, Mr. Alexander, behaved exceedingly well; but his tender frame was not adequate to the fatigue to be endured, and he had well nigh fainted on the road to Cumberland Gap. Brother Massie was captain; and finding I had gained authority among the people, I acted somewhat in the capacity of an adjutant and quarter-master amongst them. At the foot of the mountain the company separated; the greater part went on with me to Powell's River; here we slept on the earth, and next day made the Grassy Valley. Several of the company, who were not Methodists, expressed their high approbation of our conduct, and most affectionately invited us to their houses. The journeys of each day were as follow: Monday forty-five miles; Tuesday fifty miles; Wednesday sixty miles.

TENNESSEE.—Thursday 27. By riding late we reached Capt. mic's, where I had a bed to rest on.

Friday 28, Saturday 29, and Sunday 30. I spent at Gen. Russell's, whose wife is converted since I left the house last; I thought then that she was not far from the kingdom of God.

I found myself dispirited in public preaching. I afterward ordained I. Ragan and B. Vanpelt, local preachers, to the office of deacons.

Monday 31. Rode to New-River, forty-five or fifty miles; here I saw John Tunnell, very low; a mere shadow; but very humble and patient under his affliction.

NORTH CAROLINA.—Tuesday, June 1. I rode about forty-five miles to Armstrong's, and next day about four o'clock reached M'Knights on the Yadkin-River, in North Carolina; here the conference had been waiting for me nearly two weeks: we rejoiced together, and my brethren received me as one brought from the jaws of death. Our business was much matured, the critical concern of the council understood, and the plan, with its amendments, adopted.

Saturday 5, and Sunday 6. Were days of the Lord's presence and power—several were converted. We had an ordination each day. We have admitted into full connexion some steady men, with dispositions and talents for the work.

Monday 7. Rode through Salem Town; the Moravian brethren have the blessing of the nether springs, and houses, orchards, mills, stores, mechanic's shops, &c. I rode about three hundred miles to Kentucky in six days; and on my return about five hundred miles in nine days: O what exertions for man and horse:

VIRGINIA.—Wednesday 9. Came forty-five miles to I. C——'s, and next day, thirty miles to sister Jones's.

Friday 11. Rode to brother I——'s, and next day late in the evening reached Petersburg.

Sunday 13. I preached on Psalm lxxxv. 6. I was weak and unwell with excessive labour and want of rest.

Monday 14. Our conference began; all was peace until the council was mentioned. The young men appeared to be entirely under the influence of the elders, and turned it out of doors. I was weary, and felt but little freedom to speak on the subject. This business is to be explained to every preacher; and then it must be carried through the conferences twenty-four times, i. e. through all the conferences for two years. We had some little quickenings, but no great move among the people at our public preaching. Mr. Jarratt preached for us; friends at first are friends again at last. There were four elders, and seventeen deacons ordained; ten young men who offered to travel, besides those who remained on trial. We have good news from a far country—Jersey flames with religion; some hundreds are converted. The work of God does revive here, although not in the same degree as it did two years ago. In the midst of all my labour and trouble I enjoy peace within.

Saturday 19. Ended my week of business. I am crowded with letters—have much reading and writing, and the temporal concerns of the college, and the printing to attend to.

Sunday 20. I spoke melting words on Hosea xi. 8. many felt; one found peace with God. In the afternoon, I believe the power of God was felt in the hearts of some of my congregation. I I did not wonder that there was not a greater work of religion in this place, when I learned that they were sometimes three or four weeks without preaching : thus Satan tries to keep preachers and people asunder—yet some cry out, "We have no faith for Petersburg!" My dear old friend and fellow traveller W—— is smitten with boils so that he cannot go on. Stopped at brother G——'s.

Monday 21. We had the divine presence in our worship at sister Stringer's.—I am often blessed at the houses of the fatherless and widows. Now, I say to my body, return to thy labour; to my soul, return to thy rest, and pure delight in reading, meditation, and prayer, and solitude. The shady groves are witness to my retired and sweetest hours: to sit, and melt, and bow alone before the Lord, whilst the melody of the birds warbles from tree to tree—how delightful!

Tuesday 22. The Lord was with us at Finney's church; and God's dear children praised his name, whilst sinners felt and looked serious.

Wednesday 23. I preached at Paine's, an ancient, and almost worn-out place. At Ryall's, the next day, I was quite unwell; and what made the matter worse, was, that I imprudently walked out, and sat upon the ground, and took fresh cold. From Ryall's I proceeded to the old court-house, where I spoke with great pain—from head to foot was pain, all perspiration appeared to be quite stopped. I lodged at Jones's—a whole family snatched as brands from the burning.

Saturday 26. I was so unwell that I could not preach at Pride's church.

Sunday 27. Rode to brother Strong's, where, as there were many who had come expecting to hear me, I made a feeble attempt in the woods on 2 Thess. i. 5—9. my head was greatly afflicted.

Monday morning 28. I took a strong decoction of rue and wormwood. My fever breaks, and I feel a little better.—I found perfect
patience in great misery of body. Lord, make me perfect through
suffering!

Monday 28. I had a few Christians, and a few sinners at the
Widow Lackland's ; and there was a small reviving among the people. The leaven of Antinomianism prevails here, and the Methodists talk much about persons and opinions, when they should be
looking to God.

Tuesday 29. I am very weak and low in body.—Lord, sanctify
affliction, and make it a mean of health to my soul! Brother W——
preached on " He that believeth shall not make haste." I have
felt grieved in mind that there is a link broken out of twelve, that
should form a chain of union : I hope God will sanctify some providence to the explanation of this matter, and heal the whole.

Wednesday 30. Brother W—— gave us a weighty discourse
on the prophetic, priestly, and kingly offices of Christ. In great
weakness, I enlarged on 1 Peter iii. 15. and showed that it is not
enough to sanctify the Lord God in his name, word, Sabbath, ordinances, ministers, people, and worship ; but that the heart must be
filled with a holy, constant fear of, confidence in, and love to, God.
But how common is it for different denominations to ask each other
of their distinguishing peculiarities ; and how very rare it is for
them to talk closely of the dealings of God with their own souls.

July 1. As we rode on, there was a great appearance of immediate rain ; I prayed that it might pass, fearing its effects in my very
weak state ; I was mercifully preserved ; a few drops fell on me ·
only, and I found, as I proceeded, that it had rained very heavily
ahead.

We had a few unfeeling souls at Swiney's ; one man appeared to
be hardened to an extraordinary degree : I thought I felt his spirit
as soon as I came.

Thursday 2. I preached in a school-house, near brother M——'s,
with some enlargement, but, I fear, to little purpose : one woman
appeared to be under conviction.

Friday 3. I had a painful ride of twenty-five, or thirty miles, to
brother C——'s.

Saturday 4. My mind was afflicted, and my body weak. I was
led to speak on " Be ye also ready,"—and some felt the word.

Sunday 5. I was set at liberty, and there was a little shaking and
breathing after God, while I opened and explained, " And there is
none calleth upon thy name, that stirreth up himself to take hold of

thee." Afterward I rode to brother Murphy's.—I felt very weak, but patiently happy in God.

Monday 6. We had some move at Ayre's church ; brother W—— was much led out in exhortation and prayer. I spent the afternoon in reading and spiritual exercises.

Tuesday 7. We rode to Liberty, the county-town of Bedford. We set out towards Botetourt, and reached brother Mitchell's about ten o'clock the next day, and found some zeal amongst the people. Next day at E. Mitchell's, on Craig's Creek, one soul found the Lord.

Friday 10. We had a tedious, tiresome journey over hills and mountains to Pott's Creek. After a melting season at brother C——'s, we came to brother W——'s, where we were informed of the death of dear brother John Tunnell.

Saturday 11. Brother Tunnell's corpse was brought to Dew's chapel. I preached his funeral—my text, "For me to live is Christ, and to die is gain." We were much blessed, and the power of God was eminently present. It is fourteen years since brother Tunnell first knew the Lord ; and he has spoken about thirteen years, and travelled through eight of the thirteen States : few men, as public ministers, were better known or more beloved. He was a simple-hearted, artless, childlike man : for his opportunities, he was a man of good learning ; had a large fund of Scripture knowledge, was a good historian, a sensible, improving preacher, a most affectionate friend, and a great saint ; he had been wasting and declining in strength and health for eight years past, and for the last twelve months sinking into a consumption.—I am humbled.— O, let my soul be admonished to be more devoted to God !

Sunday 12. The morning was rainy. About noon I set out for the Sweet-Springs, and preached on 1 Cor. i. 23—29. A few of the gentry were kind enough to come and hear—and some were enraptured with the sermon ; for—it was very like the subject. The three following days I rested, and was very unwell. I had no place to preach, but under the trees, and preaching here seems unseasonable with the people except on Sundays.

Thursday 16. Rode to Rohoboth, where brother W—— preached, and brother A—— and myself spoke after him, and the people appeared somewhat affected.

Friday 17. We had twenty miles to Green-Brier court-house :— here some sat as critics and judges. We had to ride thirty-one miles without food for man or horse, and to call at three houses

before we could get water fit to drink—all this may serve to try
our faith or patience.

Saturday 18. Some very pointed things were delivered relative
to parents and children from Gen. xviii. 19. After being in public exercises from ten till two o'clock, we rode in the afternoon
twenty miles to the little levels of Green-Brier. On my way I
pre-meditated the sending of a preacher to a newly settled place
in the Kenhaway county.

Sunday 19. We had a warm sermon at M'Neal's, at which many
were highly offended; but I trust their false peace is broken.
There are many bears in this part of the country; not long since,
a child in this neighbourhood was killed by one.

Monday 20. Rode to Drinnon's, whose wife was killed, and his
son taken prisoner by the Indians.

Tuesday 21. I believe I never before travelled such a path as I
this day rode over the mountains to reach Mr. Nelson's, in Tyger-
Valley.

Wednesday 22. I preached at Wilson's. Here many careless
people do not hear a sermon more than once in one or two years;
this one of them told me; and that he and his wife had not been
to preaching since I was here on my last visit. I endeavoured to
apply " My people are destroyed for lack of knowledge."

Thursday 23. My horse lost a shoe on a bad road, and next day
on the mountains dropped two more; so I rode my old baggage
horse along a most dreary, grown-up path to brother C——'s.

Saturday 25. Attended quarterly meeting at Morgan-Town :—
I spoke on superstition, idolatry, unconditional election and re-
probation, Antinomianism, Universalism, and Deism.

Sunday 26. Preached on Matt. xxv. 31. to the end, brother
W—— also gave us a sermon; and a Presbyterian minister two—
so here we had it in abundance.

Monday 27. Preached at B——'s; and the next day at H——'s.
Our conference began at Union-Town on Wednesday the twenty-
ninth of July :—it was conducted in peace and love. On Thursday I preached.

PENNSYLVANIA.—Saturday, August 1. I spoke on education, from
Prov. xxii. 6. I was led to enlarge on the obligations of parents to their children; and the nature of that religious education
which would be most likely to fit them for this, and which alone
could qualify them for the next world.

Sunday 2. I ordained C. C——, I. L——, and G. C——, elders,

and four deacons. Here there is a revival among preachers and people; some of the societies are much engaged with God, and after we have had a few more conferences in Union-Town, I hope we shall drive Satan out, and have a glorious work.

Tuesday 4. Rode to B——'s; and next day came to Cressap's, where I rested the following day, and was employed in reading, meditation, and prayer. I had very solemn thoughts of God and his work: I want a closer walk with God; and to be more alone, and in prayer.

Friday 7. We had divine breathings at the chapel.

Saturday 8. We held a quarterly meeting at the widow Coulson's. There was much rain; we had many people, and but little room: these circumstances rendered the meeting in some respects uncomfortable; yet, I trust, it was profitable: many souls felt the divine power, among whom were some poor backsliders.

Tuesday 11. I had an attentive, well-behaved congregation at Squire Vanmeter's. O that they may feel the truth and effects of godliness on earth, and in heaven.

At Doctor Naves's, formerly Hyder's, I applied "O Ephraim, how shall I give thee up?" I felt a vast weight upon my spirits for these people.

Wednesday 12. We had about forty miles to ride to G——, and Brock's Gap, over a severe mountain to cross: the weather was extremely warm. I viewed and pitied the case of the people on the south fork of the south branch of the Patomac: they are Germans, and have no preaching in their own language, and English preaching is taken from them—none careth for them. I am of opinion, that if a preacher would come and continue amongst them for one year, riding up and down the river, preaching from house to house, it would answer a very good purpose.

VIRGINIA.—Came to brother Baker's, a pious German, well settled on a branch of Shenandoah-River. I had an attentive congregation of his countrymen.

Saturday 15, and Sunday 16. I preached at Rockingham, where there is the beginning of a good work. We have a church built on a hill, that cannot be hid. People came as far as thirty miles to preaching; and some found the Lord during my stay. We have some very respectable friends here.

Tuesday 18. We had a crowd of people at Bethel, who appeared very insensible. Rode on to Millers-Town, properly Woodstock: here I was permitted to preach in the Episcopal church; many attended, and behaved well, and I had light and liberty in speaking.

Wednesday 19. We had twenty-two miles to Newtown : here they have built us a spacious chapel. Our horses are stiff, and lame, and sore, and the weather is oppressively warm : we have many sick, hungry, weary rides through the heat, and over hills, rocks, and mountains.

Saturday 22, and Sunday 23. We held our quarterly meeting at Newtown : many felt the power of God—particularly at the love-feast; some were of opinion that twenty were converted.

Tuesday 25. We had a melting time whilst I opened these words, " Neither is there salvation in any other," &c. I feel a persuasion that these people will come home to God. One was deeply distressed under preaching. I rode about an hour after night, in order to reach brother Donaldson's, by which I found I had taken cold.

Wednesday 26. Our conference began at Leesburg; and we continued together until the Sabbath following : and had a happy time of peace and union.

To conciliate the minds of our brethren in the south district of Virginia, who are restless about the council, I wrote their leader a letter informing him, " that I would take my seat in council as another member ;" and, in that point, at least, wave the claims of Episcopacy ;—yea, I would lie down and be trodden upon, rather than knowingly injure one soul.

MARYLAND.—Monday 31. Preached at the Sugar-Loaf mountain with great freedom on " For Zion's sake I will not hold my peace," &c. and found the work of God had been greatly far-thered :—here I preached sixteen years ago.

Tuesday, September 1. I had a blessed season at Pigman's church, where the Lord hath wrought wonders.

Wednesday 2. There was an appearance of good at I. Holland's ; and the work goes on there.

Thursday 3. At the widow H——'s, I put them in mind of my first labours amongst them from house to house, and some sinners felt and shook. Next day at Rowe's, there was a shaking.

Friday 4. At night I preached in Baltimore, " Oh ! Ephraim, how shall I give thee up ?"

Monday 7. Our conference began ; was conducted in great peace and union, and ended on Wednesday 9.

Thursday 10. I rode to Cokesbury.

Friday 11. In the morning philosophical lectures were deli-vered ; and in the afternoon the boys delivered their orations, some parts of which were exceptionable, and duly noticed.

Saturday 12. We made some regulations relative to the order and government to be observed in the college.

Sunday 13. I preached in the college hall, on Matt. xxv. 31. to forty-six scholars ;—brothers D——, and C——, spoke after me.

Monday 14. Set out, and next day reached Duck-Creek Cross-Roads, where we held our conference for the eastern shore of Maryland and Delaware. One or two of our brethren felt the Virginia fire about the question of the council, but all things came into order, and the council obtained. Whilst in session I preached twice ; first, on Jos. iii. 5. and the second time, on Psalm cxxxvii. 6. : we had a solemn, uniting, melting season, and great power attended our last meeting.

Saturday 19. At noon I set out for Philadelphia, but my saddle horse being lame, I was compelled to ride my old horse, which is only fit to carry my baggage.

Sunday 20. Dined with brother Bond, and came on to Wilmington. Whilst preaching we had Satan inside and outside of the house, and through the windows ; I believe good was done, at which he was not well pleased.

A daughter of my old friend, Stedham, had not forgotten me ; she invited me, with much affection, to her house ; she remembered the living and dying monitions of her father, and was mindful of his friends.

PENNSYLVANIA.—Monday 21. I reached the city of Philadelphia. Our brethren have built a new chapel, thirty feet square, at the south end of the city. I feel myself fatigued and unwell, occasioned by riding a rough-going horse.

Tuesday 22. Was spent in reading, writing, and visiting.

Wednesday 23. The conference began in poor Pennsylvania district : all was peace and love. Our printing is in a good state. Our society in the city of Philadelphia are generally poor ; perhaps it is well : when men become rich, they sometimes forget that they are Methodists. I am weak, and have been busy, and am not animated by the hope of doing good here ; I have therefore been silent the whole week :—" I must needs go through Samaria."

Friday 25. There was some feeling, and profitable speaking ; we also had a love-feast. Next day, Saturday, I was closely employed in writing.

Sunday 27. Many felt and wept, whilst I enlarged on " The Lord is in his holy temple." At the new chapel, called Ebenezer, in the afternoon, my subject was 1 Sam. vii. 12. I first explained

the text; then showed the Methodist doctrine and discipline, and
the work God had wrought by them in this country.

NEW-JERSEY.—Monday 28. Rode to Burlington, the place appointed for our next conference: here I preached on "searching
Jerusalem with candles," and it was a searching season. On Tuesday night we had a shout—then came the bulls of Bashan and
broke our windows; it was well my head escaped the violence of
these wicked sinners: I hope the strong power of Satan will feel
a shake this conference. The session has been in great peace;
harmony has prevailed, and the council has been unanimously
adopted.

Wednesday 30. We had a love-feast; and a genuine, sweet
melting ran through the house. S. Strattan stood up and declared
he had followed the work of God for six months, and that he believed six hundred souls had professed conversion in that time.
There is a most genuine work in several places; viz. in Flanders,
Trenton, Burlington, Salem, and Bethel circuits—glory to our
wonder-working God! All hail, eternal Father, coequal Son, and
everlasting Spirit, in time and for ever! Amen, and Amen!!!

I delivered a discourse on Psalm cxxii. 6. On Friday I rode
through Cross-Weeks, and Allen-Town, and Cranbury, lodging at
Doctor Jaques's.

Friday, October 1. As we could not reach York, I stopped and
gave them a discourse at Elizabethtown. We afterward had a
safe, although a long passage, by water to New-York; and found
all in peace.

NEW-YORK.—Sunday 3. I preached at the old church; and in
the afternoon at the new, on Matt. xxv. 31—46. The new church
is commodious, elegant, yet plain.

Monday 4. We began our conference, and sat with close application to business until Thursday morning: all was peace, order,
and unanimity. On Thursday evening I returned to Elizabethtown.

Friday 8. Rode twenty-five miles to Trenton, and preached at
night. Next day I rode through a heavy rain to Philadelphia.

PENNSYLVANIA.—Sunday morning 10, was rainy; I however
preached at St. George's church, and again in the evening. H.
Willis is come hither to settle himself in life, and will probably go
into trade: the church has thereby lost, in part, a faithful servant.

Thursday 14 I left the city: dined at Chester; and here I saw
one whose soul was made dear to me by long acquaintance, now
feeble in body, and deeply affected in mind. Reached New-Castle,

in Delaware, and once more preached there, and had a few serious hearers.

DELAWARE.—Friday 15. I did not reach Dickinson's in time;
however, I spoke a little. I found sister Dickinson wrapt in clay,
whom I left sick about three weeks ago : she has been an attentive, devoted woman, has washed the saints' feet, and kindly served
the dear servants of God ; and I trust her soul is now in peace.
I spoke a little at Duck Creek Cross Roads, where nearly thirty
members have been added to the society since last conference.

Sunday 17. We had a gracious love feast, and a very powerful
meeting ; many bore a living testimony ; there was great life and
shouting among the people of God. In the evening I rode to brother White's.

Monday 18. At Thomas White's my soul has been made to feel
very solemn : a view of the remarkable work of God ; the death
of some, and the deep spirituality of others ; the sending out
young men for the ministry ; and the providing for the fatherless
and widows—these are all weighty matters, and greatly occupied
my mind. In the midst of all my soul panteth after God.

Wednesday 20. We rode twenty miles to Millford quarterly
meeting. They have ceiled the chapel, and put the galleries in
order ; and what is still better, there were many living souls
among them.

Thursday 21. At the love-feast many spoke of the dealings of
God with their souls. I once more visited B. Williams, and felt
my soul powerfully drawn out towards the children. The people
are alive ; but I fear they are not as much engaged as they were
this time last year.

Friday 22. Came once more to sister Sharkley's ; now my dear
old friend is gone, perhaps the Gospel must go out of the house :
I trust the dear woman is gone to heaven. I then visited the fatherless and the widow, (sister Abbitt :) I felt sweet peace, and a
solemn sense of the presence of God.

Saturday 23. Came to Lewistown. There being no preaching
appointed, we rode to the light-house : I could but praise God that
the house was kept by people who praise and love him—no drinking or swearing here. Brother H—— is a Christian and a
preacher ; and God has owned his labours. An Irish vessel had
been cast away with three hundred souls on board, all of whom
perished but about forty ; I asked him concerning it, and I learned
that they were within sight of land ; and that if they had timely
thrown themselves into the sea, they were nigh enough the land

to have been washed ashore, so that many more would have probably been saved. So much for a drunken captain, who threw these precious lives away. Brother H—— told me that he did not go near the wreck until after his return from Lewistown, with a guard; that it was reported some of the crew were as ready to plunder the goods on board as others: stricter laws are now made; and the people on this shore are greatly reformed—for which they may thank the Methodists. We have a chapel built at Lewistown; and we had an agreeable Sabbath day. The people, however, have their prejudices. Mr. W——, a minister for thirty or forty years standing, has gone (since I was here last) to give an account of his stewardship, as we must all shortly do.

Tuesday 26. I preached at the Sound chapel. Brother Everett then spoke of the sin of unbelief as the chief sin that keeps people from the blessings of the Gospel. We administered the sacrament, and in the afternoon rode to Buckingham. I rejoiced in the account brother Powell gave me of the state of religion at the Sound; he said that the Lord had owned and blest their prayer meetings; that he thought one hundred souls had been affected and shaken, and perhaps eighteen or twenty converted, in the space of eighteen or twenty months; that brother Williams, a local deacon, was in the spirit of the work; formerly he pleased all with his smooth speaking, but that now they cry out against him.

Wednesday 27. I felt glad in my soul, notwithstanding brother Lee is on forbidden ground—and, in spite of prejudice and Antinomianism, that souls are awakened by his ministry. I feel myself under some temptation; but I fight and conquer in the strength of Christ.

Thursday 28. I finished reading the second volume of the Arminian Magazine. Notwithstanding its defects, I am persuaded it is one of the best and cheapest books in America: the life' of Mr. Fletcher, the tracts, letters, and sermons are good—the poetry might be better.

Saturday 30. I feel the weakness and infirmities of flesh and blood; having rode seventy miles the two last days. At the quarterly meeting, at Garrettson's, I was unwell, but felt divine assistance in preaching.

VIRGINIA.—Sunday 31. We had a powerful love-feast; and I believe it would have been more so had God's dear children had time to speak. We had a vast crowd of people. Brother F—— preached first, and I after him: I had a solemn sense of God, and sinners were serious.

Monday, November 1. Preached at Accomack court-house, on Rom. i. 16. We had a weighty season. A poor man, who had lately professed religion, appeared to be somewhat distracted : he has been a vile sinner ; but I hope he will recover his right mind : the family is subject to derangement. There are some unreasonable things among the people here ; but we are afraid of gathering out the tares, lest we should root up the wheat also. We must continue to observe the order of God and our own discipline—attend to preaching, prayer, class-meeting, and love-feast ; and then if they will shout, why let them shout.

Wednesday 3. I preached on education, from " Come, ye children, hearken to me ; I will teach you the fear of the Lord." The word was felt by the parents. After preaching I rode to Littleton Long's. This neighbourhood is supplied with preaching by the Episcopalians, Presbyterians, Baptists, and Methodists. All is well, if the people are saved.

MARYLAND.—Thursday 4. We had but few hearers, and an uncomfortable time at our quarterly meeting in the Annamessex chapel. Next day we had a full house, and I preached on education—my text, " Train up a child in the way he should go : and when he is old he will not depart from it." After meeting we rode eighteen miles without our dinner, which, with the disagreeable weather, made me sick. Rode twenty-five miles to Broad-Creek quarterly meeting, and preached on Matt. x. 37, 38 ; and the next day on Hosea vi. 4. it was a searching time. We came off, and found the wind blowing fiercely ; but when we had entered the boat, we had a sudden calm : if this were not an answer to prayer, it was as I prayed. I reproved myself for a sudden and violent laugh at the relation of a man's having given an old negro woman her liberty *because she had too much religion for him.*

Monday 8. We held a quarterly meeting in Dorset, in a new, unfinished house.

Tuesday 9. We had a gracious love-feast ; and I addressed parents very seriously on Deut. vi. 67. I lodged with brother Henry Ennalls, who, with his wife, has been powerfully brought to God—his slaves were freed immediately. His sister, Nancy Bassett, has gone to rest : the other two have followed the example of a dear brother—God has heard their prayers.

Wednesday 10. I came to Frazier's chapel : my spirits were very low ; and I felt that there was death amongst the people.

Thursday 11. Our love-feast was living and powerful. I have

seen a wonder of grace in Capt. B——: this has been the wish of
my heart, the desire of my soul, and the answer to prayer; for
which I am thankful to God.

Friday 12. I preached At Bolingbroke to a full house on
Ephraim's mixing himself among the people.

Saturday 13. We had a gracious season at the love-feast. In
the evening I came to Allen's. The next day, being rainy, we had
but one hundred hearers at Tuckahoe ; whereas, we expected,
that had it been a clear day, we should have five or six hundred.
I preached in the evening at Choptank Bridge to a few people.

Monday 15. I see the wonders of grace ; and have had severe
conflicts : my soul is more and more established in God ; but so
many persons and things occupy my time, that I have not as much
leisure and opportunity for prayer and communion with God, and
for drinking into the Holy Spirit of life and love as I could wish.
We had a seasonable time at brother White's : I was very pointed
on 2 Peter ii. 9. Perhaps I have spoken my last admonition to
some who were present.

Thursday 18. Rode to Dover ; and next day we had quarterly
meeting at Dudley's chapel.

Saturday 20. At Duck Creek Cross Roads a spirit of prayer prevails amongst the people, and God is with them·

Sunday 21. At Cecil quarterly meeting, held at Dickinson's, we
had many people, and some life. On Monday I rode to Dr. Clayton's ; and next day to Cokesbury, where I continued until Monday the 29th. We then examined the students relatively to learning and religion—paid debts, and put matters in better order.
We have forty-five boys. The charitable subscriptions to the
establishment amount to £300 per annum.

Tuesday, December 1. The council was seated in Philip
Rogers's chamber in Baltimore. After some explanation, we all
agreed that we had a right to manage the temporal concerns of the
church and college decisively ; and to recommend to the conferences, for ratification, whatever we judged might be advantageous
to the spiritual well-being of the whole body. For the sake of
union, we declined sending out any recommendatory propositions :
we had great peace and union in all our labours. What we have
done, the minutes will show.

Sunday 5. I preached a funeral discourse on the death of Mrs.
Murray, on 2 Cor. xv. 29—31. it was, I hope, not altogether in
vain. In the afternoon I preached in Mr. Otterbine's church. I

have kept no journal during the sitting of the council; I enjoy peace of soul, but such a variety of persons and subjects agitate my poor mind.   Lord, keep me in perfect peace!

Thursday 9. The council rose after advising a loan of £1000, payable in two years, for Cokesbury; and giving directions for proper books to be printed.

Friday 10. I left Baltimore, and reached my old friend S. Turners: the girls, who were babes when I first visited this house, are now grown up, and, I trust, possess religion.

VIRGINIA.—Saturday 11. We rode through heavy rain to Alexandria in Virginia.

Sunday 12. I preached morning and evening, but the streets being muddy, and but few friends attending from the country, we had a thin congregation.

Monday 13. We set out for Stafford. The weather being uncomfortable, and the roads deep, we turned in at twenty miles, to Mr. Dawning's, who treated us kindly.

Tuesday 14. We hasted to Mrs. Waller's, where we found a few people, to whom I spoke on Rom. ii. 7, 8, 9. Finding Tommy (a son of Mrs. W.'s) had genius, I gave him a pass to Cokesbury: it may be that he may serve himself, his family, and his country :— O that he may serve his God!

Wednesday 15. Came to King George; and, cold as it was, I found nearly one hundred people had assembled at the widow Bomby's.

Saturday 18. Attended the quarterly meeting at brother Edwards's: the weather was extremely cold, and we had but few hearers.

Sunday 19. After preaching at the quarterly meeting, I visited Counsellor Carter; and spent the evening in much peace and love: he has the manners of a gentleman, the attainments of a scholar, and the experience of a Christian.

Monday 20. The weather softening, I made haste to get across the Rappahanock, and reached brother B——s, about twenty-five miles: I found myself much chilled by my ride. My soul has been kept in great peace; and, almost, in constant prayer: I wish to feel so placid as not to have any acid in my temper; nor a frown, or wrinkle on my brow—to bear all things, do all things, suffer all things from the ignorance or weakness of the children of God, or the wickedness of the sons and daughters of Satan. I think my soul momently pants after more of God.

Thursday 23. I preached at brother C——s; and was very pointed: I hope it will have the good effect of preventing the sin and vanity that too often prevail at Christmas.

Friday 24. Came to the widow Clayton's; where there has been a work of God: I preached, with liberty, from "Put ye on the Lord Jesus Christ, and make no provision for the flesh to fulfil the lusts thereof." I cautioned the people against the sins of the times.

Christmas day. I had thirty miles to Hanover. William Glendenning began before I came; when he had done, I went into the tavern keeper's porch; but I afterward judged it best to withdraw, and speak in another place. I stood in the door of a public house, and with about half of my congregation out of doors, preached on "Behold, I bring you good tidings of great joy:" the people behaved exceedingly well; and the town was very still.

Sunday 26. I had a large congregation at New-Castle, to whom I spoke on "Thou shalt call his name Jesus; for he shall save his people from their sins." William Glendenning spoke after me: I am clear he is not right in his head or heart, and am therefore resolved he shall speak no more at my appointments.

Monday 27. Preached at Colonel Clayton's. The people hereabouts are wealthy, and few attend preaching; nevertheless, I was favoured with their company, and had great liberty and sweetness in speaking to them: I feel as if God would yet work among them. It was in this neighbourhood I was laid up four years ago.

Tuesday 28. I had many people at the widow A——s; but they did not appear to be in a good frame to receive instruction: their Christmas company; sinful, worldly joy; full-feeding; together with the severity of the weather—all appeared to make against a profitable meeting.

Wednesday 29. Preached in James-City—crowded with company—I was informed of some painful circumstances relative to our dissatisfied brethren: I leave these things to God, who will bring all things to light. Contrary to my expectations, I found there was an appointment made for me to preach in Williamsburg, being the day I had intended to cross the river.

Thursday 30. I preached in the city of Williamsburg, according to appointment: I felt much liberty; and had some hope that Providence was about to open the way for a work in this place.

Friday 31. I came on to the ferry, chilled with the cold. We had to ride seven miles; the wind was high about the time we

embarked; presently a snow storm came on; and although wind
and tide were in our favour, we had rough work in crossing. Our
horses were smooth, the bottom of the boat icy, so that it was
with difficulty they could keep their feet; however kind Providence brought us safe to Cobham, whence we hasted along to
brother M——'s, and found brother Paup speaking, and the people
shouting. I preached on Ephes. v. 17, 18, 19. I afterward had an
interview with brother Paup, and a more full account of matters
relative to our disaffected brethren. Thence I rode on to brother
Blunt's; but there were none to preach to.

Sunday, January 2, 1791. Notwithstanding the snow was deep,
we rode to brother Cowling's. Few people attended; but we had
a comfortable meeting, especially at the sacrament.

Monday 3. We rode hard to get to Craney-Island, and came
within three miles by two o'clock; the people being dispersed,
we came back to brother Joliff's.

Tuesday 4. I had a few to hear, to whom I spoke on Rom. xiii.
11. I engaged R. I——, as a French teacher for Cokesbury.

Wednesday 5. We had a blessed time at Norfolk, whilst I
applied Zech. xii. 10. Many praised the Lord aloud. I was
closely employed until the moment I left town. I find the Lord
has wrought in Norfolk, Portsmouth, and the country round
about.

NORTH CAROLINA.—Thursday 6. I did not reach Chapel until
three o'clock. Next day I reached Col. Williams's, Currituck,
North Carolina. Here we had a quickening time. I possess
peace of mind; and feel no murmuring nor discontent. My horse
is very lame, and the roads in this country are very deep.

Saturday 8. After preaching at B——'s, I hasted to S——'s
ferry, on Pasquotank-River, where I waited about three hours.
The negroes were dancing. I staid behind until all the company
were over, and then crossed about eight o'clock; and about nine,
reached brother P——s.

Sunday 9. Preached at New-begun church in the morning, and
at Nixonton in the evening, in the court-house, which was nearly
filled.

Tuesday 11. Yesterday I rode to brother B——'s, within five
miles of Gates court-house. My fare is sometimes poor, my rides
are long, my horse is lame; yet, while Christ is mine, I feel
nothing like murmuring or discontent. I have passed through
Winton, Wicocon, Campbell, and Hardy counties, preaching as I
journeyed, and found a few living souls.

Sunday 16. Came to Gardener's, to quarterly meeting, where I enlarged on Peter's fall, and it was a serious, powerful meeting.

I thence rode to our late brother F——'s, whose funeral rites I performed. Although the weather was cold, the congregation was large. I was importuned to visit the town; but found there were but few who really wished me to go. I however went, and preached to them at candle light, and many of them laughed at the foolish old prophet. Perhaps when I next come to see them they will be more serious. Thence we hastened to brother Jones's, whose wife lately departed this life in the full triumph of faith— and his son is engaged in horse-racing. This brought to my mind young P——; who, after the death of his pious father, turned away the preachers, and sinned with a high hand; but the Lord followed him; and after he had spent a good deal of the substance left him by his father, he was made a happy subject of the grace of God. I will not give up all hope for young Jones.

Saturday 22. Crossed Neuse-River, at Smith's ferry, and came to the dwelling of the late Gen. Hardy Bryan; a man I had often heard of, and wished to see—but death, swift and sudden, reached the house before me. His son H—— died the 18th of last November; his daughter Mary, December 28th; and himself the 10th instant: each of them feared the Lord, and were happy souls. I felt strangely unwilling to believe the General was dead, until I could no longer doubt it: at the grave-yard I had very solemn feelings—there was some melting among the people whilst I enlarged on Psalm xii. 1.

Sunday 23. I had very great opening on 1 Thess. iv. 13, 14. It was on the occasion of the late lamented deaths. Surely this is loud preaching—it is one of the most awakening scenes of my life: how soon were these dear souls justified, sanctified, and called home to glory. Hail, happy dead!—We toil below, but hope, ere long, with you to sing God's praise above. Lord, help us to improve this providence, and always be looking and longing for glory!

Monday 24. I had a most dreary ride to Trenton: (Jones court-house) here I met with Lewis Bryan, brother to the late General:—his heart and house are open. After getting some refreshment we went to the chapel, where I preached with great freedom: there were brethren present who came to meet us from a great distance. In the evening, brothers C——, and L——, and A—— held meeting.

Tuesday 25. I preached at Lee's chapel. There is a very great change for the better since I was here three years ago:

they have now built a very decent house for worship. I was unwell in my body, but happy in my God, and resigned to his will.

Wednesday 26. Preached to a large congregation at brother D——'s, on White-Oak River.—I baptised and administered the sacrament. After dinner I rode twelve miles to L——'s, and found the people waiting : about six we began exhortation and prayer, and about midnight laid ourselves down to rest.

Thursday 27. I had many to hear at Swansbury ; the people were attentive—O that God may bless his word to them !—Surely, all shall not be in vain. I returned to brother T——'s, a mile out of town ; but the people found where I was and came out. Sometimes I am tried when I cannot enjoy my hours of retirement ; but we must bear all things, if thereby we may do good, and gain the more souls to Christ.

Friday 28. We rode sixteen miles to an old chapel on the way to Richland's ; the people and myself suffered from the weather ; however, I spoke a little, and administered the sacrament ; after which, I rode, cold and hungry, sixteen miles more to brother C. Ballard's.

Sunday 30. The truth was delivered sharply and pointedly ; but the people were wild and unfeeling.

Tuesday, February 1. I had a large congregation at the Sand-Hills. Feeling myself enlarged in spirit, although weak in body, I entered very extensively into the nature and excellencies of the Gospel. We administered the Lord's supper, and had a shaking among the people : brothers L—— and B—— were there, and we rejoiced in the Lord together. We were honoured with a little cabin at a distance from the other house, about eight feet wide and nine feet long, and were as happy as *princes in a palace*.

Wednesday 2. We had our difficulties in getting along an unknown path. Arrived at De V——'s ford ; we met with a very kind man, who gave us and our baggage a passage on a broken canoe ; then led us part of our way, and sent a servant to conduct us on. We reached Anderson's about two o'clock ; and found many people waiting ; but they appeared to be unfeeling. We were most kindly treated. The people are about to settle a newly introduced minister ; so we may go off for a year or two ; and by that time the way may be open for our return. I am charged with dreadful things about the council ; but I believe the Lord will make it appear where the mischief lies.

Crossed Cape-Fear River, and rode thirty miles to sister Turner's : here I spoke to some assembled people, some of whom felt, and my labour was not in vain in the Lord : my own soul was blessed. I was awfully impressed with the conviction that the interests of religion had been injured by backsliders and loose walkers.

Saturday 5. We had many at the quarterly meeting for that part of the country. My subject was " And Peter went out and wept bitterly."

Sunday 6. We had a little melting among the people at noon, and in the evening. Ah ! my God, how few there are who truly love thee !

Monday 7. Rode to Lockwood's Folly ; and preached at Charlotte-River to not less than one hundred people ; a vast congregation for so lonely a part of the world : the soil is very barren ; and the country, consequently, but thinly settled. We were recommended, for lodging, to a certain squire's ; but Providence so ordered it, that we came to a simple-hearted brother S——'s, where we were kindly received, and abundantly supplied with every thing necessary for man and horse. As our time would admit, I was disposed to indulge a desire I had of going by Pyraway, about twelve miles distant. We crossed Wacamaw-River : it is about one hundred and fifty yards wide : our horses ferried themselves over by swimming. I preached in the evening on " The Son of Man is come to seek and to save that which was lost."

SOUTH CAROLINA.—Tuesday 8. We came a long, dreary way, missed our road, and at last reached brother S——'s ; a distance of twenty-five miles, which our wandering made thirty miles. I rejoice to find that this desert country has gracious souls in it : O how great the change in the flight of six years ! we have now many friends, and some precious souls converted to God—glory be to the Lord most high ! I feel power to bear all things, and leave events to God : the misconduct of other men is my grief, but not my sin ; so I will trust God with his own cause.

Friday 11. We set out for Black-River, from about six miles above Kingston, having Bull-Run, Bramble Island, and great Pee-Dee to cross. Reaching Black-River, we were compelled to turn aside to Mr. S——'s rice plantation, where we procured provender for our horses, and breakfasted on our own tea.

Saturday 12. Came to Georgetown through the rain—felt myself unwell and very low in spirits.

Sunday 13. I preached a plain, searching sermon ; and some felt the word : but it is a day of small things. In the afternoon I enlarged on " How shall I give thee up, O Ephraim ?" the wicked youths were playing without, and inattention prevailed amongst those within. I was, and continued to be, under great dejection during my stay.

Monday 14. Rode forty-five miles to brother Sinclair Caperses's, under depression of spirits; and here I received letters not at all calculated to relieve me.

Charleston, Tuesday 15. I went to church under awful distress of heart : my drooping spirits were somewhat revived in the house of God. We grow here but slowly.

Thursday 17. I had a small congregation of whites. I feel the want of religion here : indeed, the gross immoralities of the place are obvious to every passenger in the streets.

I learn that in Georgia preachers of other denominations have had high disputes with ours : I am clear that controversy should be avoided; because we have better work to do ; and because it is too common that when debates run high, there are wrong words and tempers indulged on both sides.

Sunday 20. I read prayers in the morning ; and brother Ellis preached. In the afternoon brother Askew preached his farewell sermon ; and at night I was very pointed to young people, on " Remember now thy Creator in the days of thy youth," &c.

Wednesday 23. Long-looked for Doctor Coke came to town : he had been shipwrecked off Edisto. I found the Doctor's sentiments, with regard to the council, quite changed. James O'Kelly's letters had reached London. I felt perfectly calm, and acceded to a general conference, for the sake of peace.

Sunday 27. Doctor Coke preached to a very large audience in the evening : the poor sinners appeared to be a little tamed. I was much blessed in meeting the married and single men apart : I also met the married and single women. I trust there has been good done in Charleston this conference. I want to be gone into the country to enjoy sweet solitude and prayer. I have been reading three hundred pages of Taylor's sermons, where I find many instructing glosses on the Scriptures.

Tuesday, March 1. At night I made my last effort for this time : and the people were more attentive.—I let out freely against the races. I am somewhat distressed at the uneasiness of our people, who claim a right to chuse their own preachers, a thing quite new amongst Methodists. None but Mr. Hammett will do for them.— We shall see how it will end.

Wednesday 2. I left the city, something grieved in mind. I crossed the toll-bridge over Ashley-River; came to Jacksonsborough, and lodged at Bonham's.

Thursday 3. Came to Allen's tavern.—My host (a Yorkshireman) and his wife, are attentive, obliging, and cleanly : they want nothing but religion to make them superior, in their way, to almost any I have met with in America. I proceeded on to the Salt-Ketchers ; and thence to Coosanhatchie, where I was kindly entertained by Mr. Lambrights.

Friday 4. I had a very well-dressed, serious, attentive congregation, at the district court-house : I had not much liberty ; however, I endeavoured to speak plainly on " Godliness is profitable," &c. an attentive, pious, old man thanked me for my discourse.

Our horses are much hurt by long rides, having travelled one hundred miles in two days.

Saturday 5. I read, critically, Mrs. Rowe's Devout Exercises of the Heart. I wrote nearly twenty pages to Doctor Coke on the concerns of the church.

Sunday 6. Notwithstanding the heavy rain, we had many to hear at brother Stafford's : where I enforced " Let this mind be in you which was also in Christ Jesus."

GEORGIA.—Monday 7. I preached at Hudson's ferry with some freedom ; but the people appeared wild and stupid. I was alarmed at hearing a man talking large and loud, thinking he was drunk, and would come in, and disturb the congregation ; but he was, as I afterward learned, an Antinomian. I came, in a heavy storm, to brother H——'s. This day I passed Savannah Swamp, parts of which are not unlike the Santee and Kentucky lands.

Tuesday 8. We had nearly four hundred people at R——'s ; and I trust the Lord, in some good degree, breathed upon the souls present. We then rode sixteen miles, and had a comfortable evening exercise at brother R——'s.

Wednesday 9. Preached at an old church ; I was much fatigued, and felt unwell. At the invitation of Mr. C——, I came to Waynesborough. I lodged with Mr. Henry, a Jew.: we read Hebrew part of the night, and I should have been pleased to have spent the night thus occupied with so good a scholar.

Thursday 10. I preached at C——'s church ; my body was wearied with labour and want of sleep.

Sunday 13. Came to Georgetown at Ogechee Shoals, and found Satan was there. I levelled away on the parable of the sower. I come to brother H——'s.—Heard heavy tidings. My soul is calm—Let the Lord look to his own house. I hasted to Scott's : Doctor Coke came in time enough to preach ; and then we opened conference.

We sat very closely to our work ; and had some matters of moment to attend to in the course of our deliberations. I have rode about two hundred and fifty miles in Georgia, and find the work, in general, very dead.—The peace with the Creek Indians, the settlement of new lands, good trade, buying slaves, &c. take up the attention of the people.

Sunday 20. There was a shaking amongst the people whilst I spoke on Rom. x. 21.

South Carolina.—After meeting, I came away, and rode twenty miles to brother Herbert's that evening.

Whilst Doctor Coke stayed behind to preach at Ninety-six Town, I came on and made an appointment and preached at Finche's ; and some, I know, felt the word.

Wednesday 23. We crossed the Ennoree, Tyger, and Broad Rivers.

Saturday 26. We had white and red Indians at Catawba ; the Doctor and myself both preached. I had some conversation with the chiefs of the Indians about keeping up the school we have been endeavouring to establish amongst them. I asked for one of their children ; but the father would not give consent, nor would the child come. My body is weak ; but my mind has heaven and peace within. We closely employed our intervals of leisure in preparing different tracts for the press.

Lord's day 27. We found the people insensible at the Waxsaws church : some few seemed alarmed whilst Isai. xxxiii. 14. was opened and enforced.

Wednesday 30. We came to Salisbury : I felt unwell, and no freedom to speak. Doctor Coke gave them a sermon, and we then rode five miles to B——'s. Next day we reached Jones's ; and the day after (first of April) M'Knight's, where we opened conference in great peace. Many of the preachers related their experience, and it was a most blessed season of grace.

Monday 4. We rose, after sitting each night (Sabbath excepted) until twelve o'clock. Several of our brethren expressed something like the perfect love of God, but they had doubts about their having retained it.

Tuesday 5. We rested awhile at Salem on our way, and came in the evening to brother W—'s, and had a meeting there. I believe trouble is at hand :—but I trust God with his cause, and Christ with his church. My soul drinks into holiness.

Friday 8, I observed as a day of abstinence and prayer, reading and meditation. O for more of heaven! Poor Minters's case has given occasion for sinners, and for the world to laugh, and talk, and write.

Saturday 9. We had a large congregation at A——'s ; I felt life in speaking, although weak and weary in body. We rode seven miles to the banks of Dan-River, but knew not where to cross. At length we came to the Fishery ; crossed in a canoe, and walked two miles, in the night, to T. Harrison's : thus ended the labours of the day.

VIRGINIA.—Sunday 10. Doctor Coke and myself both preached at Watson's church ; and there was some little effect produced. I spent the evening with George Adams, a true son of his worthy father, Silvanus Adams, for kindness to the preachers. I am constantly weak and feverish in body ; but my soul is uncommonly happy and calm. We moved from G. Adams's to the widow Dicks's ; and thence, next day, to brother Marten's.

Wednesday 13. Came to Difficult church : where we were honoured with the company of some of the *great*: the Doctor preached a noble sermon on the Divinity of Christ ; and I urged, "It is time to seek the Lord." Afterward we preached in Charlotte and Mecklenburg ; and on Sunday following came to quarterly meeting at sister Walker's, in Brunswick. Doctor Coke went to the barn ; and I preached in the house : the rain rendered our meeting uncomfortable.

Monday 18. Near Dinwiddie court-house I waited, it being the day of the election, until our brethren returned from the courthouse, and then preached in the new church on 2 Cor vi. 17, 18.

Tuesday 19. We rode to Petersburg. We agreed to take different lodgings during the sitting of the conference—the Doctor at brother Davis's, and myself at brother Harding's.

Wednesday 20. I preached on "Our light afflictions which are but for a moment," &c. ; and there was some warmth amongst the preachers and people. The business of our conference was brought on in peace ; and there was a blessing attended our speaking on our experiences, and in prayer. The affair of the council was suspended until a general conference.

Friday 22. Late in the evening our conference rose.

Saturday 23. I preached at E. West's, to a large congregation ; and had a little spring of power.

Sunday 24. Came to Colonel Clayton's ; who was very ill. We had a large collection of people, and a good meeting : we were to have held our conference at the Colonel's, but his illness prevented. We sat at his son, B. Clayton's ; and were amply provided for : the son is not a member ; but he was very kind.

Monday 25. Doctor Coke and brother I. Ellis preached ; and there was some power attended the word. I found the Doctor had much changed his sentiments since his last visit to this continent ; and that these impressions still continued—I hope to be enabled to give up all I dare for peace sake ; and to please all men for their good to edification.

We hastened our business ; and on Tuesday, twenty-six, came to New-Castle : here I preached on " How often would I have gathered thy children together as a hen gathereth her brood under her wings, and ye would not :" I have no doubt but the people felt the word. We came on to Hanover-Town ; where the Doctor preached in the afternoon.

Wednesday 27. We rode thirty miles to the widow Collins's, Caroline county, much wearied in body, but greatly comforted in God.

Thursday 28. At eleven o'clock, at Pope's chapel, the Doctor preached on " Pray without ceasing." Myself, on " By grace are ye saved, through faith :" I was long and very close. We hasted to Port Royal, where a number of fine people were waiting, to whom the Doctor preached on " Ye are dead, and your life is hid with Christ in God :" they expressed a desire for me to preach also ; but it being late, I declined it.

Friday 29. The solemn news reached our ears that the public papers had announced the death of that dear man of God, John Wesley. He died in his own house in London, in the eighty-eighth year of his age, after preaching the Gospel sixty-four years. When we consider his plain and nervous writings ; his uncommon talent for sermonizing and journalizing ; that he had such a steady flow of animal spirits ; so much of the spirit of government in him ; his knowledge as an observer ; his attainments as a scholar ; his experience as a Christian ; I conclude, his equal is not to be found among all the sons he hath brought up ; nor his superior among all the sons of Adam he may have left behind. Brother Coke was sunk in spirit, and wished to hasten home immediately. For myself, notwithstanding my long absence from Mr. Wesley, and a few unpleasant expressions in some of his letters the dear old man has written to me, (occasioned by the misrepresentation of others) I

feel the stroke most sensibly ; and, I expect, I shall never read
his works without reflecting on the loss which the church of God
and the world has sustained by his death. Dr. Coke, accompanied
by brother C—— and Dr. G——, set out for Baltimore in order to
get the most speedy passage to England ; leaving me to fill the appointments. I had a large congregation at sister Bombry's. In
the afternoon I rode to sister Waller's, making a journey of forty
miles for this day. Next day I overtook Dr. Coke and his company at Cholchester. Brother Coxes's horse being sick, I put my
old horse in his place to carry them to Alexandria ; where we arrived about three o'clock, after riding forty miles by our reckoning. At Alexandria Dr. Coke had certain information of Mr. Wesley's death. On Sabbath day he reached Baltimore, and preached
on the occasion of Mr. Wesley's death ; and mentioned some things
which gave offence.

MARYLAND—May, Thursday 5. This day, and the two following
days we held conference in Baltimore ; and great love and sweetness prevailed throughout the sitting. I preached to a large congregation on the Sabbath, and we had a gracious time.

Monday 9. Came to Cokesbury. I found there was a vast de-
mand for money for the establishment, there having been an expenditure of £700 in five months.

Tuesday 10. Crossed Susquehannah and came to Cecil ; and next
day reached Duck-Creek. Our conference began, and was conducted in much peace and harmony amongst preachers and people.
Our meetings in public were attended with great power.

Sunday 15. Two elders and three deacons were ordained.
After the ordination, I rode to Middletown, Delaware, and preached
to a large congregation.

PENNSYLVANIA.—Monday 16. I rode to New-Castle, and had
the last interview with Dr. Coke. Surely the time to favour New-
Castle is swiftly coming. In the evening I came to Chester ; and
next day, (the 17th) arrived in Philadelphia, and opened conference. We had a tender, melting account of the dealings of God
with many souls ; and settled our business in much peace. Mr.
Hammett came from Charleston with a wonderful list of petition-
ers desiring his return : to this, as far as I had to say, I submitted ;
but ———————————— I see and hear many things that
might wound my spirit, if it were not that the Lord bears me up
above all.

Wednesday 18. I preached on " The Lord liveth ; and blessed
be my rock, and let the God of my salvation be exalted."

Friday 20. We had a fast-day ; and in the afternoon a feast of love. It was a time to be remembered : some precious souls were converted.

Saturday 21. I left Philadelphia for New-Jersey. On the road I felt much of the spirit of prayer.

NEW-JERSEY.—Sunday 22. I preached in Trenton on Joel ii. 17. Several preachers exhorted, and the Lord made sinners tremble Eighteen years ago I often slipped away from Philadelphia to Burlington one week, and to Trenton another, to keep a few souls alive : I had then no conferences to take up my time and occupy my thoughts ; and now—what hath God wrought !

We attended to the business of the conference with a good spirit. In the course of our sitting we had some pleasing and some painful circumstances to excite our feelings.

Tuesday 24. I set out for New-York. At Princeton I preached, and I trust a few felt the word. Passing through Kingston, I proceeded on to Mr. Jaques's, near Brunswick, making 32 miles. My soul is in peace ; my body weak and weary.

Wednesday 25. Rode to Elizabethtown. After dinner, I went by water to New York ; and found all in peace.

NEW-YORK.—Thursday 26. Our conference came together in great peace and love. Our ordinary business was enlivened by the relation of experiences, and by profitable observations on the work of God.

Nothing would satisfy the conference and the society but my consenting to preach on the occasion of Mr. Wesley's death, which I did on Sunday May 29: my text was 2 Timothy iii. 10, 11. I took the same subject at the old church in the morning ; and in the afternoon at the new church, varying, but retaining the substance.

Monday 30. Our conference rose ; and after love-feast, the preachers dispersed. We had had about 30 preachers at this conference, and not a frown, a sign of sour temper, or an unkind word was seen or heard amongst us :—but I am sick, and quite out-done with constant labour. Mr. Hammett's preaching was not well received : it was supposed to be aimed at our zealous men and passionate meetings : at the new church his preaching was still more exceptionable to those judicious persons who heard him. I expect some things will be retailed to my disadvantage. Be it so—I trust the Lord.

Wednesday, June 1. I preached at New-Rochelle church : the weather was unfavourable ; but we had a living meeting.

Thursday 2. We had a decent, lifeless congregation at the court-house on the Plains. In the afternoon I preached at North-Castle on Phil. ii. 12. My clay is heavy, and my spirits low.

Friday 3. I very sensibly feel the cold I had taken on my way to New-Rochelle by riding in the rain ; however, I rode to Bedford, and preached in the town-house to about 200 serious and deeply attentive hearers. Rode on to brother H——'s and was much in-disposed.

CONNECTICUT.—Saturday 4. I rode over rocks and hills, and came to Wilton ; and preached to a serious, feeling, well-behaved people at squire R——'s. In the evening I went on to Reading. Surely God will work powerfully amongst these people, and save thousands of them. We have travelled about 24 miles this day over very rough roads : the weather is cold for the season ; my horse is very small, and my carriage is inconvenient in such rocky, uneven, jolting ways. This country is very hilly and open—not unlike that about the Peak of Derbyshire. I feel faith to believe that this visit to New-England will be blest to my own soul, and the souls of others. We are now in Connecticut ; and never out of sight of a house ; and sometimes we have a view of many churches and steeples, built very neatly of wood ; either for use, ornament, piety, policy or interest—or it may be some of all these. I do feel as if there had been religion in this country once ; and I apprehend there is a little in form and theory left. There may have been a praying ministry and people here ; but I fear they are now spiritually dead ; and am persuaded that family and private prayer is very little practised : could these people be brought to constant, fervent prayer, the Lord would come down and work won-derfully among them. I find my mind fixed on God, and the work of God.

Lord's day 5. About ten o'clock we assembled in a barn at Reading, where we had, perhaps, three hundred serious, attentive people to hear—My subject was Eph. ii. 8, 9. I felt freedom, and the truth came clearly to my mind. Rode in the evening twelve miles over rocks and uneven roads to Newtown : I found multitudes of people in a Presbyterian meeting-house, many of whom appear-ed wild in their behaviour—the young laughing and playing in the galleries ; and the aged below seemed to be heavy and lifeless.— I was sick and weary ; nevertheless, I attempted to preach on Acts v. 31, 32. and endeavoured to enlarge on—1. The humiliation of Christ—2. His exaltation in his resurrection, ascension, glory,

Head of the church : a Prince to give repentance and pardon to
rebels. I felt the power of Satan, and soon ended my feeble testimony. Brother L—— preached at six o'clock. I felt much
weakened and wearied.—My impressions relative to the people in
these parts are unfavourable.

Monday 6. Came to Stepney, and found a few people waiting for
us at brother O—'s, to whom I gave an exhortation, and we had
an awakening and melting time. Came on to Chesnut-Hill, about
twenty miles from Newtown ; the people here had not had proper notice of our coming ; a few, however, being informed of it,
let others know, so that by the time I had exhorted and prayed
many joined them :. I exhorted again about forty minutes in as
pointed a manner as I well could. After meeting, we called at
E. H——'s, and obtained refreshment for man and beast ; after
conversing and praying with the family, we set out and reached
J. H——'s in the evening, where we had a small family meeting,
at which I spoke on Hosea x. 12. " Break up your fallow ground,
for it is time, yea, yet time to seek the Lord, till he come and rain
righteousness upon you." To-day I have felt weary and heavy,
and yesterday I was agitated in mind, and sorely buffeted by the
enemy—but I have peace with God.

Tuesday 7. Body and mind more tranquil and serene. Time
was when I should have thought the prospects here were very
great—the people attend in great multitudes. I find it necessary
to guard against painful anxiety on the one hand, as well as against
lukewarmness on the other. I judge that the spirits of men
must be stirred up to expect more than in former times, and pray,
preach, and converse accordingly. We came to Stratford—good
news—they have voted that the town-house shall be shut : well—
where shall we preach ? Some of the select-men—one, at least,
granted access.—I felt unwilling to go, as it is always my way
not to push myself into any public house :—we had close work on
Isaiah lv. 6, 7. some smiled, some laughed, some swore, some
talked, some prayed, some wept—had it been a house of our own,
I should not have been surprised had the windows been broken.—
I refused to preach there any more ; and it was well I did—two of
the esquires were quite displeased at our admittance. We met
the class, and found some gracious souls ; the Methodists have a
society consisting of twenty members, some of them converted ;
but they have no house of worship—they may now make a benefit
of a calamity—being denied the use of other houses, they will the
more earnestly labour to get one of their own : the Presbyterians

and the Episcopalians have each one, and both are elegant buildings.

Wednesday 8. We rested at Stratford; and had meeting in brother P——'s house : finding that most of those who attended were serious people, I spoke on our blessed Lord's words Matt. xi. 28, 29, 30. it was a time of comfort to the few seekers and believers present.

Thursday 9. Came to New-Haven, and found my appointment to preach had been published in the newspapers. Every thing was quiet; we called on the sheriff—he was absent : we then put up our horses at the Ball-tavern, near the college yard.—I was weary and unwell. I had the honour of the president S——, Dr. W——, and the Rev. Mr. E—— to hear me, and several of the collegians, with a few scattering citizens. I talked away to them very fast, telling them some little stories, whilst the sun shone full in my face. The judges looked very grave while I endeavoured to show—1. What we must be saved from ; 2. What has been esteemed by the men of the world as the wisdom of preaching ; 3. What is meant by the foolishness of preaching.—When I had done no man spoke to me. I thought to-day of dear Mr. Whitefield's words to Mr. Boardman and Mr. Pilmore at their first coming over to America :—" Ah !" said he, " if ye were Calvinists ye would take the country before ye." We visited the college chapel at the hour of prayer : I wished to go through the whole, to inspect the interior arrangements, but no one invited me. The divines were grave, and the students were attentive ; they used me like a fellow Christian, in coming to hear me preach, and like a stranger in other respects : should Cokesbury or Baltimore ever furnish the opportunity, I, in my turn, will requite their behaviour, by treating them as friends, brethren, and gentlemen. The difficulty I met with in New-Haven, for lodging, and for a place to hold meeting, made me feel and know the worth of Methodists more than ever. My body is fatigued and listless—my spirit tried and tempted : infirmities cleave to me.

From New-Haven, through a poor country, we passed on to Northbury, where there is a large Independent church. In Wallingford the meeting-house of the Separatists supplied a place for our preachers ; we have also used a neat Episcopal church— small indeed, compared with others.

I am reminded of England in travelling here ; this country more resembles my own than any I have yet seen on this side the Atlantic. I preached at five o'clock, in the meeting-house of the Separatists—a large room, and small company. My subject was 2 Cor. vi. 20. I alarmed the town by the excessive noise I made, and thereby enlarged my congregation. I felt more assisted than I expected.

Saturday 11. At Wallingford-Farms. Here has been some stir about religion; but the people say *new divinity* has put out the fire—Methodists, Baptists, Separatists, &c. &c. I felt somewhat warmed while I opened and applied " Strait is the gate, and narrow is the way that leadeth unto life." Some were tender, and some appeared a little alarmed. I then came to Middlefields, and lodged at the house of a niece of David Brainard. Here we enjoy the quiet use of a meeting-house.

Lord's day 12. Very unwell, but had to preach three times. I began at ten o'clock, on " Blessed is he whosoever shall not be offended in me." I had the attention of the people much more than I expected. In the afternoon I enlarged, under very great weakness, on " How shall I give thee up, Ephraim ?"

Came in haste to Middletown, where the committee favoured me with the meeting-house belonging to *the standing order.* I felt exceedingly low in body, while I spoke to a very large, serious, and attentive congregation, and I had liberty in preaching on 1 John iii. 23. After meeting we rode a mile out of town to get lodging. It was to the poorer classes of people that this preaching on love and charity was anciently blest.

Monday 13. Rode by Haddam, where David Brainard was born. We came through dreadful rocky ways to Capt. Lee's: a Congregational minister had just finished his sermon as we came in. As we did not wish to force ourselves on any one, we went forward to Lime, and found a free, open-hearted Baptist minister, who rose from his bed, and received us kindly. By this time we were weary and sleepy. I trust the Lord had a dwelling in this man's heart and house—his wife is a kind, loving soul ; their children obliging, and ready to serve us cheerfully.

Tuesday 14. We came over rocks, and through heat and dust, to New-London. My mind has felt but little temptation to impatience until yesterday and this day ; but, through grace, I do not yield thereto. It is both unreasonable and unchristian to murmur —it betters nothing: to deny ourselves, and to take up our cross daily, is our duty—let us not flee from it.

. New-London stands upon the River Thames—almost newly built since the war. This town suffered in the general burning carried on by Arnold in this quarter. The new meeting-house stands on an eminence ; the Episcopal church is a pleasant, well formed building. The New-Light Baptists were very kind, and some of them appeared like Methodists. My church was the court-house—my subject 2 Peter iii. 15. : I was not happy in speaking. Brother L—— gave them a sermon at half past eight o'clock. I understood there was a work of religion in this place last year ; little of it now remains. I came on to Stonington, properly so called, a distance of ten miles, over a most dreadful road for a carriage : I would almost as soon undertake to drive over the Alleghany mountain. From Stonington I came on to Westerly, crossing the line-bridge between Connecticut and Rhode-Island. I dropped a few words to the woman of the house where we dined, and saw very clearly that she felt them. I had some life in speaking to about one hundred people, at Mr. ——'s, in Charlestown, on Rev. iii. 20. One said, I had fitted the people well : another said, that I had the signs of the times.

RHODE-ISLAND.—Thursday 15. Came to Newport—the roads were comparatively good—the ferry three miles wide ; which, however, we safely crossed in a spacious open boat, excellent in its kind. In Newport are two Presbyterian meeting-houses,—one, New-Divinity, so called : three others, regular Baptists, New-Lights, and Sabbatarians ; one Friends' meeting, and one Episcopal church. We stayed two nights at our kind friend's, brother Green, a New-Light Baptist. I lectured the second night from Isaiah lxiv. 1—7. ; there was some life amongst the people, although it was late, and the congregation like our Lord's disciples before his passion. There is also a Jews' synagogue, and a Moravian chapel. I expect before many years the Methodists will also have a house for worship here. I feel the state of this people—they are settled upon their lees, and want emptying from vessel to vessel. My soul enjoys peace.

Saturday 18. We go hence to Providence, attended by our kind friend for guide. Blessed be the Lord for a refreshing rain the last night. On this journey I feel much humbled ; I am unknown, and have small congregations, to which I may add, a jar in sentiment—but I do not dispute. My soul is brought into close communion. I should not have felt for these people and for the preachers as I now do, had I not visited them : perhaps I may do something for them in a future day. We came to Bristol, and should have gone farther, but Captain G—— saw us, and took us to his house. At the request of a few persons I preached in the court-house to about a hundred people, and enforced " The Son

of man is come to seek and to save that which was lost," and found
a degree of liberty. Some time ago there was the beginning of a
work here, but the few souls who began are now discouraged from
meeting together : I fear religion is extinguished by confining it too
much to church and Sunday service, and reading of sermons. I
feel that I am not among my own people : although I believe there
are some who fear God ; and I find reason to hope that souls have
gone to glory from this town.

Sunday 19. Came to Providence. I attended the ministry of
Mr. M——, a Baptist, in the forenoon; and Mr. S——— a New-
Light, in the afternoon. In the evening I preached with some life
on Isai. lxi. 1—3. There are Presbyterians, Episcopalians, Independents or Congregationalists, here : but the Baptists appear to
be the leading people. I found a few gracious souls, and some
seeking. It has been a season of deep exercise with me while
here : I have had some weighty sensations ; I think the Lord will
revive his work in Providence.

Monday 20. I visited some serious families that truly love and
fear God. The afternoon I spent very agreeably with the old prophet Mr. Snow, aged about seventy years : he was awakened by
the instrumentality of Gilbert Tennant, whose memory I revere.
He told me much about Mr. Whitefield, and old times, and of the
ministers of old times—of himself, his awakening, and conversion
to God—of his riding thirty miles to Newport, in exceeding cold
weather, to bring Mr. Tennant to Providence.

Having obtained more knowledge of the people, my subject was
Gal. vi. 14.—plain and pointed : my audience was serious and
attentive. I endeavoured to show,

1. What it is for a man to glory in a thing.

2. What men glory in which is not the cross of Christ.

3. What it is to glory in the cross of Christ.

4. How a person may know when he glories in the cross of
Christ, viz. by the world's being crucified to him, and he unto the
world.

The people here appear to be prudent, active, frugal ; cultivating
a spirit of good family economy ; and they are kind to strangers.
They have had frequent revivals of religion : I had faith to believe
the Lord would shortly visit them again, and that even we shall
have something to do in this town. We rested a day at Easton,
and appointed meeting at five o'clock. I had good freedom on Acts
xvii. 27. and the people felt the word. We have had a solemn,
happy, and solitary retreat, and my soul entered into renewed life.

MASSACHUSETTS.—Thursday 23. We rode through dust and heat to Boston. I felt much pressed in spirit, as if the door was not open. As it was court time, we were put to some difficulty in getting entertainment. It was appointed for me to preach at Murray's church—not at all pleasing to me ; and that which made it 'worse was, that I had only about twenty or thirty people to preach to in a large house : it appeared to me that those who professed friendship for us, were ashamed to publish us. On Friday evening I preached again : my congregation was somewhat larger, owing, perhaps, to the loudness of my voice—the sinners were noisy in the streets. My subject was Rev. iii. 17, 18. I was disturbed, and not at liberty, although I sought it. I have done with Boston until we can obtain a lodging, a house to preach in, and some to join us. Some things here are to be admired in the place and among the people—their bridges are great works, and none are ashamed of labour ; of their hospitality I cannot boast : in Charleston, wicked Charleston, six years ago a stranger, I was kindly invited to eat and drink by many—here, by none. There are, I think, nine meeting-houses of the Establishment ; Friends' meeting-house, one ; Sandeminians, one ; Universalists, one ; Roman Catholics, one ; Baptists, two ; Episcopalians, two ; the Methodists have no house—but their time may come.

I preached at Slade's tavern on my way to Lynn on " If our Gospel be hid, it is hid to them that are lost." I was agreeably surprised to find a house raised for the Methodists. As a town, I think Lynn the perfection of beauty ; it is seated on a plain, under a range of craggy hills, and open to the sea : there is a promising society—an exceedingly well-behaved congregation—these things, doubtless, made all pleasing to me. My first subject was Rom. viii. 33.—in the afternoon Acts iv. 12. : here we shall make a firm stand, and from this central point, from Lynn, shall the light of Methodism and of truth radiate through the state. Our brother Johnson is simple-hearted, and hearty in the cause : we owe our entertainment and house for worship chiefly to him.

Tuesday 28. Rode to Marblehead. When I entered this town, my heart was more melted towards its inhabitants, than to any in those parts, with the exception of Lynn. After consultation, and some altercation among themselves, the committee invited me to preach in Mr. Story's meeting-house, which I did accordingly at four o'clock, on Acts xxvi. 17, 18. I was led to speak alarmingly, whilst I pointed out the Gospel as descriptive of their misery and

need of mercy: brother Lee preached in the evening to a great
number of people in and about Mr. Martin's house. Next morning, weak as I was, I could not forbear speaking to them on "Seek
ye first the kingdom of God."

Wednesday 29. Rode to Salem. Here are five meeting-houses,
two of them on the New-Divinity plan—i. e. regeneration the first
work—no prayer, repentance, or faith, until this is accomplished:
the other three belong to the Establishment—one Episcopalian;
and one Friends' meeting-house. I found no access to any. I lectured in the court-house on Rom. v. 6—9. I looked upon the
greater part of my congregation as judges; and I talked until they,
becoming weary, began to leave me. I have done with Salem until we can get a better stand. I had the curiosity to visit the cal-
vary of the witches—i. e. those who were destroyed on the charge
of witchcraft: I saw the graves of many innocent, good people,
who were put to death, suffering persecution from those who had
suffered persecution—such, and so strangely contradictory, is man.
I have felt weakness of body, and deep exercise of mind, and, at
times, good liberty in speaking—I am now convinced that the
Methodists, as a body, have the most religion, and am more and
more confirmed in my choice.

We rode to Manchester. Mr. Foster received us with great
kindness. The Selectmen granted us the privilege of the meeting-
house: I lectured on Malachi iii. 13. at five o'clock. Here are
some feeling and understanding souls. This place has been visited
for many years, and a society kept up, although the ministers did
not favour the stir; of this work, father Lee's ministry, an aged man
of that country and town, has been the principal means; for a long
time he has faithfully stood his ground, praying with, and exhorting
the people. We were invited to lodge at a place where provision
is made for the entertainment of ministers, and in the morning
money was offered. I declined accepting their invitation, and refused their money.

Friday, July 1. Came to L——'s to dinner: after praying with
them, and speaking to each in the family, I left them to God.
Thence I proceeded to T——'s, and preached at Brown's folly, to
many people—my subject, Luke ii. 10.

Saturday 2. I returned home to brother J——'s in Lynn.

Sunday 3. My first subject was "The great salvation"—In the
afternoon I spoke on Titus ii. 11, 12. and had liberty: in the evening my subject was Matt. xi. 28—30. the congregation was attentive, and my mind enjoyed sweet peace; although, outwardly, we

were uncomfortable, the meeting-house being open, and the weather very cool for the season. I feel as if God would work in these states, and give us a great harvest. My intervals of leisure have been spent in close application to my Bible, and reading Baxter's Call to the Unconverted.

Monday 4. I took the benefit of the sea-air, and began visiting.

Tuesday 5. My soul is in great peace and love. Here it is a day of small things : the people have been neglected, but now the Lord has opened their eyes. O what skill, and patience, and wisdom are needful to deal with souls! I was happy in meeting the women in class ; I found but few believers, but I do believe that God will bring them all into full liberty.

Wednesday 6. Found my mind stayed upon God. In the evening I had a large, attentive congregation.

Thursday 7. I was engaged closely in reading. I visited and conversed freely with two families. I am informed that Lynn and Lynnfield afford upwards of 2200 souls (1791.) This day brother Jesse Lee put a paper into my hand proposing the election of not less than two, nor more than four preachers from each conference, to form a general conference in Baltimore in December, 1792, to be continued annually.

Saturday 9. I preached a sacramental sermon on " Let a man examine himself, and so let him eat of that bread and drink of that cup."

Sunday 10. Preached on the great supper, Luke xiv. a very solemn, baptising, and sacramental season. The people chose to receive the elements sitting, as is the practice amongst Presbyterians. In the afternoon I enforced " What shall the end be of them that obey not the Gospel of God :" at night I spoke on " These shall go away into everlasting punishment:" the Lord was among the people, and I hope and trust some real good was done.

Monday 11. I labour under deep exercises of soul. The sea-bath I found to strengthen me. In the evening I met the men's class in Lynn, and was led to hope that a glorious work of God will be wrought here ; several people are under awakenings at this time ; my staying so long among them may be of the Lord.

Tuesday 12. We had a blessed rain after nearly a month's drought.

Wednesday 13. We came through Waltham, Sudbury, and Malborough ; at this last place there is a grand meeting house, and one not less elegant in its kind for the minister : thence we proceeded on through Northbury and Shrewsbury, to Worcester, through

rain, and with pain and weariness. Mr. Chandler received us
with kindness more than common, and courtesy anxious to please,
calling his family together with softness of address, and in all things
else being agreeable ; perhaps more so than any man I have met
with in America ; this reception shall comfort us a little in our
toil.   From Worcester, we journeyed on, passing through Leices-
ter, Spenser, Brookfields, and another town.   We dined at a place
where " the people are united, and do not wish to divide the
parish"—their fathers, the Puritans, divided the kingdom and the
church too, and when they could not obtain liberty of conscience
in England, they sought it here among wild men and beasts.   At
Greaves's tavern I saw a man from Vermont, who said the number
of their inhabitants was ninety thousand ; he invited me to send
preachers among them.

Friday 15. My mind has been dejected ; Satan has assaulted me—
I could not be fixed in prayer as I desired. We have made it
one hundred and eight miles from Lynn to Springfield. I want to
be with the Methodists again—O how unworthy of such fellowship !
yet am I seated among the princes of thy people ! At 6 o'clock I delivered a discourse in Mr. C——'s house on " It is time to seek the
Lord till he come and rain righteousness upon you:" the people were
a little moved ; and one sister under deep conviction. This place is
a haunt of soldiery : the armory being kept here : there appears to
be little religion among the inhabitants.

CONNECTICUT.—Sunday 17. Passed through Suffield to Turkey-
Hills, where I had a large and very criticising congregation,to whom
I preached my first discourse on John vii. 17.: my second subject
was Hebr. vi. 1.: there were some feeling hearts present ; the
Lord will work here. On Monday I had a crowd at Proquonac, in a
school-house, to whom I preached on 2 Cor. iv. 1, 2.: some were
frightened, some melted, and some were offended. We came to
Windsor ; Mr. S—— received us kindly, but did not fail to let us
know how lightly he thought of us and of our principles—here my
feelings were very gloomy, and I secretly wished myself out of the
way. I went to the school-house and found it crowded with people :
the Lord lifted me up whilst I opened and applied Gal. iii. 22. I
think I was given to see and feel the true state of these people ;
some of them were melted and praised God for the Gospel.

Tuesday 19. I came to the city of Hartford. At Mr. S——'s
meeting-house I was attended by three ministers : I was clear not
to keep back any part of the truth whilst I enforced Luke vii. 23.
the people were mostly serious and attentive.

I had an interview with Dorcas Brown, who was converted forty years ago, and in the history of whose experience there were some remarkable manifestations of the power of God, and of the interposition of his providence in answer to prayer in times of persecution and violence. Her son's case was also remarkable : he had been captured by the Indians, and was returned *killed;* in contradiction to this account, and the general belief, she pronounced that she should again see him in the flesh : contrary to the expectation of all but herself, he did return after an absence of three years and eight months.

Wednesday 20. At East-Hartford I felt more than usually assisted on Luke xix. 10. I had an attentive, feeling congregation. On Thursday we had a gracious shower at the quarterly meeting at West-Farmington, where I delivered a pointed discourse on Acts xvi. 31, 32. which was blessed to some souls.

Friday 22. The Episcopal church was open at Litchfield, where I preached, with very little faith, on the love of Christ. I think Morse's account of his countrymen is near the truth : never have I seen any people who would talk so long, so correctly, and so seriously about trifles.

Saturday 23. By a rocky, mountainous way, we came to Cornwall in the midst of the harvest home : we had about one hundred and fifty hearers : I had openings of mind whilst I spoke on 1 Pet. iii. 15.

Sunday 24. Came to Canaan, after preaching at a new meeting-house : here nought would satisfy but my going to the ancient Presbyterian church ; I reluctantly complied, and made a feeble attempt on Luke xi. 13. I offended, and was offended : the people seemed uneasy, and wished to be gone. This is the first, and I expect will be the last time I shall speak in that house, if not in that place. Twenty-five years ago, the people in this place had religion ; at present, it is to be feared, there is little or none : how it is I know not ; but at such places I feel dreadfully,—as if such people were the worst of all under the sun, and at the greatest distance from God.

Wednesday 27. Although under considerable affliction of body and mind, I rode over rough ways, to New-Britain ; where, in general, the people appeared unfeeling ; nevertheless, I found a few among them who felt the need of Christ : I was led to exhort them, and to pray with them—I am persuaded some are not far from the kingdom of God.

NEW-YORK.—Thursday 28. I felt some freedom at T——'s, while speaking on 2 Tim. iii. 16. : the length of the ride, and the languor of my bodily powers, had not enfeebled my mind : we found some gracious souls in the society.

Friday 29. Came to Albany. My mind felt impressed with the value of the souls in this place. By the curves I have made in my course from Hartford to this place, I suppose I have not travelled less than one hundred and fifty miles : perpetual motion is no small trial to my body and mind ; but I must cast my care upon the Lord. I am led to think the eastern church will find this saying hold true in the Methodists, viz. " I will provoke you to jealousy by a people that were no people ; and by a foolish nation will I anger you :" they have trodden upon the Quakers. the Episcopalians, the Baptists—see now if the Methodists do not work their way : the people will not pay large money for religion if they can get it cheaper.

I preached to about three hundred people in a barn at Coeyman's Patent, the new stone church not being ready. Our society is promising in this place.

Tuesday, August 2. Came to Hudson. I felt disagreeable sensations, a chill, hoarseness, headach, and fever.

Wednesday 3. The day was unusually warm, and I was sick and felt like Jonah ; I was ready to faint in my carriage ; at last, through mercy, I arrived safe at kind sister L——'s : I went to bed, took some chicken broth, and after a comfortable sleep felt revived. No more rest—I took the road again, and arrived at Rhinebeck by noon. My soul is in peace—I want more prayer, patience, life, and love—I walk daily, hourly, and sometimes minutely with God.

Saturday 6. I had a few serious people at the Mountain meeting-house. I lodged at C——'s, who was formerly a Shaking Quaker.

Sunday 7. We received the sacrament; and then went to a small grove, where we had a green carpet of nature's spreading underneath, and an umbrella of variegated leaves above us. I preached on Zech. xii. 10. to about a thousand or twelve hundred people, as it was judged : I felt solemn and recollected, and was assisted in speaking : I had some faith to believe it would be the beginning of days, and of a revival of religion.

CONNECTICUT.—Preached at Salisbury on Acts v. 31, 32. My mind is in peace.

I came to Sharon time enough to preach at three o'clock: the women crowded the house, whilst the men stood at the door, with patient attention, in the rain, which indeed many seemed scarcely to perceive ; I spoke with life and freedom on Ephes. ii. 8—10. Here are some praying souls. I read, much to my comfort, Corbit's memoirs of the secrets of his heart, brought to public view after his death.

NEW-YORK.—February 12. I preached at B——'s, on Luke xix. 10. to a number of simple-hearted people. Rode to brother J——'s to attend quarterly meeting; I felt weak and unwell, yet happy in God. My soul enters into deeper union with God, and into a sweet resignation and confidence in him for his work and church. I judge that my journey to Lynn, and my rides through the country thereabouts, have made a distance of little less than five hundred miles; and thence to Albany; nearly the same, and from Albany to New-York not much less; with, occasionally, very rough roads for a carriage: well, it is all for God, and Christ, and souls: I neither covet nor receive any man's silver or gold—food, raiment, and a little rest, is all I want.

Saturday and Sunday, 13, 14. We began our meeting in a barn at Jackson's: I had freedom whilst enlarging on Joshua xxiv. 15.: there was a large collection of people from far to our sacrament and love-feast; among these there was life, but the people about this place are dead—dead! there is a curse somewhere. I doubt if one soul has been converted to God since I was here two years ago.

Monday 15. I feel great power to trust God with his church and work: and am resolved on more frequent access to the throne of grace, not continuing so long as heretofore: I feel greater sweetness in so doing, and it tends more to an hourly and momently walk with God.

Tuesday 16. This is a day of rest from public labour. I have uncommon trials, and great liberty of spirit: my addresses to a throne of grace are frequent to-day.

Wednesday 17. Felt a good degree of liberty at B——'s on Col. i. 28. " Christ formed in you the hope of glory"—perfect in Christ Jesus—ours is not the perfection of God, of Christ, of angels; such perfection must be ours as excludes evil tempers from the heart, and yet supposes us liable to ignorance and error, while in tenements of clay. As I came along to P——'s I was ready to complain of the roughness of the roads, but I was suddenly stopped, when I beheld a poor Irish woman with a heavy child on her shoulders, and without covering for head or feet; she said she was from Canada, and thus far had begged her way:—pity for her at once stilled all murmur of complaint for myself.

On Thursday we had a gracious season at Stoney-Street, amongst sinners, seekers, and believers, while I applied Gal. vi. 10.

Saturday 20. Quarterly meeting at North-Castle : it began well ;
I was happy in mind, although unwell, whilst I spoke to the many
who attended on 1 Sam. vii. 3.

Sunday 21. Our congregation became unweildy and restless; my
subject, Luke xxiii. 3. was new, to me, at least : although my mind
enjoyed some degree of peace, my frame was agitated, and my spirits hurried. I received the olive-branch from Virginia—All is
peace—it was obtained by a kind letter from me to O·Kelly.

Saturday 27. Quarterly meeting in Newtown : I felt freedom
of mind whilst treating on Deut. v 26.

Sunday 28. We had a good sacramental time, and a melting love-
feast. There are four houses of worship in this place, but I fear
the church of Christ is very small. I have lately been led into
great depths of God, and sight of my danger and constant need of
prayer.

Monday 29. Came to New-York : the weather is warm, and here
is an awful season of affliction.

I preached at the new church on Hebr. v. 12. we had an acceptable time, and some gracious movings.

Wednesday 31. We had a serious, heart-affecting time ; many
were ready to break out into praises to God. I respect the kindness of the dear people here, and leave New York in faith that the
Lord will return to visit them.

Thursday, September 1. I visited my old friends on Staten-
Island : many whom I have preached to and prayed for, still keep
at a distance.

Friday 2. I preached in our new chapel to a large congregation
on " Ye that have escaped the sword, go away, stand not still ;
remember the Lord afar off, and let Jerusalem come into your
mind." Jer. li. 50. : it was a gracious season : after preaching the
society met, and several declared the Lord's dealings with their
souls.

New-Jersey.—Monday 5. I rode through much rain to Monmouth, New-Jersey, where I preached to a considerable congregation on " The just shall live by faith ; but if any man draw back,
my soul shall have no pleasure in him." There is some stir among
the people : at Long-Branch, within eighteen months, as I am informed, nearly fifty souls have professed conversion.

Tuesday 6. I found the Lord had not left himself without witnesses at Kettle-Creek.

Wednesday 7. At P——'s church I learn some were offended :
blessed be God ! my soul was kept in great peace.

Friday 9. At Little-Egg Harbour I endeavoured to speak very pointedly on Acts xiii. 46.—my spirit was much moved, and, I think, as a preacher and visiter, I am thus far free from the blood of saints and sinners.

Saturday 10. Rode a dreary, moscheto path, in great weakness, to Batstow works.

Sunday 11. Preached on Luke xix. 10. I advised the people to build a house for the benefit of those men so busily employed day and night, Sabbaths not excepted, in the manufacture of iron—rude, and rough, and strangely ignorant of God.

Thursday 15. Having exerted myself more than my strength would well bear last evening, I feel faint, *yet pursuing*. I gave an exhortation to a house full of people. The evening was spent with S. H——;—gracious souls, mother and children.

Friday 16. Preached at C——'s : here are some under awaken-ings ; and the prospect is pleasing. Many attended the word on the Lord's day : several of our sisters and of our brethren on this day (and on Monday at Bethel) after sacrament, testified to the goodness of God.

PENNSYLVANIA.—Tuesday 20. Rode to Philadelphia. Here, as usual, I was closely employed in writing ; I had several meetings, and some awful seasons that will be remembered in eternity—This city abounds with inhabitants—it is the London of America.

Wednesday 28. We rode to Strasburg, thirty miles, where I preached at night in a respectable tavern on Acts iii. 19. I was very plain, and had some energy in preaching, although unwell in body. I have faith to believe we shall have a house of worship, and that the Lord will have a people in this place.

Thence to M. B——'s : hitherto the Lord hath been our helper in spite of sin and Satan. We had a good time whilst I spoke on Zech. xii. 10. after sacrament several bore their testi-mony for the Lord. My soul is much humbled, and brought into close communion with God ; yea, I rejoiced greatly to find so much religion among the people. We went hence to brother M——'s, where, for two days, we had a gracious season : I preached on Acts ii. 37, 38. I had openings, and was made to feel after the souls of the people. How will Satan take advantage to raise pre-judice in the minds of many !—At first the cry was, " They are enemies to the country !" that tale worn out, it is said, " They will pull down the churches—they hold erroneous doctrines !" aye ; we will labour to raise a true spiritual church ; and if, in doing this, we injure wolves in sheep's clothing, let unfaithful ministers look to it : we shall deliver our own souls.

DELAWARE.—Came to Wilmington. Alas! for poor Wilmington —when will this people open their eyes! We rode in haste thirty miles to D——'s, but the people had met three hours before our arrival, and brother E—— had preached to them. I preached at the Cross-Roads, but the minds of the people were so occupied by the approaching election, that I fear there was little room for things of more importance.—Finding there were no more appointments published for me, I rode, through the dust, thirty-two miles to judge White's. O Lord, help me to watch and pray! I am afraid of losing the sweetness I feel: for months past I have felt as if in the possession of perfect love—not a moment's desire of any thing but God. I have an awful view of the reformed churches, and am determined to speak to the very hearts of the people. After attending a quarterly meeting at B——'s chapel, I came to W——'s; we had a large congregation: after public service, we had a meeting for the local preachers, leaders, and stewards. Next morning we had love-feast for the coloured brethren at sunrise; and at nine o'clock for the whites. We find new members are added every year; many living experiences, and miracles of grace in this society.

Friday, October 14. Came to brother L——'s. Hail, happy souls!—three out of four in this family love God.

Saturday 15. Came to Downing's chapel; had a blessed love-feast; most of those who spoke professed sanctification. My soul was filled with God. I did what I could to put those in band who had witnessed perfect love in love-feast. There is a great work of God in the lower counties of Virginia; but the Antinomian doctrines, so liberally set forth by some, greatly hinder. We have rough weather.

Thursday 20. The storm continued; it was thought no one could go out; we, nevertheless, ventured through heavy rains and came to P——'s; at night we reached D——'s, making a journey of nearly forty miles; we were wet and uncomfortable; but the Lord preserves our goings out, and our comings in.

MARYLAND.—Friday 21. Preached at brother L——'s on Hebr. viii. 10, 11, 12. I think the Lord will work in this neighbourhood, and take away the covering and the veil that are spread upon the minds of the people. Temptations have oppressed my soul, and disease afflicted my body; it is the Lord's power alone that can help me; I fear I am not so constant in prayer as I should be. I made an effort to establish a female school, under sister G—, and sister B——; and endeavoured to impress the necessity and expediency of band-meeting, on men and women, both married and single.

Tuesday 25. At M——'s, there was a living stir among some who came to the quarterly meeting from a distance. My soul is bowed down for this neighbourhood.

Wednesday, November 2. We crossed Choptank-River and came to Talbot quarterly meeting. My subject on the first day was "Oh! let the wickedness of the wicked come to an end." We had a close love-feast, and some living souls.

Sunday 6, and Monday 7. Attended quarterly meeting at Greensburg, commonly called Choptank-Bridge: we had a strict and living love-feast, and powerful testimonies.

Wednesday 15. Came to Havre de Grace, and thence hurried to Cokesbury, where I found all in peace.

Thursday 16. Came to the old meeting house at Bush, and preached on "Enoch walked with God:" the meeting-house at Bush is the second house built for the Methodists in the state: it is a poor building, remaining unfinished to this day, and likely so to continue.

Friday 17. We had a powerful, melting time, at Deer-Creek: my subject was Jeremiah xiv. 8, 9, 10.

Sunday 26. I preached at Baltimore a searching discourse on Zeph. i. 12. In the afternoon I preached at the Point, to some unfeeling souls; and in the evening performed the funeral solemnity of my dear old friend sister Tribulet, on Acts xvi. 13, 14, 15.: I was uncommonly drawn out this day, and truly laboured in body and spirit.

Monday, December 7. I went from house to house through the snow and cold, begging money for the support of the poor orphans at Cokesbury.

Rode to Annapolis and preached at night.

VIRGINIA.—Wednesday, December 9. A day to be remembered. We stopped once in forty-three miles: when we reached Oxenhill-Ferry, opposite to Alexandria, I was nearly frozen, being hardly able to walk or talk. We crossed the Patomac in an open boat, on whose icy bottom the horses with difficulty kept their feet; and still worse it would have been, had I not thoughtfully called for some straw to strew beneath them; we had five of them on board, and the waves were high.

Friday 11. Rode forty miles to Mrs. W——'s: I suffered not a little with cold: I thank God my life is spared.

Sunday 13. I could not find the way to the hearts of an unfeeling

people at the widow Bombry's ; thence we went in haste to Port
Royal ; the inhabitants, seeing us, ran together, to whom I spoke
on Acts ii. 27. : the people were respectful and attentive.

Monday 14. Rode through a storm of snow to brother A——'s.
My mind enjoys peace ; and although by constant travelling I am
kept from the privilege of being so frequently in private prayer,
yet I am preserved from anger and murmuring—my soul is wholly
given up to God.

I am now about entering upon the business of the conferences
for the present year—all is peace. Notwithstanding I have been so
highly favoured, my sufferings may be lessened by an earlier move
to the south ; I will therefore remember to be on the south side
of the Patomac by the middle of November, if circumstances allow.

Wednesday 13. Came to brother Dickenson's, Caroline county,
and waited for the preachers composing the conference in the central district of Virginia.

In the evening the brethren came together ; we opened conference, and went through a great part of our minute work ; all
was peace and love. We had searching work in speaking experiences, and in examining the young men who offered as candidates
for the ministry.

Friday 16. After fasting and prayer our conference rose. My
subject at the new chapel was 1 Chron. xxix. 15—17. Saturday I
rode to Hanover-Town.

Sunday 18. I preached at Hanover on 1 Cor. ii. 17. I rode in
the evening to brother C——'s. My mind was in peace. I
journeyed on through Richmond, Manchester, and Petersburg,
accompanied by brothers E—— and K—— ; on Friday 23d, arriving at Lane's chapel, where our conference began and ended in great
peace.

Sunday 25. I preached on John iv. 14. and had a comfortable
season ; many spoke of the dealings of God with their souls : the
examination among the preachers relative to character and experience, was very close : all was meekness and love.

Tuesday 27. We had a long, cold ride to our kind brother
Blunt's.

Wednesday 28. I preached on 1 Peter iv. 1—4.

Thursday 29. I rode twenty-five miles, through very cold weather, without taking any refreshment, to sister P——'s ; on our
way we had a meeting at brother C——'s, where many attended,
to whom I spoke with freedom on 2 Tim. ii. 19—21. : here some
wicked young men behaved quite out of character.

Sunday, January 1, 1792. On this beginning of the new year, I preached, and had liberty on Isai. lxv. 1, 2. in the evening I once more cried to the people of Norforlk, " Repent, and be converted :" my audience was attentive and tender. My body was greatly fatigued, my soul much comforted in the Lord. Religion revives here, the seed which has been sowing for twenty years begins to spring up : Norfolk flourishes ; Portsmouth declines, and is already low.

Thursday 5. Rode to W. B——'s, there were but few people. On our way thither brother M—— would stop to feed : I believe the Lord sent me to speak a word to a broken-hearted, forsaken, distressed woman. My soul enjoys peace ; but excessive labour, and bodily suffering from the cold, prevents that deep communion with God I wish for : I do little except reading a few chapters in my Hebrew Bible.

NORTH CAROLINA.—Sunday 8. I preached at the widow Hardy's to a large congregation : I felt freedom in speaking, and the souls of the people appeared tender. The prospect of our journey ahead seemed gloomy ; however, we came down in the snow, and got on board a leaky *flat*, which we were obliged to bail as we went ; the ferry was five miles wide, our horses restless, the river (Roanoak) rough, and the weather very cold ; but the Lord brought us safe to shore, twelve miles from our destined place : we were strangers to the road, and had not an hour's sun ; nevertheless, kind Providence brought us through the dark and cold to brother Ward's about eight o'clock : here I sold my carriage and took horse again.

Thursday 19. I rode with no small difficulty to Green Hills, about two hundred miles, the roads being covered with snow and ice. Our conference began and ended in great peace and harmony : we had thirty-one preachers stationed at the different houses in the neighbourhood. I find we have had a good work in the eastern district of North Carolina in the past year. For some time back I have travelled with much difficulty, having few hearers, much weakness of body, and uncomfortable weather.

Monday 23. Our conference rose. I rode twenty miles through severe cold to brother B——'s.

Tuesday 24. Brother Morrell, my fellow traveller, was unwell : we had our horses *roughed*, which detained us an hour or two after the appointed time. I reached brother T——'s, and said a little from Philip. ii. 14—16. ; but the people could not hear, their souls and their bodies were cold. Finding it was twenty-two miles to my next appointment, I set off without refreshment, intending to reach brother D——'s, near Hillsborough; on the way, however, hearing of brother S——, a local preacher, we called on him, and he gave us freely of such things as he had.

Thursday 26. I was led out with freedom on the two last verses of Hebr. xii. at M——'s. I find outward difficulties in my progress; the roads are covered with ice and snow, and the severity of the weather prevents my having an opportunity, when I wish, of spending time in private exercises; but blessed be God! I am resigned, and am kept from sin, and my soul is stayed upon God.

Friday 27. After riding thirty miles through ice and snow to Rainey's, I found many people waiting for me, and I began, without any refreshment, to speak on "This is the victory that overcometh the world, even our faith." 1 I endeavoured to point out the object of this faith; 2. Its subjects; 3. Its nature; and 4. Its victory. In our route through North Carolina we passed through Bertie, Gates, Tyrrel, Tarborough, Franklin, Wake, Chatham, Orange, Guilford, and Randolph counties. We have travelled nearly eight hundred miles since the 7th of December last past. Seldom have I been tempted to a murmuring thought; it is now the 29th of January: I want nothing but more mental and private prayer.

Tuesday 31. Yesterday and to-day we have rode about sixty miles, a great deal of the way through heavy hail and rain. I gave an exhortation at C——'s, on *seeking the kingdom of God.* Here we had all things richly to supply our wants; and what was still better, we found the Lord had souls in this family.

SOUTH CAROLINA.—February 1. I preached to a considerable congregation at M'D——'s on Acts xiii. 38.

Saturday and Sunday, 4 and 5. I attended a quarterly meeting.

Monday 6. At Flower's church. For some time past I have enjoyed much of God, though suffering under indisposition of body, and frequently in a crowd: I feel nothing but peace in my soul, and find power to trust Jehovah with his own cause.

Tuesday 7. We reached sister Port's. I find there is a great commotion among the people, excited by the conduct of W. Hammett, who has divided the society in Charleston, and taken to himself some chaff and some wheat. This is not all—they say our house will go too.

Wednesday 8. We set off after six o'clock in the morning; our horses being over-fed we did not push them, so that we did not reach Georgetown until near six in the evening. After my trials

and hard riding my cordial is to preach at night. Except Georgetown and Charleston, there are few places where I have not a
good congregation when weather permits. I can praise God—my
soul is happy in Him ; by his grace I am kept from sin, and I still
hope this dark cloud that lowers over us will yet break with
blessings on our heads.

Thursday 9. We rested; and next day came to Wappataw, and
found that brother S. C—— had moved. We then went to his
brother's, whose wife was buried that day. We were fatigued
and cold, and rejoiced to find we were not compelled to take up
our lodgings under a pine tree.

Saturday 11. Arrived in Charleston. I received a full and true
account of Mr. Hammett's proceedings. Brothers E—— and
P—— have done all things well. Mr. Hammett had three grand
objections to us.—1. The American preachers and people insulted
him. 2. His name was not printed in our *Minutes*. 3. The nota
bene cautioning *minute* was directed against him. He has gone to
the New-Market, to preach, and has drawn about twenty white
members after him. We are considered by him as seceders from
Methodism!—Because we do not wear gowns and powder ; and
because we did not pay sufficient respect to Mr. Wesley !

Sabbath 12. My subject was Isai. liii. 11. Brother H. preached
in the afternoon.

Tuesday 14. Our conference began. I preached at night on
Luke xxiv. 17. and endeavoured to show the low estate of the
interest of Christ at that time. In our conference we were unusually close in examination of characters, doctrines, and experience : we had great peace and some power amongst us, and
received the good news of eighty souls being converted in Philadelphia, and of a revival in Connecticut.

I preached a sermon to the preachers, on " Endure hardness as
a good soldier of Jesus Christ."

Saturday 18. I received an abusive, anonymous letter (I believe
from Mr. S.) on several subjects. My spirits were low ; I came from
my knees to receive the letter, and having read it, I returned
whence I came ; I judged it prudent and expedient, and I think I
was urged thereto by conscience, to tell the people of some things
relating to myself. I related to them the manner of my coming to
America ; how I continued during the war ; the arrival of Dr. Coke,
and the forming of the American Methodists into a church ; and
finally, why I did not commit the charge of the society in Charleston, to Mr. Hammett, who was unknown, a foreigner, and did not

acknowledge the authority of, nor join in connexion with, the American conference.

Sunday 19. I preached on "Who is on the Lord's side?" Mr. M——s sent in his resignation. For certain reasons we were led to pass over his character, but we were wrong; it might have been better to subject it to scrutiny, although none grieved at his going from us.

Monday 20. *I came out of the fire.*—Rode to Parker's ferry.

Tuesday 21. Came to Mr. Lambright's, and next day had a heavy ride to Maixer's, and missed my congregation after all, and so I did at Hudson's, in Georgia; however, I spoke a few words to a few people, and it was felt.

Friday 24. We had fifty miles to ride, but had the advantage of good roads. Stopped at F——'s, and then came on to brother M——'s; he and his father have kindly entertained us as the servants of the Lord.

Saturday 25. I had an attentive and feeling people at Providence, where I saw C——, and learned that poor Henry, the Jew (mentioned March 9, 1791) was dead, and died wretched in body and mind, a few months after my departure. Let preachers or people catch me in Waynesborough until things are altered and bettered. Since last Monday I have rode one hundred and eighty miles, and was obliged to ride on, though late, to prevent man and beasts being on the road on the Sabbath day. My mind was powerfully struck with a sense of the great duty of preaching in all companies; of always speaking boldly and freely for God as if in the pulpit.

GEORGIA.—Sabbath morning 26. I made frequent visits to the throne of grace, and feel my soul comforted in God's word, "Instead of thy fathers, thou shalt have sons, whom thou shalt make princes in all the land:" I feel solemn; the burthen of the work lies on me; the preachers have left, and are leaving the field.

Monday 27. We rode thirty miles to White-Oak meeting-house—a painful journey; the weather was cold, and the house open; the people, however, were attentive. It is not pleasing to the flesh to take only a little tea at seven o'clock in the morning, and then go until six at night before we have a table spread; and ah! how few Christian houses—I had my trials in the evening.

Tuesday 28. We rode through the snow to Little-River, and a few people met us at S——'s: I preached on 2 Tim. iv. 2, 3, 4. Without staying to eat, we rode on to Washington, making thirty miles this day also. We collected our conference, and had great searching and sifting, and were under the necessity of suspending one ; we were very close in examining characters and principles : each preacher spoke his experience, and made his observations relative to the work of God since last conference. Brother Hull accompanies me, and H. Herbert repairs to Alexandria in Virginia. I hope in future there will be harmony among the brethren : if souls are converted to God it answers no valuable purpose thereafter to disciple them to ourselves. I preached on the marriage supper, and took occasion to show how some are kept from, and others lose, the grace of God by the unlawful use of lawful things.

Saturday, March 4. Rode to Fishing-Creek, and had an uncomfortable time on the Sabbath at Bibb's Cross-Roads.

SOUTH CAROLINA.—Monday 6. I left Georgia, and lodged near Whitehall in South Carolina.

Tuesday 7. Rode fifty miles to brother Finch's; here the brethren gave me a meeting on Wednesday; the congregation was small, and the people unengaged ; rode that evening to Odle's, and the next day to Watter's.

Sunday 12. Preached at Smith's on Romans, v. 1, 2, 3.; and kept the holy solemn Sabbath as a day of rest for man and beast.

NORTH CAROLINA.—Monday 13. Rode forty miles to Major Moor's, cold and weary. I have read two volumes of Gordon's American Revolution, containing about one thousand pages We came to the widow M——'s : here we heard that fifty poor wandering sinners had been brought back to God in this wild place, and we rejoiced at the glad tidings.

Friday 17. I was very much chilled in riding twenty-five miles over the mountains to Wiltshire's : at 3 o'clock I preached on Hebr. iii. 12, 13, 14—I was very unwell and in much pain. There was a poor man in the house who was wild enough to swim the river on a mare with another man behind him—what a mercy that he was not drowned !

Saturday 18. I felt death in some measure at this place. Brother Hull preached and I exhorted.

Sunday 19. We had a close love-feast, and a few testimonies of the power and love of Christ : there was some little melting also amongst the people ; but it is hard to civilize, methodize, and spiritualize ; sin, Satan, flesh, and hell are against us.

We have rested two days besides Sabbaths, and rode two hundred and fifty miles in about two weeks : our entertainment is generally mean.

Monday 20. Our horses' backs being bruised, we had our difficulties in getting to Rehoboth.

We were well nigh cast away in going to the widow W——'s : it was very dark, and we were bewildered in the woods : my saddle turned, and I slipped from my horse, but received no harm. I had to walk nearly half a mile through mud and water to reach the house.

Tuesday 21. I came to Gordon's, on the Yadkin : it is seven years since I was here—dead! dead!—The world—the devil— Antinomianism in doctrine and practice. I was led out in preaching on Deut. xxxiii 29.

Wednesday 22. We started for Holstein. After riding about fifteen miles, we stopped to feed, and a woman directed us along the new way over the Elk Spur : we found ourselves in a wilderness ; the weather was very cold, and the night coming on, we were at a loss what to do ; whilst we were wishfully looking about us, to our great satisfaction we discovered a house ; it was clean and comfortable, and we were well entertained.

VIRGINIA.—Thursday 23. We made an early start for friend Osborne's, on New-River. fifteen miles distant ; here we were generously entertained. After talking and praying together, we were guided across the river, for which I was thankful. Arriving at Fox-Creek, we crossed it eleven times, and tarried that night with C——, a *nominal* member of the society of Friends, who used us very well.

Friday 24. Rode twelve miles to S——'s : after dinner, exhortation, and prayer, we came down the south fork, and crossed the middle fork of Holstein river.

Saturday 25. Came to the Salt Works, and on Sunday preached on " Happy is the people whose God is the Lord."

Monday 27. I had enlargement in preaching to an attentive congregation at Abingdon court house.

Tuesday 28. Preached at Owen's on " This people have I formed for myself."

Thursday 30. We had many people to hear at Charles Baker's, to whom I preached with some life. We took half a day to have the smith's work done in fitting our horses for the journey through the wilderness.

TENNESSEE.—Rode twenty-four miles to Mr. Y——'s on the main Holstein ; and the next day, eighteen miles to Hawkins court-house, and thence to Crabb's. We have confused accounts of Indians : our guard rested on the Sabbath day within four miles of the wilderness.

Saturday, April 1. I heard a company had arrived from Kentucky to Crabb's : this man's son and a Mr. Henderson have been killed by the Indians since I was here last.

Sunday 2. I preached to all the people I could collect.

Monday 3. We entered the wilderness and reached Robinson's station. Two of the company were on foot, carrying their packs ; and women there are with their children ;—these encumbrances make us move slowly and heavily.

KENTUCKY.—Tuesday 4. We reached Richland-Creek, and were preserved from harm. About two o'clock it began to rain, and continued most of the day. After crossing the Laurel-River, which we were compelled to swim, we came to Rock-Castle station, where we found such a set of sinners as made it next to hell itself. Our corn here cost us a dollar per bushel.

Wednesday 5. This morning we again swam the river, and also the west Fork thereof—my little horse was ready to fail in the course of the day—I was steeped in the water up to the waist : about seven o'clock, with hard pushing, we reached the Crab-Orchard. How much I have suffered in this journey, is only known to God and myself. What added much to its disagreeableness, is the extreme filthiness of the houses. I was seized with a severe flux, which followed me eight days : for some of the time I kept up, but at last found myself under the necessity of taking to my bed.

Tuesday 11. I endured as severe pain as, perhaps, I ever felt. I made use of small portions of rhubarb ; and also obtained some good claret, of which I drank a bottle in three days, and was almost well, so that on Sunday following I preached a sermon an hour long. In the course of my affliction I have felt myself very low ; I have had serious views of eternity, and was free from the fear of death. I stopped and lodged, during my illness, with Mr. Willis Green, who showed me all possible attention and kindness.

I wrote and sent to Mr. Rice, a Presbyterian minister, a commendation of his speech, delivered in a convention in Kentucky, on the natural rights of mankind : I gave him an exhortation to call on the Methodists on his way to Philadelphia, and if convenient, to preach in our houses.

Tuesday 11. I wrote an address on behalf of Bethel school. The weather was wet. and stopped us until Friday.

Friday 21. Rode to Clarke's station ; and on Saturday preached on David's charge to Solomon

Sunday 23. I preached a long, and perhaps a terrible sermon, some may think, on " Knowing therefore the terror of the Lord, we persuade men."

Monday 24. I rode to Bethel. I found it necessary to change the plan of the house, to make it more comfortable to the scholars in cold weather. I am too much in company, and hear so much about Indians, Convention, Treaty, killing and scalping, that my attention is drawn more to these things than I could wish: I found it good to get alone in the woods and converse with God.

Wednesday 26. Was a rainy, damp day; however, we rode to meet the conference, where I was closely employed with the travelling and local preachers; with the leaders and stewards. I met the married men and women apart, and we had great consolation in the Lord. Vast crowds of people attended public worship. The spirit of matrimony is very prevalent here; in one circuit both preachers are settled: the land is good, the country new, and indeed all possible facilities to the comfortable maintenance of a family are offered to an industrious, prudent pair.

Monday, May 1. Came to L——'s. An alarm was spreading of a depredation committed by the Indians, on the east and west frontiers of the settlement; in the former, report says one man was killed; in the latter, many men, with women and children—every thing is in motion. There having been so many about me at conference, my rest was much broken; I hoped now to repair it, and get refreshed before I set out to return through the wilderness; but the continual arrival of people until midnight; the barking of dogs, and other annoyances, prevented. Next night we reached the Crab Orchard, where thirty or forty people were compelled to crowd into one mean house. We could get no more rest here than we did in the wilderness. We came the old way by Scaggs-Creek, and Rock-Castle, supposing it to be safer, as it was a road less frequented, and therefore less liable to be way-laid by the savages. My body by this time is well tried: I had a violent fever and pain in the head, such as I had not lately felt; I stretched myself on the cold ground, and borrowing clothes to keep me warm, by the mercy of God, I slept four or five hours. Next morning we set off early, and passed beyond Richland-Creek:—here we were in danger, if any where: I could have slept, but was afraid: seeing the drowsiness of the company, I walked the encampment and watched the sentries the whole night. Early next morning, we made our way to Robinson's station. We had the best company I ever met with—thirty-six good travellers, and a few warriors ; but we had a pack-horse, some old men, and two tired horses— these were not the best part.

VIRGINIA.—Saturday 6. Through infinite mercy, we came safe to Crabb's. Rest, poor house of clay, from such exertions !—return, O my soul, to thy rest !

Monday 8. I came to Young's—a comfortable, quiet house, within six miles of Ratcliffe's, whose wife and children were murdered by the Indians. Here I slept comfortably.

Tuesday 9. We came to brother Baker's, where we rested two days, and had our horses shod.

Friday 12. Rode to Halfacre's, about fifty miles, and came in about eleven o'clock.

Saturday, Sunday, and Monday, 13, 14, 15. We were engaged in the business of conference at Holstein. I had a meeting with the men ; a lively one with the women, most of whose hearts the Lord touched.

Tuesday 16. We came to Russell's old place, at Seven Mile Ford ; and next day set out for Greenbrier, and reached C——'s. My spirits were too lively and disposed to gayety, which indulged, perhaps too far, made me feel mean before the Lord.

Thursday 18. Rode to Hogg's ; and next day to M——'s ; forty miles each day : the roads were better than I expected.

Saturday 20. Rode twenty miles. My weary body feels the want of rest ; but my heart rejoiced to meet with the brethren who were waiting for me. I am more than ever convinced of the need and propriety of annual conferences, and of greater changes among the preachers. I am sensible the western parts have suffered by my absence ; I lament this, and deplore my loss of strict communion with God, occasioned by the necessity I am under of constant riding ; change of place ; company, and sometimes disagreeable company ; loss of sleep, and the difficulties of clambering over rocks and mountains, and journeying at the rate of seven or eight hundred miles per month, and sometimes forty or fifty miles a day—these have been a part of my labours, and make no small share of my hinderances.

I crossed the Kanhaway at Paris's ferry. Here I conversed with a man who informed me a brother preacher had called there, and, as he said, was peevish : the dear man was just at death's door, and though his exercises and bodily infirmities may have pressed him sore, and excited expressions of discontent, he was, nevertheless, a meek and holy servant of God. My informant also mentioned another, who *had been* a member, and who would swear horribly and drink to excess : it is proper I notice, that I did not receive these accounts from a professor of religion. I thought within myself—See how we are watched : ah! we little think oftentimes how narrowly our conduct, our tempers, are observed by the world ; and poor sinners still less imagine how strictly we watch them, and how well this habit of observation, and the intimate knowledge we gain of our own hearts, makes us competent judges of their cases, and enables us so justly and so powerfully to condemn their wickedness.

Sunday 21. I preached at Rehoboth on Isai. lv. 12. there was no great move : brothers H—— and C—— both spoke after me.

"Weary world, when will it end?"

My mind and body feel dull and heavy, but still my soul drinks deeper into God. We rode about one hundred and sixty miles from the Rich Valley to Greenbrier conference ; talking too much, and praying too little, caused me to feel barrenness of soul. We had a hope that not less then ten souls were converted during the conference : at preaching, I myself having a violent headach, retired ; the Lord was with them at the sacrament ; after which, the doors being opened, many came in and the meeting continued untill nearly sunset.

We had a most solemn ordination on Thursday morning. Afterward we rode through Greenbrier by the town, on to brother W——'s, a distance of thirty-six miles. My headach still continuing, brother Hope Hull preached, and I retired to rest.

Friday 26. We rode twenty-six miles to the Little Levels. O what a solitary country is this! We have now one hundred and twenty miles before us, fifty of which is a wilderness : there is a guard at two houses on our route ; but I do not fear : nature is spent with labour ; I would not live always—hail! happy death : nothing but holiness, perfect love, and then glory for me!

Saturday 27. My body is much wearied ; my bowels being much disordered, the water, the milk, and the bread, are like physic to me. We now thought it necessary to be moving ; it was dreary work as we rode along the dreary path to D——'s ; one of my companions, as well as myself, was unwell. From D——'s we had still forty miles to go, over hills and mountains : this, I think equalled, if not exceeded, any road I had ever travelled : we at length reached Tygers Valley. We stopped at Capt. S——'s, where there were several families crowded together, for fear of the Indians. The upper end of the valley has been depopulated, one family has been destroyed since I was last here. The Captain's wife was decent, kind, and sensible. Thence we went on to W——'s, where I got some fowl soup; thence a few miles to ————, where the woman of the house was kind and attentive; but a still, a mill, a store, causes much company, and some not of the most agreeable kind.

Tuesday 30. We hasted to O——'s in the Cove, where we met with a most kind and affectionate reception. But O the flies for the horses, and the gnats for the men! And no food, nor even good water to be had. I slept well, although forced, ever and anon, to stir a little.

Wednesday 31. We had a dreary path, over desperate hills, for fifty miles; no food for man or beast, which caused both to begin to fail very sensibly: my bowels continued to be disordered, and had I not procured a little wine, I suppose I should have failed altogether.

PENNSYLVANIA.—Thursday, June 1. Both men and horses travelled sore and wearily to Union Town. O how good are clean houses, plentiful tables, and populous villages, when compared with the rough world we came through! Here I turned out our poor horses to pasture and to rest, after riding them nearly three hundred miles in eight days.

Friday 2. Wrote letters to send over the mountains.

Saturday 3. I began to feel lame, and had a severe touch of the rheumatism, accompanied with a high fever, which occasioned great pain to me while sitting in conference. I found it necessary to remove, by exchange, six of the preachers from this to the eastern district.

Sunday 11. Having been too unwell to attend preaching through the week, I now ventured in public: a great crowd of people attended, and there was some melting and moving among them. I feel the death of this district; I see what is wanting here—discipline, and the preaching a present and full salvation, and the enforcement of the doctrine of sanctification. I have been variously tried, and was constrained to be cheerful.

We have founded a seminary of learning called Union School; brother C. Conway is manager, who also has charge of the district: this establishment is designed for instruction in grammar, languages, and the sciences.

I have had some awful thoughts lest my lameness should grow upon me, and render me useless. I sometimes have fears that I am too slack in speaking in public, at conferences ; I also feel the want of time and places to pursue my practice of solitary prayer, being frequently obliged to ride all the day and late at night, that I may in time reach the appointed places to preach.

Tuesday 13. We ascended Laurel-hill, and after forty miles riding reached M——'s, quite weary. Came to I. C——'s, and found the Lord was still in this house : I preached, and felt a melting heart, and there was some move in the congregation. I find myself recruited in body and mind ; and I feel as if God would work once more amongst this people.

I was informed that Mr. Hammett had sent abroad circular letters, and had been railing against the presiding eldership, &c. I am not surprised that he should find fault with the office—its duties he was a man not likely to fulfil; yet had it not been for the power attached to it, how greatly might Mr. Hammett have confused the society in Charleston, and perplexed the preachers in the district. The Lord will see to his own house.

MARYLAND.—I preached at Fort Cumberland, in our new house, to many people. Dined with Mr. D——, at whose house I was entertained the first time I visited this town : O that each of the family may be everlastingly saved ! It is now three years since I came down this road.—Swift-winged time, O how it flies ! My body is in better health, and my soul in great peace ; I feel no wrong temper. O that my whole heart might be running out in holiness after God !

Lord's day 18. We had a solemn meeting, whilst I enlarged on " Blessed are they that hear the word of God and keep it." It was a good season.

VIRGINIA.—Monday 19. Rode to Bath. Here I had the opportunity of writing to all the connected preachers in the district.

Friday 23. In the evening I preached with some assistance on Luke xix. 10.

Saturday 24. I attended quarterly meeting at the widow Flint's. Here I had the first sight of Mr. Hammett's and brother Thos. Morrell's attacks on each other—or rather Mr. Hammett's against the Methodists, and brother Morrell's reply. Had brother M. known more, he would have replied better. Mr. H.'s quotation of a clause in my confidential letter to brother S——d, is not altogether just. He has also misquoted the *caution*, leaving out the word " District," which, when retained, shows it to have been *American*, and to have been directed against *American* apostates and impostors.

Sabbath day 25. We had a living love-feast, although the house was crowded, and warm, almost past sufferance.

Tuesday 27. I had a sweet opening at the quarterly meeting, on Ephes. ii. 12. I met the preachers, leaders, and stewards, and they resolved to enter more fully into the spirit of discipline. Next day I preached on " My Spirit shall not always strive with man."

PENNSYLVANIA.—Rode twenty-two miles to S——town, weary and warm ; the people were waiting, and I began on " An adulterous and sinful generation." This is a poor place for religion.

Friday 30. I rode nearly fifty miles through excessive heat, and felt somewhat like Jonah.

Saturday, July 1. I was taken up with writing letters, having received accounts from Cokesbury. The college seems to be the weighty concern for the present.

Sunday 2. I had heavy work—no freedom at D. W——'s : Nothing will do here but discipline. I felt my spirit much humbled before the Lord, and a willingness to suffer.

Tuesday 4. Rode to A. Kageell—it was the harvest home. I feel it my duty to press the people of God to go on to holiness of heart and life. As the next morning was rainy, we staid until the afternoon, and then rode to see our old brother M. Behem. We had a tender, feeling season on 1 John i. 8. on *Salvation from all sin.* At Strasburg, in the afternoon, we had a solemn meeting ; a young woman, who was married a few minutes before worship began, was powerfully struck under the word, and wept greatly. O may she mourn until a second marriage takes place in her soul.

Friday 7. We had a long ride to Morgantown : we came in at 11 o'clock, being much fatigued. I discoursed on the likeness between Moses and Christ, in the academical church. This building is well designed for a school and a church. I directed Esq. Morgan to one of our local preachers as a teacher.

We set out for Coventry Forge, but we missed our way, and came to brother Meredic's, in the valley. I prayed heartily for, and spoke plainly to the young people. O that the Lord would follow them powerfully !

Saturday 8. This day my soul enjoyed the presence of God. I dined at Radnor, and went into Philadelphia.

Sunday 9. I preached at Ebenezer church on James iv. 8. : at St. George's church on Mark viii. 38. I had large accounts from the eastward, and am requested to send them more preachers. After twenty years standing of the house in our hands, the galleries are put up in our old *new* church.

Monday 10 and Tuesday 11. Employed in reading and writing. I wish to be alone—O how sweet is solitude!

Wednesday 12. I sought and obtained peace between two brethren who had, unhappily, been at variance.

New-Jersey.—Thursday 13. Rode through great heat and dust to Burlington, New-Jersey. Here I had many of my old, and some new hearers : but some are much wiser than they were twenty years ago. We had a cold time of it, whilst I spoke on Hebr. iv. 7.

Friday 14. After [preaching at ——'s we rode on to brother H——'s. He is resolved, that after he and his wife are served, the remainder of his whole estate shall go to the church ; his plantation to be rented, and the annual income to be applied as the conference held for Pennsylvania and the Jerseys shall please to direct.

New-York.—Sunday 16. Preached at our church on Staten Island. I was very close on the law and the Gospel—a few felt ; but it was a dry time. Lord, help us !

Monday 17. We hasted to V——'s ferry; but found ourselves detained by the absence of both boats, so that we did not so soon as we expected reach New-York. I did not find that life and harmony here that there have been in times past. I have just now obtained and am reading Mr. Wesley's Life, the work of Dr. Coke and Mr. Moore, containing five hundred and forty-two pages. It is in general well compiled ; but the history of American Methodism is inaccurate in some of its details, and in some which are interesting. For some days past I have been occupied in reading, and and in meeting the several women's classes, and found the Lord was amongst them.

As very probably all of my life which I shall be able to write will be found in my journal, it will not be improper to relate something of my earlier years, and to give a brief account of my first labours in the ministry.

I was born in Old England, near the foot of Hampstead Bridge, in the parish of Handsworth, about four miles from Birmingham, in Staffordshire, and, according to the best of my after-knowledge, on the 20th or 21st day of August, in the year of our Lord 1745.

My father's name was Joseph, and my mother's, Elizabeth Asbury : they were people in common life ; were remarkable for honesty and industry, and had all things needful to enjoy ; had my father been as saving as laborious, he might have been wealthy. As it was, it was his province to be employed as a farmer and

gardener by the two richest families in the parish. My parents
had but two children, a daughter called Sarah, and myself. My
lovely sister died in infancy; she was a favourite, and my dear
mother being very affectionate, sunk into deep distress at the loss
of a darling child, from which she was not relieved for many years.
It was under this dispensation that God was pleased to open the
eyes of her mind, she living in a very dark, dark, dark day and
place. She now began to read almost constantly when leisure presented the opportunity. When a child, I thought it strange my
mother should stand by a large window poring over a book for
hours together. From my childhood I may say, I have neither

"—— dar'd an oath, nor hazarded a lie."

The love of truth is not natural; but the habit of telling it I acquired
very early, and so well was I taught, that my conscience would
never permit me to swear profanely. I learned from my parents a
certain form of words for prayer, and I well remember my mother
strongly urged my father to family reading and prayer; the singing
of psalms was much practised by them both. My foible was the
ordinary foible of children—fondness for play; but I abhorred
mischief and wickedness, although my mates were amongst the
vilest of the vile for lying, swearing, fighting, and whatever else
boys of their age and evil habits were likely to be guilty of; from
such society I very often returned home uneasy and melancholy;
and although driven away by my better principles, still I would return, hoping to find happiness where I never found it. Sometimes
I was much ridiculed, and called *Methodist Parson*, because my
mother invited any people who had the appearance of religion to
her house.

I was sent to school early, and began to read the Bible between
six and seven years of age, and greatly delighted in the historical
part of it. My school-master was a great churl, and used to beat
me cruelly; this drove me to prayer, and it appeared to me, that
God was very near to me. My father having but the one son,
greatly desired to keep me at school, he cared not how long; but
in this design he was disappointed; for my master, by his severity,
had filled me with such horrible dread, that with me any thing was
preferable to going to school. I lived some time in one of the
wealthiest and most ungodly families we had in the parish: here I
became vain, but not openly wicked. Some months after this I returned home; and made my choice, when about thirteen years and
a half old, to learn a branch of business, at which I wrought about

six years and a half: during this time I enjoyed great liberty, and in the family was treated more like a son or an equal than an apprentice.

Soon after I entered on that business, God sent a pious man, not a Methodist, into our neighbourhood, and my mother invited him to our house ; by his conversation and prayers, I was awakened before I was fourteen years of age. It was now easy and pleasing to leave my company, and I began to pray morning and evening, being drawn by the cords of love, as with the bands of a man. I soon left our blind priest, and went to West-Bromwick church : here I heard Ryland, Stillingfleet, Talbot, Bagnall, Mansfield, Hawes, and Venn, great names, and esteemed Gospel-ministers. I became very serious ; reading a great deal—Whitefield and Cennick's Sermons, and every good book I could meet with. It was not long before I began to inquire of my mother who, where, what were the Methodists ; she gave me a favourable account, and directed me to a person that could take me to Wednesbury to hear them. I soon found this was not the church—but it was better. The people were so devout—men and women kneeling down—saying *Amen.*—Now, behold ! they were singing hymns—sweet sound ! Why, strange to tell ! the preacher had no prayer-book, and yet he prayed wonderfully ! What was yet more extraordinary, the man took his text, and had no sermon-book : thought I, this is wonderful indeed ! It is certainly a strange way, but the best way. He talked about confidence, assurance, &c.—of which all my flights and hopes fell short. I had no deep convictions, nor had I committed any deep known sins. At one sermon, some time after, my companion was powerfully wrought on : I was exceedingly grieved that I could not weep like him ; yet I knew myself to be in a state of unbelief. On a certain time when we were praying in my father's barn, I believe the Lord pardoned my sins, and justified my soul ; but my companions reasoned me out of this belief, saying, " Mr. Mather said a believer was as happy as if he was in heaven." I thought I was not as happy as I would be there, and gave up my confidence, and that for months ; yet I was happy ; free from guilt and fear, and had power over sin, and felt great inward joy. After this, we met for reading and prayer, and had large and good meetings, and were much persecuted, until the persons at whose houses we held them were afraid, and they were discontinued. I then held meetings frequently at my father's house, exhorting the people there, as also at Sutton-Cofields, and several souls professed to find peace through my labours. I met class awhile at Bromwick-Heath, and met in band at Wednesbury. I had preached some months before I publicly appeared in the Methodist meeting-houses ; when my labours became more public and extensive, some were amazed, not knowing how I had exercised elsewhere. Behold me now a local preacher ; the humble and willing servant of any and of every preacher that called on me by night or by day, being ready, with hasty steps, to go far and wide to do good, visiting Derbyshire, Staffordshire, Warwickshire, Worcestershire, and indeed almost every place within my reach for the sake of precious souls ; preaching, generally, three, four, and five times a week, and at the same time pursuing my calling.—I think, when I was between twenty-one and twenty-two years of age I gave myself up to God and his work, after acting as a local preacher near the space of five years : it is now the 19th of July 1792.—I have been labouring for God and souls about thirty years, or upwards.

Sometime after I had obtained a clear witness of my acceptance with God, the Lord showed me in the heat of youth and youthful blood, the evil of my heart: for a short time I enjoyed, as I thought, the pure and perfect love of God ; but this happy frame did not long continue, although, at seasons, I was greatly blest. Whilst I was a travelling preacher in England, I was much tempted, finding myself exceedingly ignorant of almost every thing a minister of the Gospel ought to know. How I came to America, and the events which have happened since, my journal will show.

Yesterday I preached in New-York, on "Who is on the Lord's side ?"—I had some life in speaking, but there was little move in the congregation. O Lord, hasten a revival of thy work ! This city has been agitated about the choice of Governor : it would be better for them all to be on the Lord's side.—The standard is set up—who declares for the Lord ?—The wicked ; the carnal professors ; carnal ministers, and apostates, are the Lord's enemies.

Sunday 23. Was a melting time with many hearts in the old church : my subject, 1 John i. 6, 7. In the afternoon, although very unwell, I laboured hard in the new church, but the people were exceedingly insensible. There was a little shaking under brother Hull in the old church in the evening.

Monday 24. We set out for Lynn, and made our way through Bedford, riding fifty miles the first day : I prayed in four houses, and felt much given up on the way.

CONNECTICUT.—Tuesday 25. Rain to-day : after which, we came to Reading ; and although it was late, and the evening damp, I was unwilling to omit the opportunity of speaking to the people. Brother Hull, my fellow-traveller, went to bed very ill. God has wrought in this town : the spirit of prayer is amongst the people ; and several souls have been brought to God.

Wednesday 26. We came to Newtown and fed—thence to Waterbury : brother H. is still very ill. Here we were entertained kindly, and at small charges ; the people submitted and were attentive to prayer. Thence we continued on to Southerington : we dined at a public house, where we had cheap, good, plain usage : our host told us, " It was the misfortune of the Methodists to fall in with some of the most ignorant, poor, and disreputable people in the state." My answer was, the poor have the Gospel preached to them—that it had been aforetime asked, " Have any of the rulers believed on him ?"

Came to the city of Hartford, and thence went on to East-Hartford. I was alarming on Rev. xxi. 8. ; brother H. is still very sick ; and for my poor self, I am tempted to fretfulness ; but by grace I was kept in peace, and blessed in speaking. The next day we came through the extreme heat to Stafford, and attended a quarterly meeting, where we had a crowd of people in a new, open house : I was very unwell, and much tempted, but I had good liberty in preaching ; my subject was Colos. ii. 6. ; on Sunday I was very pointed on Rom. i. 18.

There has been a work in Tolland circuit : I suppose one hundred and fifty souls have been converted, and twice the number under awakenings in the different societies around : I felt very solemn among them. Brothers Smith, and Raynor, have been owned of the Lord in these parts.

MASSACHUSETTS.—We came through Ashford, Pomfret, Menden, and Douglass : we lodged at a tavern, where the people were very obliging, and attentive to prayer : thence we rode to Medfield's to dinner ; thence through Dover, Newton, Cambridge, Malden, to Lynn ; which we reached about midnight, having travelled sixty-five miles—my soul, meanwhile, continually filled with the goodness of God.

Thursday, August 3. Our conference met, consisting of eight preachers, much united, beside myself. In Lynn, we have the outside of a house completed ; and what is best of all, several souls profess to be converted to God. I preached on 1 John iv. 1—6.

and had, some life, but was too formal. There was preaching every night through the sitting of the conference.

Saturday 5. I preached an ordination sermon to a very solemn congregation, on 2 Cor. iii. 5.

Sabbath morning 6. I preached on 1 Cor. vi. 19, 20. In the afternoon brother A—— preached; and I afterward gave them a farewell exhortation, and there were some affectionate feelings excited amongst the people.—Many were moved, and felt a great desire to speak in the love-feast, but they had not courage. O that we had more apostolical preaching!

Monday 7. We took leave of town, making a hasty flight. We dined at Cambridge. The rain drove us for shelter under the hospitable roof of Mr. How; the kind family here accepted of family worship.

Tuesday 8. We came through Brookfield and Shrewsbury to Worcester; after resting, we briskly pursued our way to Brookfield. We found we had stopped at the wrong house; some wicked labouring young men were intoxicated, singing psalms and song tunes for their amusement; one man railed on, and cursed us because he was not told all he wanted to know.

Wednesday 9. We came to Belcher Town, and were kindly entertained at W——'s: thence we pushed on to Hadley, crossed Connecticut-River, and stopped at Northampton. Ah! where is the blessedness of which we formerly heard in this place.—I inquired of our host, but received little satisfactory information. I proposed prayer, but found it was not well received. I went to bed weary and unwell; and about half past six o'clock next morning set out again over the rocks and uneven roads, across the mountain, having passed through Worthington, Chesterfield, and Partridgefield. I wondered to see the people settled here so thickly, among the rocks, where the soil can only be cultivated by the iron hand of active, laborious industry: I should prefer any part of the Alleghany where it is not too rocky, because the land is better. We made it nearly forty miles to Pittsfield; and our journey was more disagreeable from the falling of a heavy shower. We have now rode about one hundred and seventy miles from Lynn in four days. My mind has been variously exercised, and my body much fatigued; if I have been kept from sin, to the Lord's name be all the glory! Pittsfield is a pleasant plain, extending from mountain to mountain; the population may consist of two thousand souls. There is a grand meeting-house and steeple, both as white and glistering as *Solomon's temple.* The minister, as I learn, is on the New-Divinity plan. I heard the experience of one of the first settlers in the town, who was clearly brought out of bondage ; but by resting in unfailing per-severance, he again grew cold : of late he has been stirred up and restored by the instrumentality of the Methodists. I was pleased to enjoy the privilege of retiring alone to the cooling sylvan shades in frequent converse with my best Friend.

Saturday 12. We held our meeting in a noble house, built for Baptists, Separatists, or somebody, and is now occupied by the Me-thodists. There was a large and attentive congregation, and some melting amongst the people, with whom the Lord is at work.

Sunday 13. I was so unwell, that I concluded not to go to meet-ing, but was at last persuaded along. I felt enlargement in preach-ing, and the people were tender and attentive. It has been said, "The Eastern people are not to be moved ;" it is true, they are too much accustomed to hear systematical preaching to be moved by a systematical sermon, even from a Methodist ; but they have their feelings, and touch but the right string, and they will be moved. I became weary of staying three days in one house ; Mr. Stevens was very kind, his wife was under heavy heart-awakenings.

NEW-YORK.—We set out and came to Lebanon in the state of New-York. The medical waters here are warm and very soft ; pure and light, with no small quantity of fixed air. I found a poor bath-house. Here the devil's tents are set up, and, as is common at these his encampments, his children are doing his drudgery. I baptised F——'s child : he and his wife came out from amongst the Shakers, where they had lived in celibacy many years. At the request of the people, notwithstanding my barrenness at bro-ther W——'s, I delivered a discourse on 1 Peter iii. 15.; my au-dience appeared to be strangers to our way. Mr. K——a, a Pres-byterian minister, bore his testimony in favour of the word deliver-ed, and recommended it to his people. We then came to Bethle-hem, and the next day I preached at the house of a Baptist to about three hundred people : it was a searching, moving time. I also baptised, and administered the Lord's supper ; I then went a small distance to lodge, but I felt not myself at home, the worship of God not being in the house. I now began to bring up my read-ing in the New Testament.

Wednesday 16. Came to Albany, and had a joyful, happy con-ference, twenty-one preachers being present. We constituted two deacons and four elders. Each preacher was called upon to speak of his exercises and observations since our last annual session : we ex-

amined our doctrines, and whether our faith was still firm in those
which were believed and taught amongst us. We appointed Jonathan Newman as a missionary to the whites and Indians on the
frontiers. We also sent another to Cataraqui. Before we rose,
we propounded a few questions of theology, viz.

1. How are we to deal with sinners?
2. How should we treat with mourners?
3. Which way should we address hypocrites?
4. How can we deal with backsliders?
5. What is best for believers?

We had preaching in the market-house in Albany; and notwithstanding our hurry and crowd, we were happy and had living testimonies from preachers and people. I trust two hundred have
been converted in the district since last conference.

Monday 20. I came to Coeyman's Patent, and had a degree of
light in preaching in the new church on Ephes. i. 18, 19. After
preaching we hasted to Hudson, thirty-two miles. On our way
we called on a friend whose wretched wife had made an attempt
to poison him and two others by strewing bane on the meat they
ate: the dose wrought so powerfully that they threw it up; and so
she, Satan, and hell, were all disappointed. I lodged with brother
W——: he and his wife were kind, dear souls to me, when sick
here last year—now I am well: praise the Lord, O my soul!

I had to ride thirty-five miles to Rhinebeck; the weather was extremely warm and dry. We hasted along, and arriving a little before five o'clock, found the people waiting. I preached in a
school-house, which, by enlargement makes a good church, so
called.

I had reason to fear, from former and later information, that brother ——— was not as useful nor as acceptable here as I could
wish: from a sense of duty I mentioned this to him with great tenderness. At first, it proved some trial to him; but when brother ——— and brother ——— confirmed what I had said, and I
assured him that a desire to promote the cause of God was the only
motive that led me to mention this to him, he resumed his former
cheerfulness, and we parted in peace.

It was appointed for me to preach at a place forty-five miles
distant, but the weather being extremely warm, and our horses
weary, we did not get in until eight o'clock, in consequence of
which many people were disappointed.

Thursday 24. I breakfasted at Governor Van Cortlandt's I
feel as if the Lord had been striving here.

Saturday 26. Came to the quarterly meeting at New-Rochelle. The Lord gave light and liberty in speaking. We had a meeting with the local preachers, stewards, and leaders who were present. Mr. Hammett's rejoinder has made its appearance. N. Manners has also come to town, to spread his doctrine and distribute his books : was he a gracious man, I cannot think he would write as he does against Mr. Wesley and Mr. Fletcher. Perhaps he will find it rather easier to write and print books, than to sell and pay the cost of publishing them.

Sunday 27. I preached to a vast congregation, with liberty, on 1 Cor. iii. 15, 16. Many hearts were touched, and we had a blessed season at love-feast and sacrament.

Monday 28. Came to New-York, and opened conference, twenty-eight preachers being present. We spent most of the afternoon in prayer ; and nearly all the preachers gave an account of what each one had seen and felt since last conference. The young gave us their experience, and there were several who professed sanctification. Awful H——— haunted us one day, requesting us to give him an honourable discharge from the connexion ; but we shall publish him expelled—he is the Wheatly of America.

Friday, September 1. We had a solemn love-feast, the lower floor of the house being nearly filled : several of the brethren professed perfect love ; others had lost the witness.

My mind has been so bent to the business of the conference, that I have slept but little this week. Connecticut is supplied much to my mind ; several very promising young men having been admitted this conference. The societies are in harmony, but not as lively as they ought to be. I went to hear Dr. L———, but was greatly disappointed : he had such a rumbling voice that I could understand but little in that great house. How elegant the building ! How small the appearances of religion ! Lord, have mercy upon the Reformed Churches ! O ye dry bones, hear the word of the Lord ! I was much obliged to my friend for renewing my clothing and giving me a little pocket money—this is better than £500 per annum. I told some of our preachers, who were very poor, how happy they were, and that probably, had they more, their wants would proportionably increase. My soul is humble, and by grace is kept holy : I do the best I can, and leave the event to the Lord—if others do wrong, they must answer for themselves now, and at the day of judgment.

Sunday 3. I preached a preparatory sermon, on 1 Cor. v. 7, 8. previously to the administration of the sacrament. It was ob-

served what a fitness of similarity there was between the pass-over
and the supper of the Lord. The simplicity and purity of the
latter—*bread*, instead of the flesh of an animal, and *wine*, instead
of the blood of the creature : *wine*, the blood of Christ, and *grace*
the life of our souls. It was shown who were proper communicants—true penitents and real believers. Not with the leaven of
malice and wickedness—acid, bitter, and puffing up, but the un-
leavened bread of sincerity and truth—uprightness of heart, and
sound experience.

I now leave New-York for one whole year, under the hope and
prophecy that this will be a year of the Lord's power with them.

NEW-JERSEY.—We had severe crossing the North-River : it
was much as ever the horses could do to keep their feet. We
came to Newark, and thence to Elizabethtown, in Jersey. I
now began to unbend my mind, and became very heavy. I went
up stairs, sat in my chair, rested my head, and slept solidly ; but a
kind friend would have me waked, which made me sick.

Tuesday 5. I pursued my journey through Woodbridge, and
came to Brunswick. The weather was very warm ; the roads
dusty, and our journeys long. We reached Milford town in the
evening.

Wednesday 6. Passed through Crosswicks and Burlington, and
came to Philadelphia : I found I was too late, the preachers having waited a day for me to come and open the conference.

Thursday 7. We had great peace in our conference. The
preachers gave a feeling account of the work of God. We had
more preachers than we needed this time ; both they and the people were lively : most of our brethren in the ministry can now
stand the greatest exertions.

Sabbath morning 10. We had a melting love-feast—the mouths of
many were opened to declare the loving kindness of the Lord. I
preached, but did not like their ill-contrived house. At Ebenezer
I had an attentive congregation, to whom I spoke on Philip. i. 18.
At night the *mobility* came in like the roaring of the sea : boys were
around the doors, and the streets were in an uproar. They had
been alarmed by a shout the night before, which, probably, was
one cause of the congregation being so large. Brother A——
went to prayer; a person cried out : brother C—— joined in
prayer; the wicked were collected to oppose. I felt the powers
of darkness were very strong. After ending my discourse, brother
M—— rose up and mentioned the shocking conduct he had observed among them—fighting, swearing, threatening, &c.—But where

are the watchmen ?—asleep.—Where are the magistrates ?—dozing
at home. This is a wicked, horribly wicked city ; and if the
people do not reform, I think they will be let loose upon one another, or else God will send the pestilence amongst them, and slay
them by hundreds and thousands :—the spirit of prayer has departed, and the spiritual watchmen have ceased to cry aloud among
all sects and denominations : for their unfaithfulness they will be
smitten in anger : for sleepy *silence* in the house of God, which
ought to resound with the voice of praise and frequent prayer, the
Lord will visit their streets with the *silence of desolation.*

DELAWARE.—Monday 10. I left Philadelphia, dined at Chester,
and preached at Wilmington in the evening. The next day I rode
to Duck-Creek Cross-Roads, state of Delaware, to hold conference.
We were full of business, and had life and liberty. I met the leaders and local brethren in the ministry, and we had a powerful time.
I requested them to give an account of their past and present experience ; the state of their respective families ; and the classes
they had the charge of, together with the prospects of religion
where they lived : they understood me, and spoke much to the
purpose. We parted with a good love-feast, from which the gay
and the worldly, at least, were excluded, if we did not keep out
sinners, Pharisees, and hypocrites.

Saturday 16. Rode to Camden. To Dr. Barrett, a true son of
a worthy father, we are chiefly indebted for a neat, economical
meeting-house. I had so many friends I knew not where to go.
My attendance on conferences and quarterly meetings has lately
been so constant, I found it expedient to make a sudden change and
come home. In my way I stopped at a friend's house ; the woman had been early a member ; the man, not of us : I pressed
family prayer upon her from divine authority : I saw her tears
and heard her promises. Came home to T. White's. I resolved
on the establishment of a prayer-meeting for the women before I
go hence. I have felt my soul greatly quickened of late to bear
and suffer all things, and to feel nothing but love : if we are tried
by Christian people, it is chiefly for want of grace or knowledge in
them, or us, or both—they are objects of pity, not of anger.

This day is spent in reading, writing, meditation, and prayer.
To be retired and solitary is desirable after the presence of crowds,
and the labours, various and unceasing, to which I am called : when
our Lord was pursued by the people, he, as a man, would hide
himself. I thought, if my brethren would not spare me, I must
spare myself.

I have been reading Doctor Langdon on the Revelations, and find little new or very spiritual; he is like the Newtons and all the historical interpreters—one thing is wanting. And might not an interpreter show the present time foretold by these signs, which plainly point to the *why* and *wherefore* it is, that some are Christian bishops and Christian dissertators on prophecy? A bishoprick with one, or two, or three thousand sterling a year as an appendage, might determine the most hesitating in their choice: I see no reason why a heathen philosopher, who had enough of this world's wisdom to see the advantages of wealth and honours, should not say, "Give me a bishoprick and I will be a Christian." In the Eastern states also there are very *good and sufficient* reasons for the faith of the favoured ministry. Ease, honour, interest: what follows?—idolatry, superstition, death.

Tuesday 19. Continued at Judge W——'s, and spoke a few words to a few people.

Wednesday 20. We came to Millford, and had a solemn time on Genesis vi. 3. Here I held a conference with the local preachers, and was pleased at the accounts they gave of their prospects of religion in their neighbourhoods.

Thursday 21. We had a moving feast of charity, and a close, searching time in public—my subject, 2 Tim. iii. 20, 21.

Friday 22. I came to Broad-Creek with a heavy heart. We had a blessed time in the love-feast: many souls had longings for sanctification, and some boldly professed it. I felt as if it would be long before I should again visit this house. A poor man attempted to come near me; being encouraged by my speaking to him, he approached, and told me, with a full heart, that about that time five years past, the Lord spoke through me, to his conviction, at Moore's chapel.

Tuesday 26. Attended quarterly meeting at Myle's chapel, where I met with a few serious people: the second day we had a few Church-folks—something wild.

VIRGINIA.—Thursday 28. Crossed Pocomoke to L——'s: at Dowings's at night. Brother Everett was sick. I had a large congregation at Garrettson chapel; and was much blest on Rom. viii. 29, 30. I had a comfortable conference with the leaders, stewards, local preachers, and exhorters; and we had a living love-feast.

Sunday, October 1. We had a crowded congregation, and some melting amongst the people whilst I enlarged on "Almost thou persuadest me to be a Christian." I endeavoured to point out the genuine marks of a Christian : 2. Remove the objection against these marks ; and 3. Persuade by applying to the hopes and fears of my hearers.

Monday 2. I had a kind of chill and headach, and was very un-well ; yet I rode about forty miles to Littleton Long's—I went quick to bed.

MARYLAND.—I attended the quarterly meeting in Dorset on the last day ; we had few people. Thence to Henry Ennall's, where young sister Kane was struck with conviction at family prayer : she followed us to quarterly meeting, at Easton, under deep distress ; and returning, found peace where she found conviction three days before. We had great plainness, and were much stirred up in the conference with our local brethren. The congregation was large the second day, and the people were more quiet than common—perhaps because we were so.

Thence we rode to Choptank, now Greensborough ; and preached on Ephes. ii. 17. ; and some power went through the house. I had a good conference with the local brethren ; making close inquiries relative to themselves, their families, and the societies to which they respectively belong.

I stopped a day at Judge White's, and read in haste the most essential parts of "Jefferson's Notes." I have thought, it may be I am safer to be occasionally among the people of the world, than wholly confined to the indulgent people of God : he who sometimes suffers from a famine, will the better know how to re-lish a feast.

Saturday 14. We had many gracious souls at Boardley's barn. I was greatly weakened by preaching ; but I hope souls were spiritually strengthened. We had a gracious season in conference with the local brethren, men who felt for the cause of God. Two professed to find the Lord ; and it was said two were awakened the first evening of the quarterly meeting.

Sunday 15. We had a great love-feast, the women led the way. I preached on " Thou knowest not the time of thy visitation." A larger or more attentive congregation has not, perhaps, been seen in these parts. I feel more than ever the necessity of preaching sanctification.

Monday 16. Rode to Chester-Town. Here I was warmly im-portuned to preach, and submitting to the desire of my friends, I enlarged on 1 John ii. 18. and was very pointed and alarming, at which some were offended.

Saturday 21. Rode to Back-Creek : being detained at the ferry, I did not get in until after night, which made me unwell.

Monday 23. Rode to Cokesbury—all is not well here.

Saturday 28. I came to Baltimore : here I only stopped to feed myself and horses, and then proceed on to T. C——'s, and had a little rest and peace.

Sunday 29. Contrary to my wish, I was constrained to ride to Annapolis, which I reached about eleven o'clock, and gave them a sermon on 1 Peter iii. 18. with some help and liberty.

Monday 30. We opened our district conference in great peace and love ; and so it ended.

Tuesday 31. Came to Baltimore in a storm of rain. Whilst we were sitting in the room at Mr. Rogers's, in came Dr. Coke, of whose arrival we had not heard, and whom we embraced with great love.

I felt awful at the general conference, which began November 1, 1792. At my desire they appointed a moderator, and preparatory committee, to keep order and bring forward the business with regularity. We had heavy debates on the first, second, and third sections of our form of discipline. My power to station the preachers without an appeal, was much debated, but finally carried by a very large majority. Perhaps a new bishop, new conference, and new laws, would have better pleased some. I have been much grieved for others, and distressed with the burthen I bear, and must hereafter bear. O, my soul, enter into rest! Ah! who am I, that the burthen of the work should lie on my heart, hands, and head ?

Thursday 8. Having taken cold, and had my rest broken, I went to bed to bring on a free perspiration ; and from this I received relief, my soul breathed unto God ; and I was exceedingly happy in his love. Some individuals among the preachers having their jealousies about my influence in the conference, I gave the matter wholly up to them, and to Dr. Coke, who presided : meantime I sent them the following letter.

My dear brethren,

Let my absence give you no pain—Dr. Coke presides. I am happily excused from assisting to make laws by which myself am to be governed : I have only to obey and execute. I am happy in the consideration that I never stationed a preacher through enmity, or as a punishment. I have acted for the glory of God, the good

of the people, and to promote the usefulness of the preachers.
Are you sure, that if you please yourselves, that the people will
be as fully satisfied? They often say, "let us have such a preacher;" and sometimes, "we will not have such a preacher—we will
sooner pay him to stay at home." Perhaps I must say, "his appeal forced him upon you." I am one—ye are many. I am as
willing to serve you as ever. I want not to sit in any man's way.
I scorn to solicit votes: I am a very trembling, poor creature to
hear praise or dispraise. Speak your minds freely; but remember,
you are only making laws for the present time: it may be, that as
in some other things, so in this, a future day may give you further
light.

I am yours, &c.
FRANCIS ASBURY.

I am not fond of altercations—we cannot please every body—
and sometimes, not ourselves: I am resigned.

Mr. O'Kelly being disappointed in not getting an appeal from
any station made by me, withdrew from the connexion, and went
off. For himself, the conference well knew he could not complain of the regulation: he had been located to the south district
of Virginia for about ten succeeding years; and upon his plan,
might have located himself, and any preacher, or set of preachers,
to the district, whether the people wished to have them or not.

The general conference went through the Discipline, Articles
of Faith, Forms of Baptism, Matrimony, and the Burial of the
Dead; as also the Offices of Ordination. The conference ended
in peace, after voting another general conference to be held four
years hence. By desire of my brethren, I preached once on 1
Peter iii. 8. My mind was kept in peace, and my soul enjoyed
rest in the Strong Hold.

Thursday 15. I was comforted at the women's class-meeting: I
appointed three prayer meetings for them, sister K——, O——,
and F——, to be the leaders of them: if this is regularly attended
to, I think good will follow.

Friday 16. I left Baltimore, and, contrary to my first intention,
called on the widow H——, whose daughter was awakened the
last time I was here, and still continues to be happy in the Lord.
I met the sisters here, and urged prayer meeting: perhaps it was
for this I unexpectedly came here.

VIRGINIA.—Saturday 17. Brother Ira Ellis and myself came on
to Georgetown; and thence to Alexandria, making a ride of forty

miles. Here the preachers were waiting for the district conference.

Sunday 18. I preached in our small, neatly finished house.

Monday 19. We had a close sitting in conference, and completed
our work in one day.

Tuesday 20. We set out southwardly: the day was very
stormy, and we had a gale in crossing the River at Colchester, and
came to our newly made friend Ward's, near Dumfries.

Wednesday 21. Six of us set out, and rode fifty-three miles to
D. Dickinson's, in Caroline county—so much for an American
episcopos. Travelling in such haste, I could not be as much in
mental prayer as I desired; although I enjoyed many moments of
sweet converse with God.

The mischief has begun: brother —— called here and vented
his sorrows, and told what the general conference had done. I
was closely employed in reading " The Curse of Divisions," and
my Hebrew Bible.

Sunday 25. Came to Manchester; and preached in the afternoon, and felt life amongst the people, and the preachers who
were met for the district conference. I met the preachers in band,
and found their fears were greatly removed: union and love prevailed, and all things went on well. W. M'Kendree and R. H——
sent me their resignation in writing. We agreed to let our displeased brethren still preach among us; and as Mr. O'Kelly is
almost worn out, the conference acceded to my proposal of giving
him his * £40 per annum, as when he travelled in the connexion,
provided he was peaceable, and forbore to excite divisions among
the brethren. The general conference and the district conferences have kept us a long time from our work; but after all
Satan's spite, I think our *sifting* and *shaking* will be for good: I
expect a glorious revival will take place in America, and thousands
be brought to God.

Thursday 29. Came to Petersburg—Myself, and several others
preached during our stay.

Saturday, December 1. I had a few attentive hearers at brother
Bonner's, of whom I inquired, " Where is the blessedness ye
spake of."

Sunday 2. Rode fifteen miles to G——'s chapel, where we had
a full house, and I felt life and love in speaking to the young peo-

* For a part of that year he received it, but refused, and left us to form a new and
pure church.

ple. I lodged with brother G——, and was very much moved to
lay a plan for a district school.

Monday 3. Preached at R——'s chapel : cold house and languid people. Came to brother Coxe's in the evening. I am not
conscious of inward or outward sin, yet I do not feel that inward
life I wish. I have lately read our " Cure of Church Divisions,"
and much of the word of God.

Tuesday 4. Preached at Mabry's chapel ; and the next day at
J. Mason's, where we had a full house and a comfortable time.

Thursday 6. Rode through the rain to Edward Drumgold's :
here I found a few friends and formed a constitution for a District
school, which, with a little alteration, will form a general rule for
any part of the continent.

Saturday 8. I once more visited Owen Myrick, whose wife is
gone, and from all we can learn, departed in a good old age, in
triumph to glory : the dear old man is much dispirited. We spent
the evening together very solemnly, remembering the occurren-
ces of nineteen years ago, now gone as yesterday—

> " Short as the watch that ends the night
> Before the rising sun."

The cause of his slaves was not forgotten.

Sunday 9. I came once more to Roanoak chapel, and gave them
a discourse on Eph. ii. 13. R. and I. Ellis gave an exhortation :
I met the society. We then rode six miles and got to our quarters about sunset.

Monday 10. We crossed Roanoak at Black's ferry, and directed
our course for Lewisburg. We passed Warrington, and missed
our way. We remembered the name of William Myrick, and
inquiring after him, found he lived nearly on our way ; we accordingly called on him, and were gladly received, and kindly entertained.—Memory is good in distress—had we not housed here,
we should have had our difficulties in getting to sister L——'s.

Tuesday 11. Rode to H——'s, near Lewisburg. Here I met
the preachers in conference, and were closely employed until
Saturday morning. We had about forty preachers from the two
districts in North Carolina. Our labours finished, we rode to
Neuse-River.

Sunday 16. Preached at Merritt's.

Monday 17. Rode fifteen miles to S——'s—preached on *Christ,*
the believer's *wisdom, righteousness, sanctification,* and *redemption.*

We had a difficult road in going to Haw-River, but a kind providence brought us along very well, although the weather was exceedingly cold : we crossed the stream by fording, about half past
eight o'clock, and about ten arrived at R——'s, very cold and in
much pain.—I know not why, but so it is, that I cannot feel that I
hold such sweet communion with God in cold weather as in warm ;
it may be that—

> " Nature being oppress'd,
> Commands the mind to suffer with the body."

The great love and union which prevailed at the late conference
makes me hope many souls will be converted in the ensuing year :
an account was brought in of the conversion of about three hundred
souls last year within its limits—chiefly in the Lowland circuits.—
Glory be to God! I feel that he is with us ; and I have good evidence that fifteen or eighteen hundred souls have professed to have
been converted in the United States within the last twelve months.
At Rainey's a congregation of willing, patient souls was called
hastily together, to whom I preached on 2 Peter i. 4.—I was led out
on the corruption that is in the world, arising from three grand sour-
ces,—the lust of the flesh ; the lust of the eye; and the pride of life.

Wednesday 19. I was detained until about ten o'clock, and
then rode on to S——'s, and dined : we then hastened on to Deep-
River, and lodged at Mr. B———'s. Lord, show kindness to those
who have succoured me !

Thursday 20. I took a route along a new path below the Narrows of Pee Dee; and after riding forty-five or fifty miles, came
in, cold and hungry, about seven o'clock, and found a congregation waiting : I was fatigued, and could say but little to them.

Friday 21. I rode thirty miles to Rocky-River—had few to
hear.

Saturday 22. The people were attentive and behaved well at
Anson court-house.—In the evening we had a weary ride to brother Jackson's.

Sunday 23. We attended from ten till one o'clock in a house
built of *poles*—here were light and ventilators plenty. We rode
this evening twenty miles to Mr. Blakeney's : the rain caught
us in the woods, and we were well steeped. Arriving, we found
a good house, table, and bed, which was some relief to weather-
beaten pilgrims.

Christmas eve. We rode in the rain twenty-five miles to our
kind brother Horton's, and found many people had gathered.

SOUTH CAROLINA.—Christmas day. Although the weather was cold and damp, and unhealthy, with signs of snow, we rode forty-five miles to dear brother Rembert's—kind and good, rich and liberal, who has done more for the poor Methodists than any man in South Carolina. The Lord grant that he, with his whole household, may find mercy in that day.

Wednesday 26. Preached at quarterly meeting on 1 Peter iv. 13. I was pleased to hear the young men exhort and sing after sacrament. I felt uncommonly melted—tears involuntarily burst from my eyes. God was there.

Thursday 27. I had a long, cold ride of forty-five miles to brother Bowman's, near Santee. I was overtaken on my way by rain mingled with hail, which ended in snow, covering the ground six or eight inches deep. The unfinished state of the houses, lying on the floor, thin clothing, and inclement weather, keep me in a state of indisposition.

Friday 28. We had to cross Santee, and ride thirty-five miles to dear sister Browings's. The weather still very cold.

Saturday 29. Rode thirty-three miles to Charleston, and found our little flock in peace. and a small revival amongst them.

Mr. Hammett has raised a grand house, and has written an appeal to the British conference. He represents Dr. Coke as a sacrilegious tyrant and murderer. I have no doubt but the Doctor will be able to make good his cause. As to Hammett, time will show the man, and the people who have made lies their refuge.

Sunday 30. Brother I. S—— preached in the forenoon. In the afternoon I said a little on Isai. ix. 6, 7. The blacks were hardly restrained from crying out aloud. O that God would bless the wild and wicked inhabitants of this city! I am happy to find that our principal friends have increased in religion. Accounts from Philadelphia are pleasing—souls are converted to God. There is also a move in New-York, and their numbers are daily increasing. On reviewing the labours of the last six weeks, I find we have rested about fourteen days at conferences, and rode at least seven hundred miles.

January 3, 1793. From Wednesday, December 31, to this day, Sunday excepted, we sat in conference in this city.

Friday 4. I was unwell, yet I set out and reached Mr. G——'s, on Edisto-River. A few people met me here in the evening, but I was unwell and weary, and sleepy, and very unfit for public exercise.

Saturday 5. Rode fifty miles to R——'s, and rested on the Sabbath. I had a meeting with eight or ten souls. The people in these parts are much given up to sin ; they have a little charity for the Baptists, but none at all for the Methodists.

Monday 7. We rode thirty-seven miles to T——'s ; where, had we not begged and promised to pay well for it, I know not if we should have been taken in.

GEORGIA.—Tuesday 8. We passed Augusta, and rode thirty-seven miles to H——'s, where we were treated kindly. Thence, next day, to Washington, forty-four miles. I was taken ill at brother M——'s.

Thursday 10. Met our dear brethren in conference. We had great peace and union : the Carolina preachers came up to change with those in Georgia : all things happened well. Bless the Lord, O my soul ! We now agreed to unite the Georgia and South Carolina conferences—to meet in the fork of Seleuda and Broad Rivers, on the first of January, 1794. Our sitting ended in exceeding great love.

Sabbath 13. We had sacrament, love-feast, and ordination. I felt very serious, and was very pointed on Acts xx. 26, 27. I have now had an opportunity of speaking in Washington : most of the people attended to hear *this man that rambles through the United States.* In due time I shall, with permission, visit Georgia.

Monday 14. I preached in the new house at Grant's, on " He that overcometh shall inherit all things, and I will be his God, and he shall be my son."

1. The Christian soldier has to overcome the world, sin, and the devil, with his temptations.

2. He fights under the banner of Christ, who is the Captain of his salvation.

3. His armour is described by St. Paul, Ephes. vi.

4. His inheritance—Christian tempers, and the things promised to the seven churches ; and finally, glory—" Will be his God"— giving him wisdom, truth, love—" He shall be my son"—a son partakes of the nature and property of the father, and doeth his will : so it is with those who are the children of God.

Our dear Georgia brethren seem to think some of us shall visit them no more : they appear to be much humbled, and will not give up the travelling preachers. I am now bound for Savannah ; where I may see the former walks of a dear Wesley and Whitefield, whom I hope to meet in the new Jerusalem.

Wednesday 16. We had to swim Long-Creek. We had few to
hear at H——'s ; but they felt the word, and we had a good time.

When the weather is open and the sun shines, the days are generally warm in this country, but the nights are cold, and the houses
open.

Saturday 19, Was taken up in reading Ostervald's Christian
Theology ; it is simple, plain, and interesting.

Sunday 20. I preached at Bethel on Peter ii. 24, 25. I had a full
congregation, and great freedom in speaking : the house was a miserable one.

Wednesday 23. I came to Buckhead : a few people had gathered, to whom I gave an exhortation. Reached J——'s ; making it
thirty-three miles without refreshment, being out from seven to
seven o'clock again.

Friday 25. I rode fifteen miles to my very loving friend brother
D——'s : here my mind was exercised with what I heard and felt.
Mr. Matthews wrote brother D—— he had been taught *my iniquity,*
to which Mr. H—— (his brother) gave his sanction. And why was
I thus charged ?—Because I did not establish Mr. Wesley's absolute
authority over the American connexion :—for myself, this I had
submitted to ; but the Americans were too jealous to bind themselves to yield to him in all things relative to church-government.
Mr. Wesley was a man they had never seen—was three thousand
miles off—how might submission, in such a case, be expected ?—
Brother Coke and myself gave offence to the connexion by enfor-
cing Mr. Wesley's will in some matters ; for which I do not blame
Mr. Wesley :—like other great men he had his elbow friends ; and
like other people I had my enemies.

Tuesday 29. We reached Savannah. Next day I rode twelve
miles along a fine, sandy road to view the ruins of Mr. Whitefield's
Orphan-House ; we found the place, and having seen the copper-
plate, which I recognized, I felt very awful : the wings are yet
standing, though much injured, and the school-house still more. It
is reported that Mr. Whitefield observed, whilst eating his last dinner in the house, " This house was built for God ; and cursed be
the man that puts it to any other use." The land for the support
of the school is of little value, except two rice plantations, which
we passed in our route.

I returned to Savannah, and preached on Luke xix. 10. to a serious people, with whom I had liberty.

Friday, February 1. I came to Ebenezer ; and had a pleasing
interview with Mr. Bergman ; he cannot speak much English.

The Lord has certainly something in design for this man, more than to be buried in this place. We rode through rice plantations for nearly two miles, and were entangled in the swamp.—O, how dreadful to be here in the dark!

Saturday 2. I am not enough in prayer. I have said more than was for the glory of God concerning those who have left the American connexion, and who have reviled Mr. Wesley, Mr. Fletcher, Doctor Coke, and poor *me*. O, that I could trust the Lord more than I do, and leave his cause wholly in his own hands!

This being Saturday, we rest to read and write, having rode, since Monday morning, about one hundred and twenty-four miles.

I reflected upon the present ruin of the Orphan-House; and taking a view of the money expended, the persons employed, the preachers sent over, I was led to inquire where are they; and how has it sped? The earth, the army, the Baptists, the Church, the Independents, have swallowed them all up at this *windmill end of the continent*. A wretched country this—but there are souls, precious souls, worth worlds.

I was offered the use of the court-house to preach in, but the night being cold and windy, prevented: I preached at Mr. M—'s. We want a house here, which I expect we shall obtain. I suppose there are five hundred houses of all sorts; and if I guess well, about two thousand inhabitants. There is one Lutheran church with, perhaps, fifty or sixty members. Goshen church is about forty by twenty-five, well finished: Mr. B—— and the congregation have given it to us, on condition that we supply them with preaching on Sabbath-days—once in two, or even three weeks.

I lodged at our kind W——'s. Crossed the Savannah at the Sister-Ferry; and came on to Blackswamp, and in the dark got pretty well scratched by the trees.

SOUTH CAROLINA.—Sunday 3. Preached at Blackswamp church on 2 Cor. iii. 9.: the subject was pointed; and the people were attentive.

Monday 4. I preached at Purisburg to a full house: some of the women appeared to feel the word. We had a heavy ride: I was faint, and low-spirited at the view which I could not fail to take of the state of professors and sinners. I had about fifty hearers, and was invited to a friend's house, but thought it best to pursue my journey. We came to the Salt-Ketchers bridge, where we stopped to pay our fare—but Oh, the scent of rum—and men filled with it! How shocking! Who could enter such a house! I hoped for quiet private entertainment at Red-Hill; but the gentleman refused to receive us for love, money, or hospitality's sake. I then sent brother R. to know if we could get in at the next negro-quarter : into the house we might be permitted to enter, but we could get no corn for our horses, and no bed for ourselves : overseers dare not, and their employers will not receive strangers : they are too proud to sell, and too covetous to give. At length we providentially reached a Mr. C——'s, a schoolmaster and minister : we bought some corn for our horses, and had tea, and bread and cheese for ourselves. I saw some beautiful boys at this house : had these children the opportunity of a northern education, what choice young men they might make. I was happy in the house, and pleased with two poor blacks, who were much moved under prayer. Next morning I set out about six o'clock, and passing the Fishpond, we came on slowly to Parker's ferry. I found my appointment to meet brother Jackson was not properly made ; and as it was out of my way, I made a sudden turn to G——'s, on Edisto-River. After dinner I met with —————— who offered to be our guide ; but when I began to show him his folly and the dangerous state of his soul, he soon left us, and we had to beat our way through the swamps as well as we could : he said, he had killed a negro worth £60, and a valuable horse with racing. Pushing on we found our way to the ferry, and crossed about eight o'clock.

I laid me down at nine, and rose again at seven o'clock in the morning and set out : travelling through heavy rains, deep swamps in dark nights, makes both man and beast feel the effect of yesterday's journey of forty-five miles. My mind has been severely agitated this tour ; I have rode about six hundred and fifty miles in one month, lacking one day.

Friday 8. Charleston. I have got through Mr. Wesley's Journal as far as 1782. Finding the subscription set on foot at the conference to purchase a burying-ground and build a house, was likely to succeed, we began to think about looking out for a lot. I also see a prospect of stationing two preachers here.

Sunday 10. I preached with some life on Ezek. xxxvi. 25, 26. but alas ! the people are so dissipated, and so ignorant of Gospel truth, that it is difficult to preach to them ; but I cannot spare, though they keep their course to hell. At night I spoke on Isaiah vi. 8—10. Our congregation consists of five hundred souls and upwards ; three hundred being black.

I have seen Mr. Johnson, the last President of the Orphan-House in Georgia, who confirmed what I had written respecting it.

Charleston is a growing, busy, dreadfully dissipated place. The printed list of vessels in the harbour sets forth, 53 ships, 55 brigs, 25 sloops, 25 schooners, 7 snows, and 2 barques, besides pilot-boats and coasters.

Monday 11. Met the women's class, white and black, and had a powerful meeting. They agreed to hold a prayer-meeting, once a week, amongst themselves.

Tuesday 12. I make it my work to visit every afternoon. I happily met with Mr. Wesley's Journal, bringing the date down to two years before his death. I could not but specially notice that his latter days were more abundant in labours ; and that he preached in places formerly unnoticed. He made this observation, (so fixed on my mind) that it is rare—a mere miracle, for a Methodist to increase in wealth and not decrease in grace. I have now read the third volume of Gordon's History ; Burnham's Select Martyrology ; and Memoirs of dying Saints. We have two hundred and seventeen travelling preachers ; and about fifty thousand members in the United States. Glory to God in the highest !

Saturday 16. I met the stewards and leaders : it was agreed that every other meeting should be purely spiritual—speaking experience and opening their hearts to each other.

Sunday 17. I preached on Romans iii. 11—21. In the evening was very low, but very plain on Luke xvi. 31. The building of a new house, and stationing another preacher in this city, and the state of this and the Georgia districts, with things relative to individuals in this society, do not work to my mind ; I felt as if the charm was near breaking—some wish union ; others will come back. The union must first take place with Dr. C. then with the British conference, and then with the American :—I ask ; who made us twain, and strove to scatter fire-brands, arrows, and death, through the whole continent ?

Wednesday 20. I had an interview with Doctor A. who came from the north for his health ; seeing him so low, and fearing he would die if he stayed here, I hastily invited him to ride out into the country with me.

Thursday 21. We left the city on small horses, with heavy baggage. We came to the Cypress-Swamp in the night, following a poor negro, who waded through as a guide, and not expecting to find it as bad as it was : at length we came to sister B——'s, and were kindly received ; I found no appointments were made for me, owing to brother —— being sick.

Friday 22. We set out for Santee, but missed our way, and took the road to Fourholds-Bridge, being six miles out of our course. We again directed our course to Santee ; and after coming within sight of Managoe's ferry, I took a wrong road, and went three miles up the river. We came to Mr. H.'s, where we were comfortable and had whatever we wanted.

Saturday 23. We had our difficulties in getting across the river ; the overseer had moved the flat to the middle ground, and would not suffer any one to have it ; I entreated him in behalf of the sick, but in vain. Had we waited a few minutes longer, our dear brother B. would have been there to conduct us. I have lately had cross winds ; the roads, myself, Satan, and my sick companion, Dr. A——, have all been matter of trial to me.

Sunday 24. I preached the funeral of our brother B——, on Isaiah lvii. 1. The congregation was large and attentive, but appeared stupid and unfeeling.

Monday 25. Came to brother B——'s, the weather as sultry as in the month of July in the north. We rode thirty miles.

Thursday 28. The weather was exceedingly cold, so that we declined going to the chapel, but had a comfortable meeting at brother R——'s on Ephes. vi. 10—20.

Saturday, March 2. We crossed the water at E——'s ferry, and came to father M——'s, an Englishman, from Epworth ; who was formerly converted, but living under Antinomian dotages, he lost the blessing. I trust the Lord hath again restored him by means of our labours. Here we have a chapel and society.

Sunday 3. This day was rainy, yet nearly four hundred souls came together ; but I could not fix the attention of the people, nor get them to understand.

Monday 4. Came to H——'s, and thence through Columbia, the capital of South Carolina. Brother Ellis, who is nearly risen from the dead, accompanied me from M——'s : having left one sick man, I now take up another. We came to a house five miles from Columbia ; we got a little bread, drank our own tea, had our horses fed, and paid two dollars next morning—so the matter ended.

Tuesday 5. We had our difficulties in crossing the river, which was rising ; and in beating up Cedar-Creek fifteen miles, much of it through the woods : in the evening, we came greatly wearied to R——'s, and were kindly entertained ; it may be that Providence sent us here for some good—the man and his wife feel the want of religion.

Wednesday 6. We came to Little-River-Bridge ; crossed at S——'s ferry, and at length came, thoroughly wearied, to brother Finches. I expect we have been forced to ride twenty or thirty miles out of our way among strangers on account of high waters ; my mind has been variously tried : I have been employed in improving myself in the Hebrew tones and points ; this being my horse-back study.

Thursday 7. Preached at F——'s. I consulted the minds of our brethren about building a house for conference, preaching, and a district school ; but I have no ground to believe that our well-laid plan will be executed ; our preachers are unskilful, and our friends have little money.

Friday 8. The rains continued, and the waters kept up, crossed Enoree ; high—and rising powerfully—Tyger River being impassable, we rode to Cokesbridge, and had a hungry time—came to brother W——'s, near Union court-house.

I next day preached to a few people at the open meeting-house, with some spiritual opening and sweetness. We were closely employed in writing subscriptions for the district school, and copies of the constitutions. Great rains still continue.

Thursday 14. I preached at Flat-Rock, in an open house, to an unfeeling people. Thence we came to Pacolet : the waters were up ; but for our money we got across in a flat that had drifted and was taken up.

Friday 15. Came to Father S——'s, a German ; first a Baptist, then a Methodist, but last, and best of all, a Christian.

Saturday 16, and Sunday 17. Attended quarterly meeting in Union circuit. There were no elders present. I preached on Eph. vi. 10—18. and felt a great death among the people. Sunday, we administered the sacrament and held love-feast. I desired D. A—— to preach, and brother G—— to exhort, whilst I retired to write to I. S——, desiring him to take the presidentship of Union, Catawba, Little Pee Dee, Great Pee Dee, Anson, and Santee circuits.

The people hereabouts have been poorly handled by those who, whilst they made a great profession of religion, maintained Antinomian principles and practice. I have been unwell, occasioned by the change of seasons, houses, and tables. Came to brother M.'s, on Sunday evening, to get a day of rest. I feel the want of religion in families, congregations, and societies. I have travelled about three hundred miles the last three weeks ;

and have escaped the excessive rains, but have had to wrestle with floods.

NORTH CAROLINA.—Monday 18. I spent in writing sundry letters to the north ; and in my favourite study.

Tuesday 19. I had a full house at L——'s. I felt very unfit for public exercises, both in body and mind. I have little desire to come here again :—we can hardly get entertainment. We want brethren and children here. A woman invited us to her house, but when I understood the distance, I determined to haste along, and made it about thirty miles to F.'s, in the cove of the mountain ; where we rested in peace, after getting a little Indian bread, fried bacon, and drinking some of our tea. Our lodging was on a bed set upon forks and clap-boards laid across, in an earthen floor cabin.—But worse than all the rest, these people decline in religion. I feel awful for them on this account. Next morning about sunrise we took the path up the mountain.

I sent D. A. to Dr. Busnell's to inquire if there was any expectation of my coming to Burke to preach ; for being indisposed, I intended to turn aside to Johns-River. D. A. returned ; and the Doctor's nephew pursued, and brought us to town, where I gave them a plain, pointed sermon on " The Son of man is come to seek and save that which was lost :" every one, young and old, lawyers, doctors, and clerks, were obliging, attentive, and serious. Doctor Busnell is a man I have heard of these twenty years, but knew him not until now.—He descended from the Bohemians. His son Joseph was happily brought home to God by means of the Methodists ; he lived to God, and died in Winchester about twelve months ago. The Doctor's usage to me was that of a gentleman and Christian. The transition with respect to entertainment was very great : here we had a table, bed, room, and whatever we wanted ; but all this could not give me rest, having a return of my rheumatic and nervous complaints.

Friday 22. Rode up to Johns-River ; I am heavy ; cannot attend study nor mental prayer, and company is irksome.—Oh! that my soul were always flaming with perfect love. In the evening eight of us met together and conversed on the work of God : all was love. Brother P. gave us an animating sermon on " By whom shall Jacob arise ? for he is small."

Sunday 24. I preached on 1 Cor. xiv. 3. there was a noise, and a shaking each day : some were awakened, one professed to be converted, and several to be quickened : the meeting lasted from nine A. M. to four o'clock P. M. " While he was yet speaking there

came also another." I heard there was a conference appointed at
Reese's chapel, in Charlotte county, Virginia, to form what they
call a free constitution, and a pure church ; and to reject me and
my creatures. I know not whose hand is in this ; I hope they will
call themselves by another name. Only let them settle in congregations, and tax the people, and I know how it will work. If we
(the itinerant connexion) would give the government into the
hands of a local ministry, as some would have it, and tax the people to pay preachers for Sabbath work—this would please such
men : but this we dare not do. Whenever the people are unwilling to receive us, and think they can do better, we will quietly
withdraw from them ; and if those who wish the change can serve
them better than we have done, well. Perhaps some of them may
think with ——, in Georgia, that I am the greatest villain on the
continent ; I bid such adieu, and appeal to the bar of God. I have
no time to contend, having better work to do : if we lose some
children, God will give us more. Ah! this is the mercy, the justice of some, who, under God, owe their all to me, and my *tyrants*,
so called. The Lord judge between them and me! There appears
to be a general quickening in the Yadkin circuit, and about eight
souls have professed conversion there in the last three months.

Monday 25. I rested and prepared to cross the *Harmon harim*—
the multitude of mountains.

Tuesday 26. We wrought up the meanders of Johns-River to
the Globe, and met a few people at Mr. Moor's, a Baptist, a very
kind head of a respectable family.

Wednesday 27. We began our journey over the great ridge of
mountains ; we had not gone far before we saw and felt the snow,
the sharpness of the air gave me a deep cold, not unlike an influenza.
We came to the head of Watauga-River. Stopped at Mr. S——'s,
and had some enlargement on " The promise is to you and to your
children," &c. My soul felt for these neglected people. It may
be, by my coming this way, Providence will so order it, that I
shall send them a preacher. We hasted on to Cove's Creek, invited ourselves to stay at C——'s, where we made our own tea,
obtained some butter and milk, and some most excellent Irish potatoes : we were presented with a little flax for our beds, on
which we spread our coats and blankets, and three of us slept
before a large fire.

Thursday 28. We made an early start, and came to the Beaver-
Dam ; three years ago we slept here in a cabin without a cover.
We made a breakfast at Mr. W——'s ; and then attempted the

iron or stone mountain, which is steep like the roof of a house. I
found it difficult and trying to my lungs to walk up it. Descending
the mountain we had to jump down the steep stairs, from two to
three and four feet. At the foot of this mountain our guide left us
to a man on foot; he soon declined, and we made the best of our
way to Dugger's ford, on Roans-Creek. We came down the river,
where there are plenty of large, round, rolling stones, and the
stream was rapid. My horse began to grow dull: an intermittent fever and a deep cold disordered me much. I was under
obligations to Henry Hill, my new aid, who was ready to do any
thing for me in his power. Perhaps Providence moved him to
offer to travel with me, and his father to recommend him. Twenty
years ago a rude, open loft did not affect me—now it seldom fails
to injure me.

TENNESSEE.—Friday 29. We took our journey deliberately.
We passed Doe-River at the fork, and came through the Gap—a
most gloomy scene—not unlike the shades of death in the Alleghany mountain. Mr. L——, a kind Presbyterian, fed our horses
gratis. I must give the Presbyterians the preference for respect
to ministers. We prayed, and came on to ——. a kind people;
but to our sorrow we find it low times for religion on Holstein and
Watauga Rivers. In Green circuit there is some increase. My
way opens; and I think I shall go to Kentucky. I laid my hands
on what is called " The Principles of Politeness," imitated from
Chesterfield: it contains some judicious remarks, and shows the
author to have been a man of sense and education—but of no
religion. He recommends some things contrary thereto.

Tuesday, April 2. Our conference began at Nelson's, near
Jonesborough, in the new territory. We have only four or five
families of Methodists here. We had sweet peace in our conference.

Wednesday 3. I gave an exhortation after brothers H—— and
M'H—— had preached, and there was a melting among the people.

Thursday 4. I had a happy time at my old friend C——'s; I
am pained for his children, who are yet unconverted.

Friday 5. Rode to Nolachucky, and attended a meeting at
Squire E——'s, where I had about two hundred hearers. We
have formed a society in this place of thirty-one members—most
of them new. There are appearances of danger on the road to
Kentucky; but the Lord is with us. We have formed a company
of nine men (five of whom are preachers) who are well armed
and mounted.

Saturday 6. Rode to Green ———, and crossed the grand island ford of Nolachucky : the low lands are very rich, the uplands barren. Stopped and fed at Green court-house ; here was brought a corpse to the grave in a covered carriage drawn by four horses. Solemn sight! Be instructed, O my soul! A whiskey toper gave me a cheer of success as one of John Wesley's congregation! I came on alone through heavy rains, over bad hills and poor ridges, to brother Vanpelts, on Lick-Creek—he is brother to Peter, my old, first friend on Staten-Island : I was weary, damp, and hungry ; but had a comfortable habitation, and kind, loving people, who heard, refreshed, and fed me. We had a large congregation at brother Vanpelt's chapel, where I had liberty in speaking. I left the young men to entertain the people a while longer, and returned and read Mr. Wesley's Sermon on Riches.

If reports be true, there is danger in journeying through the wilderness ; but I do not fear—we go armed. If God suffer Satan to drive the Indians on us ; if it be his will, he will teach our hands to war, and our fingers to fight and conquer.

Monday 8. Our guard appeared, fixed, and armed, for the wilderness. We came down to E——'s, and were well entertained. Thence we proceeded on to the main branch of Holstein, which being swelled, we crossed in a flat ; thence to R——'s, where I found the reports relative to the Indians were true ; they had killed the post and one or two more, and taken some prisoners. I had not much thought or fear about them.

Tuesday 9. We came off ; there were only eight in our company, and eight in the other—two women and three children. We had two poor sinners, that set themselves to work wickedness ; they would not let us go foremost ; so we took it patiently, and followed up to the Cumberland station. I went to Robinson's station, where the soldiers behaved civilly. We gave them two exhortations, and had prayer with them. They honoured me with the swinging hammock (a bear skin) which was as great a favour to me as the governor's bed ; here I slept well.

KENTUCKY (East line)—Wednesday 10. We hasted on our way, meeting with our troubles at the foot of Cumberland mountain ; we then went foremost, and travelled at a great rate, the roads being uncommonly good. We fed on the banks of Cumberland-River, and kept up the head of Rich Lands. We then pushed through Little and Big Laurel to the Hazle Patch, Hood's station. Here there was high life below stairs—talking, laughing, &c. We had a troop of poor, very poor sinners ; I gave dreadful offence by

a prayer I made. After resting here from three to six, we urged
our way along the new road to Rock-Castle. Fed at the deserted
station, and hasted to Willis Green's, but missing our way, did not
get in until eight o'clock ; a supper at that time was good, and a
bed was better, having not slept in one for three nights, and having
rode one hundred miles in two days. I felt so well in the morning I was ready to set out for Salt-River. I went to Danville, and
set myself down in Mr. Rice's church ; thence to F. Clark's,
where I was not expected, but was quite welcome. I left my aid
and pack horse at G——'s, to rest.

Saturday 13. We rode thirty-three miles down to a quarterly
meeting at Humphries chapel. Here my presence surprised the
brethren. The state of the work here appears to be low. I had
some light, life, and liberty in preaching, and some felt the word.
We closed our meeting after several had joined in prayer. Lord
remember the labours of this day! Let not thy faithful word fall
to the ground! From the quarterly meeting we came to Col.
Harding's. He has been gone some time, as a commissioner, to
treat with the Indians ; if he is dead, here is a widow and six
children left. I cannot yet give him up for lost. We had a large
congregation at W——'s, where I was led out on Psal. xxxiv. 17—
20. I cannot stand quarterly meetings every day—none need desire to be an American bishop upon our plan, for the ease, honour,
or interest, that attends the office : from my present views and
feelings, I am led to wish the conference would elect another
bishop, which might afford me some help.

Tuesday 16. Rode thirty miles without food for man or horse.
I was uncomfortable when I came into the neighbourhood of
W——'s : there is a falling away among the people. Lord help
me to bear up in the evil day ! Let me not disquiet myself, and
kill man and horse in vain !

Thursday 18. I rode sixteen miles to Clarke's station to attend
the quarterly meeting. My winter's clothing, the heat of the
weather, and my great exertions in travelling, cause me to be
heavy with sleep ; yet, blessed be God, I live continually in his
presence ; and Christ is all in all to my soul !

Friday 19. I preached a short, pointed sermon ; and the preachers and members were moved.

Sunday 21. We had sacrament and love-feast ; and some spoke
much to the purpose : my subject was Hebr. vi. 4—8. The congregation was very large. I endeavoured to show, 1st. How far people
may advance in the grace of God ; 2d. By what degrees they may

apostatize ; 3d, The impossibility of a recovery when they arrive at a certain degree of wickedness : 1st, Because they sin against God, Christ, and the Eternal Spirit, and lose all they ever felt or knew ; 2d, Every means is lost upon them ; to sin against the remedy, is to be undone without it.   The difference between those who are recoverable and those who are not—such are not who deny the work to be of God, persecute, and say the devil was the author of it ; the others acknowledge the work that it was of God, and have some regard for his people.   Lastly ; that the only security pointed out by the apostles against apostacy, is to go on to perfection.

Tuesday 23.   I was at Bethel—the place intended for a school.

Sunday 28.   We had sacrament and love-feast, and some living testimonies.

Monday 29.   Rode through the rain to Lexington.   I stopped at C. White's once more.   Oh that God may help him safe to glory !   Came to brother Morgan's.   I felt awful and solemn, and some dejection of mind.   Ah ! want of religion is too visible in most houses.

Tuesday 30, Wednesday May 1, Thursday 2.   We spent in conference ; and in openly speaking our minds to each other.   We ended under the melting, praying, praising power of God.   We appointed trustees for the school ; and made sundry regulations relative thereto : we read the Form of Discipline through, section by section, in conference.

Friday 3.   I preached on Habakkuk iii. 2.   I first pointed out the distinguishing marks of a work of God ; 2d, The subjects ; 3d, The instruments ; 4th, The means.   If ever I delivered my own soul, I think I have done it this day.   Some people were moved in an extraordinary manner, shouting and jumping at a strange rate.

Saturday 5.   Came to Bethel to meet the trustees.

Sunday 6.   We had an awful time whilst I opened and applied "Knowing therefore the terror of the Lord, we persuade men." It was a feeling, melting time, among old and young ; and I am persuaded good was certainly done this day.   I feel a good deal tried in spirit ; yet, blessed be God, I still have peace within ; God is all to me : I want more faith to trust him with my life, and all I have, and am.

Tuesday 8.   We rode down to the Crab Orchard, where we found company enough ; some of whom were very wild : we had a company of our own, and refused to go with them.   Some of them gave us very abusive language ; and one man went upon a

hill above us, and fired a pistol towards our company. We resolved
to travel in our order, and bound ourselves by honour and conscience to support and defend each other ; and to see every man
through the wilderness. But we could not depend upon wicked
and unprincipled men, who would leave and neglect us, and even
curse us to our faces. Nor were we at liberty to mix with swear-
ers, liars, drunkards ; and, for aught we know, this may not be the
worst with some. We were about fourteen or fifteen in company ;
and had twelve guns and pistols. We rode on near the defeated
camp, and rested till three o'clock under great suspicion of Indians :
we pushed forward ; and by riding forty-five miles on Wednesday,
and about the same distance on Thursday, we came safe to Robinson's station, about eight o'clock.

Friday 11. We rode leisurely from the edge of the wilderness ;
crossed Holstein, and about one o'clock came to brother E——'s,
it being about sixteen miles.

TENNESSEE.—Saturday 12. We came to brother Vanpelt's, with
whom we rested on the Sabbath. I have travelled between five and
six hundred miles in the last four weeks, and have rested from
riding fifteen days at conferences, and other places. I have been
much distressed with this night work—no regular meals, nor sleep ;
and it is difficult to keep up prayer in such rude companies as we
have been exposed to ; I have also been severely afflicted through
the whole journey.

Monday 14. Was a day of great trial ; we rode about forty-six
miles—stopped at ——, where, through carelessness, I nearly had
been burnt up.

Tuesday 15. At eleven o'clock we came to B——'s. The subject was, " Let this mind be in you which was also in Christ Jesus." Sisters W——, and H——, making some clothing, and re-
pairing my burnt raiment next day, we could not move until eight
o'clock. We then set out without a guide, missed our road, and
came in about two o'clock : we found the people patiently waiting,
to whom I preached on " Ye will not come to me that ye might
have life."

VIRGINIA.—Thursday 17. Came to Abingdon—felt very heavy ; I
however preached in the court-house to a very genteel people on
the words of Joshua, " Ye cannot serve God," &c.

Saturday 19. Came to Sister Russell's—I am very solemn. I
feel the want of the dear man, who, I trust is now in Abraham's
bosom, and hope ere long to see him there. He was a general of-
ficer in the continental army, where he underwent great fatigue : he

was powerfully brought to God, and for a few years past was a
living flame, and a blessing to his neighbourhood.—He went in the
dead of winter on a visit to his friends ; was seized with an influenza, and ended his life from home—O that the Gospel may continue in this house! I preached on Hebr. xii. 1—4. and there followed several exhortations. We then administered the sacrament
and there was weeping and shouting among the people : our exercises lasted about five hours. I have little rest by night or day—
Lord, help thy poor dust! I feel unexpected storms—within
from various quarters ; perhaps it is designed for my humiliation.
—It is a sin in thought I am afraid of; none but Jesus can support
us, by his merit, his spirit, his righteousness, his intercession, i. e.
Christ in all, for all, through all, and in every mean, and word, and
work.

Monday 21. Rode to C——'s, and was well steeped in rain :
here I wrote a plan for a district school.

Wednesday 23. We rode forty-five miles to H.'s, where we
had many people. About five o'clock, on our way over the hills,
we felt the rain without, and hunger within : next day we crossed
Walker's Mountain, and in the evening met brother M——, at
Munday's.

Friday 25. Came to Rehoboth, in the sinks of Green-Briar ;
where we held our conference. I was greatly comforted at the
sight of brothers B. J. and Ellis Cox. We had peace in our conference, and were happy in our cabin. I learn that mischief is
begun in the lower parts of Virginia ; J O'Kelly, and some of the
local preachers, are the promoters and encouragers of divisions
among the brethren.

Tuesday 29. We passed the Sweet Springs, and crossed a rough
mountain to brother Drew's, on Pott's creek. I wrote many letters
to the south district of Virginia, to confirm the souls of the people, and guard them against the division that is attempted among
them. Came to E. Mitchel's. Crossed James-River, near the
mouth of Craiges-Creek; but was prevented by the rain from
pursuing our journey. We spent the evening comfortably at sister
Pryer's.

Friday 31. Rode forty-five miles to Moore's furnace ; and lodged
with kind brother R.

Saturday, June 1. We came to Staunton, a very unpleasing place
to me. There is an Episcopal church, a court-house, good taverns
and stores here. We went to Mr. ——'s, expecting to find a
friend ; after making the trial, we thought it best to return and

take lodging in a tavern. Thence we proceeded on to Rocktown, a beautiful place ; here I felt myself stiff, and weary, and troubled with rheumatic pains : sweet sleep was quite welcome. My congregation was small, the people not having proper notice of my coming. Satan has been sowing discord here, and has hindered the work of God ; but I hope the approaching quarterly meeting will be a blessing to them ; and that we shall not toil in vain. The loss of sleep, and other circumstances, made me very heavy, and brought on a sick headach, which I had not felt for some time. I spent the evening with Doctor Dulany. Rose, and took the rain next morning as usual, having had rain for eight or ten days successively. On my way I was met by an old German, who shook me by the hand, and said he wished he might be worthy to wash my feet—Yea, thought I—if you knew what a poor sinful creature I am, you would hardly look at one so unworthy, but Jesus lives—O precious Christ—thou art mine and I am thine !

Came to Newtown : the roads exceeding mirey, and our horses very tired : we are glad to get a little rest at brother Phelp's. My soul has been much tried by Satan, and I am pained for the work of God. In my six month's travel I find that six acceptable preachers are preparing to settle themselves in the world, and leave the itinerancy.

Thursday 6. We came to Winchester ; where they have built an excellent house, and we have better times than I expected : here nothing would do, but I must preach, notwithstanding the lanes and streets of the town were so filled with mire, owing to the late rains.

Friday 7. We rode to Bath, that seat of sin : here we continued to rest ourselves : my public work was a sermon on the Sabbath. A number of our society from various parts being here, I have an opportunity of receiving and answering many letters. I am afraid I shall spend nine or ten days here to little purpose ; I employ myself in reading à Kempis, and the Bible : I also have an opportunity of going alone into the silent grove, and of viewing the continent, and examining my own heart. I hope for some relief from my rheumatic complaint which has so oppressed me for six months past. The people here are so gay and idle, that I doubt there being much good done among them. The troubles of the east and west meet me as I pass.

MARYLAND.—Sunday 17. A number of us crossed the ferry at the mouth of Great Capon ; and made our way through great heat to Oldtown, thirty-two miles : we were obliged to ride moderately,

or the excessive warmth of the weather might have killed our
horses. We had no small consolation in uniting the brethren from
three districts in conference; whose names only were before
known to each other. I gave them one sermon on " Pray for the
peace of Jerusalem: they shall prosper that love thee." Our conference sat three days successively, very closely employed.

Friday 21. We rode thirty-five miles to F.'s, and thirty-five more
the next day to Fort Littleton. Our roads are rough; I am sick;
our fare is coarse; but it is enough—I am to die. I have been
under violent temptations—Lord, keep me every moment! Our
horses were out of the way, so that we could not pursue our journey. I was desirous to be doing good somewhere; and was led
to speak to a woman unknown to me, and urged her to pray three
times a day: she appeared tender; and with tears promised so to
do—perhaps this labour may not be lost. I have had the happiness to hear that my labour of this kind at the widow H.'s, when
there last, was successful, and that a woman was wrought upon to
give herself to God, and found peace. We collected the little
persecuted society, to whom I preached on " All that will live godly
in Christ Jesus shall suffer persecution :" they were poor, but
very kind. Thence we proceeded on to Juniata ; crossed to Mif-
lin-Town, and came to H. M.'s.

Thursday 20. I had some little time to read, write, and pray.
My congregation was careless and unfeeling. I enforced David's
charge to Solomon. Methinks it ought to be with those who
have to do with souls, as with a tender, feeling physician that
attends a patient :—does the fever rage, or the delirium continue?
his countenance is sad; and when labour and medicine fail, and
the symptoms continue or grow worse, he is then forced, as a skilful
physician, to pronounce his patient incurable—whilst a quack flat-
ters and sees no danger : such is the difference between a true minister of Christ and a false teacher, when applied to the souls of
men.

Thursday 27. Was to me a day of trial. We set out late towards
Northumberland : night coming on, we stopped at Penns-Creek.
Next morning we went to Northumberland to breakfast. It has a
little chapel (that serves as a school-house) belonging to the Methodists. We have a few kind, respectable friends, whose circumstances are comfortable. I gave them a sermon on John xiv. 6.;
and in the afternoon paid Sunbury a visit. The people here are
almost all Dutch. I was enabled to speak alarming words on
Acts iv. 12.

July 2. After preaching on " the grace of God appearing to all men," we wrought up the hills and narrows to Wyoming. We stopped at a poor house.; nevertheless, they were rich enough to sell us a half bushel of oats, and had sense enough to make us pay well for them. We reached Mr. P——'s about eleven o'clock. I found riding in the night caused a return of my rheumatic complaint through my breast and shoulders. But all is well, the Lord is with us.

Thursday 4. Being the anniversary of the American independence, there was a great noise among the sinners : a few of us went down to Shawanee ; called a few people from their work, and found it good for us to be there.

Sunday 7. The Lord has spoken in awful peals of thunder. O, what havock was made here fifteen years ago! most of the inhabitants were either cut off, or driven away. The people might have clothed themselves in sackcloth and ashes the third, if in white and glory the fourth of July. The inhabitants here are very wicked ; but I feel as if the Lord would return. I hope brothers F——, I——, and P——, will be owned of the Lord. The man at whose house I was to preach, made a frolic the day before ; it was said he sent a mile across the river for one of his neighbours, taking him from his work, and telling him he was about to bleed to death : this falsity was invented, I suppose, to incline the man to come : the people would not come to his house. I had to walk a mile through burning heat to preach ; I was severely exercised in mind, hardly knowing where to go to get a quiet, clean place to lie down.

Monday 8. I took the wilderness, through the mountains, up Lackawamy on the Twelve-miles Swamp ; this place is famous for dirt and lofty hemlock. We lodged in the middle of the swamp at S——'s ; and made out better than we expected. Next morning we set out in the rain, without breakfast : when we came to the ferry, a man took us to his house, and gave us some bread, butter, and some buckwheat, and then charged us four shillings and twopence, although we found our own tea and sugar,—the place we should have called at was a little further on the way.

On the 5th, after very sultry weather, there came a whirlwind, and a very great storm ; in which there fell hail of such a size that three stones filled a pint measure : this went through Hudson, some distance from us.

New-Jersey.—Wednesday 9. We came to Broadhead's, and were totally unknown ; I was sick, and stopped for breakfast—they suspected we were preachers; one asked brother Hill who I was : being informed, the mother, son, and daughter came running with tears to speak with me.—I stopped, and gave them a sermon at Marbletown. I found the work of God going on among the Low Dutch :—these, of all the people in America, we have done the least with.

NEW-YORK.—Saturday 12. We rode to Coeyman's Patent ; we had a good quarterly meeting ; many newly converted souls testified of the goodness of God, and of the power of his grace. From thence to Albany with reluctance ; and lectured, being Sabbath evening : I felt the wickedness of the people : but we had a melting season among the preachers in our conference. Great changes will be made among the preachers from this conference ; some will be sent to New-Jersey ; others to Rhode-Island and Massachusetts. The people of Albany roll in wealth : they have no heart to invite any of the servants of God to their houses ; unless a great change should take place, we shall have no more conferences here. I am tired down with fatigue and labour, under great weakness of body. Yet I must haste to Lynn—it may be, to meet trouble. But my days will be short.

> " My suffering time will soon be o'er ;
> Then shall I sigh and weep no more :
> My ransom'd soul shall soar away,
> To sing God's praise in endless day."

We hope two hundred souls have been awakened, and as many converted in Albany district the past year. Our friends are happy here, not being distressed with divisions in the church, nor by war with the Indians, as they are to the southward. According to our reckoning, we make it about four hundred and forty-seven miles from Oldtown to Albany—to come the mountainous road through the woods ; and to come by Baltimore, Philadelphia, and New-York, it is six hundred miles.

Saturday 19. The congregation being small, and the preachers sleepy, made it a task for me to preach at Rowe's chapel.

Sunday 20. There was a breath of life in the love-feast. I was enabled to be close in preaching on Matt. xviii. 3. " Except ye be converted, and become as little children, ye cannot enter into the kingdom of heaven." In my introduction I showed that the being converted here mentioned, is the same word which in other places is translated, " born again ;" answering to the new creation and resurrection. In this discourse I took occasion to show the misera-

ble state of the unconverted, both present and future, and the exercises that converted souls do, and must pass through ;—that they
must be made as little children, wholly dependent on God ; possessing meekness of spirit, and freed from the guilt, power, and nature
of sin.   My mind enjoyed peace ; but I was grieved at seeing a
number of young, unfeeling sinners assembled at a tavern on the
Lord's day.

CONNECTICUT.—Monday 21. We rode fifteen miles to Sharon,
two miles from Litchfield—there is a little move among the people of this place.

Tuesday 22. Came to H——'s. I rested in a very solitary
shade, and was comforted in my own mind. Perhaps the old man
is right who says, not many of this generation will enter into the
promised land, but their children. Came to East-Hartford, and find
it still a day of small things. Falling under deep dejection (such
as I had not known for months,) I concluded to preach this evening for my own consolation on "Thou that teachest another,
teachest thou not thyself?" We passed through and spent a night
at Windham—a pleasant town. Thence through Canterbury and
Plainfield : where our preachers from Connecticut have visited—
but it is a dry land—little rain in a double sense. Thence I came
upon the state of Rhode-Island ; stopped in Coventry, and found
that the two preachers stationed here have been running over almost the whole state, and had formed but few societies. When I
came to Providence, I. Martin told me, that under the present difficulties they had agreed not to forward the preachers of the Methodists among them, nor to befriend them ; I asked for a tavern,
and was directed to General T—'s, where I was used well : some
were displeased at our praying ; and acted much like Sodomites.
Oh! the enmity and wickedness that is in the human heart. In the
morning I was visited by Mr. Wilson ; I gave him my mind freely,
and left him : the secret of the matter was, that many in that congregation would have been kind to us, but meeting with Mr. ——,
coming from Ireland, (once a travelling preacher) he settled with
them : their convenience suited his interest. But the people can
hear us in the school-house ; and if any are awakened, they will
join the church over the bridge.

MASSACHUSETTS.—We had heavy work for man and horse to
reach Easton—our money grew short.

Sunday 27. Reading the Scripture in the congregation appeared
to be a new thing among the people. I gave them a lecture

under the apple-trees on Isaiah xxxv. 3—6.; and trust my labour was not lost.

Monday 28. We rode upwards of thirty miles, through great heat, to Lynn. On our way we fed our horses, and bought a cake and some cheese for ourselves ; surely we are a spectacle to men and angels! The last nine days, we have rode upwards of two hundred miles, and, all things taken together, I think it worse than the wilderness: the country abounds with rocks, hills, and stones ; and the heat is intense—such as is seldom known in these parts.

Tuesday 29. Preached in Lynn on 2 Chron. xv. 2. the prophecy of Azariah by the Spirit.

I. We are to seek Jehovah in the means ; by the direction of the word and Spirit; through Christ, by repentance and faith.

II. The Lord will be with his people, as a Father and God ; in his wisdom, love, truth, and mercy ; at all times, and places ; in every strait and difficulty.

III. We should be with God as his children, to fear, trust in, worship, and serve him.

IV. The breach of the covenant by idolatry, departing from the love, fear, and confidence they have in him.

V. That the Lord will withdraw from such souls.

August. We have only about three hundred members in this district ; yet we have a call for eight or seven Preachers : although our members are few, our hearers are many.

Sunday 3. We had preaching at six, twelve, two, and seven o'clock, and administered the Lord's supper also. I have now finished my work at Lynn. Circumstances have occurred which have made this conference more painful than any one conference beside.

Monday 4. We rode to Cambridge. On our way we called on Mr. Adams, and found him and his wife under deep exercise of mind. We then came to Walktham, where many attended. Things appear strange here ; but several souls are under awakenings, and there is hope the Lord will work. The harvest is great ; the living, faithful labourers are few.

We hasted to Westham ; and found a congregation at the Baptist meeting-house. From Westham we came two miles to Needham ; here the majority of the people prefer the Methodist preachers ; and want to pay them by a tax on the people ; but brothers Smith and Hill absolutely refused this plan ; for which I commend them. I gave them a sermon, and found some feeling souls.

Wednesday 6. We passed several little towns, and came to Milford, about nineteen miles from Needham; here they have a good priest's house, and meeting-house; all appear to be in peace and fulness of bread. About three hundred were soon collected, to whom I preached on " The love of Christ constraineth us," &c. The man at whose house we lodged was very kind, and told me his father held society meeting in the house where we preached; and, except conditional perseverance, preached our doctrines. We rode through Minden, Douglas, Thompson, Woodstock, up to Pomfret; missing our way, and being very unwell, as I have been for some time with an inflammation in my throat, we concluded to turn in at a tavern, and spend the night in pain: pain begets invention. I now began to think, What shall I do? I am my own physician. I sent for two blisters; applied both to my ears; and then began to march to Ashford. I turned in at Mr. W.'s, and met brothers T. and S. and was dragged out to baptise an household, whilst I had a fever; the weather was excessively warm, like Carolina: I had an awful night.

CONNECTICUT.—Saturday 9. Came to brother H.'s: here I grew worse: this night I had some discharges, and was somewhat relieved. For a few days I have felt some pain in my left foot: it now inflamed more and more, until I could scarcely put it to the floor; I applied a poultice, and spent the Sabbath in private; and was closely engaged in reading the Scriptures.

Monday 11. Our conference sat at Tolland. Lame as I was, I went through the business; and notwithstanding I was tired out with labour, heat, pain, and company, I must also preach; so I submitted; and endeavoured to apply 2 Tim. ii. 24—26. Being unable to ride on horseback, I drove on in a carriage through the rain, over the rocks in the dark, and came to Doctor Steel's at Ellington.

Yesterday the pain seized my right foot. I am now not able to move from my horse to a house; an attack of this kind generally terminates in about eight days.

Thursday 14. Came in brother S.'s carriage to Hartford. From what we can gather, we are encouraged to hope that upwards of three hundred souls have been awakened; and more than two hundred converted to God, the last year: if this work goes on, Satan will be labouring by all means, and by every instrument. From Hartford I came to Middletown. I slept at E. F.'s, who was the first separate minister on the west of Connecticut-River; a man who had laboured, and wrote much: had his learning been

equal to his piety and good sense, the *standing order* would have
trembled under his hand. Who would think his church would vote
him out, when old and gray headed, because he could not subscribe
to the new divinity? He is now, as he saith, like a broken vessel;
upwards of fourscore years of age: his wife and children favour us.

I came to New-Haven; thence to Derby; and had a return of
the inflammation in my throat. Came to West-Haven—very unwell. I had heavy work to get to Reading, being lame in both feet:
I laid myself down on the road-side, and felt like Jonah or Elijah.
I took to my bed at Reading.

Monday 18. Rode ten miles on horseback, and thirteen in a carriage, to Bedford, and rested a day at dear widow Banks's, where I
was at home. Oh, how sweet is one day's rest!

NEW-YORK.—Wednesday 20. When I came near the White-
Plains, my horse started, and threw me into a mill-race knee deep
in water, my hands and side in the dirt; my shoulder was hurt by
the fall. I stopped at a house, shifted my clothes, and prayed
with the people. If any of these people are awakened by my
stopping there, all will be well. This day I made out to ride
thirty-three miles.

Thursday 21. Came to New-York. The weather is extremely
warm. Great afflictions prevail here—fluxes, fevers, influenzas.
It is very sickly also in Philadelphia. I have found by secret
search, that I have not preached sanctification as I should have
done: if I am restored, this shall be my theme more pointedly
than ever, God being my helper. I have been sick upwards of
four months; during which time I have attended to my business,
and rode, I suppose, not less than three thousand miles. I kept
close house in New-York until Sunday 24.; then I attempted to
preach on Romans xiii. 10—12. The weather being warm and
dry, I caught an influenza which held me four days—and this in
addition to my fevers and lameness. The effects of this weather
were sensibly felt by every member of conference, some of whom
were so indisposed that they could not attend. We made a collection of £40 for the relief of the preachers on the frontiers of
New-York and Connecticut.

We have awful accounts from Philadelphia; which made me
feel too much like a man, and too little like a Christian.

NEW-JERSEY.—Monday, September 1. I rested. Tuesday 2,
dined at Elizabethtown on my way to Philadelphia. Wednesday 3, I
reached Trenton, and received a letter from brother M—k—y, requesting me to come to Burlington, and that it was doubtful

whether it were prudent to go into Philadelphia on account of the
contagion that then prevailed in that city : I did not reach Burlington so soon as was expected, and the preachers went on to Philadelphia. I preached in Burlington, and the people were very
solemn.

PENNSYLVANIA.—Friday 6. We rode to the city. Ah! how the
ways mourn : how low spirited are the people whilst making their
escape! I found it awful indeed. I judge the people die from
fifty to one hundred in a day : some of our friends are dying, others
flying.

Sunday 8. I preached on Isai. lviii. 1. "Cry aloud, spare not,
lift up thy voice like a trumpet, and show my people their trans-
gressions, and the house of Jacob their sins." The people of
this city are alarmed; and well the ymay be. I went down to
Ebenezer, (a church in the lower part of the city) but my strength
was gone : however, I endeavoured to open and apply Micah vi. 9.
The streets are now depopulated, and the city wears a gloomy aspect. All night long my ears and heart were wounded with the
cry of fire! Oh! how awful! And what made it still more serious,
two young men were killed by the fall of a wall : one of them was
a valuable member of our society. Poor Philadelphia! the lofty
city, He layeth it low! I am very unwell; my system is quite
weak; I feel the want of pure air. We appointed Tuesday 9th to
be observed as a day of humiliation : I preached on 1 Kings viii.
37—40.; and had a large and very serious, weeping congregation.
The preachers left the city on Monday; I continued in order to
have the minutes of conference printed.

Wednesday 10. We left the city—solemn as death! The people
of Derby and Chester are sickly : and they are greatly alarmed
at Wilmington. I found a quiet retreat at friend Bond's, near
New-Castle.

MARYLAND.—Came to the quarterly meeting at the Cross-Roads :
where there were crowds of people : I gave them a sermon
on "Yea, in the way of thy judgments have we waited for thee."
I showed, 1. That God sent pestilence, famine, locusts, blasting,
milldew, and caterpillars, and that only the church and people of
God know, and believe his judgments. 2. That God's people waited for him in the way of his judgments; and 3. That they improved
and profited by them. About one o'clock we set out and rode
thirty-two miles to Thomas White's; and spent one day at my
former home.

Sunday 14. We rode twenty miles to Millford, and had a comfortable love-feast; I preached to many on 2 Chron. vii. 13—15. I preached a laboured sermon at Quantees quarterly meeting : the second day brother G. preached on "There remaineth therefore a rest to the people of God." My finishing stroke' was 'to show them the way to ruin—so we parted.

Thursday 18. We rode to Accomack ; and had a comfortable quarterly meeting at Downing's. I met the located official members, and we had sweet fellowship together.

Sunday 21. After a gracious love-feast and preaching on Jer. xvii. 9, 10. I returned, weak in body, and under dejection of mind, to C——'s chapel, a ride of twenty miles : this is one of the most awful places I ever visited, according to my feelings : I had only courage to exhort for a few minutes. Brother S——, one of our elders, gave it as his opinion that two hundred people had died in the bounds of Somerset circuit the last summer.

I searched the continent for the Travels of Sin and True Godliness ; now, they are printed and bound together, and sell well ; our Americans are not fools : no books sell like those on plain, practical subjects ; as the Saints' Rest, Baxter's Call, Alleine's Alarm, and Thomas à Kempis.

I came to B. E——'s to quarterly meeting : we had a solemn time, though our congregation was small.

Friday 26. We came to Easton, twenty-five miles ; here the people pretended to be afraid of my communicating the infection of the yellow fever, although I had been out of Philadelphia from the 9th to the 26th Instant. I gave them a long discourse, and then rode to Hillsborough ; and thence to Judge White's. Sickness prevails in every house ; but there are not so many deaths as might be expected from general afflictions.

Monday 29. I preached at quarterly meeting on " The Lord is good ; a strong hold in the day of trouble, and he knoweth them that trust in him." 1. Originally, independently, communicatively good. 2. He knoweth, loveth, approveth, and delivereth those that put their trust in him.

Tuesday 30. I came early to Churchhill ; and felt myself solemnly engaged with God. In the evening I was enabled to give a close, alarming exhortation on the present alarming and awful times.

October, Wednesday 1. I endeavoured to enforce, at Worten's, " Let us search and try our ways, and turn again to the Lord." The wind being contrary, we rode twenty miles to brother B—'s.

through dust and drought. Brother B—— conveyed me to North-
East on Thursday ; and Friday 3, after disputing the passage at
the ferry with Mr. R——, I rode to Cokesbury. I had left Philadelphia, and knew not that a pass was necessary until I came to
the ferry. Mr. Barney, who was a health-officer, behaved like a
gentleman, and gave me a true and honourable certificate. I
found matters in a poor state at college—£500 in debt, and our
employers nearly £700 in arrears.

Thursday 9. Came to Baltimore ; passed the guard against the
plague in Philadelphia, set for prudence, one hundred miles off.
Oh ! the plague of sin ! Would to God we were more guarded
against its baleful influence ! I was sick, weary, and feeble ; yet,
preaching being appointed for me in town, I sounded the alarm on
Jer. xiii. 16. " Give glory to God before he cause darkness," &c.

Friday 10. I hasted to Annapolis.

Saturday 11. Attended a quarterly meeting at Bignal's, in a
large tobacco-house, where I enlarged on the weighty words of
our Lord " Because iniquity shall abound, the love of many shall
wax cold."

Monday 13. I opened and applied the charge given by David to
Solomon, at G. R——'s, well adapted to the children of the Methodists.

Tuesday 14. I had a large congregation of serious women at
Capt. Weems's. To these I preached on John xiv. 16.   1. Christ
is the way to God by precept, example, and power. 2. The
truth ; the true Messiah, revealing the truths of God, the standard
and judge of all. 3. The life, by his merit and spirit, leading to
the knowledge of God in his perfections and glory.

Wednesday 15. I enlarged on " Without me ye can do nothing,"
and applied it to sinners, Pharisees, hypocrites, backsliders, believers, and sanctified souls.

Saturday 18. I attended a quarterly meeting at H——'s ; where
I exhorted the people to " Forget the things that are behind, and
to reach towards the things that are before"—i. e. Establishment
in grace ; walking with God ; resignation to his will ; meekness,
humility, perfect love, a glorious resurrection, and eternal glory—
" Leave the things that are behind"—see Hebr. vi. 1. and v. 12.
" Leave these ;" so as not to rest in conviction, repentance,
faith, justification, nor in church ordinances, as being the whole of
religion, or any part thereof, any farther than as they lead us to
Christ. We had some life in the love-feast, and in public service :

but there is a dearth here. The circuit has suffered for want of a preacher.

Sabbath 19. I came to Baltimore, and preached on Amos iii. 6, 7, 8.

Monday 20. Our conference began. I was well pleased with the stations, and the faithful talk most of the brethren gave us of their experience and exercises. I preached a charity sermon on " Hath God cast away his people." We collected £27, which was augmented to £43, and applied it to the supplying the wants of the distressed preachers.

Sunday 26. I preached, and ordained elders and deacons, at the Point, and at night in town spoke on Jeremiah ix. 12—14.

Monday 27. I left Baltimore in a cool, stormy day. We dined with Capt. White, on the north branch of the Patuxent, and had only time to warm, eat, drink, and pray. We hasted on to S. Turner's. We stopped on the way at the house of some old, forgotten English people : I talked plainly to the poor old woman, and commended the family to God in prayer. I rode to my old friend A——'s, and spent the evening in Christian conversation, writing, and prayer.

VIRGINIA.—Tuesday 28. Five of us came to Stafford courthouse. The next day we dined and prayed at F——'s, and in the evening reached Collins's, an old stand in Caroline county.

November, Friday 1. We breakfasted at Ellis's tavern, and next day rode to Richmond and Manchester, and came to B——'s, and preached to a congregation mostly women. Thence we proceeded to J. A——'s. I was so hoarse it was with difficulty I spoke to the people. In six days we have rode two hundred and twenty miles.

Sunday 3. We had to ride ten miles to quarterly meeting at T——'s chapel. I did not expect to be heard ; but, to my great surprise, I had not spoken long before my voice was clear. We had a melting time under brother John Easter—was much blessed with the local brethren. Brothers W—— and A—— were recommended to the office of deacons, and ordained. Brother W—— with two others, are appointed to wait on me at the ensuing conference—what for will then be better known.

Tuesday 5. I rode to brother B.'s, and the next day preached at Charity Chapel. It was a day appointed by the bishop and committee of the Episcopal church to be observed as a day of fasting. I feel my mind greatly eased relative to those who have lately separated from us and set out as reformers. Let the Lord look to his own church.

Thursday 7. We had a serious congregation at Cumberland quarterly meeting : some appeared to be much engaged.

My Sabbath day's journey was from sister L——'s to a new chapel in Prince Edward, twenty miles, where, after preaching on Matt. xxiv. 12—14. I was led to say a few things for myself—as to my coming to and staying in America : of the exercise of that power which was given by the first and confirmed by the last general conference. Many of the people thought me not that monster I had been represented. I thought this the more necessary here, as great pains had been taken to misrepresent and injure me in this congregation and neighbourhood. So it is ; when I am absent some will say what they please of me. After sacrament we came, weary and hungry, to brother R——'s, by whom we were kindly entertained. My soul is staid on the Lord, although Satan will push at me by means of the world, the flesh, and false brethren.

Tuesday 12. I preached at brother T——'s, on Nottaway-River. The people here have been unsettled by the divisions which a few persons have endeavoured to make in our societies.

Thursday 14. Rode from brother N——'s to Salem, and, after preaching, to brother M——'s, in Brunswick, making it about thirty miles, without eating or drinking.

Friday 15. I had a few serious souls at Roses-Creek. Here I received the happy tidings from John Dickins, that he, with his family, have been preserved during the late contagion in the city of Philadelphia.

Sunday 17. At Meritt's chapel ; the weather was rainy and uncomfortable, and brother E—— very unwell. The next day I rode from brother F——'s, about twenty miles, to preach a funeral discourse on the death of our dear brother Cox. The Lord's power was present. Brother Bruce preached at Jones's chapel on " Sowing to the flesh." I was happy in God at brother P——'s, in the evening. The next day I staid at the chapel until it appeared as if I was well nigh chilled through, and to cure me had to ride twelve miles to brother Moss's : thence twenty miles to brother Bonner's, where I met several of the brethren in great peace and love. Came to J. Smith's, and had a good season on Eph. iv. 22—25. The seeds of discord have been sown here, but they have not taken deep root. Several of the preachers came in, and we spen the evening, and were happy together.

Sunday 24. Hasted to Petersburg. Came in a little before noon, and preached on Isai. lxvi. 4, 5.

Monday 25, and the following days, were spent in conference. The preachers were united, and the Lord was with us of a truth. There were fifty-five preachers present. I had some difficulties respecting the stations; but there was a willingness among the brethren to go where they were appointed, and all was well.

Our disaffected brethren have had a meeting at the Piney-Grove, in Amelia circuit, and appointed three men to attend this conference. One of these delegates appears to be satisfied, and has received ordination amongst us since he was delegated by them; the other two appeared, and we gave them a long talk. My mind has been closely employed in the business of the conference, so that I have slept only about sixteen hours in four nights.

Friday 29. Rode nineteen miles, and preached at Mrs. Cox's barn. The next day we reached brother Mooring's, in Surry.

Sunday, December 1. My mind was in a state of heaviness. I endeavoured to preach on 2 Cor. xiii. 5. It is heavy times here; but the work is the Lord's, and I wish to leave it all to him. In discoursing on the above text I pursued nearly the following method—

I. Such as profess to have experienced religion should examine whether they have not let some fundamental doctrines slip.

II. Examine into the nature and effects of faith; it is the substance of things hoped for, in a penitent state; and the evidence of things not seen, in a justified state.

III. They should know themselves, whether they are seekers, believers, or backsliders.

IV. They should prove themselves, to themselves, to their ministers, the world, and the church of God.

V. That if they have heart-religion, Christ is in them—the meek, loving, pure mind of Christ.

Monday 2. Came to Ellison's chapel, in Sussex.

Tuesday 3. Preached at Lane's chapel: it was low times and cold weather. Thence to my old friend Moss's, near Sussex court-house. I have lately read Blair's Sermons, where I find some very beautiful things: they contain good moral philosophy; and his Sermon on Gentleness, is worthy the taste of Queen Charlotte; and if money were any thing towards paying for knowledge, I should think that sermon worth two hundred pounds sterling—which some say the Queen gave him.

Thursday 5. After riding several miles out of my way, I came to dear brother and sister Parham's—two Israelites indeed. I was unwell, yet spent the evening comfortably. Next day I had a long ride to Pelham's, in Greensville; where I enlarged, to a small, serious congregation on 2 Cor. xii. 15.—the grand subjects of the faithful minister's care.

Saturday 7. Rode through the rain to Woolsey's barn—now Dromgoole's chapel.

Next day we had but twenty miles to ride for our Sabbath day's journey. Came to Roanoak, and enlarged on Eph. iii. 7, 8.—In which I showed, 1st, How a minister of Christ is made ; 2d, To whom he is to preach ; 3d, What he is to preach, viz. the unsearchable riches of Christ ; 4th, The humble opinion the ministers of Christ entertain of themselves.

NORTH CAROLINA.—Monday 9. Crossed Roanoak in a flat, with seven horses ; but we were mercifully preserved. Came to Warrenton. I had a violent pain in my head, and my horse's back being injured, I stopped at Myrick's, having rode only twenty miles.

Tuesday 10. Came to Lewisburg, and held our conference at Green Hills, about a mile from town. Great peace and unity prevailed amongst us. The preachers cheerfully signed an instrument, expressing their determination to submit to, and abide by what the general conference has done.

Friday 13. Our conference rose : it was agreed that the next conference should be held in Petersburg : there the preachers from North Carolina, Greenbriar, the Centre and South Districts of Virginia, may all meet, and change properly, and unite together for their own and the people's good.

Saturday 14. Rode to father P. B——'s :—Oh that the last days of ancient Methodists may be the best ! I have a cold and pains ; but there is ease in peace, and love, and communion with God.

Sunday 15. We had as many people at father B——'s as we could find room for : I delivered some alarming words from Isaiah lxv. 2.

Monday 16. Rode up Neuse ; fed at Tomkins's, and hasted to the widow Carson's, (about forty miles.)

Tuesday 17. After riding about twenty-six miles to R——'s, I gave them a short discourse on " The foundation of God standeth sure :" after eating, we had to ride sixteen or eighteen miles in the evening home with brother M'Gee. In the morning we crossed Deep-River, in a flat, not without danger. Thence down Caraway creek, to Randolph Town ; thence to Huwary, at Fuller's ford.

Here we were assisted by some young men with a canoe. Thank the Lord, both men and horses were preserved. The young men *sometimes prayed* and *sometimes swore.* After riding three miles, came to Wood's, but Russel's was the place of preaching, where I found some who had heard me in Virginia many years past; I laboured to speak, although my throat was very sore : the hearts of the people appeared to be cold, as well as their bodies.

Friday 20. I had to ride thirty miles by two o'clock ; but was so poorly I declined preaching. Saturday and Sunday I spent at I. Randle's : I gave place to brothers M‘K—— and B——. On Sunday evening, I gave the family a discourse at W. Randle's.

Monday 23. Crossed Rockey-River : this is a bold stream : it rises in Mecklenburg, North Carolina ; and after running eighty or ninety miles, empties itself into Pee Dee, a little below Montgomery.

SOUTH CAROLINA.—Came to Blakeney's, on the waters of Lynch's creek : here I preached to about forty people ; it being Christmas day.

Thursday 26. We crossed various branches which empty into Pee Dee about ten miles below Ports-Ferry : we passed the hanging rock to J. H——'s.

Friday 27. We set out at sunrise : the weather was cold and frosty : we made it twenty-two miles to Camden. After dinner we crossed the river, and came to Marshall's.

Saturday 28. We set out very early, and came through pine and oak barrens, twenty-five miles : about one o'clock I was willing to sit down and rest. I have lately felt all the grace I had put to trial : through mercy I am kept from sin, and long to be perfect in faith and patience, love and suffering : I am sometimes tempted to wish to die ; but I fear it is wrong : I rather chuse to wait the Lord's time.

Sunday 28. With some difficulty I attended at the meeting-house near Marshall's.

Monday 30. We rode forty-five miles to brother Cook's, on Broad-River ; and the next day to brother Finch's : here we are to have about thirty preachers from South Carolina and Georgia. We were straitened for room, having only twelve feet square to confer, sleep, and for the accommodation of those who were sick.—Brother B—— was attacked with the dysentery.

Wednesday, January 1, 1794. We removed brother B—— into a room without fire. We hastened the business of our conference as fast as we could. After sitting in a close room with a very large fire, I retired into the woods nearly an hour, and was seized with a severe chill, an inveterate cough and fever, with a sick stomach : with difficulty I sat in conference the following day ; and I could get but little rest ; brother B——'s moving so frequently, and the brethren's talking, disturbed me. Sick as I was, I had to ordain four elders and six deacons ; never did I perform with such a burthen. I took a powerful emetic. I was attended by Doctor D——.

I found I must go somewhere to get rest. The day was cloudy, and threatened snow ; however, brother R. E—— and myself made out to get seven miles to dear old brother A. Yeargin's house. The next day came on a heavy fall of snow, which continued two days, and was from six to ten inches deep. I had to let some blood : I made use of flaxseed, and afterward of betony tea, both which were of use to me. I must be humbled before the Lord, and have great searching of heart.

Monday 13. Rode thirty miles ; although the weather was damp and unpromising, and came to Herbert's store, on Broad-River. I was so weak that my exercise and clothing almost overcame me. The next day we passed Connelly's ferry ; and got nothing for ourselves until we had rode forty-six miles to Colonel Rumph's, where we had every thing, and were free and comfortable.

Sunday 19. Rode to the Cypress, where I could not rest without giving them a little sermon.

Monday 20. I reached the city of Charleston. Here I began to rest : my cold grew better. Doctor Ramsey directed me to the use of laudanum, nitre, and bark, after cleansing the stomach with an emetic. The kindness of sister Hughes was very great. I have written largely to the west, and declined visiting those parts this year. The American Alps, the deep snows, and great rains ; swimming the creeks and rivers, riding in the night, sleeping on the earthen floors, more or less of which I must experience, if I go to the western country, might at this time cost me my life. I have only been able to preach four times in three weeks.

I have had sweet peace at times since I have been here ; the love of meetings ; (especially those for prayer) the increase of hearers ; the attention of the people ; my own better feelings ; and the increasing hope of good that prevails among the preachers, lead me to think that " the needy shall not always be forgotten, nor the expectation of the poor fail." I have been pleased in reading Prince's Christian History, of about four hundred pages : it was a cordial to my soul in the time of my affliction. It is Me-

thodism in all its parts. I have a great desire to reprint an abridg-
ment of it, to show the apostate children what their fathers were.
I have read Gordon's History of the American Revolution: here
we view the suffering straits of the American army; and, what is
greatly interesting, General Washington's taking his farewell of his
officers—what an affecting scene! I could not but feel through the
whole of the description. What, then, was the sight! O, how
minds are made great with affliction and suffering! Poor Beverly
Allen, who has been going from bad to worse these seven or eight
years—speaking against me to preachers and people, and writing to
Mr. Wesley and Doctor Coke, and being thereby the source of most
of the mischief that has followed; and lastly, having been agent for
Mr. ——, is now secured in jail for shooting Major Forsyth through
the head. The Major was marshall for the federal court in Georgia, and was about to serve a writ upon B. A——: the master-piece
of all is, a petition is prepared, declaring him to have shown marks
of insanity previous to his killing the Major! The poor Methodists also must unjustly be put to the rack on his account, although
he has been expelled from amongst us these two years.—I have
had my opinion of him these nine years; and gave Doctor C——
my thoughts of him before his ordination: I pity, I pray for him—
that if his life is given up to justice, his soul may yet be saved.

Friday, February 14. I enjoy peace of mind, and am closely employed in reading my Bible; and a collection of sermons delivered at Bery-street 1733, by Watts, Guyse, Jennings, Neal, Hubbard,
and Price, containing upwards of five hundred pages.

Sunday 16. I preached in the morning on Phil. ii. 30. and in the
evening again. I was tried in spirit: I had not more than one
hundred white people to hear me. Brother S. and myself let
loose; and according to custom they fled: they cannot, they will
not, endure sound doctrine.

Monday 17. I was employed in reading and visiting.

Tuesday 18. I feel restless to move on, and my wish is to die in
the field. I have had a time of deep dejection of spirits, affliction
of body; loss of sleep, and trouble of soul. I have, in the course
of my stay here, had frequent visits from the blacks; among whom
I find some gracious souls.

Wednesday 19. I find this to be a barren place; I long to go to
my work. When gloomy melancholy comes on, I find it best to
think as little as may be about distressing subjects. Thursday,
Friday, and Saturday, I visited sundry families. It seems as if a
strange providence holds me here: I am sometimes afraid to eat,

drink, or even to talk, unless it be of God and religion. I shall certainly feel a Paradise when I go hence. I am not unemployed; yet I might be much better occupied for God and souls.

Tuesday 25. Last evening we had a love-feast; and the poor Africans spoke livingly of the goodness of God. I am now preparing to leave this city, where I have experienced consolation, afflictions, tribulations, and labour.

Friday 28. I now leave Charleston; the seat of Satan, dissipation and folly : ten months hereafter, with the permission of divine Providence, I expect to see it again. My horse proving unruly, and unwilling to take the boat to Hadrill's point, we changed our course, crossed at Clemon's ferry, and then came the road to Lenoir's ferry : we passed the plantations of the great, lying east and west; their rice fields under water. We got no refreshment until we came to S——'s, thirty-four miles, except the little our horses got at the ferry.

Saturday, March 1. We set out in great spirits, having sixteen miles to the ferry; where we were detained six hours. We hoped to have been in Georgetown by sunset. Now we thought of travelling until midnight : we came to Cedar Creek, which we found in a bad state. We stayed at the ferry; being persuaded we could not reach Georgetown time enough for meeting.

Sabbath morning. We directed our course westward, and came along, drooping and solitary, to M——'s ferry, about twenty-five miles. We rode up to a large house, and were asked in to drink brandy : three men and two women appeared to be set in to drink the *pure stuff*, glass after glass; we were glad to retreat. There came on a storm of rain, with thunder and lightning. I was unwilling to go to ——, expecting the same kind of Sabbath devotion there. We travelled a most dreadful road to Black-River, and had plenty of water above and below us. After riding fifteen miles, we came to the widow B——'s, where we got a shelter; still we had our fears: there is such a quantity of water in the swamp and lowlands, that our feet are kept very uncomfortable, and some places are impassable. Isaac Smith, in all these difficulties and trials of swamps, colds, rains, and starvation, was my faithful companion.

After riding twenty-seven miles without eating, how good were the potatoes and fried gammon! we then had only ten miles to brother Rembert's; where we arrived about seven o'clock. I confess my soul and body have been powerfully tried.—What blanks are in this country—and how much worse are the rice plantations! If a man-of-war is " a floating hell," these are standing ones ; wicked

masters, overseers, and negroes—cursing, drinking—no Sabbaths; no sermons. But hush! perhaps my journal will never see
the light; and if it does, matters may mend before that time; and
it is probable I shall be beyond their envy or good will. O
wretched priests, thus to lead the people on in blindness!

Thursday 6. We had family meeting at brother R——'s : I gave
them a long discourse on the last words of David, 2 Sam. xxiii. 5.
"Although my house be not so with God, yet he hath made with
me an everlasting covenant, ordered in all things and sure, for this
is all my salvation and all my desire, (pleasure or delight,) although
he make it not to grow." 1. I considered how we enter into covenant with God. 2. On man's part it is ordered to repent, believe,
love, obey, suffer, &c. and in a word, to attend to every duty God
hath enjoined. 3. That this is all the delight of a gracious soul—
that his eternal all is rested upon the covenant relation he bears to
the Lord. David appears, 1. To have been looking to Solomon's
peaceable kingdom. 2. To Christ, who was to come of David's
seed. 3. Parents, and gracious souls, may say the commonwealth,
the church, their families, &c. are not as they could wish; yet God
is their portion. What distresses were experienced in the families
of ancient saints! see the history of the families of Adam, Noah,
Abraham, Isaac, Jacob, Eli, Samuel, David, and others of whom we
read. My time is short—this may be my last to speak, or theirs
to hear: we are not only creatures of a year, but of a day, an
hour.

Sunday 9. I preached on Romans v. 20, 21.

Monday 10. We held a little conference to provide for Charleston, Georgetown, Edisto, and Santee : some are afraid that if we
retain none among us who trade in slaves, the preachers will not be
supported, but my fear is that we shall not be able to supply this
state with preachers.

Tuesday 11. I had to preach to the respectable people of Camden—where I suppose I had two hundred hearers in the court-
house. It was heavy work, my body and faith being both weak—
some trifled; some felt; and perhaps more understood.

Wednesday 12. We missed our way to the chapel called Gran-
nies-Quarter ; and made it thirty miles to Horton's, at the Hanging-
Rock, on a very warm day, without any refreshment, except a
little biscuit.

Thursday 13. Rode thirty miles more to the Waxsaws, after
preaching at the chapel in the woods. I went to brother T——'s,
where we had a room to ourselves ; and our horses were richly

fed : this was a great favour—such as we do not generally receive
in this country.

Saturday 15. We set out under discouraging prospects ; having
had a heavy rain the night before. We came to Shepherds ;
where we had to swim our horses along side a canoe, and had they
not struggled powerfully, and freed themselves from among the
bushes and grape-vines, they had certainly drowned : we returned
across the stream, and then brought them down the creek, to a place
where there were no trees in the way, and we got safe across.

Sunday 16. The waters being still high, our passage difficult,
and having no inclination to travel on the Sabbath, we continued at
S——'s, where we stayed the night before. Notice was circula-
ted through the neighbourhood, and by eleven o'clock there was
collected a congregation of sixty or seventy people.

Monday 17. We set out, and passed Charlotte, in Mecklenburg ;
here I learned that meeting was appointed for me at A——'s. I
came to L. Hill's, where I met with N. W. and D. A. having rode
thirty-four miles. By the time I reach justice White's I shall
make out to have rode about one thousand miles in three months ;
and to have stopped six weeks of the time with great reluctance.
I preached at —— on 2 Tim. ii. 12—17. I, 1. Gave the marks
of a Christian ; one of which is, that he suffers persecution. 2.
The marks of heretics and schismatics ; the former oppose the
established doctrines of the Gospel ; the latter will divide Christians. 3. That we must continue in what we have been taught
by the word, the Spirit, and faithful ministers of Christ. 4. That
the Holy Scriptures are the standard sufficient for ministers and
people, to furnish them to every good work.

Thursday 20. I directed my course in company with my faithful
fellow-labourer, Tobias Gibson, up the Catabaw, settled mostly by
the Dutch. A barren spot for religion. Having rode in pain
twenty-four miles, we came, weary and hungry, to O——'s tavern ;
and were glad to take what came to hand. Four miles forward
we came to Howes-Ford, upon Catabaw-River, where we could
neither get a canoe nor guide. We entered the water in an improper place, and were soon among the rocks and in the whirl-
pools : my head swam, and my horse was affrighted : the water
was to my knees, and it was with difficulty we retreated to the
same shore. We then called to a man on the other side, who
came and piloted us across, for which I paid him well. My horse
being afraid to take the water a second time, brother Gibson
crossed, and sent me his ; and our guide took mine across. We

went on, but our troubles were not at an end: night came on, and it was very dark. It rained heavily, with powerful lightning and thunder. We could not find the path that turned out to Connell's. In this situation we continued until midnight or past; at last we found a path which we followed till we came to dear old father Harper's plantation; we made for the house, and called; he answered, but wondered who it could be; he inquired whence we came; I told him we would tell that when we came in, for it was raining so powerfully we had not much time to talk: when I came dripping into the house, he cried "God bless your soul, is it brother Asbury? wife, get up." Having had my feet and legs wet for six or seven hours, causes me to feel very stiff.

Friday 21. We set forward towards brother White's, and took our time to ride twelve miles.

Saturday 22. My soul enjoys peace; but Oh! for more of God! This campaign has made me "groan, being burthened." Bad news on my coming to the mountains; neither preachers nor elders have visited Swanino since last October; poor people—poor preachers that are not more stable: but all flesh is grass, and I am grass. I have provided brothers G. and L. for the westward. I wrote a plan for stationing; and desired the dear preachers to be as I am in the work: I have no interest, no passions, in their appointments; my only aim is to care and provide for the flock of Christ. I see I must not leave Charleston till the third or fourth week in March; then the rains will subside, and the creeks and rivers be passable; and so shall we escape the danger of drowning ourselves and horses. I feel that my sufferings have been good preaching to me—especially in crossing the waters. I am solemnly moved, in not visiting my Holstein and Kentucky brethren. It may be their interest to desire the preservation of my life: while living I may supply them with preachers, and with men and money. I feel resolved to be wholly the Lord's; weak as I am, I have done nothing, I am nothing, only for Christ! or I had long since been cut off as an unfaithful servant; Christ is all, and in all I do, or it had not been done; or when done, had, by no means, been acceptable.

NORTH CAROLINA.—Sunday 23. My subject at justice White's was Hebr. ii. 1, 2, 3. I had more people than I expected. I have visited this place once a year; but M. K—— and L. have both failed coming at all; I pity them and the people. If I could think myself of any account, I might say, with Mr. Wesley, "If it be so while I am alive, what will it be after my death?" I have written several letters to the westward to supply my lack of service. I am mightily wrought upon for New-Hampshire, Province of Maine, Vermont, and Lower Canada.

Saturday 29. Started for Nolenten's and came part of the way alone. After winding about the creeks and hills, came to a cabin: here I found a few serious people, to whom I preached on 1 Tim. iv. 8. after which I spent the evening with dear brother S. in his clean cabin.

Sunday 30 After riding about five miles, I came to a meeting-house : it was a cabin half floored, with long open windows between the logs.

Monday 31. I had the house filled with serious people, and found much to say on Ruth i. 16, 17. whatever weight there might have been in the discourse, I was happy in my own soul.

Tuesday, April 1. I was very happy whilst riding alone down to Doctor Brown's : on my way, I saw Babel, the Baptist-Methodist house, about which there has been so much quarrelling : it is made of logs, and is no great matter. I am astonished at pro-fessors, old professors, neglecting family and private prayer—Lord, help! for there is but little genuine religion in the world.

Wednesday 2. Came to E.'s meeting-house, near Hunting Creek, in Surry county : here I met with some old disciples from Mary-land, Delaware, and Virginia, who have known me these twenty-two years. Our meeting was attended with mutual pleasure : my soul enjoyed much sweetness with these people. There has been some trouble amongst them ; but I know God is with them. I was secretly led to treat on sanctification at W.'s ; and if the Lord will help me, I am resolved to speak more on this blessed doctrine. After preaching, I came to Cokesbury school, at Hardy Jones : it is twenty feet square, two stories high, well set out with doors and windows ; this house is not too large, as some others are : it stands on a beautiful eminence, and overlooks the Lowlands, and river Yadkin.

Monday 7. I set out alone, and missing my way, got entangled in the bush and thickets, and made it about twenty miles : although it was a trial to me, it might be intended to prevent the poor peo-ple from being disappointed who came late.

I had the pleasure of dining and drinking tea with a Moravian minister, who has the charge of the congregation at Muddy-Creek. Next day I called at Salem.

I rode twenty miles to Levin Ward's, on the head waters of Dan-River, Stokes county. I was greatly fatigued, but having no

appointment to preach, after a good night's rest, I was much refreshed. Having little opportunity of being alone, I wandered
into the field for solitude. I met with P. S from old Lynn, a
child of Providence : after passing solemn scenes at sea, he was
taken and left in the Lowlands of North Carolina. First a Christian, then a preacher. He was stationed in Guilford ; but offered
himself a volunteer for Swanino ; which station hath been vacant
nearly six months ; one of the preachers appointed there being
sick, and the other married ; and now because I have power to
send a preacher to these poor people, some are pleased to account
me, and call me a despot.

Friday 11. I went to Simpson's house. I was greatly chilled,
and unable to preach. The house was very open, but brother B.
sounded away bravely. It appeared as if my fingers were nearly
frozen. I went home with brother C. and had every thing comfortable.

Saturday 12. I had a small congregation, but a good time with
some feeling souls at brother J.'s, on my choice subject, Hebr.
iii. 12. We have rumours of war with England. But the Lord
reigneth, although the earth be so much disquieted. I spent the
evening with brothers B. and S.

I was in the clouds on Sunday 13. : my body was full of pain,
and my mind much dejected. I came through Rockingham, and
saw my old friends : lodged with father Low, who is seventy-six
years of age, and happy in God.

Monday 14. Brother Sands set out for Swanino. Had I ventured
to Kentucky, how should I have stood the wilderness, with four or
five days of such cold, rainy weather as we have lately had ; I was
thankful to God that I changed my course. I feel wholly devoted
to God, and greatly wish to see more fruit of my labour.

Friday 18. I rose early—crossed Pudding-Creek, Banister, and
Bearskin, and came to brother C——'s, five miles from Pittsylvania
court-house. I met with my old friends Jones and W. D. and had
a comfortable meeting.

VIRGINIA.—Monday 21. Rode with brothers B. and M. (who met
me the day before) to brother Landrum's, and gave them a short
sermon. I was happy in the company of the dear preachers.
Oh ! my soul, trust thou in the Lord ! O for Zion's glory ! come
Lord Jesus, come quickly !

Wednesday 23. I attended the funeral of R. O. ; who, I learn,
died of a consumption, in the fear and love of God. I was too
systematical for my congregation, who were wild and unawakened.

I baptised a few children, then crossed Symes-Ferry, and came twelve miles to brother Spencer's, in Charlotte county : here report saith, that there is sad work with those who have left us, and who are now exerting themselves to form as strong a party as they can ; the principal of these are J. O'K. E. A. J. K. and J. C. I learn by a letter from J. Ellis, that matters are not desperate : this letter, with some others, I shall reserve for a future day. If the real cause of this division was known, I think it would appear, that one wanted to be immoveably fixed in a district ; another wanted money ; a third wanted ordination ; a fourth wanted liberty to do as he pleased about slaves, and not to be called to an account, &c.

Thursday, Friday, and Saturday, I spent in private application.

Sunday 27. I had a crowded congregation at Reeve's chapel, those who had just left us appeared very shy. I was very unwell, and said but little on the division : I told them how long I had been in the country, how I had laboured, and what I had gained. After all we shall see what the end of all this work will be.

Wednesday 30. I preached (though not of choice) at Charlotte court-house, here Mr. —— met me and charged me with saying at —— "that they would take off my head." I told him I did not remember to have said so, but if I did, I must certainly have meant the Episcopacy of our Church ; he answered, that in that I was very right, he strove to do it with all his might ; yet he talked of *union*, and hoped I would do my part—At what ? Why to destroy, first, the Episcopacy, and then the conference—or at least its power and authority. I went to Major R.'s and was treated very kindly.

Saturday, May 2. I had a serious congregation, and a good meeting at C's. Came to Pride's church, in Amelia county, where there are no very great prospects. I was at the kind widow C.'s, on Appomattox-River, thence to brother H.'s ; where I was attended by brothers F——, M——, B——, T——, and W——. I learn I am set forth as an enemy to the country, that I am laying up money to carry away to England, or elsewhere ; but in the midst of all, I bless God for peace in my spirit. Let them curse, but God will bless, and his faithful preachers will love and pity me.

Friday 8. After preaching at S——'s chapel on Peter's denial, I rode to brother G——'s, twenty miles ; my mind was heavy, my body weak and feeble ; O, that I had in the wilderness a lodging place ! I ordained brother G. and baptised his son Philip ; a dreadful rumour followed me from last Sabbath. I felt humble

and thankful that I could suffer ; I think more of religion now than
ever. O, my God, I am thine ; glory to Christ for ever!

Monday 11. Rode forty miles to S——'s, and preached the
next day ; but it seemed as if my discourse had almost as well
have been Greek, such spiritual death prevails among the people.
After preaching, brothers H. B. W. and myself rode to brother
W——'s, in Campbell county.

I preached in the court house at New-London, where I had a
large, serious, and polite congregation ; I dined with my old friend,
countryman, and neighbour, Joseph Perkins, who is superintendent
of the armoury.   In this county (Bedford) there are thirteen
societies of Methodists, three or four of which are large ; there
are about ten local preachers, who labour for Christ and souls.

Saturday 16, and Sunday 17. Was quarterly meeting at Wilson's
chapel. The first day I gave place to brother B——. Sabbath
day, after sacrament, and love-feast, I preached on Rev. iii. 20.
The people within were serious, those without had their own talk
and entertainment. I kept the Sabbath in the crowd in the best
manner I could. I came off under rain and clouds to a town called
Liberty, and preached in the court-house, but did not find freedom
to eat bread or drink water in that place. Why should I receive
aught from those who renounce my service? I went to friend
S——'s, who has a godly wife, and was kindly entertained ; I wish
to serve the Methodists who can hear with candour ; but I am not
fond of preaching at places where the prejudices of the people run
so high.

Friday 19. I had about one hundred and fifty hearers at Edson's,
and had liberty in preaching ; brothers M. and B. assisted me. My
soul is in peace and perfect love. I purpose to preach present
conviction, conversion, and sanctification. I might do many things
better than I do ; but this I discover not till afterward. Christ is
all to my soul ; if my labours are not blest, yet my soul shall rejoice
in the Lord and be blest.

Thursday 21. Came to M—— on Mill-Creek, in Botetourt's
county, where I was met by brother I. E. who assisted me next
day in preparing the minutes.

Saturday 23. Preached at Fincastle, and had very few to hear
except our own people ; came the same evening to E. M——'s,
where we were to hold our conference : here I met the brethren
from Kentucky, and received a number of letters.

Sunday 24. I was enabled to preach a searching discourse to
near one thousand souls on Isa. lii. 8.

Monday 25. We were closely employed in the business of the conference.

Wednesday 27. We went over the mountain to Rockbridge county. We crossed the north branch of James-River, half a mile from the town of Lexington; dined at the Red House, and came to Mr. F——'s on the south branch of Shanadoah. Thence I urged my way by Stanton through the rain, without any boots; and having sold my oil cloth a few days before, I was wet from head to foot. My mind is in peace, waiting till my change come—hanging on Jesus for everlasting rest. We have a valuable house here, (Newtown) and three local preachers; at Charlestown a good house and one local preacher; I feel as though it would be a long time before I go through this country again. For some days I have had an inflammatory complaint in my ear, it is now removed into my mouth.

I spent Monday 25th, and Tuesday 26th at brother ——'s, and was very much indisposed. Came to Winchester; here is a good meeting-house. I had many to hear my very feeble testimony on Romans v. 10. Doctor —— made a gargle of rose leaves, nitre, and spirits of vitriol, which was of use to my throat. I came on Thursday to J. H.'s, and employed brother A. to preach, my throat continuing very bad. I found my mind greatly resigned to the will of God under my affliction.

Sick, wet, and weary, I found a comfortable retreat in the house of R. Hamson; I have not been so thoroughly soaked in two years; I think I have need of a leathern coat that will stand all weathers. I got two men to *canoe* me across the river; they brought me over safe, and appeared to be satisfied with a quarter of a dollar each. Saturday was an awful day to me; my ear was exceedingly painful.

Sunday, June 1. I ventured to the church in the rain, and bore a feeble testimony for nearly an hour on 2 Pet. i. 4.

It was with difficulty I could attend the conference; my throat, and passage to the ear being inflamed, and I had also a chill and high fever. We had preaching morning, noon, and night, and had peace and consolation in our deliberations. On the last day of the conference I delivered a discourse on 1 Cor. i. 5. and we concluded with a solemn sacrament.

I next came to Shanadoah county. We have had awful rains or about two weeks—to these I have been exposed in my afflicted state.

Sunday 8. Preached at Newtown, little notice being given, and few people attending.

Monday 9. Rested at brother Phelp's. My mind is in peace; but I feel the spiritual death of the people; they are not what they were in religion. I am now on the head branches of Opec-ken. I stopped awhile at J. H.'s, and then came on to Shepherds-Town. It was a very instructing time to me; I cannot pretend to preach; yet I talk a little to the dear people, who flock to see and hear me by hundreds. I hope to be as much resigned to a life of affliction as a life of health; and thus may I be perfect in love and wholly crucified with Christ! I concluded after my high fever, and my being forced to bed, that it was out of the question for me to attempt to speak; but when I saw the people coming on every side, and thought " This may be the last time," and considered I I had not been there for nearly five years, I took my staff, faintly ascended the hill, and held forth on 1 John i. 6, 7. and felt strengthened, having a clear view of the word of God.—After meeting, we administered the sacrament, and I then returned to my bed. I preached at Fredericktown. Rode to Liberty; when I came there, I was so faint, and my strength so spent, that I felt as if I could by no means attempt to preach; but after brother R. had sung a hymn and prayed, I made a feeble attempt on Gal. i. 11, 12.

MARYLAND.—Tuesday 17. I rode twenty-three miles to the stone chapel, where I preached on Peter's denial of his Lord.

Wednesday 18. I once more came to Baltimore; where, after having rested a little, I submitted to have my likeness taken: it seems they will want a copy; if they wait longer, perhaps they may miss it. Those who have gone from us in Virginia, have drawn a picture of me, which is not *taken from the life.* We called a meeting at Cokesbury, and made some regulations relative to the salaries of the teachers, and the board of the students. I return-ed to Baltimore, and spent Sabbath day 22 there, and found the people but dull. Brother M'C. took his stand at the wind-mill between town and Point. My soul was quickened whilst applying these words, " Every knee shall bow, of things in heaven, things on earth, and things under the earth, and every tongue shall confess that Jesus Christ is Lord to the glory of God the Father;" I was grieved to find the hearts of the people so cold in religion: the world is a thief, stealing the heart from God.

Monday 23. Set out for Philadelphia. Spent a day at college.

Wednesday 25. I reached J. H——'s, very unwell with bodily infirmities, but I found Christ with me. Next day we breakfasted with brother M——, at Newport, dined at Chester, and preached in the evening at Philadelphia, after riding forty miles. I was weak and heavy in body and soul. I spent Friday in writing to my brethren in various parts who called for my advice.

PENNSYLVANIA.—Sunday 29. I preached at the new African church. Our coloured brethren are to be governed by the doctrine and discipline of the Methodists. We had some stir among the people at Ebenezer. In the evening we had a cold time at the great church on Amos iv. 11. This has been a hard day's work.

NEW-JERSEY.—Monday 30. I rode to Trenton an exceedingly warm day, and preached in the evening. We rode to Kingston; thence to Brunswick; thence to Bonham-town, and were weary enough when we got to Mr. B——'s. Poor brother S—— almost fainted, and went, outdone, to bed.

Came to Elizabethtown, and was grieved at the conduct of some of the preachers. Oh, how careful should each one be lest he become a stumbling-block and destroy precious souls! As I cannot help, so neither am I to answer for other men's sins.

Wednesday, July 2. I gave them a close discourse on 2 Cor. vii. 1. I had four Methodist and one Presbyterian minister to hear me, and we had some life in our souls.

Thursday 3. Came faint and weary to Powles-Hook, and felt my mind solemn and devoted to God. Thence crossed over to New-York, and found my friends kind and full of the world.

NEW-YORK.—Friday 4. Was the anniversary of Independence, I preached on 2 Pet. iii. 20, 21 : wherein—

I. I showed that all real Christians had escaped the pollutions of the world.

II. That it is possible for them to be entangled therein again and overcome.

III. That when this is the case they turn from the holy commandments delivered unto them.

IV. That the last state of such is worse than the first : for God is provoked, Christ slighted, the Spirit grieved, religion dishonoured, their understanding is darkened, the will is perverted, the conscience becomes insensible, and all the affections unmoved under the means of grace; they keep the wisdom of the serpent, but lose the harmlessness of the dove.

At dinner Mr. P—— spoke a word in favour of Mr. G——
(who was once with us, as also *he* had been) this brought on an
explanation of matters : my answer was, 1. That I did not make
rules, but had to execute them. 2. That any one who desired me
to act unconstitutionally, either insulted me as an individual, or the
conference as a body of men. I hardly know sometimes where
to set my foot ; I must be always on my guard, and take heed to
what I say of and before any one. Lord, make me upright in heart
and life before thee and all men !

Sunday 6. My mind was much agitated about trifles. I preached
in the morning on Hebr. xiii. 12. and we had a little move at
the sacrament. At three I preached in the new house, and again
in the evening at the old house, and gave a close exhortation to
the society.

Monday 7. Came to Berian's, near Kingsbridge, and thence to
the White-Plains, and dined with Lawyer H——, a member of our
society. I preached at Chester court-house to about one hundred
people : here are some living, gracious souls. Came in the
evening to King-street. I am not conscious of having sinned, but I
feel the infirmities of flesh and blood, and am in continual heaviness through manifold temptations. We had a sultry afternoon,
and a rough ride over the rocks and hills to Bedford, where I had
a feeble time in the town-house, on the fall of Peter. I was
sick, sore, tempted, and grieved :—and bade Bedford farewell !

CONNECTICUT.—Thursday 10. Came to Norwich, sixteen miles :
thence to Fairfield, twelve miles ; and in the evening reached Po-
quonack, making nearly forty miles, in very great debility of body.

Friday 11. We came to New-Haven ; thence to North-Haven ;
thence to Middlefields : the rain took us as we crossed the mountains, and made it heavy work. We found it poor times. Were I to
be paid by man for my services, I should rate them very high : it
is so painful at present for me to ride, that a small sum would not
tempt me to travel forty miles a day. I bless the Lord for daily
afflictions of body and mind : O may these things terminate in my
total resignation to the will of God !

Saturday 12. The rain detained us till noon ; I then came to Middletown, and preached at three o'clock in the Separate meeting-
house with some life. I lodged with the old prophet, Frothingham.
After this dear old man had laboured and suffered many years,
and had been imprisoned three times for the cause of Christ ; after he grew old and his memory failed, and he could not receive

the *new divinity*, they mistook and wrested his words ; and his con-gregation turned him out to starve :—but the Lord will provide.

Sunday 13, Was a great day—we had a love-feast, and I preached in the court-house, morning and evening, and brother S—— in the afternoon.

Monday 14. Rode fourteen miles to the city of Hartford ; and preached once more in Strong's church—and I roared out wonder-fully on Matt. xi. 28—30. Next day we came five miles to Spen-cer's, in Hartford ; where we have a neat house, forty by thirty-four feet. Thence I rode fifteen miles to Coventry, where I had a large congregation, and a comfortable meeting.

Wednesday 16. We had to make our way through heat, rocks, and dust, to Gargle's, at the wonderful water-works erected on the falls of the river : and thence to Pomfret's ; making in all thirty-three miles.

Thursday 17. We came a very rough path of five miles, to Douglass, then hasted twelve miles to Menden ; thence to Milford, three miles : we stopt at Mr. ——'s, and brother R—— went for-ward to supply my place : I was not able, nor was there time to speak much after he had done : the heat was intense—and there was very little shade, this country being long since untimbered.

Friday 18. Rode nineteen miles to Needham : if possible the heat and dust were greater than before, so that by the time we reached the appointment, we were nearly spent ; here we met with brother T——, and was grieved at the account of the impro-per conduct of ——, which causes noise, smoke, and fire enough.

Saturday 19. Came to Waltham to a quarterly meeting : at three o'clock I gave them a discourse on *the little flock*, to comfort the affrighted sheep. Sabbath day, we had love-feast at eight o'clock, sermon at half past ten o'clock, and again in the afternoon : there was some life in the love-feast, and sacrament also.

MASSACHUSETTS.—Monday 21. I came to Boston unwell in body, and with a heavy heart. I passed the road and bridge from the University to Boston. A noble road and grand bridge. We have very agreeable lodging in this town : but have to preach, as did our Lord, in an upper room. We had a prayer meeting, and the Lord was present to bless us.

Labour, and affliction of body and mind, make my poor heart sad, and spirits sink : why art thou cast down, O my soul, and why art thou disquieted within me ? hope thou in God : thou shalt yet praise him !

Tuesday 22. I took up my cross and preached in a large room, which was full enough, and warm enough ; I stood over the street ; the boys and Jack-tars made a noise, but mine was loudest ; there was fire in the smoke, some, I think, felt the word, and we shall yet have a work in Boston : my talk was strange and true to some.

Wednesday 23. I now go hence to Lynn ; once the joy, now the grief of our hearts : but we must go through all for Christ and souls.

Sunday 27. I gave them a sermon in the forenoon, and another in the afternoon. I could but rejoice in the prospect of leaving Lynn on Monday morning. The society here began in union. It is now incorporated in order to prevent the Methodists from being obliged, by law, to pay congregational tax.

I left Boston, and passed Roxbury, Dorchester, Milton, Stoughton, and Easton ; making it upwards of forty miles.

Tuesday 29. Rode through Attlebury to Providence—I had no freedom to eat bread, or drink water in that place. I found a calm retreat at Gen. Lippelt's, where we can rest ourselves : the Lord is in this family ; I am content to stay a day, and give them a sermon.

RHODE-ISLAND.—Thursday, August 1. I left Gen. Lippelt's and set out for New-London.

CONNECTICUT.—Friday 2. Brother R. preached in the evening in New-London.

Saturday 3. I made my appearance in the court-house, and preached to about seven hundred people with considerable freedom.

Sunday 4. We had love-feast in the upper room of the court-house ; where some spoke feelingly : our sermon and sacrament took up three hours. God is certainly among these people. We have set on foot a subscription to build a house of worship, and have appointed seven trustees.

Monday 5. Was one of the warmest days we have known. We left New-London and came through Norwich, twelve miles : this is a well improved country ; producing fine clover, oats, and flax.

We passed Windham, and Mansfield. We were met by a powerful thunder gust ; but stepping into a house, escaped its effects : this is one advantage which we have in travelling in the eastern, rather than the western country ; in the latter, oftentimes there is not a house for miles ; in the former there are houses always in

sight. We passed fine streams and excellent meadows; but the
heat was excessive, and we had no shade except now and then a
spreading tree : our horses were as though they had been rode
through a brook of water. We purchased our dinner on the way,
and it was sweet : we laboured hard till eight o'clock, and came
sick and weary to father P——'s, not less, in my judgment, than
forty miles.

Thursday 7. A day of rest and affliction of body : came to Tolland
very unwell. I find my soul stayed upon God in perfect love, and
wait his holy will in all things.

Saturday 9. I preached in a school-house at the north end of
Tolland, and had the house filled.

Sunday 10. Brother R——, though sick, went to Coventry, and
I was left alone at Tolland ; where I preached in the forenoon on
Acts ii. 37, 38. with some freedom ; and in the afternoon on
Colos. ii. 6. and found it heavy work. After meeting I was taken
with a dysentery, (attended with great sinking of bodily powers)
which held me most of the night. Monday I was better, and
preached in a school-house at Ellington. I felt great dejection of
spirit, but no guilt or condemnation. Ah! here are the iron walls
of prejudice ; but God can break them down. Out of fifteen
United States, thirteen are free ; but two are fettered with ecclesiastical chains—taxed to support ministers, who are chosen by a
small committee and settled for life. My simple prophecy is, that
this must come to an end with the present century. The Rhode-
Islanders began in time, and are free :—hail sons of liberty ! Who
first began the war? Was it not Connecticut and Massachusetts ?
and priests are now saddled upon them. O what a happy people
would these be if they were not thus priest-ridden! It is well for
me that I am not stretching along, while my body is so weak and
the heat so intense ; brother Roberts is with me, and we both only
do the work of one man in public. I heard —— read a most
severe letter from a citizen of Vermont, to the clergy and Christians of Connecticut, striking at the foundation and principle of the
hierarchy, and the policy of Yale-College, and the Independent
order. It was expressive of the determination of the Vermonters
to continue free from ecclesiastical fetters : to follow the Bible,
and give liberty, equal liberty, to all denominations of professing
Christians. If so, why may not the Methodists (who have been
repeatedly solicited) visit these people also.

Tuesday 12. I rode over the rocks to the Square Ponds, and
found our meeting-house as I left it two years ago, open and un-

finished. We have here a few gracious souls : I preached on
Luke xiii. 24. and lodged with brother C——, who was exceedingly kind to man and horse.

Wednesday 13. Came to brother M——'s, on a branch of the
Alemantick. Our friends and the people in North-Stafford had
appointed for me to preach in Mr. ——'s meeting-house : to this
I submitted, but it was not my choice : I was loud, plain, and
pointed, on Rom. viii. 6, 7. Mr. —— was present, and after
meeting kindly invited me to his house. The soil of this country
is naturally poor, but made rich by cultivation : it is blest with
good stone to build chimneys, and to make walls or fences, that
may boast of strength and duration to the end of time.

I went beyond my strength at brother M——'s ; we had a crowd
of hearers, and some melting among the people. I felt myself so
moved that I could not be calm. I gave them a sermon in West-
Stafford, on Hebr. iii. 12, 13, 14. I am awfully afraid many in
these parts have departed from the love, favour, and fear of God.
I was led to treat particularly on unbelief, as the soul-destroying
sin : it keepeth men from turning to God ; and it is by this sin that
the heart first departs from God ; to prevent which, Christians
ought to exhort one another daily, lest they be hardened through
the deceitfulness thereof, and so become cast-aways. Came to
Esq. S——'s : In the evening, I felt much hurt by the exertions
I had made for precious souls.

Saturday 16. I rode up the hills, where we had some close
talk ; I observed there was good attention, and some melting in the
congregation. I came to L. S.'s ; here some of the young people
are with us, and the old people prefer hearing the Methodists
preach to the hearing of sermons read.

Sunday 17. I came to the new chapel in Wilbraham, forty by
thirty-four feet ; neatly designed on the Episcopal plan. I was unwell and under heaviness of mind. I preached to about four hundred people, who were very attentive, but appeared to be very
little moved. The standing order have moved their house into
the street, not far from ours ; and they think, and say, they can
make the Methodist people pay them : but I presume in this they
are mistaken.

Monday 18. Came to S. B.'s—and was at home, feeling comfortable in body and mind.

Tuesday 19. I preached at Mr. R.'s ; and was led on a sudden
to open and apply Phil. ii. 12, 13. ; 1. Who are addressed ? Christian believers ; 2. The leading subject—future and eternal salva-

tion ; to avoid legality, Antinomianism, and lukewarmness ; 3. That he hath, and doth work in them to will and to do; to resist temptation ; to be sanctified ; and to be finally saved ; 4. They should work out their own salvation, by being found in every means of grace ; attending to mercy, justice, truth, and love ; 5. With fear, where many have failed ; with trembling, where many have fallen. Some were not well pleased at this Anti-Calvinistic doctrine ; but I cannot help that. I have been much tried, and much blessed ; weak in body, but, I trust, happy in Christ—in the precious love of Jesus.

Wednesday 20. I had a quiet retreat at brother W.'s. My mind enjoys peace ; and my soul shall breathe after the salvation of dearly bought souls. Mr. S. a minister of the standing order, held a meeting near us at the same time : whether this were in opposition or not, he knoweth. I preached on " Seek the Lord, and ye shall live."—1. The death to which those are exposed who have not found the Lord ; 2. The life those do and shall enjoy who have found, and do live to the Lord—a life of faith, love, and holiness here, and glory hereafter ; 3. We must seek him in all the means of grace. Rode in the evening to father A.'s, in Springfield ; a kind family. Here I gave them a short sermon on Acts ii. 22. ; I showed 1. What we must be saved from ; 2. That we cannot save ourselves ; 3. On whom we must call for salvation ; 4. That whosoever thus calls on the name of the Lord, without distinction of age, nation, or character, shall be saved.

Friday 22. We came to mother K.'s, in Enfield, a capital town in Massachusetts. The inhabitants one hundred and fifty miles up the river, send down the white pine logs by means of the freshets at the breaking up of the winter and frost : the people up the stream mark them ; and the people here take them up, and are paid for it, or purchase the logs. It is said, that if the proprietor is paid for two-thirds of those he puts into the river, he is content, and well rewarded for his labour.

Sunday 24. I was well attended at the Separate meeting-house, where I applied Acts v. 29—33. We had a solemn sacrament; but O! my soul is distressed at the formality of these people. Brother Roberts preached in the afternoon to a crowded house, and at five o'clock I had to preach to a few sermon-stupified hearers of different denominations. Oh my Lord ! when wilt thou again visit the people of this place. I have read Lowman on the Jewish Government : strange that it should be so much like the British

government, and ancient New-England : but the wonder ceases
when we know the writer was an Englishman. Now I suppose I
have found out how the Bostonians were moved to call the General
Assembly a court, and their members deputies—they followed
Lowman.

Tuesday 26. I rode twelve miles to Wapping. I was happy to
have an opportunity of retreating a little into much loved solitude
at Capt. S——'s, a man of good sense and great kindness. I had
some enlargement on Isai. lv. 6—9. and was enabled to speak with
power and demonstration. I preached at T. S——'s barn : my
spirits were sunk at the wickedness of the people of this place.
My subject was Isai. lxiv. 1—7. O what mountains are in the
way! Idolatry, superstition, prejudice of education, infidelity,
riches, honours, and the pleasures of the world. Ver. 7. " None
calleth."   Prayer of every kind is almost wholly neglected.
" That stirreth up himself." Oh! how might men address their
own souls : as, O! my soul, hast thou had conviction, penitence,
faith, regeneration ? Art thou ready to enter the unseen, unknown
state of happiness, and stand before God ? or wilt thou be content
to make thy bed in hell?

I lodged at the oldest house in Windsor, with another brother
S——, not unlike the captain. Notwithstanding his certificate
from the Methodists he has been taxed to pay a ministry he heareth
not. O liberty ! O priestcraft ! So all that withdraw must pay
the ministry.

I can scarcely find a breath of living, holy, spiritual religion
here, except amongst a few women in East-Hartford. If there
should continue to be peace in America, yet I am afraid that God
will punish the people himself for their wickedness—it may be
by pestilence, or civil discord, or internal plague.

Saturday 30. We were called upon to baptise a child, which
Mr. —— refused to do, because the parents owned the covenant
and have now broken it. This is the way to bind people to the
good old church.

Sunday 31. My affliction of body and mind was great at Spencertown, yet I had a solemn time in preaching in the new tabernacle
to about four hundred people on Luke xxiv. 45—48. After an
hour's recess we came together again, and some were offended,
and others convicted, while I enlarged on " The promise is to
you and your children." I was in public exercise about five
hours, including sacrament, and was so outdone with heat, labour,
and sickness, that I could take but little rest that night.

Monday, September 1. I rode to the plains of Ellington, and next day to Wilbraham, and was kindly treated by S. S——. I preached at the next house, and we had a dreadful talk to a miserable, faithless people. We rode two miles in the heat, and I was near fainting, and felt almost like Jonah.

Thursday 4. We opened our conference with what preachers were present. I was still weak in body. I lodged with Abel Bliss, whose son was educated, *and not spoiled*, at Cokesbury.

Friday 5. We had a full house, and hasted through much business.

Saturday 6. Brother L. R—— and myself preached. My subject was Mal. iii. 1—4. I treated on the coming and work of John the Baptist; the coming, work, and doctrine of Christ, and his changing the ordinances and priesthood, with the ministry and discipline of the church.

Sunday 7. We spent from eight to nine o'clock in prayer: a sermon, three exhortations, and the sacrament followed. We parted at three o'clock, and I came to Enfield, and got my dinner at seven o'clock in the evening.

Monday 8. We spent this day on the road; passing Windsor and East-Hartford, and came to the city. The next day we reached Middletown, where I was taken ill. We have a call for preachers to go to New-Hampshire and to the Province of Maine.

Wednesday 10. We rose at three, and set out at five o'clock, and breakfasted at North-Haven. We came in the evening to Stratford, and had a little meeting, although I was heavy, sick, and sleepy.

Thursday 11. We rode to General W.'s. Here I learn they guard Kingsbridge, and will not suffer any one to pass from New-Haven. It is also said, the pestilential fever prevails in the city of New-York, having been brought there by a brig from the Islands. I thought it best to stop, and consult the preachers in the Albany district, before I go into the city. As the yellow fever is so prevalent in the West Indies and our vessels continually trading there, the United States will partake, I fear, of their plagues; and so the Lord will punish us for our sins and prodigality. I only wish to be holy; and then, let come whatever the Lord pleases. I came through Poquonnock, Fairfield, and Norwalk; but there is no room for the Methodists in those places.

We had a pleasant ride, within sight of Long Island, on the salt-water creeks, where there are tide mills which work very swiftly and powerfully. Brothers R. and P. left me to attend the quarterly meeting at Dan-Town, and I spent my time in retirement.

Friday 12. I filled my minute-book, and read freely in the Bible ; this book is so much hated by some ; as for me I will love and read it more than ever.

Saturday 13. Very warm and I was very faint. I preached in a new open house, and had a sweet comforting time on Luke xii. 31, 32. Here I met brother Dunham from Upper Canada, who wants more preachers in that province.

Sunday 14. Although very unwell, I crept out to administer the sacrament, and preached a little on Rom. xiii. 11. I must needs go through Bedford. O ! how should I learn, whatever I think, to say but little ; it was the sin of meek Moses, when pressed hard, to speak unadvisedly with his lips. This country is so rough and ridgy that we cannot get forwards except it be along the road to the landing, or to some capital place.

NEW-YORK.—My horse having wandered and left me, I borrowed a horse, and on Monday rode to lawyer H.'s ; and the next day came in a carriage to New-Rochelle : after preaching on Hebr. iii. 12. I lodged near the place I preached at twenty-three years ago.

Wednesday 17. I came near Kingsbridge, and found that it was not as had been reported concerning the malignant fever in New-York ; perhaps a dozen might have taken the infection from a vessel ; but it hath not spread, and the weather became propitious by rain and pure winds. On Thursday the 18th I came into the city.

Sunday 21. I preached in the old house on Psalm cxxxii. : at the new church in the afternoon on Psalm i. : and at Brooklyn in the evening. Here our brethren have built a very good house. The labours of the day, pain of body, and my concern for the peace of the church, tended to keep me from proper rest, and caused an awful night.

Monday 22. We opened conference, and sat closely to our business. Several of our preachers want to know what they shall do when they grow old—I might also ask, what shall I do ? Perhaps many of them will not live to grow old.

Tuesday 23. I preached with liberty ; but on Thursday night I had a powerful temptation before I went into the church, which sat so heavily on me that I could not preach ; yet I trust I was kept from sin. My sleep is so little, that my head becomes dizzy, and

distresses me much : four hours' sleep in the night is as much as I
can obtain. We concluded our work ; and observed Friday as a
day of abstinence and prayer, and had a good time at our love-feast.

Sunday 28. Preached at ten o'clock at Brooklyn. In the afternoon at the new church on " Wo to them that are at ease in
Zion !" I ordained seven deacons and five elders ; and in the evening, at the old church, I preached again : we had the best time at
the last, at least it was so to me. All day I was straitened in my
throat, and in my heart. We collected two hundred and fifty dollars for the relief of the preachers in distress.

This has been a serious week to me : money could not purchase
the labour and exercise I have gone through. At this conference
it was resolved that nothing but an English free day-school should
be kept at Cokesbury.

Monday 29. I did not sleep after three o'clock in the morning.
Came to the boat at seven o'clock, but could not get across till one
o'clock ; which, to my no small grief, prevented my attending my
appointment on Staten-Island.

NEW-JERSEY.—Tuesday 30. Rose at three o'clock. Set out at
five o'clock, and rode forty-two miles to Milford, and preached ;
but I found this heavy work.

Wednesday, October 1. I had some life in preaching at Cros-
week's meeting-house. I then came to brother Hancock's, and
took sweet counsel with my old friend, whose wife I received as a
member of society twenty-two years ago. I was in suspense about
going through Philadelphia, lest I should not reach Baltimore in
due time. Now report saith that they have stopped the Baltimore
stage on account of the malignant fever, which rages powerfully
at the Point. There is a great stir among the people concerning
the western insurrection ; the people have risen up against government on account of the excise law relative to the distillation of
spirits. A number of the militia are called out : thus trouble comes
on in church and state. O, my Lord, give us help ; for vain is the
help of man !

Thursday 2. I came to Burlington ; and as I had not had a day
to myself for some time, I took one now, to read, write, and fill up
my journal, &c. I feel for the church, and continent : but the
Lord sitteth above the water-floods, and remaineth a King for ever.
I preached at Burlington, and the people were serious.

PENNSYLVANIA.—Saturday, October 4. Brother M. and myself
came to Philadelphia ; and on

Sunday 5. I preached three times; and was not a little fatigued with this day's labour: I felt assisted, and had some openings in preaching.

Monday 6. Our conference began, and our matters were talked over freely. Our session continued until Friday, by which time I felt tired of the city, and had a desire to be on horseback. I have felt liberty in preaching to the citizens, and indulge some hope of a revival of religion among them.

Saturday 11. Rode thirty-five miles to sister Grace's, at Coventry, who, with her daughter and granddaughter, are, I trust, happy in God. I visited this house twenty years ago. Sister Grace, when in a dilirium, was singing and talking about God. I spent a solitary Sabbath at her house, and was happy in speaking at her door, (she being sick.)

Monday 13. Brother Cook and myself had a heavy ride of nearly fifty miles to J. H——'s, which we accomplished by travelling a little in the night.

Tuesday 14. I preached at Bethel, on Back-Creek; and on Wednesday 15 crossed Elk-River, and came to quarterly meeting at Hart's meeting-house. I spent the evening with my dear son in Jesus, D. S——: I cannot give him up.

MARYLAND.—Thursday 16. Crossed Susquehannah, and came to Cokesbury college. I found it £1200 in debt, and that there were between 5 and £600 due us, £300 of what we owe ought now to be paid.

Saturday 18. We came to Perry Hall. The preachers were afraid to go into Baltimore, but the brethren from there came out to calm their fears and invited them in. I have been hurried, and have not as much time for retirement as my soul panteth for—yet I desire nothing but Christ.

Monday 20. We rode to Baltimore; and in the afternoon opened our conference: we had about fifty preachers, including probationers: our business was conducted in peace and love. Myself and others being unwell, we sat only six hours in the day.

Tuesday 21. I gave them a sermon on Exodus xxxii. 26. We had a list of names from Fairfax; who required an explanation of a minute in our form of discipline, relative to the trial of members: inquiring whether the "select members were as witnesses, or judges, and had power to vote members in or out of society." (Sec. 8. p. 56.) We answered them.

Our collegiate matters now came to a crisis. We now make a

sudden and dead pause ;—we mean to incorporate, and breathe, and take some better plan. If we cannot have a Christian school, (i. e. a school under Chirstian discipline and pious teachers) we will have none. I had peace of mind, but not much rest.

Sunday 26. We had a comfortable love-feast, but were prevented from attending our other meetings by the excessive rains. The next day I came to Elk-Ridge ; where I saw, after twenty-two years' labour, a well designed frame of a new house for public worship ; a few good women are trustees. The storm prevented me from having a congregation here also. Came to J. Holland's, where I had a few hearers, and had a comfortable time ; it was like paradise regained among the old Methodists.

VIRGINIA.—Thursday 30. Crossed the Patomac, at the mouth of Goose-Creek ; and came, unexpected by the brethren, to Leesburg. Thence we journeyed on through Prince William and Fauquier counties. We passed Germantown, and came along Rogues-Road, to Norman's ferry, on Rappahannock. After a disagreeable journey, and being exposed to uncomfortable weather, on Tuesday, the 4th of November, we came safe to father Kaubler's, in Culpepper county. Thank the Lord, there is here and there a house for God. At father K.'s I had many women and but few men to hear. Some of the men are gone to war, some to their sports, and some have no desire to hear.

We rode ten miles to brother Frye's : after a long absence of ten years I am here again. My mind is in great peace, and the preachers and people appear pleased to see me. I learn that about the month of June last died the great politician Richard Henry Lee, of Westmoreland county ; one who took an active part in promoting the independence of the United States of America. O, when will liberty be extended to the sable sons of Africa ! We trust the happy period will come, when universal light shall shine through all the earth, and Jesus shall reign

> ————————" Where-e'er the sun,
> Does his successive journeys run ;
> His kingdom spread from shore to shore,
> Till sun shall rise and set no more."

Thursday 6. I had some life, and there was a small stir on the minds of some at Frye's, where we had a crowd of preachers and people.

Friday 7. Crossed one of the south branches of Rappahannock, called the Rapid-Ann, and came thirty miles to J. L——'s in Louisa county.

Saturday 8, and Sunday 9. Attended the quarterly meeting at Lastley's meeting-house ; we had a large congregation, a quickening sacrament, and life in the love-feast. I feel it necessary to retire and humble myself before the Lord : I have been crowded with company, and have had much talk, and I find a solitary walk very agreeable.

I attended a few appointments in Hanover, and Goochland counties ; and on Saturday 15 came to the city of Richmond, about five o'clock, and preached to a few people in Mr. Parrot's storehouse.

Sunday 16. We came to a church near brother B——'s, where were gathered many people, among whom were some sons of division. Here were many pale faces, and (as I was told afterward) some who had been making solemn promises in their affliction, wondered how I should know, and speak so pertinently on that subject. Thence we came to brother I. M.'s, in Chesterfield ; and the next day crossed Appomattox and Nottaway rivers, and reached to B. Jones in Brunswick county, on our way to Brunswick quarterly meeting at Meritt's chapel. It was rather a dull time, although I had some freedom in speaking, and we had a good love-feast.

Saturday 22, and Sunday 23. Attended a quarterly meeting at Jones's chapel in Sussex county, where we had many people : I preached on Deut. ix. 12.—too applicable to many of these souls. The rumour of the small-pox being at Petersburg, and only ten or twelve, out of seventy or eighty of the preachers, having had it, it caused us to think of holding our conference at sister Mabry's in Greenville county, where there are fifteen or sixteen houses that will receive and entertain the preachers. After sending brother Hutt to Petersburg, it was, by a mojority of the preachers present, judged most prudent to hold the conference at the place just mentioned.

Monday 24. About thirty preachers were collected together. I am crowded too much for my head and heart : when I sit and hear people talk on unprofitable subjects, it clouds my head and grieves my spirit, even if I say nothing.

Tuesday 25. We opened our conference, and had great siftings and searchings, especially on the subject of slavery. The preachers almost unanimously entered into an agreement and resolution not to hold slaves in any state where the law will allow them to manumit them, on pain of forfeiture of their honour and their place in the itinerant connexion ; and in any state where the law will not admit of manumission they agreed to pay them the worth of their labour, and when they die to leave them to some person or persons, or the society, in trust, to bring about their liberty. After raising and applying what money we could (which was about £50) we calculated that one fourth of the preachers at this conference had received for their salary the past year about £10 ; one half from about 12 to £15, and one fourth their full quarterage (sixty-four dollars). We had great peace, and not one preacher objected to his station. We sent an apology to our brethren in Petersburg for not having held conference there, according to appointment, for reasons already assigned. We were greatly obliged to our friends in Greenville for accommodating the conference. Men and horses were well entertained— all for love.

Monday, December 1. I rode twenty-seven miles, and on Tuesday 2, I preached at F. B——'s, twelve miles from Petersburg.

Wednesday 3. Came to J. Smith's, and had a comfortable season. Brother S—— has been on the verge of eternity, and was blest with delightful prospects of glory, but the Lord has raised him up again.

Thursday 4. Came to Grave's chapel, very unwell ; here lived brother Lewis Lloyd, who left this world this year. He was an old preacher, and professed perfect love fifteen years before his death, and finally departed in the triumphs of faith.

Friday 5. I preached at Rivers's chapel, and made it twenty miles by the time I reached brother Petham's in Greenville. I was heavy in body and spirit. I am not conscious of having sinned, yet I suffer on account of the people. I delighted myself in reading some of Doddridge's Sermons to Young People. To the young persons present I preached at brother P——'s on Saturday ; and on Sunday 7, rode twenty-eight or thirty miles to brother Paup's, on Roses-Creek, where I enlarged on Peter's fall. Our burdensome stone, Ebenezer, now gives us some trouble and care. If we can employ good men, keep up discipline, and maintain credit, it may come to something.

Monday 8. I performed the funeral rites of sister W——, on Waquae-Creek, Brunswick county. We had a full house of unfeeling people, and the word of the Lord was a burden. I opened the Bible on Jer. xiv. 10. Let any one read it as an awful portion—it may be it is as true to these people as it was to Israel. I had a meeting with the trustees of Ebenezer school. Matters

are very discouraging ; people in general care too little for the
education of their children.

Tuesday 9. Preached at Williams's meeting-house. These are
a poor people, not impoverished with slaves ; but they have a good
meeting-house, with a glass window behind the pulpit, so that we
can see to read without raising a shutter and receiving all the wind
that comes, though this is in Lunenburg county, near Mother
Ogburn's, where we used to have our melting seasons twenty
years ago. We dined with the gracious aged people, and in the
evening crossed Meherrin, and came to S. Holmes's, an ancient
stand in Mecklenburg. Next day I preached at Salem, where
there is the best house we have in the country part of Virginia.
In this neighbourhood there has been a society standing for twenty-one years. Rode in the evening to brother Spedd's—rich and
full, and a friend to freedom.

Thursday 11. Preached and administered the sacrament at
Youngs's chapel ; and came in the evening to T. Jones's. Dear sister Jones is gone to rest, after two years of deep affliction. She
has had a painful journey through life; but her persecutions and
troubles are now at an end ; and heaven will compensate for all.
She made choice of Job iii. 17. for her funeral text ; and with great
deliberation disposed of her property. I preached her funeral on
Friday 12th, and found it a serious day to me. I never saw her more
than twice or thrice, and we have interchanged a few letters. She
was doubtless a woman of sense, vivacity, and grace. She wrote
to admiration—all in raptures. She would pray in any place, and
before any people ; she reproved with pointed severity, and sung
with great sweetness.

NORTH CAROLINA.—Saturday 13. We crossed Roanoak, and
came to Mr. Smith's, in Granville county. On Sunday 16th crossed Mountain and Grassy Creeks, and came to brother Owens's,
whose wife is a true daughter of D. Grant, my dear old friend in
Georgia. He was among the last fruits of that great man Mr.
Davies, when he laboured in Hanover in Virginia, forty years ago.

Monday 15. Crossed the head streams of Tar-River, which are
only small branches, and rode on to R——'s (where I had an appointment ;) and found I had another twenty-five miles forward at
L——'s : so I left brother C—— to fill up my place, and went
forward to the latter ; where I preached to about two hundred
people. I feel weak in body and mind, yet find my soul stayed
upon God. " Still onwards I go," fainting yet fighting.

Thursday 18. I have a long journey to Charleston, (S. C.) and but fifteen days to perform it; having appointed to be there the 1st of January.

Friday 19. We rode twenty-five miles through a powerful fall of rain; but we wrought our way through the swamps, floating and sinking as we went.

Saturday 20. It snowed as powerfully as it rained yesterday; however, we set out for Salem about nine o'clock, and forded two creeks; but the third we swam. Brother Ward went in, and after a pause I followed; but being cloaked up, my horse nearly slipped from under me: one foot was *properly* soaked. I walked about one mile and rode another, and reached the town about twelve o'clock, just as they were ringing the bell. Feeling the want of a fire, I went to the tavern; but I found but one fire-place there; I sat down with the company, and dried my feet a little, until my companions came along. I have need of power, (and I am accused of having too much) to stand such days as this: my soul is kept in peace and communion with God; and, through grace, I will not murmur at my sufferings whilst the salvation of souls is my end and aim. We found a home at father Hill's, from Maryland, about three o'clock, having rode nineteen miles to-day, and thirty yesterday. I was thankful for a house and friends, and an opportunity of putting into port. It is a comfort to remember there remaineth a rest for the people of God.

Sunday 21. I came to Cokesbury school; and after preaching on 1 Cor. xv. 58. I rode down to brother Charles Caton's. Here a few souls have been brought to God since I was in these parts in May last.

Monday 22. We were detained some time at Long's ferry by a wagon, and a number of horses. Mrs. —— entertained us very kindly, and her husband gave us a hearty welcome when he came home, and found out who we were. It was expected by some that I should preach at Salisbury, but I did not; so we rode on and reached the widow B.'s about eight o'clock at night, having rode thirty miles.

Tuesday 23. We set out at sunrise: the morning was cold and frosty. We rode ten miles and fed at A.'s; thence we hasted twenty-five miles to J. R.'s, took a late dinner, and rode to W. R.'s, making upwards of forty miles. Next day we had to swim Rocky-River; we then passed Newtown, and made it thirty miles to Jackson's.

Thursday 25. Christmas day. We changed our course, and took the grand Camden road to great Lynch's Creek, thirty miles. When I came to Mr. Evans's and told my name, I was invited to stay ; and it was well for us that we did.

Friday 26. I came off about sunrise ; and made forty miles to *Publius* James Rembert's : I was hungry, sore, and very low spirited ; here we found a warm house, comfortable table, (which was very acceptable) good bed and fire, with very kind friends. Lord, dispose us to humility before Thee, and bless our benefactors ! James Rogers and Samuel Cowls were my faithful attendants. I hear my friend John Hughes, of Charleston, is dead. From what I learn of him in his last illness, I trust the dear old man is gone safe. William Adams and Captain Darrell of the same place, have been cast away and drowned ; strange changes take place in a very short time. O my God ! help me to be each moment on my guard, ready for death and judgment. The land we came through yesterday is poor, and but thinly settled—a plantation once in three or four miles. The long-leaved lofty pines have a grand appearance.

Sunday evening 28. Rode after preaching to brother Bradford's. Monday 29th to Bowman's. Tuesday 30th we had to wrestle with Santee Swamp for three hours, having to wade the flat ground then under water ; but through mercy we got safe over at last. We hasted on, and came in the evening to the house of a very kind Frenchman, who entertained us gratis.

Wednesday 31. Myself with the main body of the preachers came into the city of Charleston. I felt faint and unwell after the fatigues I had passed through on my journey.

Thursday, January 1, 1795. Being New-Year's day, I was called upon to preach, unwell as I was, which I did on Psalm xc. 12. We entered on the business of our conference, and continued until Wednesday 7th. We had preaching every night during the sitting of conference. It was the request of the conference that I should preach them a sermon on Tuesday night ; with which I complied, and made choice of Jer. xxiii. 29—32. In times past I have endeavoured to keep on travelling all the year, but I now judge it meet to stay in Charleston a little longer and then take the field : yet it is with fear and trembling.

Sunday 11. Brothers I. C. and G. being about to leave the city, I gave place to them to perform the services of the Sabbath. I heard part of a discourse by Mr. Furman on partial and total backsliding: I thought he spoke well, and that it was an excellent sermon. I doubt if he had more than seventy white hearers. A vast number in the city do not attend to the worship of God any where.

Monday 12. The remaining members of the conference left the city. Brother Bruce and myself must now lay our shoulders to the work. I have my feelings and fears about staying in Charleston; but grace is sufficient: I wish to give my all to God; and whether I read, write, preach, or visit, to do it all to his glory; and to employ my precious time profitably.

And am I yet alive, with death so near? How many of my friends in this city, and in other places, are gone into eternity! I hear very little from the preachers in the north.

Tuesday 13. I had a comfortable season in the church, on the words of St. Paul to the Galatians, "Am I therefore become your enemy because I tell you the truth." In this discourse I observed, how great was the affection between the Christian societies in ancient Galatia, and St. Paul, until the Judaizing teachers came in among them. The province of Galatia was in Lesser Asia; and when the ancient Gauls, or Galatæ, wanted to extend their province, they penetrated through Italy and Greece, and went into Asia, and pillaged the country as far south as Babylon: but one hundred and twenty thousand being defeated by a handful of Jews; and Attalus, king of Pergamus, having forced them from his territory, they settled here. Among these the Gospel was planted by St. Paul, Acts xvi. 6.; who had but just left the country when the schism began by means of the teachers of the ceremonial law. In this church there have been a great number of bishops, and some councils, and Synods; but for near eight hundred years the tyranny of the Mahometans, Saracens, and Turks, hath almost exterminated the very name of Christianity. I observed, 1. That there is a proper portion of truth which is applicable to every one's case; 2. That it is a bad sign when a man is esteemed an enemy for telling the truth, as if falsehood alone were pleasing.

Wednesday 14. I preached at brother Wells's on "It is good for me that I have been afflicted, that I might learn thy statutes:" this cannot be the language of any but gracious souls. Sinners think all these things are against them, and wonder what they have done more than others, that they are thus afflicted. I treated of afflictions of body and mind; personal and family; in the church and in the state. Ah! my Lord, by whom shall Jacob arise? for he is very small.

Sunday 18. I preached in the morning on Exod. xx. the first and second commandment. In the afternoon, on the affliction and conversion of Manasseh, 2 Chron. xxxiii. 12, 13. One young man behaved amiss, for which I reproved him : perhaps he might be among those in the evening who made a riot, broke the windows, and beat open the doors.

Tuesday 20. I read Mr. Flavel on keeping the heart ; where I found some weighty sayings. I preached in the evening, and brother Bruce exhorted. Mr. —— came home with me, pleading and crying to God, and acknowledging his sin : who knoweth but he will turn, repent, and find mercy ! The desperate wickedness of this people grieves and distresses my soul, so that I am almost in continual heaviness ; yet, through grace, I trust I am kept from sin. I spent part of this week in writing and reviewing some explanatory notes on our form of discipline.

Sunday 25. I preached morning and afternoon. My soul, at seasons, wadeth through deep waters for this city and society ; it cannot, in my opinion, continue long in its present situation—perhaps a dispensation of mercy or judgment is near.

Wednesday 28. I finished reading the history of the French Revolution, containing about eight hundred pages, and a surprising history it is. They have had heavy struggles with monarchy, aristocracy, and democracy ; and have had martyrs of each and every form.

Thursday 29. I am sensible of not being enough in prayer ; this gives me pain. There came on a violent, awful storm of rain, and what should I do upon the road in such weather ? Charleston is, to me, one of the most serious places I ever was in.

Saturday 31. I was in a most distressed, gloomy state of body and mind. I employed myself in reading, writing, and prayer— but very uncomfortably.

Sunday, February 1.

> "Still heavy is my heart,
> Still sink my spirits down."

I went to the church, and lectured on the second table of the law ; attending particularly to our Lord's comment on each precept. In the afternoon I enlarged on Jer. xxxi. 33. ; and I do hope there was some stir in the hearts of the people ; I had an afflictive night, by the labours of the day. I began reading " Berridge's Christian World Unmasked." How like the man and his conversation, which I have heard by the hour thirty years ago ! I think there is some tartness in his Christian remarks on the Checks, and dear Mr. Fletcher, of whom I have heard Mr. Berridge speak in terms of very great respect. I was insulted on the pavement with some as horrible sayings as could come out of a creature's mouth on this side of hell—When I pray in my room with a few poor old women, those who walk the streets will shout at me. The unparalleled wickedness of the people of this place, and the spirit of contention among the professors of religion, most severely agitate my mind. I now spend my time in running hastily through the first volume of the Hebrew Bible.

Thursday 5. I was deeply dejected. I have been lately more subject to melancholy than for many years past, and how can I help it : the white and worldly people are intolerably ignorant of God ; playing, dancing, swearing, racing ; these are their common practices and pursuits. Our few male members do not attend preaching ; and I fear there is hardly one who walks with God : the women and Africans attend our meetings, and some few strangers also. Perhaps it may be necessary for me to know how wicked the world is, in order that I may do more as a president minister. There is some similarity between my stay here, and at Bath in Virginia. O how I should prize a quiet retreat into the woods !

In reading Mr. Wesley's Journal, Vol. I. page 154. he observes, " I set myself carefully to read N. Machiavel's celebrated Book. I began," says Mr. W——, " with a prejudice in his favour, having been often informed he had been misunderstood and greatly misrepresented ; I weighed the sentiments it contained ; compared one passage with another, and endeavoured to form a cool, impartial judgment ; and my most deliberate judgment is, that if all the other doctrines of devils which have been committed to writing since letters were in the world were collected together in one volume, it would fall short of this ; and should a prince form himself by this book, so openly recommending hypocrisy, treachery, lying, robbery, oppression, adultery, and murder of all kinds, Domitian or Nero would be angels of light compared to that man." No wonder that Doctor —— should say that the Methodist preachers were men of true Machiavilean principles : *judge, reader :* this is the justice, this is the mercy we are to expect from some priests : and why ? because we spoil their reading trade.

Sunday 8. I preached on Psalms viii. 4. Brother Bruce entertained us on " That your faith should not stand in the wisdom of men, but in the power of God." I met the society, read the Rules

of Discipline, and gave a close talk about conformity to the world.
I have now finished the first volume of Mr. Wesley's Journal. I
admire his candour and the soundness of his sentiments ; but I need
say but little, as it will be shortly published and speak for itself.

Monday 9. The people have high work below stairs laid off
for each day this week. The western regiment parades to-day,
the eastern to-morrow ; Wednesday is the President's birth-day ;
Thursday, Friday, and Saturday, come on the races. I intend to
keep close to my room, except when attending meetings in the
evenings. I am in the furnace ; may I come out purified like
gold ! It is a dark Providence holds me here. Mr. Phillips is here,
and in want of money. Our friends opened their hearts and gave
him twenty or thirty dollars. He is not clear on Original Sin ; so
that we cannot, nor dare not employ him; yet, notwithstanding his
sentiments, I hope he is a good man ; but good or bad, he ought
not to starve.

Monday 16. I rode out to take the air ; and saw the wandering
air-balloon. I am persuaded there are gracious souls among Mr.
Hammett's people ; some of whom have left him, and will, perhaps, return. I was employed in reading Mr. Wesley's Journals ;
and I am now convinced of the great difficulty of journalising.
Mr. Wesley was, doubtless, a man of very general knowledge,
learning, and reading, to which we may add, a lively wit and humour ; yet, I think I see too much credulity, long flat narrations,
and coarse letters taken from others in his Journal : but when I
come to his own thoughts, they are lively, sentimental, interesting,
and instructing. The Journal of a minister of the Gospel should
be theological : only it will be well to wink at many things we
see and hear, since men's feelings grow more and more refined.

Sunday 22. I had no small inflammation in my ear ; yet after I got
to preaching, I was long and loud ; warm, and very pointed : our
congregations are uncommonly large. I was recollecting, by the
help of Mr. Wesley's Journal, how long it had been since I became
acquainted with the Methodists. I was awakened, (as I think,)
when about thirteen years six months old ; at the age of sixteen
I began to read and pray in the public congregation ; one year six
months after this, publicly to exhort and expound God's holy word ;
at twenty-one I travelled much ; and in the beginning of my
twenty second year, I travelled altogether. I was nine months in
Staffordshire, and other adjoining shires ; two years in Bedford-
shire circuit, and two in Salisbury circuit.

Mr. Wesley, in his Journal, seems to think that the cause of the hinderance of the work of God is wholly and entirely in man. But may we not ask, with reverence, hath not God sometimes, for his own purposes, withheld his power, that no flesh might glory in his sight, but feel that He is all in all?

Wednesday 25. We had a love-feast for the Africans ; and many gave in their experiences with life.

In the evening we had a love-feast for the whites. I have had a long stay here, and now rejoice in the hope of going again into the field to work. Nothing would have kept me here but the hope of preserving my health the other ten months of the year ; which will enable me to run through North and South Carolina, the New Territory, Virginia, Maryland, Delaware, Pennsylvania, Jersey, New-York, Connecticut, Rhode-Island, Massachusetts, Province of Maine, New Hampshire, Vermont, and sometimes Kentucky.

Friday 27, we observed as a general fast. I was weak in body and afflicted with the headach ; yet I met the people in the church, and read Joel ii. 12—18. I prayed, I wept before the Lord : I fasted from two o'clock on Thursday until half past five on Friday. I wish we could have solemn monthly fasts, and love-feasts before sacrament. I hope the Lord will look upon us generally throughout the continent, and take away our reproach.

Mr. Wesley lived to see two general revivals of religion, one at the beginning, the other about thirty-six years ago ; though, doubtless, they had generally a gradual growth of religion : we also have had two revivals—one at the beginning, the other about seven years ago : the third revival has now taken place in England, and I hope ours will soon follow.

Saturday 28. I attended the meeting of the stewards, and directed that each of the three stewards, in rotation, should receive and pay all moneys, for one third of the year, and then give place to another for the same time. I also appointed a clerk to attend particularly to the books.

Sunday, March 1. I preached in the forenoon and afternoon ; and it was thought the arrows of the Almighty flew abroad. We had a melting sacrament with white and coloured people : about half a dozen of Mr. Hammett's people from Trinity attended. The people have had much dust cast in their eyes in this place, but now they begin to see more clearly.

I am now about packing up in order to take my leave of this city : I am sure faithful preaching will be blest. I have effectually out, and we should not have strength to ride over the barren sands. We accordingly set out, and rode twenty-two miles to G.'s ; tried it since I have been here: my parting subject was 1 Cor. xvi. 23, 24. the congregation was very large : and if the people are prudent, and the preachers faithful, we shall have a work in this place. The poor Africans brought their blessings, and wishes, and prayers : dear souls ! may the Lord provide them pastors after his own heart !

Thursday 5. I left this seat of wickedness, not without both grief and joy. I never saw so great a prospect here, and doubt if there hath been such an one since the place was first settled. We crossed Ashly-River about ten miles from town ; here was a bridge of value, which was so damaged by the worms and barnacles, that it stood only two years. Sister G. her family, and a wagon were on it when it gave way ; it sunk with them into the water, but they received no injury. We rode thirty-five miles, eating some biscuit with a little wine and water, and came to Mr. Eccles's, Beach-Hill, near Edisto-River. I was somewhat wearied, but happy in my solitary retreat. I think I have not spent my time in vain in Charleston : first, I have had near as many hearers as I could have found in the country : secondly, there hath been real fruit among the white and coloured people ; and such as may, with care, be preserved. I gave them a sermon at Squire Eccles's near two hours long. My soul has peace ; and by the help of God I must hasten eastward and heavenward.

Saturday 7. We came to Lindsey's ; and after preaching to about sixty people, had to ride twelve miles to Cattle-Creek after four o'clock : nor was that the worst ; a storm of thunder and rain came on, and had we not stopped, we should have been steeped from head to foot.

Sunday 8. We had about four hundred people at the church, among whom were a few that loved and feared God ; and many that are stupid, and have become hardened under the preaching of the Gospel. I spent Monday 9 at brother M.'s, and felt the society in the city near my heart.

Wednesday 11. We rode to S.'s, where I gave them a long talk on " The grace of God that bringeth salvation," &c. I thought the weather was too fine to continue so long ; so we made a push and rode eighteen miles to P.'s at the Ponds ; where we supped and breakfasted at our own expense ; and bought provision for our horses. About midnight the rain began to patter on the long shingles—what could we do ? if we stayed, our provision would be where we stopped to eat, and feed ; and then rode eighteen miles more to the widow Pope's, on Little Seleuda.

Saturday 14. I came to A.'s chapel ; but the weather was so exceedingly cold, and the house so open, that we went to the dwelling house, where I preached and prayed, and (the people said) stormed and scolded. When meeting was over, I saw the new still-house, which, as George Fox said, " Struck at my life ;" and we found it necessary to deal plainly with brother —— about his distillery, and to tell him what we apprehended would be the consequence if persisted in—Its natural tendency would be to corrupt his family, and the neighbourhood ; and to destroy the society. O, that the snare of Satan may be for ever broken ! We came to G.'s meeting-house, where we had as wild and disorderly a congregation as could well be without words and blows. I preached a little, and stormed a great deal, but all would not do. It was an awful day to me ; but I hope my labour was not wholly in vain. I lodged at D. Earpes's, who came from Berkley to Seleuda, and has been a preacher twenty years ; I ordained him deacon, and joined his daughter to a husband. Thence I came to J.'s, where there was another wedding : I had work enough—the bishop—the wedding—I could hardly keep them serious. I preached on Isai. xxxv. 3—7 and had an open time.

Wednesday 18. I rode to R——'s and preached.

Thursday 17, and the two following days, we had work enough to write subscription papers to be sent abroad for the purpose of collecting £100 to finish Bethel school, and secure the land : but my expectations are small ; the people have so little sense of God and religion. Saturday, I opened the new house on 1 Thess. v. 14. ; and on Sunday we had a sermon and love-feast.

Tuesday 24. Crossed Enoree at Anderson's ford, in a canoe ; and Tyger at Crenshaw's ford, and came to brother G——'s, near the Fish-Dam ford, on Broad River. What a confluence of waters flow into the Santee in about two hundred miles, on a straight line, from the mouth ; and in its meanders, three hundred or more !

Wednesday 25. I preached and administered the sacrament at a store near the Fish-Dam ford : this part of the country hath been settled about forty years.

Thursday 26. I found some assistance on Jer. xxxi. 34, 35. at Gregory's meeting-house, in the woods ; and I hope it was not altogether in vain. Last night I spent an hour with the blacks in their quarters, and it was well received by them : it will never do to meet them with the whites; by this means our preachers lose all their fruit; many reasons might be assigned for this. O, my soul, rest in the Lord from moment to moment! All the places I have visited this week are new, and I hope the Lord will work at some, or all of them. I exhorted our people to learn their slaves to read; (this is greatly wanting) they would then understand preaching much better. We crossed Pacolet, and came to P——'s; my mind was under deep exercises on account of the state of religion in this neighbourhood.

Sunday 29. Was an awful day—perhaps the most awful I shall ever spend in this place. My comfort was in the woods with the Lord.

Monday 30. I rode forty miles to M——'s: my body is weak, and so is my faith for this part of the vineyard. God is my portion, saith my soul. This country improves in cultivation, wickedness, mills, and stills; a *prophet of strong drink* would be acceptable to many of these people. I believe that the Methodist preachers keep clear, both by precept and example; would to God the members did so too! Lord have pity on weeping, bleeding Zion!

Wednesday, April 1. We rode thirty miles through a barren country, and came, weak and hungry, to brother B——'s clean, comfortable house; and had all things agreeable. I find it hard to ride eight or nine hours without any other nourishment but a little bread and tea.

Friday 3. Was a rainy day. I had some talk with a few blacks, and was comfortable and happy; we lose much by not meeting these people alone. I find, generally, that those who are held by professors of religion are hard to move.

NORTH CAROLINA.—Saturday 4, and Sunday 5. Quarterly meeting at Daniel Asbury's meeting-house. I notice many attend preaching at such times as these, who appear wild, and do not know how to behave themselves. In the afternoon I met the poor blacks by themselves, and was greatly blessed.

Monday 6. We crossed Catabaw, rode thirty-five miles, and came to brother Fitzhugh's, where we met with kind treatment to sweeten the bitter cup of a hard and hungry day's ride.

Thursday 9. Crossed Hunting-Creek, and came to A——'s meeting house in Surry county: here I had near three hundred hearers, to whom I preached on Hebr. v. 12—14. and had more enlarged views of this subject than I ever had before. We have had a good work here; fifty souls are lately brought in; appearances are greatly changed for the better since I was here eleven months ago.

Friday 10. We came to G——'s, in Wilkes county.   I feel awful —I fear lest darkness should be felt here.   Ah, Lord, help me to go through good and evil report; prosperity and adversity; storms and calms; kindness and unkindness; friends and enemies; life and death, in the spirit and practice of the Gospel of Jesus Christ!

Sunday 12. I preached the funeral of grandmother G——, aged eighty-seven or eighty-eight years.

Monday 13. We took our acceptable departure—I cannot live where God is not acknowledged. I passed through the heart of Wilkes county. Here is a poor prospect of religion among all sects. We came in the evening to the house of a poor, honest man. Bless God! we can embrace the poor cabins, and find shelter. The people are kind and free with what they have.

Wednesday 15. I preached on Hebr. iv. 1. to many people, collected from various parts, at brother White's, on John's River, and was greatly assisted.

Thursday 16. We had preaching, and were engaged in writing letters and copying the minutes. My soul enjoys sweet peace; but I see an awful danger of losing that simple walking and living in the enjoyment of God.

Friday 17, I observed as a day of rigid fasting—this I cannot do more than once a month. I am frequently obliged to go on three cups of tea, with a little bread, for eight or nine hours, and to ride many miles, and preach, and perform my other ministerial labours.

Sunday 19. We had a crowded congregation, and a moving season at the sacrament. Monday and Tuesday we directed our course up John's River.

Wednesday 22. Crossed the Ridge, and kept on to the westward. We went Major J. White's path, and found it abundantly better than the old one. We reached the top of the Ridge in about six miles; here we found ourselves among fruitful hills; then we had a good path for six miles more, except where there were some laurel branches and roots. We stopped at S——'s. and it was well we did, or we should have been well nigh starved, both man and horse. I went on to D——'s, and thence to Nelson's, where I met with brothers B——, A——, and W——, ancient men among us. I stood the fatigue, and sleeping three in a bed, better than I expected. From White's to Nelson's is eighty miles. We crossed the Wattawba about twenty times. At supper we ate of

the perch that are taken in great plenty from Smith's fish spring.
I judge there must be a subterraneous communication from that to
the river. I felt uncomfortable in my mind, as I feared the Lord
had left this place. I was led to speak with life and power on
" Will ye also go away ?" I spent a night with brother Whitaker;
I wish his wife may not love him to death.

TENNESSEE.—Monday 27. We hasted to F. Earnest's, on Nola-
chucky-River; where we hold our western conference. Here
six brethren from Kentucky met us, and we opened our conference
with twenty-three preachers, fifteen of whom were members.
We received every man's account of himself and his late labours;
and inquired of each man's character among his brethren. Our
business was conducted with great love and harmony. Our brethren have built a meeting-house, and I must needs preach the first
sermon; which I did on Exod. xx. 24. Notwithstanding it was a
time of great scarcity, we were well and most kindly entertained.

Friday, May 1. We rode thirty miles to Holstein, without food
for man or horse: but when we came to brother Baker's we had
food and friendship. My feelings were disagreeable. In addition to the heat of the weather and the fatigue I have gone
through, I have not slept five hours a night, one night with another, for five nights past.

Saturday 2. On our way we called to see father A. where we
fed and prayed; and in the evening reached Abingdon; being the
time and place of the sitting of the district court.

VIRGINIA.—Sunday 3. I gave them a sermon, and although it
was so public a time, we had great decency in the congregation.
Rode thirteen miles in the evening.

Monday 4. We rode thirty-five miles to the head branches of
the main Holstein, and the next day reached Alfred's, on New-
River.

Wednesday 6. We rode to Pepere's ferry, and made it thirty-
five miles to M'Daniel's. Thursday, we rode to brother W.'s,
near Fincastle, thirty-eight miles: the toils of this journey have
been great, the weather sultry, the rides long, and roads
rough. We suffered from irregularity in food and lodging; although the people are very kind, and give us the best they have,
and that without fee or reward; so that I have only spent about
two shillings in riding about two hundred miles. I hope posterity
will be bettered by my feeble efforts. I have rode two hundred
and twenty miles in seven days and a half, and am so exceedingly
outdone and oppressed with pain, weariness, and want of sleep,

that I have hardly courage to do any thing.—Hail, happy day of rest! It draws nigh, and this labour and toil will soon be at an end!

Saturday 9. I conferred with the travelling and local preachers at E. Mitchell's. Sunday 10, the preachers and people were solemn whilst I enforced " Grieve not the Holy Spirit of God."

Monday 11. I rode forty miles to Mr. Blaker's at the Calf-Pasture, and the next day thirty-five to Moore's. Wednesday 13, rode twenty-four miles to Rock-Town, and preached at three o'clock; and again the next day. Here I met the trustees of our school, to whom I read my Thoughts on Education. In the evening I left the town, and on Friday 15, rode forty miles.

Saturday 16. I had a hard push to Newtown quarterly meeting, where, after delivering a short discourse, I held a conference with the local preachers and leaders. I enjoyed myself among these people; they are not quite as lively as heretofore, but God is still with them. Sabbath day, after sacrament, love-feast, and ordination, I preached with some freedom on 2 Peter iii. 17, 18. Upon the whole my soul is refreshed; although I have been on the run, and have wrote none in my Journal for more than a week.

Monday 18. We rode to Charlestown, Jefferson county, and lodged with a pious physician. Next morning breakfasted with J. H——, and then came to Harper's ferry, where the impending rocks impress the mind of the traveller with terror; and should they fall, would crush him to pieces : this scene is truly awful and romantic. We came to S. Phillip's, but were not expected until next week : so I directed my course to Baltimore.

MARYLAND.—Wednesday 20. I passed Fredericktown; thence to Liberty Town, where I stopped, conversed, and prayed, and then came on to brother Warfield's, thirty miles.

Thursday 21. We set out for Baltimore; the rain came on very heavily; I have not felt, nor seen such, since the sixth of March, since which time I have rode about one thousand two hundred miles. This day I heard of the death of one, among my best friends in America—Judge White, of Kent county, in the state of Delaware. This news was attended with an awful shock to me. I have met with nothing like it in the death of any friend on the continent. Lord help us all to live out our short day to thy glory! I have lived days, weeks, and months in his house. O that his removal may be sanctified to my good and the good of the family! He was about sixty-five years of age. He was a friend to the poor and oppressed; he had been a professed churchman, and was united to the Methodist connexion about seventeen or eighteen years. His house and heart were always open; and he was a faithful friend to liberty in spirit and practice; he was a most indulgent husband, a tender father, and an affectionate friend. He professed perfect love, and great peace, living and dying.

Sunday 24. I preached twice in town, and was delivered from my gloomy state of mind. I spent part of the week in visiting from house to house. I feel happy in speaking to all I find, whether parents, children, or servants; I see no other way; the common means will not do; Baxter, Wesley, and our Form of Discipline, say, "Go into every house:" I would go farther, and say, go into every kitchen and shop—address all, aged and young, on the salvation of their souls.

Wednesday 27. I read "The Dawn of Universal Peace;" and the second and third volume of Walker's Sermons. Thursday, my mind was under deep exercises, unknown to all but God alone.

Saturday 31. I met the Africans, to consult about building a house, and forming a distinct African, yet Methodist church.

Friday, June 5. I came in peace to Cokesbury. Stayed on Saturday; and gave them a sermon *on the shortness of time:*—thence came through dust and heat to North-East. Sunday, I preached within the frame of a house that is begun, to a number of sinners.

Monday 8. I preached twice; and came in the evening to Mr. Bassett's, on the Manor. I have great inward distress in my soul. I felt, when in prayer, as if the Lord would restore sister Moore to health; time will determine whether the impression is of the Lord.

Tuesday 9. We hasted on to Georgetown. Some are of opinion that —— will receive £200 per annum or more, Glebe subscriptions, &c. this is more than 64 dollars; and even that he seldom received among us. He was always very generous, and did not serve us for money. He did certainly run well. I was low in body and mind; and very flat in preaching. Dear brother B——, who attended me with his carriage to North-East the last time I was here, is now gone to rest. Oh! how short is the life of man! we must needs come on to Chester-Town. Still languid in body, and my spirits under an awful fit of dejection at reviewing the state of persons and things. I was quite unwell, and crowded with company: my subject in town was Psalm li. 9—13. We then rode fifteen miles home with brother C——; my body and spirit still very low. O! my Lord, help me through all my afflictions. Ah! what a comfortable thing it is to be among the ancient Methodists! But this is not always my place; indeed, it cannot be.

Tuesday 11. Still under awful depression. I am not conscious of any sin, even in thought; but the imprudence and unfaithfulness of others bear heavily on my heart; I feel a degree of willingness to decline, die, and enter into rest. For the first time, I visited Centreville, and preached in the new house : some of the people felt awful. I saw Doctor Hall, who is greatly changed since 1792, and under deep exercise about preaching ; so that he cannot attend to his practice, and appears to be lost in thought. I wrote to him to try Baltimore : it is a pity such a man of sentiment, learning, and fine feeling, should be lost. I rode home with R. W. he is rich in the world, but wants more of the life of religion : he appears still to love the preachers, and the cause of God. I received information that Doctor M——'s wife, before she died, manumitted her favourite servant-maid ; not long after the Doctor himself was called away ; but before his removal he manumitted all his slaves. This man claimed no high Gospel light, and professed no more religion than the generality of the world among us do. I have a hope that God is preparing me for greater usefulness in my latter days. Oh how happy should I be, if after labouring thirty years, as I sometimes fear, to very little profit, if it should hereafter appear that hundreds have been converted by my ministry ! Of late I have had but little to do, but pray, preach, ride, converse, and take my necessary refreshment.

Saturday 13. We crossed Choptank-River at Ennall's ferry ; we had nine men, three horses, and a carriage on board, and a very indifferent boat, but through a kind Providence we got safe over. When I first landed I felt a damp on my spirits, which I feared was ominous of persons and things. Our friends were loving at the Dorset quarterly meeting, but not very lively ; however there was some stir in the love-feast. At eleven o'clock we had nearly a thousand people collected, but they are awfully hardened. We had a heavy time : I felt much like what I suppose Jonah felt. We were furnished richly with the comforts of life. I came to the dwelling-house of my dear friend Judge White (whose death I have already mentioned)—it was like his funeral to me. I learned since I came here, and I think it worthy of observation, that just before he died, unknown to his wife, he had showed Samuel, his son, his books, and given directions concerning his house, &c. He then came to his wife, and said, "I feel as I never felt before," and gave certain directions concerning his burial.

DELAWARE.—Wednesday 17. I had a solemn season at Dover. I spent the evening with Doctor A. Ridgeley, in the late dwelling-house of his father. In some houses we serve the fathers, not the children; in some the children, not the fathers; and in some we serve both parents and children.

Thursday 18. I preached at Duck-Creek Cross-Roads, where there has been a great revival of religion.

Friday 19. I set out for Philadelphia, and came to Whiteclay and Redclay Creeks. I saw my old friend S. H—— once more. I must needs preach, although I had rode thirty-five or forty miles. Next day I called at Chester, and found my dear sister Withy unwell and in trouble. O may I meet her in heaven at last!

PENNSYLVANIA.—Sunday 21. I preached in the city of Philadelphia three times, not with the success I would wish. I was exceedingly assisted in meeting the classes, in which I spent three days, and am now of opinion that there is more religion among the society than I expected.——I trust both they and myself will remember this visit for days to come. I was also much quickened in meeting the local preachers and leaders, who spoke feelingly of the state of their souls and the work of God. I now go hence to meet new troubles, and to labour while feeble life shall last.

Thursday 25. I rode to Cross-weeks.

Friday 26. Although very poorly I reached brother B——'s. I was happy in this family, and addressed most of them concerning their souls.

NEW-JERSEY.—Saturday 27. I came to Elizabethtown, and found brother Morrell (who had been bled and physiced almost to death,) on the recovery. My troubles are greater than ever: my body is weak, and my spirits very low. At the request of my friends, I stayed in town until Sunday, and was assisted in a manner I least expected, in preaching to about eighty people from 1 Cor. xv. 58.: after sermon I called the society together, and had a melting time in speaking personally to each. I attended the Bowery church in the afternoon; and the minister spoke largely on "That your faith might not stand in the wisdom of men, but in the power of God."

NEW-YORK.—Monday 29. I came to New-York the new way by Newark bridges, which are well established over Second and Passaick rivers: it is the nearest way to New-York, and preserves the traveller from heat in the summer, and cold in the winter: from moschetos, and delays by winds, and other incidents. I began meeting the women's classes, and felt happy, and found the Lord was amongst the sisters.

Saturday July 4. Being the anniversary of Independence, the bells ringing, drums beating, guns firing ; and orations on liberty, and equality too, are not forgotten. I see the need of being more watchful among the best of men : a spirit of love exists among the preachers ; but we are far from being as spiritual as we ought to be. The Rev. Mr. Ogden was kind enough to present me with his first volume On Revealed Religion ; it contains a soft, yet general answer to the deistical atheistical oracle of the day, Thomas Paine : it is a most excellent compilation, taken from a great numbur of ancient and modern writers on the side of truth ; and will be new to common readers. So far as I have read, I can recommend it to those who wish for full information on the subject. I met the official members of the society ; and had some close talk on the doctrine and discipline of the church : I asked if they wished to be Methodists ? But how could I suppose any thing else, when they had been a society of nearly thirty years standing ?

Sunday 5. I preached in Brooklyn in the morning, and returned to assist in the sacrament in the afternoon at the new church ; I then met the black classes ; and preached at half past six ; I closed my day's work by meeting two men's classes.

Monday 6. I met nine classes ; so that I have now spoken to most of the members here, one by one. I left the city in peace, and received of their bounty towards bearing my expenses. We came to Stamford ; where I preached in a private house.

CONNECTICUT.—Rode thirty-three miles to Stratford ; the prospects here are great as to the fruits of the earth. My body was weak and my faith still more so ; however, I gave them a sermon on John iii. 19—21. ; and the house was crowded inside and out.

Friday 10. We had a very warm ride, fourteen miles, to New-Haven. I think it is as sultry here as it was the tenth of June in Delaware. Nothing would do but I must preach in Doctor Edward's meeting-house ; which I did, on these words, " Yea, doubtless, and I count all things but loss for the excellency of the knowledge of Jesus Christ my Lord."

Saturday 11. I came to Middletown : we had a prayer-meeting, and I spent some time in visiting from house to house.

Sunday 12. Brother Roberts being indisposed, I had to give them two sermons at the farms, and one at the court-house.

Monday 13. We had some life at Middle-Haddam. Tuesday 14, preached at New-London about six o'clock, where I found most of the preachers present. Wednesday 15, we opened our conference, which consisted of about twenty members, and sat until noon on Saturday. We had great peace in our conference ; but some exercises relative to externals, arose from the ancient contest about baptism, these people being originally connected with those that are of that line. O! what wisdom, meekness, patience, and prudence, are necessary! Our brethren were exceeding kind ; and I hope this conference will be for the good of the people in this place, and thousands besides.

Monday 20. We took our leave of town, and set off for our respective appointments. Two of our British brethren from the West Indies, Harper and Kingston, who had fled here to save their lives, (i. e. if possible to recover their health,) were with us : I was pleased to see our preachers ready to give their strange brethren a little of the little they had. I came to Norwich, fifteen miles, and preached at eight o'clock A. M. in the academy, (formerly the Separate meeting-house.) It was a most awful time of heat.

RHODE-ISLAND.—Tuesday 21. We rode twelve miles to Plainfield ; and after resting and feeding, we came to Coventry, in Providence. My fatigue and indisposition made me glad to get to bed. The people here have made some attempts to improve the state of the roads ; and really they need it, for they are properly made up of rocks and stones.

Wednesday 22. At brother L——'s I ordained D. M'C—— from Passamaquoddy ; who is as one born out of due time. He has been labouring between the British and American boundaries. I consider it fifty hard miles from New-London to General Lippelt's : we have been the best of three days riding it, through the intense heat ; and last year I rode it in one day. I feel a moving towards these people, as though the Lord would get himself a name, and have a people to praise him in this place. I feel myself greatly humbled before the Lord, for the peace and union in our late conference ; and the satisfaction expressed by the preachers on receiving their stations.

Thursday 23. We came in the evening to Providence : when we entered the town, some drunken fellows raised a cry and shout, and made a sacrifice of the Methodists to hell. Mr. —— is now pastor of, and the Tennant-house is shut against us. I wished to ride on, and not to stop in town ; but Mr. Robertson, an ancient Englishman, constrained us to turn in with him. We dined at Milton ; and made it thirty miles to Boston, where I preached twice on the Sabbath, (though very unwell) in a room that will hold about two hundred and fifty people. It seemed as if we

hardly had either cursing or blessing among the people here. I
have no doubt but that if we had a house, we should command a
large congregation ; but we labour under great inconveniences
where we preach at present. I feel myself feeble in body and
faint in spirit ; yet Christ is mine, and I hope to be his in time and
for ever : Amen.

MASSACHUSETTS.—Monday 27. I rode through some rain to Lynn.
I was much shut up and distressed in my public exercises : my congregations were large and lifeless. Since I have been in Lynn, I have
visited Woodsend and Gravesend, met five classes, visited about
one dozen families, and talked to them personally about their souls,
and prayed with them. I have filled up intervals in reading my
Bible, and the second volume of Mr. Wesley's Sermons. Oh, how
I wish our preachers and people to read his Journals, Sermons, and
Notes ! My body is afflicted, but my soul is serene.

Thursday 30. I preached on Isaiah lv. 10, 11. Friday was an
excessively rainy day. My spirits were sunk into dejection. I
feel no passion, but grieve and sorrow : to *move, move*, seems to be
my life. I now lament that I did not set off with the young men to
the Province of Maine. There are some tender, gracious souls in
this town ; especially among the members of society.

Sunday, August 2. Was a very warm, sultry day. I rose in the
morning very feeble in spirit, and attended prayer-meeting at six
o'clock. I preached three times ; administered the sacrament, and
met two classes, and was not so fatigued as I expected I should
have been. I have had some refreshing seasons ; and now I bid
farewell to Lynn for two years. I rode a solitary way through
Malden, Mistick, and North-Cambridge ; and preached at Waltham, at five o'clock, to a few people : the great rain prevented
many from attending. Brother Roberts took an intermittent fever
when we were at New-Haven, and hath laboured and suffered, sick
or well, until he is almost dead. I received from the quarterly
meeting held in Fairfield circuit, what I should be glad to receive
once a year from every circuit in the Union. It was as follows :—
" The preachers of the Methodist Episcopal order who have travelled on this circuit since the last conference, have so conducted
themselves that their characters are unimpeachable." Signed by
the local preachers, exhorters, stewards, and leaders.

Tuesday 4. Brother L—— and myself came ten miles to Fram-
ingham, where I preached to a simple-hearted people ; and
although weak in body, I felt enlargement of heart ; here the so-

ciety appeared to be all tenderness, sweetness, and love. After
riding thirty miles to Milford, (being an excessive day of heat and
hunger,) I preached on Isaiah xxxv. 3—6. To my great surprise,
whilst I was preaching, brother Roberts, whom I had left sick at
Waltham, came in ; I was amazed that he should ride thirty miles
through such heat without eating or drinking ; it was enough to
make a well man sick.

Thursday 6. We set out for Thompson in Connecticut, whence
we came to dear brother Nichols's : if I had not eaten, I could not
have stood the labour of thirty miles, and preaching. I found there
was religion among this society ; the ancient people are stirred up
by the Baptists, and the young ones by the Methodists.

Saturday 8. We rode twenty-six miles to Wilbraham ; I was well
nigh spent, and brother Roberts was ready to drop on the road
side. I spoke late ; the weather was warm ; I took but little rest
for my body, and my mind was powerfully tried various ways.

Sunday morning 9. My first subject was the parable of the sower,
afterward the sacrament was administered : I thought it a dull
time; but others did not think so. I gave them another discourse
in the afternoon on " The promise is to you and to your children."
It was a running exhortation, chiefly application. In the evening brother Roberts, though weak in body, gave them a sermon on
" My little children for whom I travail in birth again till Christ be
formed in you." I see but little prospect of good being done here
whilst the people are so divided.

Monday 10. I stopped and gave an exhortation at Springfield :
After a thunder-gust, we came on to Agawomin. If I accomplish
the tour I have in contemplation, it will make about six or seven
hundred miles to the city of New-York. I was stopped by the
rain : but when I cannot do one thing another offers ;—I could
read, write, pray, and plan. I laid out a plan for my travels in 1797 ;
through Connecticut, Rhode-Island, Massachusetts, Province of
Maine, New-Hampshire, Vermont, and New-York : making a distance of twelve or fifteen hundred miles. I set out for Williams-
town on the banks of Hoosack, on the west borders of Massachusetts ; I lodged at sister H.'s ; I was well steeped in water, although
my cloak saved me in a good degree as is frequently the case.
My rest was interrupted. To labour hard all the day, and have
no sleep at night, ill suit the flesh. Well might St. Paul say, " If
in this life only we have hope in Christ, we are of all men most
miserable." To labour and to suffer by night and by day, meet

reproach, give up father and mother, wife, children, country, liberty, ease, health, wealth, and finally, sometimes life itself in martyrdom :—all this may be required.

VERMONT.—Friday 21. We rode in the afternoon into the woods of Bennington, and preached at brother D.'s, and had a melting, comfortable season with about fifty souls. There are sinners, Deists, Universalists, &c. and they all have something to say about religion. I have felt awful for this place and people ; but God is able of these stones to raise up children unto Abraham. I feel my soul stayed upon God, although I am in heaviness through manifold temptations.

Saturday 22. Brother Roberts and myself parted : he went to Pownell, and myself to Ashgrove, where we have a society of about sixty members : they originated with P. Embury, who left the city of New-York when the British preachers came there. He continued to pursue his purpose of forming societies in the country ; but dying in a few years, the society was left, and were without preaching by the Methodists for fifteen years : we have now a neat little chapel here.

Sunday 23. I had a free, open time, with a few feeling souls on Luke xi. 1. In the afternoon, I visited a neglected people among the hills, and had an attentive congregation. This day I enjoyed peace of soul, and was happy in Christ.—After riding fifty miles, I found myself at home at this place, (Ashgrove.)

CONNECTICUT.—My soul has been much quickened this Sabbath, and I find a difference between being amongst saints and sinners. We came through Cambridge county, now Washington ; and passed Argyletown, named after Argyle, in Scotland. We came to brother M——'s ; we and our horses were quite weary ; but it is enough, the Lord is with us ; let this suffice at all times, and in every place. We came through a mere wilderness of swamp : the roots of the white pine, beech, and hemlock were a good deal in our way. We reached Westfield, where is a considerable settlement, and a promising society.

NEW-YORK.—We passed Skeynesborough, and turned our course eastward through some rough ground, and came to Hampton township, where we held a quarterly meeting at brother M—'s, in a pleasant vale. We rode through considerable heat, nearly twenty miles, without obtaining any refreshment! I have reason to praise God that I have been able to travel from Lynn to this place ; the distance, the way I have come, I compute to be four hundred

miles ; I am now within a mile of the line of Vermont. There
is only one county, in the state of New-York, between this and
Lower Canada. There is a place called Plattsburg, where they
have often solicited us to send preachers. I find some similarity
between the northern and western frontiers.

Sunday 30, was a high day : we had sacrament and love-feast,
and many opened their mouths boldly to testify of the goodness and
love of the Lord Jesus : the porch, entry, kitchen, and the lodging rooms were filled : one soul professed conversion. I find
that two hours' close meeting flags the minds of God's children :
many of the people of the world are filled with prejudice because
they are shut out.

Sister S——, an ancient woman, and a professor among the Baptists, was sent for by her father to turn the head and heart of her
son from the Methodists : but she had grace and sense to know
that God had been at work upon his soul ; and with tears and
prayers wished him God speed.   Mr. G——, who had heard great
and bad things of the Methodists, was surprised to hear that a son
of his died a Methodist, in New-York ; and still more so, when he
was visited by another son, who had joined society in Waltham.
When this son came home, the father and family were alarmed,
finding that he had met with something that had greatly changed
him : after this, the prejudices of the dear old man were dissipated, and he came five miles to our quarterly meeting. I rode
forty miles : I conclude that for thirty-five miles of this road there
are ten or twelve houses for every mile, including those which
extend to the mountains on either side of the road. Notwithstanding
the roads are somewhat hilly, they are good for travellers. I labour
under great exercise of mind from various quarters ; and my own
infirmities of body and mind are neither few nor small.

Wednesday, September 2. We had a solemn meeting at Bethle-
hem, in Asbgrove.   Thursday 3, we had a warm-hearted people
at R——'s, and a better time than weakness of body or mind could
promise. On Friday, we came to Lansingburgh, and thence to Troy ;
at last we got to Coeyman's Patent, weary, sick and faint, after
riding thirty-six miles.

Saturday 5. We were crowded with people : I suppose we had,
perhaps, a thousand at the stone church, at Coeyman's Patent ; and
I felt some life and warmth amongst them.

Sunday 6. In the morning we had baptism, ordination, sacrament, and love-feast ; some spoke with life of the goodness of God.

I gave them a discourse at eleven o'clock, and then went to bed with a high fever. Brother Roberts pleased, and, I trust, profited the people with a discourse, after I had done.

Monday 7. I rose very unwell, and had to ride thirty-five or forty miles through the rain: I came in much wearied, and found a comfortable lodging at Mr. I——'s.

Tuesday 8. I am somewhat better in body, but clouds and darkness still rest upon my mind.

Thursday 10. We rode twenty miles to Marble-Town (properly so called at present) I preached on Hebr. xii. 28, 29. I felt awful; there appeared to be very little devotion among the people. Our southern friends are battered on the subject of slaves, and these are in peace; it will not do; we must be Methodists in one place as well as another.

Saturday 12. We reached brother Garrettson's; and Sunday 13, I preached at R——'s chapel. Then returned to Rhinebeck chapel, and preached on Hebr. xiii. 5. God once put into brother Garrettson's hands great riches of a spiritual nature, and he laboured much; if he now does equal good according to his temporal ability, he will be blessed by the Lord, and by men.

Tuesday 15. We made it twenty miles to the wreck of an old Presbyterian meeting-house, at Wapping-Creek, called the *hollow;* where I gave them a discourse on "Judgment beginning first at the house of God"—and there was some little motion, but the Methodists were not on their own ground.

Wednesday 16. Brother R—— gave us a close, good sermon on "My people have committed two evils," &c. I then enlarged on "My grace is sufficient for thee;" our meeting continued till three o'clock; we got no dinner, and had to ride twelve miles to get to our supper and lodgings. We stopped at Governor Van Courtlandt's, who reminds me of General Russell—we had all we needed, and abundantly more than we desired. Rest, rest, how sweet! yet how often in labour I rest, and in rest, labour.

Sunday 20. I had a comfortable time at Croton chapel, on Rom. i. 16. I returned to General Van Courtlandt's, and dined with my dear aged friends. Shall we ever meet again? We came to Fisher's, near the White Plains chapel, to hold conference. My soul is kept solemn; and I feel as if earth were nothing to me; I am happy in God, and not perplexed with the things of this world.

Tuesday 22. A few of us met in conference; the main body of the preachers not coming in until about twelve o'clock. We went through the business of the conference in three days, forty-three preachers being present. I was greatly disappointed in not hearing the preachers give a full and free account of themselves and circuits. Although we sat ten hours in each day we did not close our business until Thursday evening, after sitting each night till twelve o'clock.

NEW-JERSEY.—Friday 25. We crossed Hudson-River twenty-six miles above the city of New-York, and came on the waters of Hackensack; a river that is only thirty miles long and navigable two thirds of the way: we then came to Passaic-River, crossed at Second-River, and made out this day to ride forty miles, much fatigued.

Saturday 26. We rode about thirty-two miles with very little to eat; however, we had the pleasure of seeing the famous Brunswick bridge, which is now nearly finished. It is the grandest of the kind I have seen in America. I was *properly* wearied; and prepared to rest on Sunday. I was sorely tried yesterday; more so than I have been these six weeks past.

Monday 28. We came to Monmouth; we would have gone to Shrewsbury, but time and horses failed us. I learn that the ancient spirit of faith, prayer, and power, is taking place in a few places below. I was shocked at the brutality of some men who were fighting, one gouged out the other's eye; the father and son then beset him again, cut off his ears and nose, and beat him almost to death. The father and son were tried for a breach of the peace, and roundly fined; and now the man that hath lost his nose and ears is to come upon them for damage. I have often thought that there are some things practised in the Jerseys which are more brutish and diabolical than in any of the other states : there is nothing of this kind in New-England—they learn civility there at least. We rode twenty miles to Emley's church, where the great revival of religion was some years ago. I felt a little of the old, good spirit there still. Thence we journeyed on to Penny-Hill, fifteen miles, where I was enabled to speak strong words. Thence I came to New-Mills, and gave them an alarming talk on —Judgment beginning at the house of God.

PENNSYLVANIA.—Saturday, October 3. I came through the sand to Philadelphia, and on Sunday evening I preached on " All seek their own, not the things which are Jesus Christ's." In doing which—

I. I pointed out the things that are Jesus Christ's.

II. How these are to be sought.

III. That men are not to seek themselves wholly, or partially, in the ministry of Christ, but that *self* must be altogether out of the question.

Monday 5. We opened our conference, and went on with great peace, love, and deliberation, but were rather irregular, owing to some preachers not coming in until the third or fourth day. We made better stations than could be expected, extending from Northampton, in Virginia, to the Seneca Lake.

Friday 9, we observed as a day of fasting and prayer. I preached at eleven o'clock on Joel ii. 15—17.

Saturday 10. Our conference rose.

Sunday 11. I preached in the morning at the African church, in the afternoon at Ebenezer, and in the evening at St. George's, where, to my surprise, the galleries were filled. I applied "Knowing therefore the terror of the Lord, we persuade men." I had work enough, being often compelled to digress to call the attention of the wild people.

Monday 12. After getting a copy of the minutes I came to Chester, and dined with Mary Withy, who hath lived a widow in this house thirty-one years, and hath kept one of the most complete houses of entertainment in America. She hath sold out for £3000, and is to give place in three weeks. I came late to Wilmington, and preached on Col. i. 10. The great hinderance to the work of God here is the loose walk of professors of religion. Thence, by T. H——'s, I proceeded to North-East Forge, and lodged with my dear son, D. Sheredine.

MARYLAND.—Wednesday 14. We came to Cokesbury. Here we undertook to make an inventory of all the property belonging to Cokesbury college, and found the sum total of the amount to be seven thousand one hundred and four pounds, twelve shillings and nine pence.

Saturday 17. I came to Baltimore to attend the quarterly meeting; brother Whatcoat and myself filled up Sunday the 18th, and were crowded with people.

Tuesday 20. Our conference began. We had preachers from the Northern-Neck; and what is called New-Virginia, (Pitt District,) and the west of Maryland—about fifty-five in number. On Friday night there was a public collection for the assistance of the preachers who were deficient in their quarterage.

Sunday evening 25. I preached on "Then shall many be offended, and shall betray one another." As I wished not to be idle

I concluded to spend a good part of this week in meeting classes. The Africans of this town desire a church, which, in temporals, shall be altogether under their own direction, and ask greater privileges than the white stewards and trustees ever had a right to claim.

Thursday 29. Was a very solemn day of thanksgiving : the subject I made choice of was Psalm cxlvii. 20. " He hath not dealt so with any nation." This I applied spiritually—

I. To ourselves as individuals.

II. As it applies to our families.

III. To the society and ministry.

IV. As it applies to the continent.

In the afternoon I preached at the Point on " In every thing give thanks."

Saturday 31. I left town and came to Elk-Ridge, where I found a little time for reflection and prayer.

Sunday, Nov. 1. I preached and administered the sacrament on the Ridge. After twenty-three years preaching here, we have a small society. I dined at the widow Howard's, and had an interview with sister Pue, who appeared to be deeply oppressed with the loss of her valuable husband. It is now more than twenty years since the doctor attended my ministry ; and I have to hope was deeply awakened. In the latter part of his life he was much afflicted ; he called upon God, and I trust died in peace. I doubt if there hath been a man of his profession of equal skill, continuation, and attention, in the state of Maryland. Mr. Fletcher, when near his end cried out, " My poor, what will become of my poor ?" So the Doctor, when on his death-bed, " What will become of my patients ?"

Monday 2. After riding forty miles, I came late in the evening to Georgetown, and found a congregation waiting at the new chapel. Although wearied and unwell, I felt some liberty in speaking ; and I am persuaded that good might have been done here if professors had not traded away their characters. It is strange, that people professing no religion, look for justice and perfection in all Christians, and forget themselves.

VIRGINIA.—Thursday 5. I reached Faulks. Friday 6, preached at the widow Bumbury's, to about sixty-six hearers, after riding about sixty-six miles from Alexandria.

Saturday 7. I rode about forty-two miles, and found a quiet retreat at brother E——'s. Next day I had about four hundred hearers.

Wednesday 11. I had about three hundred hearers at Lancaster meeting-house. Came in the evening to the widow Diggs's. Friday 13, after preaching to a few people at the widow Woodland's, we set out at one o'clock for Bowles's ferry, and crossed in forty minutes, although it was three miles over : we landed in Essex county, and rode eight miles to brother Mann's, where I preached fifteen years ago.

Saturday 14. I visited brother L. R. Cole, and spent the day with him and his agreeable wife. Brother Reuben Ellis is certainly married, for the first time ; may it be for the glory of God, and the good of his church, and comfort of the dear man and his wife !

Sunday 15. I preached to some souls within and round the house, with a mixture of rich and poor, tame and wild people, at mother Cowles's !—I am amazed at the dear aged woman—the additional labour to which she submits, although now between seventy and eighty years of age, and possessing such strong mental powers !—it is surprising.

Monday 16. After a rainy morning I rode to Paup's chapel, and had nearly a hundred people. I spent the evening with Mrs. J. Ellis, brother Paup, and brother Perry :—I was not so spiritual as I might have been.

Tuesday 17. Crossed Mattaponi at Frazie's ferry, and Pomonkey at Putney, and came to Colonel Cleaton's : the weather was cold, and the wind and hunger were both pinching. We were kindly entertained at P. Davies's : Stephen, his brother, is dead, and hath left the chief of what he had to the church. He hath appointed me his trustee to dispose of it, and J. Ellis his executor. I feel the burden of the connexion ; my only hope is, that the Lord of the harvest will send labourers into *his* vineyard, not *mine*.

Thursday 19. I preached at Richmond ; and the next day came, cold and hungry, to my affectionate, kind, adopted son, J. Harding's, in Petersburg. Here several of the preachers met me, to accompany me to the quarterly meeting in Brunswick. I received an original letter from Mr. L——, not like what I wrote ; so I bid him farewell : I will not give him another opportunity to abuse me ; neither shall I lay to heart what he saith to afflict me. I attended the quarterly meeting at Meritt's chapel, and there was some move among the people. I rode to J. Paup's, and had some consultation about Ebenezer school.

Monday 23. I preached at W——'s chapel, and in the evening, came, cold and hungry, to L. Holmes's, in Mecklenburg.

Tuesday 24. Our conference began at Salem chapel; there were present about fifty members, and sixteen probationers—we had close work ; and great harmony in sentiment.

Saturday 28. Brothers A—— and C—— preached; and we had a warm, living season.

Sunday 29, was a great day. I preached on 1 Tim. iii. 15, 16. ; and there were ten elders and nine deacons ordained. This part of the connexion has regained its proper tone, after being kept out of tune for five years by an unhappy division. We were kindly entertained by our friends and brethren ; preachers and people were blest ; and we parted in peace.

Monday 30. I had a few people, and several preachers at brother Seward's. The next day at Wolsey's barn, (now Drumgold's chapel) I had a few people, they having had but short notice : here religion appears to be in a low state : I spent the evening with brother E. D—— ; his house is not with the Lord, as he prayeth and longeth ; yet I trust God hath made an everlasting covenant with the father, well ordered and sure.

Wednesday, December 2. I preached at my old friend W. Owen's, whom I first knew at Portsmouth ; we had a small house, and a good meeting. In the evening I came to my aged friend M. M——'s ; whom I have known these twenty years, although never at his house before.

NORTH CAROLINA.—Monday 7. I preached at brother Clayton's, near Halifax ; and then hasted to brother Bradford's, where we had a small congregation the next day. Yesterday evening William Glendenning stayed here : he talked very boldly to R. W—— ; alleging that he was free, &c. I expect he will go on without fear or wisdom, until many of the Methodists will not receive him into their houses and hear the abuse of their ministers, people, and discipline.

We crossed Tar-River and Town-Creek, and came to T. Sheppard's, where we had all things richly to enjoy. I had my trials, and my spirit was greatly afflicted and humbled : I was glad to get alone to pour out my soul unto God.

Saturday 12. This hath been to me a day of trial and consolation. It is wonderful to see how the people in this country are hid by swamps and creeks.

Sabbath day 13. We set out in the midst of the rain to Span's meeting-house ; I had ten hearers, to whom I preached on Luke xii. 32. We came to brother Span's, who has sold off his property, and is about to move to the high lands of South Carolina : the reason he assigns is laudable ; and I think God will be with him. It rained powerfully in the night, which brought me under great exercise about getting along, having been so often stopped by, and dipped in the rivers and swamps.

Monday 14. We crossed Neuse-River at Whitefield's ferry, the river rising very fast. We passed North-East and Goshen bridges, and Bear-Swamp ; all of which we crossed in safety, though not without fear : my feet were wet, my body cold, and my stomach empty, having had no dinner. I found a good fire, a warm bed, and a little medicine, each necessary in its place. No people make you more welcome to their houses than these ; but is Christ welcome to their hearts ? I am sensible of the want of more religion among them.

Friday 18. After riding about twenty miles, I preached at Father V——'s ; I felt strangely set at liberty, and was uncommonly happy. Here we left Goshen circuit, and Samson county.

Saturday 19. We crossed the south branch of Black-River, and came to Elizabethtown, about fifty miles above Wilmington : we had a very cold day, and nothing to eat for thirty miles. Brother M'Rea met us near the town and took us to his house ; and it was well he did, or we might have been lost in the woods. But the kindness of the people in supplying our wants made up for our toil—Lord, comfort them who comfort us ! Here we had a quiet retreat, and spent the Sabbath in public and private exercises.

Monday 21. We set out by sunrise, and had to work our way through the swamps, where I feared being plunged in headforemost. I have lately been much tried several ways ; and much comforted. We came down Brunswick county, North Carolina, twenty miles to Norman's, within the line of South Carolina. Cross where you will between the states, and it is a miserable pass for one hundred miles west. I was much led out on Rev. xxi. 6—8. This country abounds with bays, swamps, and drains ; if there were here no sinners, I would not go along these roads. I am in want of rest, and should be glad of better fare. O, for patience, faith, courage, and every grace ! Sometimes I feel as though I could rejoice to die and go home : but at other times the work of God is in my way, and sometimes my own unworthiness.

SOUTH CAROLINA.—Thursday 24. We came to Kingston, where I preached in an old Presbyterian meeting-house, now repaired for the use of the Methodists. I spent the evening with W. Rogers, formerly of Bristol, where our wants were richly supplied : thus, sometimes we abound and at other times suffer want ; and we may balance the one with the other.

Christmas-day 25. We set out at six o'clock for Georgetown, and came to Urania Ferry, which we crossed and came to Waca-maw-River : we were detained at the two ferries about three hours, and rested one, and came to Georgetown about four o'clock in the evening ; having rode thirty-seven miles without eating or drink-ing, except a low land hard apple, which I found in my pocket. The vanity of dancing in this place is in a good degree done away, and they have no play-house, and the people are very attentive: I trust that time and patience will bring all things about; that we shall not ride so many hundred miles in vain, and that so many prayers offered up, and tears shed for their welfare, will not be lost. After ten years' labour we have done but little, but if we could station a preacher here, we might yet hope for success. I found brother Cannon had not laboured in vain ; he hath established class meetings among white and black ; and the good would have been still greater had prayer meetings been properly kept up. We try to do good, but who among us try to do all the good they can ? for myself, I leave no company without fears of not having dis-charged my duty. Were it not for Jesus, who would be saved? When I have preached, I feel as though I had need to do it over again ; and it is the same with all my performances. Brother Blanton, my faithful friend, who freely offered himself to go to South-Carolina, now my companion in travel, had not preached for a month, so I thought it time for him to begin again, which he did in the evening. I preached on Psalm xii. 1. and on the Sabbath I preached on Deut. v. 12—14. In the afternoon the people were attentive and somewhat moved. I find the scene is changed in Georgetown ; we have a number of very modest, attentive hear-ers, and a good work among the blacks. The Methodists begin to stand on even ground with their antagonists.

Monday 28. We directed our course towards Charleston, and crossed Santee at Lanues's ferry, which is the best I know on the river. In the evening we reached Mr. C——'s : I felt for the man of the house, and was pleased in having the privilege of praying with them, and enjoyed great sweetness therein.

Tuesday 29. We came to our dear brother Jackson's on Cain Hoy River : here we had the pleasure of hearing of some revival of religion among the children and domestics of the Methodists.

Wednesday 30. We reached Charleston, having made it about seventy-four miles from Georgetown, along an excellent road.

Here are the rich, the rice, and the slaves; the last is awful to me. Wealthy people settled on the rice lands of Cooper-River hold from fifty to two hundred slaves on a plantation in chains of bondage: yet God is able of these stones, yea, of these slave-holders, to raise up children unto Abraham. My soul felt joyful and solemn at the thoughts of a revival of religion in Charleston. I find several young persons are brought into the fold of Christ.

Thursday 31. Several of the preachers came into the city to conference. We had a melting time at the love-feast at brother Wells's.

Friday, January 1, 1796. I gave them a sermon suited to the beginning of the year, and the sacred fire was felt. Saturday 2, we began our conference. Lord's day 3, was a day of extraordinary divine power, particularly at the sacrament; white and black cried out and shouted the praises of God—yea,

"Clap your hands, ye people all,
Praise the God on whom ye call."

Monday 4. We again entered on the business of conference; present, about twenty members and seven graduates. Tuesday 5, continued our business; we have great peace and love—see eye to eye, and heart to heart. We have now a second and confirmed account that Cokesbury college is consumed to ashes, a sacrifice of £10,000 in about ten years! The foundation was laid in 1785, and it was burnt December 7, 1795. Its enemies may rejoice, and its friends need not mourn. Would any man give me £10,000 per year to do and suffer again what I have done for that house, I would not do it. The Lord called not Mr. Whitefield nor the Methodists to build colleges. I wished only for schools—Doctor Coke wanted a college. I feel distressed at the loss of the library.

Thursday 7, we observed as a day of fasting and humiliation, to seek the blessing of God on the conference. We began, continued, and parted in the greatest peace and union. We concluded to send J. J—— and J. R——, alternately, as missionaries to Savannah and the ancient parts of Georgia. Friday 8, most of our brethren took their leave of the city, and I had time for recollection. We have in some cases had to station one preacher where formerly there were two: I trust the cause to God, and he will support it for his own glory; I must look more to him and less to men, whether aged, middle-aged, young, married, or single, of great or small abilities. My mind is variously exercised about staying here:

I lament the partiality of the people for and against particular preachers.

Sunday 10. I gave them a discourse on Hab. ij. 1, 2. "I will stand upon my watch, and set me upon the tower, and will watch to see what he will say unto me, and what I shall answer when I am reproved. And the Lord answered me, Write the vision, and make it plain upon tables that he may run that readeth it." At noon brother Hill made an attempt to preach in the street opposite St. Michael's church, but was prevented by the guard; however, it wrought right, for many were led to attend the church in the afternoon and evening meetings : there appears to be great moving one way or another.

Monday 11. My soul is stayed upon God, momently looking unto him. In reading Mr. Winterbotham, I compared the great talk about President Washington formerly, with what some say and write of him now : according to some he then did nothing wrong ; it is now said that he was always partial to aristocrats and continental officers : as to the latter, I ask, Who bought the liberty of the states ? the continental officers :—and surely they should reap a little of the sweets of rest and peace : these were not chimney-corner whigs. But favours to many of the officers now would come too late—a great number of them are gone to eternity, their constitutions being broken with hard fare and labour during the war. As to myself, the longer I live, and the more I investigate, the more I applaud the uniform conduct of President Washington in all the important stations which he has filled.

Sunday 17. My spirit felt awful through the morning : I preached to a full congregation, and had a solemn season ; and in the afternoon I preached on Luke viii. 10. Monday 18. I am still employed in reading : I admire the sterling truth contained in Mr. Wesley's writings on divinity.

Thursday 21. Precious time—how it flies! I was greatly entertained and comforted in spirit in receiving from brother Southerland an account of the great, confirming blessing, he hath experienced to his soul. Oh! that we could receive such accounts from every family! I have written to several of my ancient friends in Philadelphia. I may say of letters as it was said of silver in the days of Solomon, "I make no account of that :" I suppose I must write nearly a thousand in a year.

Sunday morning 24. I was so poorly as to be hardly able to rise from my bed ; however, I made out to deliver two discourses in public to large congregations. Monday, I wrote, visited, and rode; I read but little. Oh! time, precious time, how swiftly doth it fly!

Wednesday 27. I have great reason to praise God that I am in a house, and not exposed to the dreadful rains and freshets that have taken place. We learn by late accounts that corn, rice, cattle, bridges, and we know not what, are swept away and destroyed by the late uncommon rains. I feel myself humbled before God, under a sense of my not having been as faithful to him as I might have been. I am rather too much delighted with reading on paper, what I have read with my eyes in my travels through the continent.

Sunday 31. Was much taken up with the work of the Lord: I preached in the morning and afternoon.

Monday, February 1. I have wrote in the most pointed manner to my dear brethren at Baltimore, to establish prayer meetings in every part of the town. My mind is unhappy; I wish to be gone into the country to be about my Master's work.

We had a prayer meeting, but the spirit of prayer and supplication did not appear to be among the people. I have peace with God; but my soul is in continual heaviness for Zion.

Wednesday 3. I had near two hundred and fifty of the African society at the love-feast held for them in the evening. Oh, my God! display thy power. I received good news from Jesse Lee concerning the prospect of religion in Boston, Providence, and the District of Maine—that the preachers, societies, and quarterly meetings are lively. My soul at times is in heaviness through manifold temptations. I felt an impression on my mind when at prayer that I felt too much, and might fret myself because of evil doers; I resolve, through grace, to be more resigned to the Lord, and less distressed, least I should lightly sin against God or myself in unnecessarily injuring my health.

Friday 5, I spent in reading and writing, and observed it as a day of fasting and prayer. I felt myself under dejection of spirit. Ah! what a dreary world is this—my mind is under solemn impressions—the result of my reflections on God and souls. I will endeavour not to distress myself above measure. If sinners are lost, I cannot save them, neither shall I be damned for them. I was happy last evening with the poor slaves in brother Wells's kitchen, whilst our white brother held a sacramental love-feast in the front parlour up stairs. I must be poor: this is the will of God concerning me.

The Methodists have now about ninety thousand members of
society in Europe, about seventy thousand in America and the
Islands, and about four hundred in Africa.

Sunday 7. We had an awful, solemn season, while I discoursed
on the two thieves that suffered with our Lord, and still more so
in the afternoon on our Lord's comment on the sixth commandment: it was dreadfully loud and alarming. I believe that
believers, seekers, and sinners felt the word, and I was pleased
to hear that some were stricken with the power of God. I
feel very weak in body, and find that age makes an alteration.
But my soul is truly happy in the Lord, and his work is reviving
amongst us.

Sunday 14. I began the solemnity of the day by opening and
applying our Lord's comment on the seventh commandment, which
is designed to condemn the adultery of the heart. It appears to
have been the will of our Lord not to give liberty for a second
marriage while a former husband or wife is living. St. Paul undoubtedly understood it so, even when heathen husbands left their
wives, or wives left their husbands.

Wednesday 19. The city now appears to be running mad for
races, plays, and balls. I am afraid of being out of my duty in
staying here too long: my soul is among the lions; yet Christ is
mine, and I trust my supreme desire is, " Holiness to the Lord."
My soul longeth to be gone like a bird from a cage. I have been
employed in visiting from house to house, and lament the super-
ficial state of religion among the white people who are called
Methodists. I have thought if we had entered here to preach
only to the Africans, we should probably have done better.

Sunday 21. I delivered two discourses on our Lord's Sermon on the Mount, and was loud, long, alarming, and not very
pleasing.

Monday 21. I felt myself indisposed, owing to the exertions of
the day past.

Wednesday 24 and Thursday 25, I was employed in putting my
thoughts together on the unlawfulness of divorce—of having more
than one wife, or taking a second on any consideration while the
first is living. I begin to feel comfortable at the thoughts of
leaving this city shortly. This makes me fear I ought not to stay
here so long. It is true, I have a thousand or twelve hundred
hearers, and two or three hundred of these change with the day.
My soul possesseth peace, but great unworthiness cleaveth to me.
I am apprehensive I injure myself by giving too intense applica-

tion to reading. In my early days I contracted a habit for this, and I cannot easily give it up.

Sunday 28. My morning subject was Philippians i. 8, 9. In the evening I treated on *wolves in sheeps' clothing :* some laughed, some wept, and some were vexed. Ah how I wish to make my escape and be gone ! I must pay for this indulgence with pain of mind : I feel for these souls : many of them who have been sitting under my ministry, appear to be more hardened now than when I began first to preach to them ; and no wonder, seeing they have so insulted the Spirit of God.

Wednesday, March 2. For my unholiness and unfaithfulness, my soul is humbled : was I to stand in my own merit, where should I be or go, but to hell ? The time drawing nigh when I expected to leave the city, I was visited by my poor Africans, and had their prayers and best wishes. And now, what have I been doing ? I have preached eighteen sermons, met all the classes, fifteen in number, wrote about eighty letters, read some hundred pages ; visited thirty families again and again But who are made the subjects of grace ? Such are my impressions, that I am apprehensive God will work more in judgment than in mercy ; and that this will be an eventful year to the inhabitants of this place. In the course of my stay here I have written more than three hundred pages on subjects interesting to the society and connexion.

Thursday 3. I left the city ; the rain of yesterday and to-day has made the road extremely wet and muddy ; it was in our favour that we came over the Causeway at Ashley-River, without swimming. We came in the evening, dripping, to father E——s, having rode thirty-four miles.

Friday 4. We crossed Edisto-River, and came to Island-Creek. At a pole-house I talked awhile on 1 Chron. vii. 14. and administered the sacrament. My feet were as if they had been steeped in water.

We had to ride three miles for lodgings, hungry, wet, and weary. Since half past eight yesterday we have rode upwards of sixty miles. I am now turned fifty years of age, and feel it hard to flesh and blood to go upon the old line, as in former days. God is at work in this place, so that we do not labour and suffer altogether in vain. I was under some difficulties about getting along, owing to the great rains, which have so raised the water courses that they are impassable. We at length directed our course towards Augusta ; with deep wading, by the assistance of brother B——, and by the blessing of Providence, we came to father E——'s, a

Lot in Sodom. It is all right that I should come to see these aged
people, and preach to the young ones. I am weary, but I will travel on : I only want more of the spirit of faith and prayer. I feel
very sensibly for my dear Charleston people ; I doubt not but
they think of and pity me. My feet have been wet every day,
for four days successively ; but the kindness of the people help-
eth me greatly over these troubles.

Wednesday 9. Rode twenty-five miles to Chester's. Here I
learned Edisto was impassable. If we had not hasted along as we
did, we should not have passed it in proper time, and I should have
been prevented from visiting Georgia this year also. There are
so many water courses, and so few ferry's, that going through this
country in any certain time is like a lottery.

Thursday 10. We sent notice through the neighbourhood, to
collect a congregation ; so I had the privilege of preaching to a
people I had not addressed for six years. Oh! my soul, how dost
thou travail for souls night and day!

GEORGIA.—I crossed W——'s ferry ; the point on the south
side is washed like a beach, and the house swept away by the late
freshets ; I saw how the flood had ploughed up the street of
Augusta : I walked over the ruins for nearly two miles, viewing
the deep gulfs in the main street. I suppose they would crucify
me if I were to tell them it is the African flood ; but if they could
hear me think, they would discover this to be my sentiment. I
was honoured with the church to preach in ; where I had about
four hundred respectable hearers. I have delivered my own
soul—it may be once for all. I have rode about one hundred and
ninety miles from Charleston into Georgia ; I have attended four
meetings ; and have not had, in all, above six hundred hearers.

Wednesday 16. I rode fifteen miles to Whiteoak ; I was sick ;
the house was very open, and the wind blew powerfully. Dying!
—dead!—unpleasing appearances! We swam our horses across
Little-River, and had to ride fifteen miles after preaching to get
our dinners.

Friday 18. I was very much outdone before I reached Comb's
meeting-house, which was very open. I was very warm in preaching. I rode to G——'s in the evening, making it nearly twenty
miles : when I came there I was so indisposed, that I was glad to
go to bed. Next morning I felt better, and rode to the school at
Coke's chapel ; where, after preaching, I partially examined the
scholars.

Thursday 24. I had a few wealthy, and, I fear, wicked people at Pope's chapel; I preached on our Lord's weeping over Jerusalem. We had deep wading across Long-Creek, and made it nearly twenty miles to ———, very kind, but no religion here. Since I have been in Georgia, I have had a blessed time of consolation in my own soul. I must needs go through Petersburg. I had to ride to Curltail-River, and thence to the head of Reedy-River, twenty-eight or thirty miles. We got no food for man nor horse until we came to D——'s; I preached to his father twenty-two years ago.

SOUTH CAROLINA.—Tuesday 29. I held forth about an hour and a half on Acts iii. 26. We set out again about two o'clock, and had to ride for our dinner *only twenty miles*. We crossed Muddy, and Lick Creeks, Little and Great Bush-River. These afford bodies of excellent land.

Wednesday 30. We had a meeting of the trustees of Bethel school, and it was agreed it should be a *free school;* and that only the English tongue and the sciences should be taught. I drew up an address on behalf of the school in order to raise three hundred dollars per annum, to support a president teacher. I dined with my unshaken friend, W. P. an Israelite indeed. He hath all things richly to enjoy, and a good conscience also. He was formerly a travelling preacher amongst us, and laboured for and with us nearly as long as he was able. The weather is as warm here as in the month of June to the north. I was so weary with riding that I could not sleep.

Sunday, April 3. A multitude of sinners came together at W. S——'s. I feel myself still faint and feeble, and would not live always.

Monday 4. I crossed Fair-Forest, and came to J. G.'s, where I had to stop and rest. Since I came into South Carolina, I have rode through Newbury, Spartansburgh, Union, and Lawrence counties. There is a general complaint of the want of corn in these parts; and no wonder, when we consider the great storm which they have had, and the number of stills in the country: the people here drink their bread as well as eat it. I am so very poorly in body that close study injures me. I crossed Lawson-Fork at the high shoals, a little below the Beauty-Spot. I could not but admire the curiosity of the people—my wig was as great a subject of speculation as some wonderful animal from Africa or India would have been. I had about one hundred people at the meeting-house, some came to look at, and others to hear me. We must needs go

off without any dinner, intending to ride nearly forty miles to
father Moore's, in Rutherford county, (N. C.) After brother M.
and myself had preached, we passed the Cow-Pens, where Morgan
and Tarlton had their fray. We made it nearly twenty-five miles
to the Upper Island ford, on the main Broad-River; and after
travelling until seven o'clock at night were glad to stop at brother
S——'s, ten miles short of the place we intended to reach when
we set out.

NORTH CAROLINA.—Wednesday 6. We came to Moore's : I was
at a loss how to address myself to these people—it may be for the
last time : it was laid on my heart to speak from our Lord's lamen-
tation over Jerusalem. I felt awful among them.

Saturday 9. We came to Cane-Creek, in Burke county. We
dined on some peach-pie in the woods. In the afternoon there
arose a most dreadful storm of rain, with thunder and lightning :
it was very awful ; we cried to God for man and beast, and were
preserved. We came in about seven o'clock, and were received
by T. B. with great kindness.

Monday 11. We crossed Lovelady's ferry and came to Connell's, where I met with several preachers. After preaching, I
was going to administer the sacrament, and discovered that what
they had provided for wine was in reality brandy ; so I desisted.
Here I met Doctor B——ll, who is still praying and waiting for
the consolation of Israel. I rode a mountainous path six miles to
father W——'s, where we dined. Ah! what a round of continual
running is my life. Of late, feeble as I am, I cannot help thinking
of Cumberland, in Tennessee ; and trying to go there : if I must
go to Kentucky, I think it is time to go to Cumberland also.

Thursday 14. We took our departure from Johns-River, up
the branches of Catabaw : on our way we met with a half dozen
living creatures, like men and women, who seemed quite pleased
with their mountain wedding ; they were under the whip, riding
two and two as if they would break their necks ; one had a white
cloth like a flag, and the other a silk handkerchief ; when they
had spent their fire, they called at a still-house to prime again.
I ascended about one mile up a mountain, and came to M. Davenport's : here I felt deep dejection of mind as well as great
weakness of body, and as if I could lie down and die ; owing, in
some measure, I presume, to the great fatigue I underwent in
ascending the mountain, which was very steep.

Saturday 16. We set off at six o'clock, and directed our course
up Tow-River ; thence up the Rocky-Creek through the gap of

the Yellow Mountain, to the head waters of Toe-River; we had
to ride till eight o'clock at night. My mind is still under deep
depression.

TENNESSEE.—Sunday 17. I preached at Dawe's to about two
hundred people; and then met the society, and had a melting season. The milk and water of this country are both as physic to
me; I am afraid that such shocks as these, will, some time or
other, overset me.

Monday 18. I rested at D——'s; my body very feeble, and
mind under exceeding dejection, with imaginary and real evils.

Tuesday evening, the preachers came in from Kentucky and
Cumberland.

Wednesday 20. Our conference began in great peace, and thus
it ended. We had only one preacher for each circuit in Kentucky;
and one for Green circuit in Tennessee. Myself being weak,
and my horse still weaker, I judged it impracticable to attempt
going through the wilderness to Kentucky; and have concluded to
visit Nolachucky. I wrote an apology to the brethren in Kentucky
for my not coming, and informed them of the cause.

Monday 25. On the banks of Nolachucky I parted with our
dear suffering brethren, going through the howling wilderness. I
feel happy in God. Sinners appear to be hardened, and professors
cold; the preachers, although young men, appear to be solemn and
devoted to God, and doubtless are men who may be depended upon.

NORTH CAROLINA.—I came to C——'s, where I saw a Baptist
minister, who had moved from Georgia to Kentucky; he appeared
desirous of returning again. I was told he expressed his fears,
that the ministers in Kentucky will be a curse to each other, and the
people too: good religion and such good land, are not so easily
matched together. We came to D——'s, and had a full meeting.
Brother Hill and his aids had a great time on the Sabbath; and I
trust the time to favour this people is come.

Sunday, May 1. We came to Acuff's chapel. I found the family
sorrowful and weeping on account of the death of Francis Acuff,
who from a fiddler became a Christian; from a Christian, a preacher;
and from a preacher, I trust, a glorified saint: he died in the work
of the Lord in Kentucky. I found myself assisted in preaching on
Ephes. ii. 1, 2. The house was crowded, and I trust they did not
come together in vain. I was somewhat alarmed at the sudden
death of Reuben Ellis, who hath been in the ministry upwards of
twenty years; a faithful man of God, of slow, but very solid parts;

he was an excellent counsellor, and steady yoke-fellow in Jesus. My mind is variously exercised as to future events—whether it is my duty to continue to bear the burden I now bear, or whether I had not better retire to some other land. I am not without fears, that a door will be opened to honour, ease, or interest; and then farewell to religion in the American Methodist connexion; but death may soon end all these thoughts, and quiet all these fears.

VIRGINIA.—Thursday 5. I came to ——'s; thence to the unmeaning meeting-house, and found a wild, wicked people, to whom I preached on Gen. xix. 18. An appointment had been made for me to preach in Abingdon. As I expected there would be no opportunity, as the court was then sitting, I concluded to go off to Clinch, but was informed there would be (by the will of the judges) an adjournment of the court for my preaching: I therefore went and preached at three o'clock, and had the judges, some of the lawyers, and very few of the citizens to hear me. As sentence was passed on a poor criminal this day, and two more were burnt in the hand, I judged I ought to meet the solemnities of the day, and spoke on " Knowing therefore the terrors of the Lord, we persuade men;" but was shut up in my own mind.

Saturday 7. I escaped from Abingdon as out of a prison, and rode to Clinch. I passed by Mr Cummings's—he hath not laboured for nought; few men have a better house or plantation : but his plea is, " He put his life in his hand :" and so have I, every time I have crossed the wilderness and mountains. I expect a crown for my services : were I to charge the people on the western waters for my services, I should take their roads, rocks and mountains into the account, and rate my labours at a very high price. We crossed North-Holstein, and came to D——'s, sixteen miles ; where we had a congregation of about two hundred people.

TENNESSEE.—Saturday 14. We passed Russell court-house, and intended to go to B——'s, but were met by a most violent storm of rain, thunder, and lightning. We had a most dreadful crack; the fire and scent were like the discharge of a great gun ; I was much alarmed for nearly a mile with expectation or fear of what would overtake us. We found shelter from part of the storm in a poor cabin, where some people had stopped on their way to Cumberland. Cold, labour, and being in the rain, causes me to feel very unwell.

Sunday 8. In the morning I awoke very unwell; I took a few drops of camphorated spirits, Bateman's Drops, and paregoric, and found some ease, although my headach and fever still continued. I made out to preach to about two hundred people.

Monday 9. I hobbled over the ridge, through the capital part of Russell county, sixteen miles to B——'s : these people have lived in peace ever since the death of Ben, the half-blooded Indian war-rior, who was shot through the head while carrying off two women. He was a dreadful wicked wretch, who by report may have been the agent of death to nearly one hundred people in the wilderness, and on Russell. Here I preached to a few insensible people ; and had time to read, write, and sleep in quiet. Yesterday our pray-ers were requested on behalf of F. D——. This day in the eve-ning brother K—— was called upon to perform her funeral so-lemnities. Perhaps she has been as great a female sufferer as I have heard of. The following account, in substance, was taken from her own mouth, some time ago, by J. Kobler, who performed her funeral rites.

Her maiden name was Dickenson. She was married to a Mr. Scott, and lived in Powell's Valley : at which time the Indians were very troublesome, often killing and plundering the inhabitants. On a certain evening, her husband and children being in bed, eight or nine Indians rushed into the house ; her husband being alarmed, started up, when all that had guns, fired at him. Although he was badly wounded, he broke through them all, and got out of the house : several of them closely pursued him, and put an end to his life : they then murdered and scalped all her children before her eyes, plundered her house, and took her prisoner. The remainder of the night they spent around a fire in the woods, drinking, shouting, and dancing. The next day they divided the plunder, with great equality ; amongst the rest of the goods was one of Mr. Wesley's hymn-books ; she asked them for it, and they gave it to her, but when they saw her often reading therein, they were displeased, called her a conjurer, and took it from her. After this they tra-velled several day's journey towards the Indian towns ; but, said she, my grief was so great I could hardly believe my situation was a reality, but thought I dreamed. To aggravate my grief, one of the Indians hung my husband's and my children's scalps to his back, and would walk the next before me. In walking up and down the hills and mountains, I was worn out with fatigue and sorrow, they would often laugh when they saw me almost spent, and mimic my panting for breath. There was one Indian who was more humane than the rest ; he would get me water, and make the others stop when I wanted to rest : thus they carried me on eleven days' journey, until they were all greatly distressed with hunger : they then committed me to the care of an old Indian at the camp, while they went off a hunting.

Whilst the old man was busily employed in dressing a deer-skin, I walked backward and forward through the woods, until I observed he took no notice of me ; I then slipped off, and ran a considerable distance and came to a cane-brake, where I hid myself very securely. Through most of the night I heard the Indians searching for me, and answering each other with a voice like that of an owl. Thus was I left alone in the savage wilderness, far from any inhabitants, without a morsel of food, or any friend to help, but the common Saviour and friend of all : to Him I poured out my complaint in fervent prayer that he would not forsake me in this distressing circumstance. I then set out the course that I thought Kentucky lay, though with very little expectation of seeing a human face again, except that of the savages ; whom I looked upon as so many fiends from the bottomless pit ; and my greatest dread was that of meeting some of them whilst wandering in the wilderness.

One day as I was travelling, I heard a loud human voice, and a prodigious noise, like horses running ; I ran into a safe place and hid myself ; and saw a company of Indians pass by, furiously driving a gang of horses which they had stolen from the white people. I had nothing to subsist upon but roots, young grape-vines, and sweet-cane, and such like produce of the woods. I accidentally came where a bear was eating a deer, and drew near in hopes of getting some, but he growled and looked angry ; so I left him, and quickly passed on. At night when I lay down to rest, I never slept, but I dreamed of eating. In my lonesome travels, I came to a very large shelving rock, under which was a fine bed of leaves ; I crept in among them, and determined there to end my days of sorrow. I lay there several hours until my bones ached in so distressing a manner that I was obliged to stir out again. I then thought of, and wished for home ; and travelled on several days, till I came where Cumberland-River breaks through the mountain.

I went down the cliffs a considerable distance, until I was affrighted, and made an attempt to go back, but found the place down which I had gone was so steep that I could not return. I then saw but one way that I could go, which was a considerable perpendicular distance down to the bank of the River. I took hold of the top of a little bush, and for half an hour prayed fervently to God for assistance ; I then let myself down by the little bush until it broke, and I went with great violence down to the bottom. This was early in the morning, and I lay there a considerable time with a determination to go no further. About ten o'clock I grew so thirsty, that I concluded to crawl to the water and drink, after which I found I could walk. *The place I came through, as I have been since informed, is only two miles, and I was four days in getting through it.* I travelled on until I came to a little path, one end of which led to the inhabitants, and the other to the wilderness ; I knew not which end of the path to take—after standing and praying to the Lord for direction, I turned to take the end that led to the wilderness; immediately there came a little bird of a dove colour near to my feet, and fluttered along the path that led to the inhabitants. I did not observe this much at first, until it did it a second or third time ; I then understood this as a direction of Providence, and took the path which led me to the inhabitants. Immediately after her safe arrival she embraced religion, and lived and died a humble follower of Christ.

Sunday 15. How gladly would I have attended my bed, rather than my meeting ; but it was fixed otherwise, and I had to stand in the door, pressed with people, and preach to about three hundred hearers. There was some stir among them. I felt better in soul and body after meeting than I did before. We passed through Wythe county, and rode seventy miles in two days.

Thursday 19. I was crowded with stupid sinners of various descriptions, to whom I preached on Joshua xxiv. 19. " Ye cannot serve God," &c. It was a matter of surprise, that I not only refused to stay a night, but that I did not eat bread nor drink water in that place.

Friday 20. We rode forty miles to Indian-Creek, about fifteen miles above the mouth. We had no place to dine until we arrived at father C——'s, about six o'clock. If I could have regular food and sleep, I could stand the fatigue I have to go through much better ; but this is impossible under some circumstances. To sleep four hours, and ride forty miles without food or fire is hard : —but we had water enough in the rivers and creeks. I shall have rode nearly one thousand miles on the western waters before I leave them ; I have been on the waters of Nolachucky, to the mouth of Clinch ; on the north, middle, and south branches of Holstein ; on New-River, Green Briar, and by the head springs of Monongahela. If I were able I should go from Charleston (S. C.) a direct course, five hundred miles, to Nolachucky ; thence two hundred and fifty miles to Cumberland ; thence one hundred to

Kentucky; thence one hundred miles through that state, and two hundred to Saltsburg; thence two hundred to Green Briar; thence two hundred to Red-Stone, and three hundred to Baltimore. Ah! if I were young again! I was happy to have a comfortable night's sleep, after a hard day's ride, and but little rest the night before. I have now a little time to refit, recollect, and write. Here forts and savages once had a being, but now peace and improvement.

Monday 23. I rode to Rehoboth chapel in the sinks of Green Briar, where we held conference with a few preachers. Here I delivered two discourses. Thursday crossed Green Briar River, and had to pass along a crooked and dangerous path to Benton's. My mind is in peace.

Friday 27. I felt myself very heavy : my mind unprepared for the congregation at Gilboa meeting-house, and could not preach with any satisfaction. After meeting the society, I came away much clouded. We came off from brother C——'s about four o'clock, aiming at the Little Levels; but darkness came on, and we had to climb and blunder over the point of a mountain, in descending which my feet were so squeezed that the blood was ready to gush out of the pores : I could hardly help weeping out my sorrow : at length we came to brother H——'s, where the kindness of the family was a cordial, and we went to rest about ten o'clock, and all was well.

Sunday 29. I was very warm in body and mind at M'Neale's. In the afternoon (contrary to my sentiment and practice on the Lord's day) we took our departure, purposing to reach Morgantown on Wednesday evening, in order to attend an appointment made for me on Thursday, the second of June. We reached my old friend Drinnon's, who received us gladly, and entertained us kindly. Next day (Monday) we opened our campaign through the mountains, following a path I had thought never to travel again. Frequently we were in danger of being plucked off our horses by the boughs of the trees under which we had to ride. About seven o'clock, after crossing six mountains and many rocky creeks and fords of Elk and Monongahela Rivers, we made the *Valley of Distress*, called by the natives Tyger's Valley. We had a comfortable lodging at Mr. White's; and here I must acknowledge the kindness and decency of the family, and their readiness to duty, sacred and civil. Thence we hastened on at the rate of forty-two miles a day. We had to ride four miles in the night, and went supperless to *the Punchins*, where we slept a little on hard lines.

After encountering many difficulties, known only to God and ourselves, we came to Morgantown. I doubt whether I shall ever request any person to come and meet me at the levels of Green Briar, or to accompany me across these mountains again, as brother D. Hitt has now done. Oh! how chequered is life! How thankful ought I to be that I am here safe, with life and limbs, in peace and plenty, at kind brother S——'s.

PENNSYLVANIA.—Thursday, June 2. I gave them a discourse on "Work out your own salvation with fear and trembling." I had half a dozen preachers and a congregation of serious hearers, and some wept. I was informed of an awful circumstance. A man, aged seventy years, strangled his own son to prevent his appearing as evidence against him for theft.

Thursday 9. We crossed Great Yohogany, and came to Connel's-Town, where we had a good time. I preached on Acts iii. 26. Sister C——, who professed to find peace six or seven years ago, when I prayed with her, was now sick ; I gave her counsel and medicine, and trust I left her better in soul and body.

Saturday 11. I rode to Union-Town, and after a solemn meeting, I sat in conference with the preachers.

Monday 13. We left Union-Town and rode about thirty-five miles, and the next day forty-five to J. F——'s.

MARYLAND.—Wednesday 15. I came to Old-Town, and preached to a few people at brother J. J. Jacobs's, and the next day rode nearly forty miles to father F——'s.

Friday 17. We rode forty-two miles, and were weary enough.

Saturday 18. I came to brother S. Philips's, and was glad to lay me down and rest, having rode about two hundred miles on uneven roads in five days and a half.

Sunday 19. I was musing in my own mind how I could best spend the morning of that day. I concluded to call the family into the room, and address them pointedly, one by one, concerning their souls : I did so, and hope it was not in vain. In the afternoon I preached on the twenty-third Psalm.

Tuesday 21. I preached in Frederick-Town at ten o'clock, and at Liberty-Town at five o'clock.

Wednesday 22. I had some life at the new meeting-house on the Ridge. I borrowed a horse to ride nine miles, and then made out to get to Baltimore. O what times are here! The academy is crowded, they have five teachers, and nearly two hundred scholars. I will now take a view of my journey for some months past. From the best judgment I can form, the distance is as follows

from Baltimore to Charleston (S. C.) one thousand miles ; thence
up the state of South Carolina two hundred miles ; from the centre
to the west of Georgia two hundred miles ; through North Carolina one hundred miles ; through the state of Tennessee one hundred miles ; through the west of Virginia three hundred miles ;
through Pennsylvania and the west of Maryland and down to Baltimore four hundred miles. I was employed in town as usual in
preaching and meeting the classes, &c. I continued in town
until Thursday 30, and then set off, and came in the evening to
Esquire G——'s, our ancient lodging, and was received with
their usual kindness.

Friday, July 1. Came to Abingdon and saw the walls of Cokes-
bury, with some pain of mind. We came in the evening to Mr.
Dallam's, whose house was the first home I had in these parts.
Sister Dallam is worn out with affliction : but her confidence in
God continues and appears to grow stronger.

Saturday 2, and Sunday 3. I attended Cecil quarterly meeting ;
and spent Monday 4th at Mr. Bassett's ; I was so unwell, that if my
company had not been entertaining I should have been in bed.

Wednesday 6. We had a solemn season at Dudley's chapel : it
was like a Sabbath.

Thursday 7. I rode to Choptank (now Greensborough) through
excessive heat ; S. Cook was watching for me, and when I came she
could hardly bear my presence ; she seemed as deeply affected as
if I had been her father, knowing the great affection that subsisted
between her deceased father and myself. I am now happy that it
is not in me to weep as do others, or I might never wipe my eyes.
I preached on Isai. lvii. 18—21.

Tuesday 10. I went to meeting under great heaviness ; and
there was some among the people. I dined with Wm. Moore,
where I prophesied seventeen years ago. How few are left now
that heard me then !

Monday 11. The heat has been for some time, and still is, excessive ; I doubt if it be not equal to that in Georgia and the
islands. We rode fifteen miles to Quantee's chapel ; where we had
a number of gay people ; but it appeared as if they did not understand or even hear what I said. We have reason to praise God
for an abatement of the heat of the weather, which, had it continued, would have been insupportable. We had excessive rain,
attended with thunder and lightning.

We came to Snow-Hill, on Pocomoke-River. I called on the
weeping widow Bowen, whose late husband, after being the princi-

pal in building a house for divine worship, died in peace. Here I met about one thousand people : being unable to command the congregation from the pulpit, I stood in one of the doors, and preached to those who were in, and to those who were out of the house.

I rode eight miles to the sea shore ; when we came near we felt the cool sea breeze very powerfully. I lodged with S. Evans, whose house I visited sixteen years ago : here are two people above seventy years of age, who have lived together forty-eight years.

Tuesday 19. We rode forty miles to Lewistown ; we stopped to dine near H——'s grand mill seat. My spirits of late keep up greatly, not being subject to depression as heretofore. It cleared away about noon, and gave us the opportunity of riding two miles out of Lewistown, after preaching to the brethren and the Africans. I dined with Mr. Shanklin, whose house was the first that was opened to me in this place. We then urged our way up the county, and escaped the rain until we came within two miles of Milford ; it then poured down very heavily, and we came in dripping about eight o'clock.

Friday 22. We had a living love-feast : many opened their mouths, but spoke too much of what was past. We had an exceeding great company, to whom I preached on Isai. lxii. 12. The two following days, Saturday and Sunday, I attended Dover quarterly meeting ; where I suppose we had nearly two thousand people. It was a living, open season : there was great sweetness and love among the brethren.

Monday 25. About thirty-five minutes before I began meeting, I received the last loving request of our dear brother William Jessop, which was to preach his funeral sermon : I had my difficulties in speaking, and the people in hearing of a man so well known and so much beloved : he was always solemn ; and few such holy, steady men have been found amongst us. I stopped at Middletown, Wilmington, and Chester, in my way to Philadelphia.

PENNSYLVANIA.—Thursday 28. I preached on Psalm xxiii. 24. I have thought that we should preach as if we expected no help from the people ; yea, as if we believed that enemies of God and us were in the congregation. I began meeting classes in the city. I had some pleasure in receiving news of a revival of religion in the south ; likewise from the eastern states. But there are great failures among the preachers on account of health, &c. preventing their travelling and standing to the work. Brother Blanton has given me an account of the late fire in Charleston, and says that about five hundred houses are destroyed.

Saturday 30. I began reading Mr. Fletcher's Portrait of St. Paul : the notes are significant, and show what a minister of the Gospel ought to be, and what he may be through grace.

Sunday 31. I had some life and more liberty at Ebenezer in the morning at five o'clock : I must needs attend the second African church ; and at half past seven o'clock, in the great unwieldy house and congregation in Fourth-street, I preached on John i. 17.

Monday, August 1. I drew the outlines of a subscription, that may form part of a constitution of a general fund, for the sole purpose of supporting the travelling ministry ; to have respect,

First, To the single men that suffer and are in want.

Secondly, To the married travelling preachers.

Thirdly, To the worn-out preachers.

Fourthly, The widows and orphans of those who have lived and died in the work.—And

Fifthly, To enable the yearly conference to employ more married men ; and finally, to supply the wants of all the travelling preachers, under certain regulations, and restrictions, as the state of the fund will admit.

Thursday 4. I was called upon by the African society in Campington to open their new house, which I did on Rom. i. 16—18. and had an unwieldy congregation of white and black   Brother D. gave a lively exhortation on the new birth.

Friday 5. Having concluded on the presentation of the subscription, I hasted with it from house to house. After dinner we came to Germantown, where I preached in the academy at six o'clock to a large congregation of women. I lodged once more at the house of mother Steele and her daughter Lusby ; having had an acquaintance of twenty-two years.

NEW-JERSEY.—Sunday 7. It being rainy in the morning, my congregation was not very large at Trenton. I preached on Isaiah lxii. 10. 1. The charge to the ministry to go through the gates as ministers and Christians. 2. Prepare the way—removing all the difficulties. 3. Cast up the highway—repentance, regeneration, and sanctification. 4. Gather out the stones—wicked ministers and people. 5. Set up the standard—i. e. form the Christian church ; give the standard of Christian doctrine and experience. In the afternoon I preached on Hebr. x. 38. It is a dry time, and we cannot get along : I was sorry I did not preach in the street.

Monday 8. We directed our course through the Jerseys towards
New-York ; passing through Penny-Town, and along an agreeable,
well-improved part of the country.

Tuesday 9. We made our way twenty-five miles to brother
M'Collough's, near Schooley's Mountain—properly a remnant of
the Blue Ridge. After a good meeting at brother M'C.'s, we went
to lay the foundation of a new meeting-house : we sung part of
Dr. Watts's hymn on *the corner-stone*, and prayed : I then had to
lend a hand to lay the mighty corner-stone of the house : we then
sung and prayed, and retired to brother Budd's, an Israelite indeed ;
my never-failing friend in time, and I hope will be to all eternity.

Wednesday 10. I thought it good not to be idle, so I went to
Hackets-Town, and preached on " The promise is to you, and to
your children," &c. we had few people, but a feeling, serious time.
Thence we rode to Dover, where we had many people at a short
warning : I admired the solemnity of the women ; the men appeared to be outdone with the heat and labours of the day.

Friday 12. We rode twenty miles to brother Dickinson's : he is
now an official character among us, and can remember, when he
was a child, how godly men came to the house of his father,
preaching, praying, and talking about religion, as was the case at
my father's house when I was a child.

Saturday 13. I rode to Elizabethtown, where I preached : the
next day I met the classes. Having heard many things of Mr.
Austin, many of which were very wild, I went and heard for myself : he explained the 22d chapter of the Revelation of Jesus
Christ to St. John, and applied it to the Millennium and reign of
Christ upon earth : his foretelling the time and place of the coming
and kingdom of Christ ; General Washington being Zerubba-
bel, and himself Joshua the high priest, and the ploughing up
of a certain field—all this appeared to me like wildness of the
brain.

Monday 15. We rode to New-York : whilst crossing the ferry
some foolish, wicked people uttered so many *damns* that I was a
little afraid the Lord would sink the boat : I asked a man if he
had any chalk to lend me that I might mark down the curses the
company gave us on our passage of thirty or forty minutes. I
was taken up in meeting classes and visiting from house to house
a good deal of my time in the day, and I frequently preached at
night. I read Watson's Apology for the Bible.

Sunday 21. I went over to Brooklyn, where we have a small
society : I had very few hearers except those who came from the

city. I administered the sacrament, and we had some life. We then returned to the city, where I preached in the afternoon to about one thousand six-hundred people, some of whom were wicked and wild enough. The preachers had pity upon me, and desired me to preach only twice this Sabbath. In my own soul I feel happy, but on account of the church of God, and poor sinners, awful. It appears as necessary to preach conviction and conversion among our own, as among other congregations. Oh! when will the Lord appear as in ancient times!

Monday 22. I met three living classes; several among whom professed perfect love. The weather is excessively warm and dry : people are sickly, and dying, especially children ; I find my body very weak : preaching at night, added to the moschetoes, causes me to sleep very little.

Wednesday 24. We have still very great heat : it appears to me to be *unhealthy, judgment weather* : I feel almost spent. I generally walk three or four miles a day, pray ten or twelve times, in the congregation, families, and classes ; my sleep is interrupted with pain and heat.

Thursday 25. I was much fatigued in meeting classes and visiting from house to house ; but the Lord was present to bless, which gave me consolation. In the evening we had a full house ; I was uncommonly assisted in preaching; and there was much weeping in the congregation. It is impossible to preach to these people till you are well acquainted with them ; but here I have no continuing city : next week I go hence.

Sunday 28. I preached in the morning at the old church ; in the afternoon at the new church, on Hebr. ii. 3. and in the evening at the old church again on Rev. iii. 2, 3. besides meeting six classes in the course of the day ; in general I have had no extraordinary assistance in preaching of late. Brother L—— preached twice in the north end of Broadway ; the congregation appeared serious and attentive. Notwithstanding the labours of the day were considerable, I was not much wearied. In meeting the society, I observed to them, that they knew but little of my life and labours, unless in the pulpit, family, or class meetings, that they were unacquainted with my labours even in that city, much less could they tell where I had been, and what I had been doing for one year.

Tuesday 30. I delivered my concluding discourse on Isaiah lvii. 18.; 1. The penitent backslider ; 2. The Lord hath seen his ways ; 3. Healing him ; 4. Leading him ; 5. Restoring comforts to him : we had some serious, feeling souls at our meeting.

Wednesday 31. I had a meeting with the leaders in close conference, and found it necessary to explain some parts of our discipline
to them, particularly that of the right of preachers expelling members, when tried before the society or a " select number," and
found guilty of a breach of the law of God, and our rules ; and
that if an appeal were made, it should be brought before the quarterly meeting conference, composed of travelling and local preachers, leaders, and stewards, and finally be determined by a majority
of votes. I found it also needful to observe there was such a thing
as heresy in the church ; and I know not what it is if it be not to
deny the Lord that bought them ; and the eternity of the punishment of the damned, as is virtually done by the Universalists.
Schism is not dividing hypocrites from hypocrites, formal professors
from people of their own cast : it is not dividing nominal Episcopalians from each other ; nominal Methodists from nominal Methodists ; or nominal Quakers from nominal Quakers, &c. But *schism*
is the dividing real Christians from each other, and breaking the
unity of the Spirit. I met the trustees ; and after going hither
and thither, and being much spent with labour through the day ; I
gave them a discourse at the new house, (in the evening) on Acts
xx. 32. My attempt was feeble but faithful.

Friday, September 2. I left the city, stopped at father Oakley's,
twenty miles from New-York, where a few people came together,
to whom I preached on Acts iv. 12. and at night I was enabled to
take a little rest.

Saturday 3. Notwithstanding the rain I rode twelve miles to the
White-Plains quarterly meeting, where I enlarged on Ephes. vi.
13—18. ;—being Paul's exhortation to the use of the whole armour of God. I was in great heaviness through temptation and
infirmity of body. I lodged with Elijah Crawford : this house is
for God.

Sunday 4. I was very low, but attended the love-feast ; I stood
in one of the windows, and preached very loud to a large congregation on Hebr. xii. 25. There were some feeling, gracious souls
present. I was desired to preach in Bedford, but declined it for
several reasons. I cannot stand such constant exertions. I have
felt very severe pain in one of my shoulders, much like that I experienced after Cecil quarterly meeting. I lodged with brother Davis, where we had the company of one who may be a disciple of
mine : I hope to see him yet in the kingdom of grace and glory :
if he should live to read these lines he will know who I mean.

Monday 5. I rode fifteen miles to the widow Banks's to tarry for a night. My soul is in peace, and Christ is mine ; but trouble will come : I am not yet all immortal and at rest ; my rheumatic affections are very severe ; I was imprudent in making, and my indisposition prevented my attending my appointments.

CONNECTICUT.—We came off in the morning for Reading ; fed at Ridgefield, and reached my journey's end about one o'clock, about twenty-three miles. On my way I dined with lawyer Smith, and preached at Sanford's on 1 Peter i. 13—15.: in doing which, I pointed out, 1. The most leading features that formed the character of the people addressed—elect—begotten again—scattered abroad by persecution and by the ministry of the word—suffering ministers and saints of God ; 2. The subject on which they were addressed— to *gird up the loins of their mind*, and hope for great grace when Christ shall appear to overthrow Jewish superstition and heathen idolatry—*obedient children*—to fear, trust in, and love the Lord; and to keep all his commandments : to be holy, according to the nature and will of God, and his great and gracious promises.

Wednesday 7. We had very bad roads over hills and mighty rocks, to Oxford, twenty-eight miles ; and after dinner, eight miles more to Derby ; where I preached in brother H——'s house to about sixty people, on " If the righteous scarcely be saved," &c. I felt my pain, but could thank the Lord for all things.

Thursday 8. Was a day of pain to my body, but peace to my soul. I have been of late attending quarterly meetings, and have felt great heats and colds, and changes of weather. We came to New-Haven, where I preached in brother Thacher's house, near the foundation of the college ; we were crowded, and I was elaborate on Romans i. 16—18.

Friday 9. We rode solitarily on the sand to Middletown. We dined with Captain Hall, who received us kindly, and entertained us comfortably.

Saturday 10, and Sunday 11. We had many brethren and sisters from distant towns, at the quarterly meeting : here I preached on 1 Peter iv. 12—15. and on Isaiah lxii. 12. ; and was much at liberty, and a little comforted at the love-feast and sacrament. Walking backward and forward tended to fatigue my body as well as speaking. As I thought, so it is, the preachers have been very acceptable to the people this year.

Monday 12. I came to Old-Haddam. Here they have built a new meeting-house ; and there are some gracious souls here. I sen-

sibly felt the effects of heat and the labours of the day. We made
it fifteen miles to father Wilcox's. I conclude, that since I have
left New-York I have rode about one hundred and forty miles,
and a great part of the way is rough and rocky; my body is full
of infirmities, and my soul of the love of God. I think that God
is returning to this place; and that great days will yet come on in
New-England.

Wednesday 14. Was an exceedingly warm day. The Episcopal
house here is grand indeed. We passed Hadlime, thence to Mill-
ington, where we had many to hear at kind brother P——'s.

Thursday 15. I had twenty miles to New-London. My brethren have given me work enough. I feel like a man of a feeble
body, but my soul enjoys a sweet calm, and pure love; I cannot
seek or desire any thing but God. I refused to go into the court-
house to preach, but we had a gracious season at a dwelling-house.

Friday 16. We came to Pogustonick, a little town of attentive
people: I preached on "The Son of Man is come to seek and to
save that which was lost:" an aged man cried out, and rising up at
the close of the meeting, delivered his testimony: what he is I
cannot infallibly say; he spoke in too high terms of me to my face.

Saturday 17. I came with a heavy burden to Norwich landing;
I held forth in the academy made out of a Separate meeting-
house: there were few present beside the brethren from other
towns; I enlarged on "If ye be reproached for the cause of
Christ, happy are ye, for the spirit of glory and of God resteth
upon you; on their part he is evil spoken of, but on your part he
is glorified." The persons under sufferings—those who were
the friends to, and followers of Jesus—partakers of the spirit of
God, as a spirit of glory teaching them to believe, to love, and
suffer, and give glory to God and Christ.

Sunday 18. We held our feast of charity at eight o'clock: it
was a sweet, refreshing season; several talked very feelingly,
among whom were some aged people; many praised God for the
instrumentality of the Methodists in their salvation. My spirit
felt awful this morning; and my body unwell; however, at the
time appointed I began preaching on Romans viii. 6—8. A Uni-
versalist had his book and pen, or pencil, I suppose, ready to take
down my discourse; I said "Stop, let that gentleman write;" but
it appeared as though his fingers or heart failed him: brother
P——g had preached a sermon in that house, which had been
printed and traduced. Serious impressions appeared to be made
on the minds of some of the audience. After spending about four

bours in the congregation, (including sacrament and love-feast) I
passed the afternoon in retirement at my lodgings, being unwell.
This day I was led out greatly for New-England ; I believe God
will work among this people ; perhaps they have not had such a
time here for many years : the power of God was present ; some
felt as at heaven's gate—two or three aged women spoke as on the
borders of eternity, and within sight of glory.   Cold as the evening was, I was under the disagreeable necessity of riding ten
miles ; I crossed the Illymantink at Loyd's bridge, and came in
late to brother Fuller's.   I was pleased to hear an aged mother,
(formerly a Separatist) tell the dealings of God with her before
her daughter (now brother Fuller's wife) was born.

Monday 19. We rode through Windham, Scotland, and Abingdon.
After dining at Captain P——'s, we rode on to Thompson ; a few of
the preachers were present, and we were able to form a conference. We talked together, and rejoiced in the Lord.   That
evening and the next morning, Tuesday 20 and Wednesday 21, we
were closely employed ; we had about thirty preachers, some of
whom were from the Province of Maine, three hundred miles distant, who gave us a pleasing relation of the work of God in those
parts.   I delivered a discourse on Acts xxvi. 18, 19. and we ordained seven deacons and five elders.   About four o'clock I took
my leave of town, and stopped at Eastford, and saw father ——, a
solemn saint—lamenting the decline of religion among the Baptists.

Thursday 22. We rode thirty-five miles to East-Hartford,
where I gave a discourse to a few on Zeph. iii. 12, 13. Friday
23, we rode to Waterbury, where I preached in the Separate
meeting-house at four o'clock. Had we not have fallen in with
Mr. B. we might have missed our way and not have reached the
place till sunset.

Saturday 24. We passed along an exceedingly uneven and rocky
road through Salem and Oxford ; the appointment was not made
in the latter place, so we dined on what came to hand. Came on
to New-Stratford, and thence to the widow B——'s in North Stratford. I have been under great heaviness, and was unwell in body.
We have rode upwards of one hundred miles in the last three
days ; but still I must go on ; there is no rest. I attended at
Chesnut-Hill, and preached on 1 Thess. i. 5.: a flatness among
these people was very visible. This was the first house that was
built for the Methodists in Connecticut, and it is not finished yet.

Monday 26. We rode along to Fairfield, Norwalk, and arrived
at Stamford, about twenty-eight or thirty miles. On our way we

stopped to feed our horses, and found a woman that was sick, with
whom I talked and prayed. I felt as if I should not preach again
in haste, if at all, in Stamford. We crossed the state line and came
to New-Rochelle, in the state of New-York, twenty-three miles—
heavy and hungry. We stopped at Clark's, where I preached on
Isai. lxii. 1. and we were crowded with people. I enjoy peace
of mind, but am deeply tempted ; yet few minutes pass in which
my soul is not engaged in prayer.

NEW-YORK.—Thursday 29. I preached on Luke xii. " Who
then is a faithful and wise servant," &c. I began to confer with the
brethren as they came in, and do the business by scraps, as we
could come at it. We were in doubt whether some of the preachers
would come at all, on account of the rumours of the yellow
fever, which still appeared in parts of the city. On Friday we
entered fully into our work ; and on Saturday we concluded our
short conference, the preachers being desirous to depart. We had
a solemn, peaceable sitting ; and so also were our congregations.
I preached at our house in John-street on Mark ix. 1. " There
be some standing here which shall not taste of death until they
have seen the kingdom of God come with power," but I had little
opening.

Sunday October 2. I preached at the house in John-street on
Ephes. iv. 11—13. and had great enlargement : the feelings of the
people were touched, and my own also, as if it had been the last time,
as it probably may be with some of my hearers, if not myself : I
could not have been much more moved ; it was with difficulty I could
continue speaking. In the afternoon, at the new house, there was
also a move in the congregation whilst I enlarged on 1 Cor. iv. 10,
11. I ordained in both houses, in all eight deacons and seven
elders, and was on my feet six hours in the course of this day.

Monday 3. In the morning the weather had a stormy appearance, so that no passage was to be had at Powles Hook. We were,
as yet, safe on shore, but brothers R—— and E—— went to
Whitehall, where they found a boat that would sail, *sink or swim*,
for Van Deezer's Landing, upon Staten-Island : I did not like the
appearance of things, but submitted to go, with a high tide and the
wind at N. E. We passed the bay, ten miles over, in the space of
an hour : when we were within one mile of the dock the wind
shifted to N. W. and blew powerfully : the people on shore were
alarmed, and had the skiff ready to take us up, expecting we
should fill and sink, or be beaten off and strike the rocks : after

some time we secured the boat, landed the men, but left the landing of the horses for better weather. We dined, and rode up to the Blazing-Star, greatly against my inclination. At the ferry, the men were unwilling to move, and kept us on the bleak marsh sometime : when they came, they told us in anger, it was at our own risk of men and horses if we ventured. We suddenly turned and went to a friend's house, fed, and dried a little, and then rode twelve miles more, and stopped within a mile of Amboy ferry.

NEW-JERSEY.—Tuesday 4. We came to the ferry ; and after being detained about an hour, we made out to get a passage. Here we met with the preachers who had been retarded in their journey by the late storm. I pushed along, weary and unwell, to brother Hutchinson's ; and next day, faint, though cheerful, we reached Burlington.

Thursday 6. We reached Philadelphia about noon ; my mind is in peace, but my body and spirits fail. Here I met my old friend Andrews, from Hartford, in England, after twenty-six years' absence. Friday I rested a little, and arranged the minutes for the present year.

PENNSYLVANIA.—Saturday 8. Was spent in preparing for the ensuing conference.

Sunday 9. At Zoar chapel, the church of the second African society, in Camping-Town, I enlarged on " Ye were as sheep going astray, but are now returned to the shepherd and bishop of your souls." In the afternoon, at Ebenezer, my subject was Psalm lxxxi. 11—16. In the evening in Saint George's my discourse was like a storm from Mark xvi. 19, 20. I observed that Jesus sent out his disciples ; when he went to rest, they went to labour. The signs of their mission were miracles, and the signs that followed their ministry, convictions and conversions ;—the hinderances they had to expect, and the qualifications granted them every where ; and his not leaving them without witnesses.

Monday 10. We opened a conference of between forty and fifty preachers ; we had great love and great riches also : never before have we been able to pay the preachers their salaries ; at this conference we have done it, and had two hundred dollars left for debts and difficulties the preachers had been involved in. I was pleased to hear such wholesome talk by our plain countrymen. I sat with great pleasure and heard G. R—— on " We beseech you that ye receive not the grace of God in vain ;" as also I. W—— on " Feeding the flock of God ;" and J. P—— on " The fountain opened for sin and for uncleanness."

Friday 14, we set apart as a day of fasting and humiliation, and for ordination. I was pleased to dismiss the conference from their confinement in business, and gave a discourse on "Humble yourselves under the mighty hand of God." I now felt willing to rest both mind and body. We heard by the newspapers of the arrival of Doctor Coke in the United States.

Saturday 15. We dined at Chester with my dear old friend M. Withy, and came in the evening to Wilmington.

DELAWARE.—Sabbath day 16. The morning was rainy, but we had a few serious people to whom I preached on Rev. ii. 1—7. My soul enjoys sweet peace. Being in haste to get to Baltimore, we rode on the Sabbath afternoon to my old friend S. Heansey's; of this I am not fond, and where necessity does not compel me, rarely do it. I turned out of the way on Monday to preach at Bethel, in the place of Doctor Coke; my subject was, "Let us labour to enter into that rest, lest any man fall after the same example of unbelief." It was a happy season. In the course of the day I rode thirty-five miles and lodged at North-East.

Tuesday 18. We rode to Perry-Hall, and were entertained with the greatest kindness.

MARYLAND.—Wednesday 19. We came to Baltimore, where about a hundred preachers were met for general conference. They agreed to a committee, and then complained; upon which we dissolved ourselves. I preached on "The men of Issachar that knew what Israel ought to do;" and again, on "Neither as being lords over God's heritage, but being ensamples to the flock:" there were souls awakened and converted. No angry passions were felt amongst the preachers; we had a great deal of good and judicious talk. The conference rose on Thursday, the 3d of November: what we have done is printed. Bishop Coke was cordially received, as my friend and colleague, to be wholly for America; unless a way should be opened to France. At this conference there was a stroke aimed at the president eldership. I am thankful that our session is over. My soul and body have health, and have hard labour. Brother Whatcoat is going to the south of Virginia, brother M'Claskey is going to New-Jersey, brother Ware to Pennsylvania, and brother Hutchinson to New-York and Connecticut: very great and good changes have taken place.

Friday, November 4. We reached the widow Dorsey's by riding an hour in the night. I took a cold; and a boil on my face makes me uncomfortable.

VIRGINIA.—Saturday 5. We rode twenty miles ; and on Sabbath morning we came directly to Alexandria. Doctor Coke preached on " The wise men that came to Jesus :" brother Whatcoat and myself exhorted.

Monday 7. We came to Captain Ward's : he is gone to sea, but his wife made us welcome. Tuesday 8, we rode through *awful* Fredericksburg to Todd's tavern : men and horses being weak and weary we contentedly stopped.

Wednesday 9. We came about thirty miles to Ellis's tavern, and there, as well as at T——'s, we were kindly and genteely entertained at a reasonable expense. The next day we stretched on to Richmond :—and who could be kinder and more pleased to see us, and make poor sickly travellers welcome, than Mr. Parrot and wife ? Here I persuaded Dr. Coke to rest a day.

Saturday 12. Brother Whatcoat and myself came to brother Waltham's, near Chesterfield court-house. We preached to a few people, refitted a little better, and the next day came to brother Featherston's, where I gave them a short discourse. We dined and came on to Petersburg, and spent the evening at J. Harding's. I was much pained with the boil on my face, and another on my eye. Here I heard Dr. C. preach, and I gave an exhortation.

Monday 14. I must needs call and see my old friends, Wood, Tucker and wife, and talked a little, prayed, and parted. We then went forward, calling on Richard Graves, an old disciple. Thence to mother Maybury's, in Greensville, where I have often had a comfortable night's lodging.

Thursday 15. Our conference began at brother Batt's, a most convenient house, and very kind people. We sat in great peace, and good order. A few preachers declined travelling. We elected and ordained six elders and nine deacons. The deficiencies of the preachers amounted to upwards of £194 Virginia currency.

Sabbath day 20. Dr. Coke gave a comment on the 20th chapter of the Revelation of Jesus Christ by St. John, and then a sermon on Luke xiv. 26. " He that loveth father and mother more than me," &c. I then gave a short exhortation, and ended the service of that pleasant day.

Monday 21. I visited, perhaps for the last time, mother Maybury, who is aged and swiftly declining. I also visited brothers B. and D. and then rode once more to Robert Jones's, in Sussex county.—Here I had a few moment's leisure to write and recollect myself, after being so closely employed in conferences and company.

Tuesday 22. I preached at Jay's chapel to about one hundred people, with whom I had a comfortable season on 2 Peter iii. 17, 18. I noticed, 1. The appellation, *beloved*. 2. That of the *wicked*, which I distinguished into three classes—1. Those that make no profession of religion, and are openly wicked. 2. Those who have been awakened and may have enjoyed religion, but have fallen from it. 3. Those who profess the highest attainments in religion and yet live in known sin :—*the error of the wicked*, infidelity in theory, or practice, or both : which embraces the abovementioned classes of the wicked—*grow in grace*—to grow in the graces of the Spirit, the knowledge of our Lord and Saviour, now and for ever ; the glory due to Christ in his kingdom of grace and glory.

Wednesday 23. I rode to brother Davis's, about twenty-seven miles. On my way I visited brother Grains and mother. Brothers Pennington, Briggs, and Evans, are gone to rest. My soul enjoys much peace, and is big with hope that we shall have a greater work in this district than we have ever yet had : I feel happy among the few ancient disciples who are left. I preached once more at Lane's chapel, and the Lord was with us : my subject was Jer. xxxii. 38, 39. We have lost about twenty members of this society by O'Kelly ; we have about forty left.

Friday 25, was a cold day, but we rode twenty-five miles to brother Joseph Wood's, in Isle of Wight county : some of our brethren riding on before, called a night meeting, and we were comforted together.

My mind of late hath been in great peace. I am glad I have not contended with those violent men who were once with us. We ought to mind our work, and try to get souls to Christ ; and the Lord can give us children " That we shall have after we have lost our former," that shall say in our hearing, " Give place that there may be room for us to dwell." We had a very *winterly* morning, but we rode to brother Blunt's, where I preached to many people on Zeph. iii. 12, 13. Notwithstanding my name has been so cast out as evil, and my character traduced, I ordained brother B—— and another brother, after taking from the former a written declaration of his opposition to slavery. My dear aged friends told me their troubles and sorrow, which the divisions in the societies had caused.

Sabbath day 28. Through hard necessity I rode sixteen miles to brother Cowling's in Isle of Wight county, and had three rooms in the house filled, and there were some of the coloured people out of doors, notwithstanding the coldness of the weather. My subject was Hebr. x. 37—39. I spoke with great rapidity for nearly two hours, administered the sacrament, and ordained brother Powell to the office of a deacon. It was time for me to visit this quarter again, lest some should think I was afraid to come. But who hath been at the planting of the Gospel in the sixteen United States? Had I none but Virginia to visit I could show myself oftener.

Monday 28. We crossed a small ferry, and came through Suffolk to brother Jolliff's, twenty-two miles. I had solemn thoughts while I passed the house where Robert Williams lived and died, whose funeral rites I performed. The weather is remarkably cold for the season, the ice being more than an inch thick on the streams. I was amazed to hear that my dear, aged friend, Benjamin Evans (now gone to glory) was converted to the new side by being told by J. O·Kelly that I had offended Mr. Wesley, and that he being about calling me to account, I cast him off altogether. But, *quere*, did not J. O·K. set aside the appointment of Richard Whatcoat? and did not the conference in Baltimore strike that *minute* out of our discipline which was called *a rejecting of Mr. Wesley?* and now does J. O·K. lay all the blame on me? It is true, I never approved of that binding minute. I did not think it practical expediency to obey Mr. Wesley, at three thousand miles distance, in all matters relative to church government; neither did brother Whatcoat, nor several others. At the first general conference I was mute and modest when it passed, and I was mute when it was expunged. For this Mr. Wesley blamed me, and was displeased that I did not rather reject the whole connexion, or leave them, if they did not comply. But I could not give up the connexion so easily, after labouring and suffering so many years with and for them. After preaching at Jolliff's we rode to Portsmouth, and preached in the evening, where we had many people at a short warning My subjects this day were 1 John i. 3, 4 and Isai. i. 9. We visited Norfolk, and preached at noon, Wednesday 30, on 1 Peter ii. 11, 12.—at night on 1 Cor. xv. 58.

Thursday, December 1. I returned to Portsmouth, and preached on 1 Pet. v. 10. Thence, through damp weather, we rode back to Jolliff's, where we had preaching, exhortation, and sacrament, and the Lord was with us.

NORTH CAROLINA.— Friday 2. We had a long, cold, hungry ride to Gates county, in North Carolina.

Saturday 3. We had a blessed season in Colonel Baker's new house on 1 John iii. 1, 2, 3. I have felt unwell by these changes :

sometimes preaching makes me sick, and at other times makes me well. Yesterday we rode nearly forty miles ; to-day we laboured, and our horses rested. I feel solemnly given up to God in toil and suffering.

Sabbath day 4. We rode fourteen miles to Winton, where I preached to an attentive congregation, from town and country, on St. John's Gospel i. 4. I remembered my old friend Boon ; I was invited to and most kindly entertained at the house of one of his daughters. So it is, when the dear, aged parents go off, they leave me their children. Thence to Northampton county, twenty-eight or thirty miles, and came in about six o'clock. We had to day, as on Friday last, to breakfast about six or seven in the morning, and to dine about the same hour in the evening. My soul hath been in great peace. I rode to see Richard Whitaker and his wife, after several years' absence : I felt truly solemn when I found myself at the old house where the father and mother died. I remember well what passed when I was here last—the distress of the doctor and his kindness to me in the year 1785.

Tuesday 6. We had a rainy morning. Crossed Roanoke at Edwards's ferry, and came to Champion's : I resolved to preach, although only a part of two families were present. We dined, and hasted to mother Whitaker's, about twenty four or twenty-five miles.

Wednesday 7. We had a very sharp morning. I preached at brother Bradford's on 1 John iv. 16—18. Yesterday on " The promise is to you and to your children," &c. I parted with my dear brother Whatcoat, after travelling together about seven hundred miles. It was painful to part, yet I was well pleased he had not to drive the rough way, and that through the rain. In this I loved my brother better than myself. We had a comfortable season at sermon and sacrament this day. I felt myself at home in brother Bradford's family.

Thursday 8. I came again to the widow Philips's, on Swift-Creek; the house was filled—my subject was awful, Amos viii. 11. " Behold, the days come, saith the Lord God, that I will send a famine in the land ; not a famine of bread, nor a thirst for water, but of hearing the words of the Lord." I observed—

I. The great and interesting things contained in the word of the Lord.

II. The benefits and blessings communicated by the faithful preaching and hearing, believing and obeying the word of the Lord.

III. The causes and effects of this famine; deaths, removals, backslidings of ministers and people, and had reference to ancient times.—Dreadful effects—the want of means to civilize, moralize, and spiritualize mankind.

I felt differently to-day from what I did yesterday; it was like beating upon a rock; but the Lord can give a blessing. We are greatly blessed with healthy weather.

Friday 9. We came to Tarborough. They had made a fire in the small apartment of the court-house, and I thought it was for preaching, but it was for dancing, and the violin lay on the table. Mr. Clement was kind enough to stop the scene, and we had a serious congregation to hear, to whom I preached on Hebr. viii. 9—11. There were two or three houses open to me in town, but I lodged three miles out at brother Toole's. We rode on Saturday 10th twenty-eight miles, without food or rest for man or horse, until we came to brother Forbes's, Pitt county, where I spent the Sabbath, and preached on Rom. ix. 27. I had many hearers, but it was cold times, both literally and spiritually; my soul was solemn—my body unwell.

Monday 12. I rode to father Barrows's: I was much led out on Hebr. iii. 12—14. In those words, 1. Christians are cautioned against a most dreadful end. 2. The means to prevent it; and, 3. The example of backsliders. The end interesting and great—to hold fast the beginning of their confidence. The means—by exhorting one another daily. We rode twenty miles to father Ormonds; the people came before the rain, but had to return home through it; my subject was, "The little flock;" and I had considerable opening. I feel nothing painful, but the want of a revival of religion; my soul feels as if the Lord will yet do wonders among this people.

Wednesday 14. We rose early, and rode in haste to Cox's ferry, on Neuse-River: the weather was damp and chilly. We had very few to hear at the meeting-house: it was a day of great trial, and I was beset on every side.

Thursday 15. We made a forced march of twenty-five miles to Newbern; we had no refreshment for man nor horse. Having an inflammation in one of my ears, and having fasted so long, I was very unwell; but a sermon was expected, and delivered on these words, "Because thou knewest not the day of thy visitation:" my hearers were numerous and serious. I had never viewed the situation of this town before: it is the image of Charleston (S. C.) Neuse and Trent have a likeness to Cooper and Ashley rivers. This is a

rowing place. Our society here, of white and coloured members,
onsists of one hundred. I every day see and feel the emptiness
f all created good, and am taking my leave of all : what is worth
ving for but the work of God? I wrote to our brethren in the
ity stations, not to neglect the sick an hour, nor an absentee from
lass one week ; indeed we ought to be always abounding in the
/ork of the Lord ; to attend to old and new subjects, to our work,
nd to every means, like men labouring to find out new means for
ew difficulties. Should piety, health, and trade attend this New-
ern, it will be a very capital place in half a century from this.

Friday 16. I had great openings on Rom. i. 15—17. I know
ot when I have visited a place with such pleasing hopes and feel-
ıgs : I trust there hath been something more than man in this.
)h ! how greatly was my heart knit to these people!

Saturday 17. I preached at ten o'clock the second part of the
ame theme, Phil. i. 27. I was exceedingly close on the duties,
pirit, and practice of the Gospel. We had to ride fifteen miles to
,ee's, upon Trent. I felt solemn and sorrowful at leaving my dear
eople at Newbern ; they wished to give me money, but love is
etter than gold. .

Sunday 18. We had much rain : but few came to meeting. Find-
ıg we had twenty miles to Bryans's, we wished to move to Le-
nuel Hatches's, who was very kind.

Monday 19. We had to ride early : my horse trots stiff ; and
o wonder, when I have rode him, upon an average, five thousand
ıiles a year for five years successively. I preached on Hebr. iii.
', 8. I felt as if the Lord and his messengers had left this place.
Iy spirit was grieved at the conduct of some Methodists, that
ıire out slaves at public places to the highest bidder, to cut, skin,
nd starve them ; I think such members ought to be dealt with :
ın the side of oppressors there is law and power, but where is jus-
ice and mercy to the poor slaves? what eye will pity, what hand
vill help, or ear listen to their distresses ? I will try if words can
e like drawn swords, to pierce the hearts of the owners.

I have heard by a person from Baltimore, that by means of the
veekly society meeting, our people are all on flame : thank God that
t came into my heart to recommend it to them! this also shall com-
ört us in our toil. I have rode upwards of thirty miles this day.

Tuesday 20. At the rich lands, but amongst spiritually poor
)eople. I had about thirty hearers, and here are a few precious
ouls. Father Ballard and family still stand by us. I had some
reedom on Hebr. iii. 14. 1. Wherein believers are partakers of

Christ, past, present, and to come—in wisdom, righteousness, sanctification, and redemption. 2. The beginning of their confidence stedfast to the end ; without which, they cannot be saved or safe. I described the nature, effects, and fruits of this confidence in God, in Christ, in the Holy Spirit ; in the Scripture promises, precepts, threatenings, in, and of heaven, earth, and hell.

Wednesday 21. We had a cold ride of about twenty miles to Stone's Bay; where there are a few people, (who have been forsaken by the preachers) to whom I preached on Hebr. x. 38, 39.

Thursday 22. I came to Nixons's, on the road to Wilmington ; here I found a kind people, but the preachers had left them because they did not immediately join in fellowship. Perhaps I was called this way to feel for souls in and round about Wilmington : if we had men and money, it would be well to station a preacher in such places as Wilmington.

Friday 23. We had an excessively cold ride through heavy sands to Wilmington ; when we came to the town wharf there was neither flat nor ferry ; the causeway was under improvement ; the only expedient therefore that remained was to cross at Negro-Head. We came up the sand hills to Wright's ferry. It was truly cold and very bleak on the water, while in a trifling flat ; and I feared one or both the horses would be thrown out of it. We were driving through the woods till seven o'clock, and the weather exceedingly cold ; at last we came to Rolks's, on Town-Creek. We could not spare ourselves the next day, but came off blowing and biding our fingers. We passed Lockets-Folly and Shallot-River, and came up to father Gause's, where we met with friendship, fellowship, and love, and held meeting on Christmas day, it being the Sabbath.

SOUTH CAROLINA.—Monday 26. We came to Little-River, and thence to Kingston, where we lodged with our Mr. Rogers, after riding about forty-five miles. Tuesday 27. I gave a sermon in the chapel, and on Wednesday 28, rode thirty-seven or forty miles to Georgetown. Here we have nearly one hundred Africans in society, while we have only seven or eight whites, our doctrine being too close, and our discipline too strict. After riding the above distance in the cold, without any regular meal, I was hardly fit for the pulpit at night ; however I gave them a talk on " Glory to God in the highest, and on the earth peace, good will towards men." I observed on this, as I had on some former occasions,—that the redemption and salvation of mankind by Jesus Christ was the bright-

est display of the justice, mercy, truth, love, and holiness of God ;
yet in such a manner as that justice should not destroy, but give
glory to mercy ; and that mercy should not destroy, but glorify justice and mercy in Christ to sinners : justice in the sufferings of
Christ, and in the punishment of incorrigible sinners.   The truth
of God shineth also : it only belongs to a God to preserve and display all his attributes and perfections : in this plan we may say
mercy and truth are met together, righteousness (or justice) and
peace have kissed each other ; and all the truths of God held sacred, with reverence let it be said, God would no longer be God,
to act unlike himself, or to be unjust, unmerciful, or unholy, or
untrue ; or to swallow up or violate one attribute by exerting
another.   What should we think of a governor or judge that would
pardon all criminals indescriminately and unconditionally ?—where
would be the exercise of justice ?

Thursday 29. Hearing of a sacramental occasion at Boon's
chapel, I rode thirteen miles to attend it ; it was up Santee, on the
upper branches of Sand-Pitt : my subject was " Christ hath once
suffered for sins, the just for the unjust, that he might bring us to
God."   We were entertained elegantly, and with great hospitality, at Mr. Boon's.

Friday 30. We set out in the rain, crossed Santee, (we had a
quick passage for once) and rode about fifty miles, and came to
brother Jackson's about nine o'clock.   Here our rapid march was
ended : I rested two days.—Serious news from Baltimore—the
academy, and our church in Light-street, with brother Hawkins's
elegant house, all destroyed by fire ! The loss we sustain in the
college, academy, and church, I estimate from 15 to £20,000 :
it affected my mind ; but I concluded God loveth the people of Baltimore, and he will keep them poor, to make them pure ; and it
will be for the humiliation of the society.

January 1, 1797. Being Sabbath day, I lectured on Psalm lxxxiv.
and 2 Cor. v.   Monday 2. I came to Charleston, and preached
in the evening on Eph. v. 15, 16.   Tuesday 3. We began conference, and sat some days six or seven hours.   We had pleasing accounts of the growth of religion in Georgia as well as in this state.
We had a sermon every evening, and many to hear.

Sunday 8. My subject was John xiv. 21—23.   I do not yet feel
myself in the Spirit of the work.   Monday 9. Our conference
rose. We have been blessed with some young men for the ministry. By letter from James M'Cannon, in Baltimore, I learn that
our people have had the offer of the Episcopal church, and the

English and German Presbyterian churches, until we can rebuild.
I began reading the Bible and Winterbotham's View of the United
States. We have sent out subscriptions for the Methodist Magazine. The like severity of weather hath not been known here
for fourteen or fifteen years; the gardens and oranges appear to
be destroyed; the want of moisture may have increased the
effects of the frost. I have felt my soul filled with love, for the
general union in the ministry, and for the church: my mind is
stayed upon the Lord alone. Tuesday 9. Our dear brethren set
out for their circuits. Wednesday 10. In the evening we met the
society in the manner I had recommended to the brethren in New-
York, Philadelphia, and Baltimore. We were much blessed; it
was a gracious season. Brother Wells appears to be dying swiftly.
I purpose to go out only every other night, as I am called to duty
every morning with fifty or a hundred Africans. I lament the
wickedness of this city, and their great hatred against us. I spent
Thursday, Friday, and Saturday, in reading, writing, and visiting
the sick.

Sunday 15. Notwithstanding I had taken medicine on Saturday,
and was unwell, I preached on John vi. 66—69. We were much
crowded, and more so, when Dr. Coke preached in the evening.
Monday 16. The remnant of the preachers left the city. I rode
up the path, and attended the Doctor to Clement's ferry. At
night I met the seeking Africans in brother Wells's kitchen. This
evening I prayed with brother Wells for the last time; he expressed his confidence in God, and freedom from guilty dread and
horror.

Tuesday 17. I was called to the house of brother Wells, just
departed this life. His widow I found in prayers and tears, as also
the dear children and servants. We appointed his funeral to be at
four o'clock to-morrow. The scene was serious. I learned he
wished to see me once more: I visited him every day that I could
with propriety. It is twelve long years next March since he first
received Henry Willis, Jesse Lee, and myself, into his house. In
a few days he was brought under heart distress for sin, and soon
after professed faith in Christ; since that he hath been a diligent
member in society. About fourteen months ago, when there was
a revival of religion in the society, and in his own family, it came
home to his own soul; he was quickened, and remarkably blest,
and continued so to be until his death. His affliction was long and
very severe. The last words he was heard to say that could be
understood were that " he knew where he was, that his wife was

with him, and that God was with him." He hath been a man of sorrows, and hath suffered the loss of two respectable wives and a favourite son ; sustained heavy loss by fire, and was subject to a great variety of difficulties in trade and merchandise. He was one much for the feeling part of religion ; a gentleman of spirit, and sentiment, and fine feelings, a faithful friend to the poor, and warmly attached to the ministers of the Gospel. This was a solitary day, and I laboured under uncommon dejection. I preached in the evening, and was in great heaviness.

Wednesday 18. We committed the dust of our dear brother Wells to the old church burying-ground, in Cumberland-street. Doctor Coke performed the funeral rites, and delivered an oration ; I also gave a short one. My serious gloom continued.

Thursday 19. We were closely attentive to the notes on the Discipline.

Friday 20. Visited Mr. Grant, declining swiftly in a consumption. He appeared to be somewhat awakened to a sense of the state of his soul and body.

Saturday 21. Till noon my heart sinketh, and I am ready to conclude we are not sent to the whites of this place, except a very few ; but to the poor Africans. I find this a suffering, holy time.

Sunday 22. I preached Mr. Wells's funeral sermon on Rev. ii. 10. I observed, 1. Who it is that speaketh. 2. To whom he was speaking. 3. What might be supposed and granted concerning the angel of the church—that he had professed the convicting and converting grace of God ; that he had suffered poverty, temptation, and persecution. 4. What it is to be faithful to God—to fear him, as also to trust in his providence and grace ; faithful to Christ and to the Spirit, to the church of God, to his family and citizens ; faithful unto death, even martyrdom. I gave a brief account of Mr. Wells's life and death. I was exceedingly weak in body and mind before I began preaching, but was considerably liberated. I had a solemn, attentive congregation, and was glad to come home and spend the evening in solitary reading and prayer. I have to meet the African people every morning between five and six o'clock, at my lodging, with singing, reading, exhortation, and prayer.

Monday 23. We were at work upon our notes on the Discipline. Tuesday 24, I was very unwell, yet I must needs preach a little on 2 Cor. vi. 2. My body is weak, and my soul is distressed on account of sinners. I have made out to read the third volume of Winterbotham's General View of our continent ; this I do, because I have some hope of visiting British America before I die.

Wednesday 25. My mind oppressed and my body afflicted, I was close at work, heart, head, and eyes. No justice for Cumberland-street Methodists—a young Scot shouted in the church, and after he was taken out of the house struck three or four men, no bill was found against him ; and we are insulted every night by candle-light.

Thursday 26. Still unwell. The three following days I was confined to the house with a fever. I wrought at our work : O, that it may be for the glory of God and the good of his church! I have numbered the chapters, and versed Scriptures in it. I am resolved to visit more, if spared to get through this weighty business. Mr. Grant, after three years warning with a consumption, is gone ; I trust God had mercy on his soul. Doctor Coke preached in the morning, brother Hill in the afternoon.

Sunday 29, and Monday 30. I consulted a physician, who judged my disease to be an intermittent fever, and such it proved itself : on Tuesday 31, I was taken about two o'clock with a powerful ague, which held me till nearly nine o'clock. I presume it has been working for two weeks ; I probably took it by going out at the death of brother Wells. Wednesday, February 1. I took the powders of Columbo after the bilious pills. Thursday 2, my fever did not return. Friday 3. Growing better, I had serious thoughts about going home to God. Of late I have been kept uncommonly happy. My depression of spirits at times is awful, especially when afflicted ; that which is deeply constitutional will never die but with my body. I am solemnly given up to God, and have been for many months willing to live or die in, for, and with Jesus.

Wednesday 8. I was better, and was enabled to read, write, ride, and visit.

Thursday 9. To-morrow my dear Coke sails for Europe. My mind is in peace, but I am not pleased with such confinement. I now take a decoction of the bark. I am under great obligations to Doctor Joseph Ramsay for his peculiar attention to me in my affliction, without fee or reward for his services. By letter from John Dickins, I learn the work of God greatly revives in New-York among the aged people and little children. I have lately read the second volume of Mr. Wesley's Sermons.

Friday 10. This day Doctor Coke is waiting to sail for Ireland. Strangers to the delicacies of Christian friendship know little or nothing of the pain of parting. Glad tidings of great joy from New-York.—A second glorious work is begun there, twenty souls converted, a great love-feast, and Sabbath evening meeting held until one o'clock in the morning. This news hath given a spring to us in this city.

Saturday 11. I visited a little.

Sunday 12. I attended my station, and stood upon my watch-tower. My subject was Eccles. v. 1. " Keep thy foot when thou goest into the house of God."

I. The house of God—the temples, first and second, and syna-gogues, were called houses of God. A place built for the worship and service of the Lord ; the congregation and church.

II. The exercises and ordinances of the house of God ; reading and preaching the word of God ; prayer and praises ; baptism and the Lord's supper. In his temple every one shall speak of his glory.

III. The manifestations God is pleased to make of himself in his own house to the souls of his people.

IV. How people should prepare for and behave in the house of God. To keep their eyes and ears—fix their attention on the Lord and Master of the house.

V. The wicked called fools, and the sacrifice they make. Ig-norant of themselves, of God, of Christ, and true religion, and the worship of the Lord, and do not consider it is God, Christ, and sacred things they make light of.

We were full, and I put my strength to the test. In the after-noon from Ezekiel xxxvi. 25—27. I showed the evils God threatened, and prophesied the removal of, by his servant to his nominal professional people, Israel.

I. Their stony heart ; their idols and filthiness.

II. The blessings promised and prophesied—a new heart, a new spirit, the in-dwelling and sanctifying influence of the Spirit.

III. The blessed consequential effects—" I will cause you to walk in my statutes, and ye shall keep my judgments to do them." The law, the judgments of God, because of the penalty annexed—thus saith the Lord to the renewed soul, " Thou shalt have none other gods but me." " Lord," saith the Christian, " I want none other but thee." Saith Jehovah, " Thou shalt not make to thyself any graven image." The pious soul saith, " I will not ; the work of my hands cannot save my soul : I will not take thy name in vain. I love thy day—thy love hath written thy law upon my heart, and love to my neighbour engages me to fulfil my duty to him also." " The meek shall inherit the earth," as a sacred charter from the Lord—this is their claim, security, and defence.

I was wearied with the duties of the day, and had only retired to rest when the alarm of *fire* was cried—it proved only to be a kitchen, and by the activity of the people it was soon extinguished.

Monday 13. I have peace, and am as well in health as I could expect. Bless the Lord, O my soul! I was taken up with handing about a subscription for the new house. Our people appear much afraid to move in this work.

Tuesday 14. I met the stewards on the subject of the new house. We have adjourned on the question. If materials fall in their price, and if we can secure £400, shall we begin? Oh we of little faith! It is a doubt if we had fifty in society, and £100 on hand, when we laid the foundation stone of Cumberland-street house, which cost us (including the lot) £1300. The society has been rent in twain, and yet we have wrought out of debt, and paid £100 for two new lots, and we can spare £100 from the stock, make a subscription of £150, and the Africans will collect £100.

Wednesday 15. I felt much better, and rejoice in hope of going hence.

Thursday 16. Was a solitary day; my soul was in heaviness, and my body weak. I was employed in writing letters, and reading the Bible with critical attention.

Friday 17. I thought I would fast, refraining from food till six o'clock; I felt very weak, had a fever and headach, and was glad to go to bed at seven o'clock. I feel pain to be gone, and do not expect much peace of mind, or health of body, until I go to my old solitary country life. I judge that discipline, and the doing away of certain things, have contributed somewhat to the late revival of religion in New-York.

Sunday 19. I entered on my duty. I had not an opening to preach, so I made an explanatory discourse on Isaiah lv. 1—7.; and it appeared to be of use. My leading heads were,

I. The spiritual blessings held forth in the temporal good things, waters, wine, milk—Water to quench thirst, cleanse, and heal, as to drinking, bathing, &c. all expressive of the grace of God to our souls; comforting, cleansing, healing. Wine for the sickly, tempted, dispirited ones; milk for babes.

II. The grand qualifications—thirst and no money; and to come, no merit, no righteousness.

III. The reasoning—" Wherefore do you spend your money," &c. i. e. make great sacrifices for pleasure, and yet are disappointed; such is the case of those who seek after ceremonial righteousness.

IV. His offering Christ.

V. The promise of the increase of the kingdom of Jesus Christ among distant and unknown nations.

VI. *When* they are to come to seek the Lord, viz. " while he may be found."

It was a melting season. In the afternoon I preached on Rom. viii. 31. " What shall we then say to these things ; if God be for us, who can be against us ?"

I. I viewed the whole chapter. The character and distinguishing marks of the people of God.

II. How he will order himself on the side of his people, in his justice, mercy, truth, power, and love : " If God be for us ?"— this is a modest supposition. I observed, he will not aid our persecutors—their help is departed from them ; that he sanctified persecution ; and sometimes would cut off the enemies of his church and people ; that some were enemies from policy, others from heretical principles, some from enmity of heart ; others would think their fathers, mothers, husbands, wives, &c. were misguided and deluded. I stood on my feet about three hours this day, was much wearied and slept but little.

Monday 20. I was weak—the weather uncommonly warm. I rejoice in hope of leaving the city next Monday, if the Lord spareth me.

Tuesday 21. My mind has been greatly afflicted, so that my sleep has been much interrupted, yet there was a balm for this ; a poor black, sixty years of age, who supports herself by picking oakum, and the charity of her friends, brought me a French crown, and said she had been distressed on my account, and I must have her money. But no ! although I have not three dollars to travel two thousand miles, I will not take money from the poor. I am very unwell, my soul and body is distressed : ah ! that such trifles should affect me. I have read four books of Moses critically.

Wednesday 22. Was a sorrowful day to me : I am thinking God is teaching me I ought not to stay in this place after this manner ; perhaps I shall never stay here again for so long a time. I am kept from sinning, yet not from deep and sore temptation.

Thursday 23. Brother James King came to town to take the charge in this city as assistant preacher to Benjamin Blanton.

Friday 24. I began to prepare for my departure hence.

Saturday 25. My mind is happy in the expectation of leaving this city on Monday.

Sunday 26. I judged it best to be plain and explanatory upon
the Lord's supper, 1 Cor. v. 7, 8. Our congregation was large, and
the sacramental occasion very solemn. My farewell discourse was
on 1 Sam. xii. 23, 24. I observed on the duty of those who have
the charge of souls ;

I. To pray for them.

II. To teach them the good and the right way; which is to
fear the Lord, and serve him in truth, sincerity, and purity of
intention.

III. The motives to induce them—the consideration of the great
things God hath done for them.

What good have I attempted to do here ? I assisted the Doctor
in the notes on the Discipline. I have preached every Sabbath
except two ; formed a plan to erect a house in the west end of
the city suburbs, to be equal to that in Cumberland-street ; I
have made peace between a dying man and his brother-in-law, in
which two families were concerned, and I cured a poor African's
sore leg by applying a poultice of bread and milk.

Monday 27. I felt a fever, yet rejoiced to leave Charleston.
Many came to see me. I have persuaded one person to give up
the use of what I feared would be her ruin ; she promised she
would ; if so, all will be well. On my way I felt as if I was let
out of prison. Hail! ye solitary pines! the jessamine, the red-
bud, and dog-wood! how charming in full bloom! the former a
most fragrant smell. We reached Monks-Corner, and were most
agreeably entertained at Mr. Jones's. We came on the next day
and had but hard fare till we reached Nelson's ferry : it being a
rainy day, the gentlemen were regaling themselves with cards :
blunt Frank Asbury asked for dinner, but told them he could not
dine upon cards ; the cards were very politely put away, and every
necessary mark of attention paid : Mr. Gurdine, who commands
several ferries on this river, is a complete gentleman. We came
off in the rain, and it fell very freely. Through the swamp we
had deep wading, and steeped our feet ; we wrought along as night
came on ; and after riding four miles in the dark, dirt, and rain, we
came to the widow Bowman's : here I found shelter and was kindly
entertained. Her husband was a godly, gracious man, and died in
the Lord some years ago.

Wednesday, March 1. We rested and refitted. Thursday 2. We
had a cold day at Gibson's ; my subject was 1 John v. 13—15. I
was very unwell, under infirmities of body and mind. Thence we

rode five miles to Mark Moore's, where I preached on 2 Peter iii.
18. and had a comfortable time.

Friday 3. We had a dry, cold, hungry, long ride of thirty miles
to Bradford's, where I dined, and preached at three o'clock, and
felt resolved to give them one plain talk on Hebr. iii. 7, 8. 1. The
voice of God, is the Gospel of Jesus Christ as preached by himself. 2. What is comprehended in hearing his voice—attending,
believing, obeying. 3. How men harden their hearts—by delays,
and by inward and outward sin ;—the Holy Ghost saith, To-day, in
the word, in the ministry, in the hearts of men.

Saturday 4. At Rembert's new chapel I preached on Matt. xi.
28—30. where I had some living sweetness.

Sunday 5. After love-feast and sacrament, I preached on 2 Cor.
vi. 6—10. but had not much satisfaction. Religion is reviving here
among the Africans ; several are joined in society : these are the
poor ; these are the people we are more immediately called to
preach to.

Monday 6. I preached in the court-house at Camden, set apart
for a meeting-house : my subject was, " Knowing therefore the terror of the Lord, we persuade men." 1. I treated on the divine character of Christ, as judge—his perfections, and relation to the persons who are to be tried. 2. The characters to be judged—infi-
dels, sinners, Pharisees, hypocrites, backsliders, believers ; true
and false ministers. these are to be tried, found guilty, or ac-
quitted ; sentenced and punished ; or applauded and rewarded. I
received a second letter from New-York, informing me of the
revival of religion there among the aged and young people. I
rode fourteen miles to G——'s quarter, a small house among the
sand hills ; thence eight miles to brother Horton's, whose brother,
a Baptist, had lately departed this life ; he was blest in his end.

Wednesday 8. We rode thirty-two miles to the Waxsaws, hungry and faint : at Wren's I was led out on " Let us not sleep as do
others." The next day, at quarterly meeting, I preached on Isa.
i. 9. : there was a noise and shaking. This evening a little
circumstance gave me great pain ; I broke my skin in two places.
We rode on Friday and Saturday seventy miles. We passed
through a large settlement of Presbyterians ; Mr. M'Crea, their
minister, gave us a kind invitation to lodge at his house ; but we
wished to cross the river at Martin's Ferry, and stay at the widow
Featherston's.

NORTH CAROLINA.—Sunday 11. We were at Daniel Asbury's.
My leg was inflamed by riding, and I found it necessary to poultice

it. I sat down and taught the people on "He that cometh to God must believe that he is and that he is a rewarder of them that diligently seek him." We had a living meeting in the evening; some souls were greatly blest.

Monday 12. We rode into Iredell county, thirty-three miles. We were caught in the rain, which threw me into a chill, followed by a fever; in this situation I came to, and preached at brother Fitzgerald's. Between four and five o'clock, brothers Dean and Dyson, (Methodists) Hall and Bowman, (Presbyterians) had filled my appointment in the preceding part of the day.

Tuesday 13. I preached at the church in the forks of the Yadkin on Isaiah xxxv. 1—4. I had to ride eight miles in the rain to Templeton's.

Wednesday 14. I rode five miles to Mr. Hoy's, and treated on the *rest that remaineth to the people of God*. In the afternoon I rode twelve miles to father Bruce's, where I found myself at home.

Thursday 15. We had to ride fifteen miles through the rain to Oxford's. After preaching on Hebrews ii. 1. we rode eight miles to Paynes's. The weather was very damp: I felt the chill through me. The next morning I was seized with a fever which held me more or less until Sabbath morning, when I preached at Perkins's and Connelly's meeting-houses; at the former on Hebr. ii. 3. and at the latter on 2 Cor. latter part of the vith chapter. Here as many as eight preachers came to meet me; some of them one hundred miles. I feel myself very unwell, and am afraid that almost every rain will bring on a relapse of the fever. My mind of late is much resigned to the will of God; I feel I have nothing here but the church of God; I would not throw my life away nor hold it back, if the Lord called for it in labouring, travelling, and suffering. I conclude I have rode one hundred miles this week, and the weather has been very uncomfortable, the roads bad, and our lodging in some very open houses; to which I may add my preaching in new and unfinished meeting-houses in March, which is a searching, changeable month, especially near the mountains.

Sabbath day 19. At Connelly's new church I preached on 2 Cor. vii. 1. I only intended to give a short discourse.

Monday 20. I had but twenty miles to ride to Esquire White's, at the Mulberry Grove. Here I left Doctor S. B——l; but death hath now removed him. I still continued to feel feverish and feeble, and thought it needful to take mountain bark.

Tuesday 21. I preached once more at Johns-River; my subject was 1 Cor. i. 24, 25. As I thought it would be my last, I exerted myself until my chill and fever returned : I also administered the sacrament and baptised children.

Wednesday 22. I set out on my journey for the west ; and it had a serious influence on my mind to leave brother Hill behind, who I fear hath a confirmed consumption, and I too so unwell. It began to rain violently before we came to Henley's : I took shelter in a house from the rain, and talked and prayed with a poor woman. We dined at Mr. Henley's, calling at Wakefield only to talk and pray.—I cannot well pass by my friends without calling. We hastened across Lynville Mountain, which is awfully barren, and came on to Young's Cove ; the storm followed us, with thunder, lightning, and rain. We arrived after some of the people were gone ; but some returned, and I gave them but a small talk, being very weary in walking down the mountains, and over the rocks.

Thursday 23. I came to Davenport's : my subject was " Godliness is profitable," &c.—Grace in the heart, in all its operations : bodily exercise for a little time is useful for health—for the present world—for the means of grace.—Godliness promiseth every thing we can wish for in the present and future life ; answering all the purposes of civil, domestic, and Christian life :—justice, mercy, and truth ;—every duty and relation ; all the joys and all the sufferings of life ; all the lawful use of lawful things ;—and prepares for the enjoyment of God, Christ, the Eternal Spirit, angels, and glory.

Friday 24. I was unwell : the clouds were lowering. We had rode but a mile when the rain began : brother Jones's house was at hand ; here we stopped two hours, until some of the rain fell to the earth : there was a short cessation, and about half past twelve o'clock we set out again, rode six miles, and were driven into Mr. Cook's by thunder, hail, and rain ; here we stopped to talk with God and man. Hard necessity made us move forward ; the western branch of Toe-River, that comes down from the Yellow Mountain, was rapidly filling ; and was rocky, rolling, and roaring like the sea, and we were compelled to cross it several times. When we came to ascend the mountain, we had a skirmish of rain, thunder, and lightning—it was distant—it was mercy. I found hard work to ride where Thomas White had driven his wagon, for which he deserves a place in my journal and a premium from the state. When we had ascended the summit of the mountain, we found it so rich and mirey, that it was with great difficulty we could ride along ; but I was wrapped up in heavy, wet garments, and unable to walk through weakness of body ; so we had it, pitch, slide, and drive to the bottom. We then came upon the drains and branches of Great Toe-River. From Fisher's we had to ride through what I called the *shades of death,* four miles to Miller's ; here we had to cope with Toe-River, and near the house came into deep water ; my horse drove to the opposite bank above the landing, and locked one of his feet in a root or something like it, but freed himself : at last we made the house, the people received us kindly, and gave us such things as they had. We could only partially dry our garments. We heard heavy tidings of a deep rocky ford yet to be passed in our way across Toe-River.

TENNESSEE.—Saturday 25. We were escorted by three brave young Dutchmen. After riding three miles we began to scale the rocks, hills. and mountains, worming through pathless woods, to shun a deep ford. I thought, ride I must, but no—the company concluded to walk : I gave my horse the direction of himself, under Providence. I had to step from rock to rock, hands and feet busy, but my breath was soon gone, and I gave up the cause and took horse again, and resolved that I would ride down the hills, although I had not rode up them : at last (hit or miss, Providence is all) into the path we came, and thence kept down the river and over to Little Toe, bearing down the stream ; when we had passed the Gap, we wished to feed ; but the man had no corn to sell : we tried, man and horse, to reach Nathan Davies's ; where we arrived and were made comfortable. I was much spent with the labours of this day. Hearing of the quarterly meeting at Dunworth's, I rode on Sunday 26th twelve miles, and arrived time enough for me to give them a feeble, yet faithful talk on Isa. i. 9. I am of opinion it is as hard. or harder. for the people of the west to gain religion as any other. When I consider where they came from, where they are, and how they are, and how they are called to go further, their being unsettled, with so many objects to take their attention. with the health and good air they enjoy, and when I reflect that not one in a hundred came here to get religion ; but rather to get plenty of good land, I think it will be well if some or many do not eventually lose their souls. I was met by our brethren Kobler, Burke, and Page. I rested on Monday and Tuesday to take breath and medicine. I find myself so hardly put to it at times that I can only journalize a little. We concluded as there are not proper stations on the Cumberland path, it will not do for me to lodge on the ground : the general opinion is against it. We are to try to go to Kentucky next week.

Wednesday 29. I rode to William Nelsons, and after dinner to Nathan Davies's. Thursday morning I was very weak, and have slow, but almost continual fevers. I preached with great difficulty in the afternoon, and returned to William Nelson's. This night I felt a total change of mind. The weakness of my body, and the cold and unsettled state of the weather, made me, with the general advice of the preachers present, give up the cause ; they also advised me to make the best of my way to Baltimore, and not to ride in the rain. It may be, the Lord intends to lead me in a way I have not yet known ; it is perhaps best that I should go with all expedient haste, from conference to conference, only stopping at the towns and chief places on Sabbath days. Live or die, I must ride. After all the disappointments, perhaps every purpose is answered but one. I have sent brother Cobler to take charge of Kentucky and Cumberland, by visiting the whole every quarter : brother Bird I have stationed in the Holstein district. I have written a circumstantial letter to brother Poythress and the Kentucky conference I have made a plan for the stationing of the preachers, at least those of any standing : and now I will make the best of my way to Baltimore ; perhaps there may be some special call for me there : I must, as the burden of meeting the conferences, ordaining, and stationing the preachers resteth on me, save myself. I am peculiarly concerned for the cities : the prosperity of the work of God depends much on having proper men for any and every part of the work.

Friday 31. It being rainy I rested. Saturday, April 1. The weather was clear and cold : we set off for brother Baker's. My horse hath the honour of swimming Holstein River every time I visit this country.

Sunday 2. I felt better than I had done since I crossed the mountains. I preached on Acts iii. 26. and was for pushing on again about fifteen miles farther, to Edward Coxe's : we got lost, and were an hour in the night.

Monday 3. We made a stretching ride of about forty miles, and were another hour in the night, and came to Half-Acres. I was *properly* outdone, and my fever returned and held me thirty hours.

Tuesday 4. I reached the widow Russell's : I am scarce able to read, write, sing, or pray ; nevertheless, after I had rested, I preached in the evening.

VIRGINIA.—Thursday 6. We took our way up Walker's Valley ; after riding about eight miles my weakness came on, and I was addressed by name and earnestly requested to stop and take refreshment and rest at Mr. M'Carty's; here we were richly provided for: the mother and daughter are most agreeable and kind. After commending ourselves and this affectionate family to God, we came to Benoni Banning's; as I was told, so I found this family—most attentively kind: we stopped here Friday, Saturday, and Sunday.

My fever never left me, as I thought, from Monday until Friday night. I am kept cheerful, but very weak. My diet is chiefly tea, potatoes, Indian-meal gruel, and chicken broth. My reading is only the Bible: I cannot think much, and only write a few letters. I think of my charge, of the conferences, and the church, and of my dear parents, who will probably outlive me—I must be made perfect through sufferings. I rest in rainy weather, and have to ride from eighty to one hundred and twenty miles in a week. The way we now go we have sometimes to ride thirty miles to get to a house. From the 9th of April to the 27th of May I have kept no journal. The notes of our travels and troubles taken by Jonathan Bird and Joshua Wells, will tell a small part of my sorrows and sufferings. I have travelled about six hundred miles with an inflammatory fever, and fixed pain in my breast. I cannot help expressing the distinguishing kindness of some families where I have been forced by weakness to stop—Captain Shannon, on Walker's creek—my friend Scarborough, on the sinks of Green Briar—Colonel Moffatt and brother Young in Augusta: neither can I forget Mr. Lee and Moore—the Harrisons, at Rocktown, and brother and sister M'Williams—Sisters Phelps and Reed, in Winchester, and my dear, kind friend Doctor Tiffin. By a strange providence I was cast upon Ely Dorsey, on Linganore, who nursed me as if I had been his own father.

MARYLAND.—From the 27th of May until June 10, no journal. We rode nearly forty miles from Linganore to Baltimore. I lodged at brother Hawkins's retreat, about one mile from the city. I lounged away a week in visiting a little.

Sunday, June 18. I was only able to speak about fifteen minutes. I recover but slowly. The constant resort of the wealthy and poor visiting me, made me much ashamed that they should look after such a worthless lump of misery and sin.

June 25. I met the male members of the society Sabbath morning, as I had met the sisters and the official members in the preceding week. I obtained the liberty of the managers of the African academy to congregate the fathers as well as to teach the children. We had nearly five hundred coloured people. Brother Willis preached on Acts vii. 7. and I added a few words. In the afternoon I gave a short exhortation at Mr. Otterbine's church, on Howard's Hill. I am now waiting for the making of a sulky. Thomas Barber, from Birmingham (England) took a second likeness of me, at the desire of my mother, to send to England. I am trying to organize the African church. I made interest for the use of Mr. Otterbine's church for Sabbath in the morning and evening for the white people. I have attempted to promote society meetings at Old-Town and the west end of the city, either at the Dunker's meeting-house or Mr. Otterbine's church. My feelings or my fears premonish me this will be a sickly summer. I visit, dine, and ride out every day—but it is very hard work for me to eat, drink, talk, and do nothing. As I am not a man of the world the most of the conversation about it is irksome to me. I am taken from house to house, and the brethren wish the pleasure of seeing me, and those who are acquainted with their families will come to see me also.

July 3. I attempted to preach in Doctor Allison's church, and felt more assisted than I expected.

Tuesday 4. I was taken in a chariot to Perry-Hall in company with sister Fonerdon. I felt the effects of my exertions on the Sabbath, the want of rest, rising early, and riding to Mr. Gough's. In my mind I felt almost as in old times. God hath not left this house. I felt great love to the family in praying for them in the family and in the closet. I had an open and free conversation with Mr. Gough about his soul. I conversed with the servants also, and had freedom in prayer, although I felt weakness of body. I wrote a few letters and read a little in the Bible. The weather is excessively warm.

Saturday 8. I cannot now as heretofore spend ten hours out of sixteen in reading the Bible in English or Hebrew, or other books, or write letters from morning until night. My bow is weak, if not broken; but I have more time to speak to God and souls. Sabbath day I performed at Mr. Gough's alone.

Wednesday 12. I borrowed a servant at Mr. Gough's, and came on to Mr. Sheridan's house, North-East Cecil county; here I borrowed another servant, and on Friday I rode to Wilmington, and stopped at Allen M'Lane's, now living there.

PENNSYLVANIA.—Saturday 15. Warm as it was, I reached Philadelphia: and Sabbath evening 16, I felt free to labour a little, feeble as I was, and enlarged on John xiv. 1. I have great reason to be thankful for my sulky; I should soon be silent without it. I rode to Germantown to see aged mother Steel, and sister

Lusby, and found freedom, although I could hardly walk or talk;
yet must needs speak to the women of the house about their
souls. Dined at brother Baker's retreat, and came back to the city
very sick, and went to bed.

NEW-JERSEY.—Tuesday 18. I came off to Burlington; and was
much grieved to hear my appointments had been made, and not
attended in consequence of my illness.

Wednesday 19. Dined at Crossweek's, at brother Abbott's, once
a travelling preacher, now a merchant. We came on to father
Hutchinson's; here I was almost outdone with excessive heat. I
stopped four days, but found it hard work to sit still.

Monday 24. We came to Brunswick; dined, prayed, and rejoiced to hear that God had kindled a living fire here, through
the instrumentality of a brother from Elizabethtown. We came on
to Elizabethtown, forty miles; it was ample labour for man and
horse: here I was sick again.

Tuesday 25. I rode to Newark, and dined with Mr. Ogden, a
steady friend. After the rain, I came to New-York; here I spent
a few painful days, being unable to visit or be visited.

NEW-YORK.—On Monday I came to Shotwell's, very unwell;
and the next day to Kingsbridge: here I was compelled by affliction to spend two weeks. I then rode to New-Rochelle, and
lodged at Mr. Sherwood's. Finding myself swelling in the face,
bowels, and feet, I applied leaves of burdock, and then a plaister
of mustard, which drew a desperate blister. I had such awful
sore feet, I knew not but that they would mortify; and only after
two weeks was I able to set them to the ground. I took cream of
tartar, and nitre daily to cool, and keep open the body; I also
made use of the bark.

Sunday, September 12. I began to walk once or twice across
the room.

Monday 13. We began our route to Wilberham; we had not
rode far over the rocks before I was taken very unwell. We
stopped at Byram, at father Banks's: I was soon put to bed with a
very high fever that held me through the night. I now began to
conclude it was not the will of God I should proceed, and the
brethren would not persuade me to go on; brother Totten returned with me to mother Sherwood's. I have had slight fevers,
but expect to rest until about the first of October, which I hope,
with riding a little every clear day, will restore me to health.

Thursday 16. I visited Nicholas Underhill's wife, who is near
her trying hour; I hope it was good for me, for her, and the fa-

mily. I take a small potion of bark each day, and one third of a common dose of cream of tartar and nitre, and hope I shall yet be raised up. My mind is stayed upon God : and I hope to be more holy ; but I fear I shall never be able to ride and preach as I have done in former days, so as to be more useful. I have now much time to think of, and review my whole life.

The kindness of this Sherwood family is great ; my dear mamma, and Betsy Sherwood, and Jonathan and Bishop also : if I had not been at home here, what additional distress of mind would have attended me ! my friends also were welcome to come and see me. Sabbath-day, at the widow Sherwood's, I had the pleasure of hearing our brother Matthias make a pointed, profitable, and powerful discourse. It is now eight weeks since I have preached—awfully dumb Sabbaths ! I have been most severely tried from various quarters ; my fevers, my feet, and Satan, would set in with my gloomy and nervous affections. Sometimes subject to the greatest effeminacy ; to distress at the thought of a useless, idle life : but what brought the heavy pang into my heart, and the big tear to roll, that never rises without a cause, was, the thought of leaving the connexion without some proper men of their own election, to go in and out before them in my place, and to keep that order which I have been seeking these many years to establish. My aged parents were dear to me in their advanced age and dependant state : like myself, they have spent what they had to spare for many years, nearly forty, in keeping open doors for the Gospel and people of God : this burden hath been laid upon them. I am happy that I can now ride a little every clear day for my better health, and can eat and sleep better. I am left too much alone : I cannot sit in my room all day making gloomy reflections on the past, present, and future life. Lord, help me ! for I am poor and needy ; the hand of God hath touched me, and I think Satan *forts* himself in my melancholy, unemployed, unsocial, and inactive hours.

Sunday 18. I was strongly impressed in my mind months ago that this summer and fall would be marked with heavy afflictions. Oh Philadelphia ! I have had very little faith for that city ; I have often remarked the general contempt of the Sabbath ; the constant noise of carriages ; there is a perpetual disturbance of worshipping assemblies. It is true, one event cometh on the righteous and the wicked ; but God will stand to his word—he hath punished, he will punish those that rob him. If report be true, the distress of the Philadelphians is great ; three-fourths of the citizens are fled.

Monday 19. I felt strength of faith and body, as if I should be raised up again. I rode for recreation nine miles. The clouds are dispelled from my mind—O that my future life may be holiness to the Lord—prudent and exemplary to many! I wished to speak to a poor African whom I saw in the field as I went out, and as I came along on my return, he was at a stone wall within eight or nine feet of me : poor creature! he seemed struck at my counsel, and gave me thanks. O, it was going down into the Egypt of South Carolina after those poor souls of Africans I have lost my health, if not my life in the end—the will of the Lord be done!

Wednesday 20. I rode about fourteen miles. I met a messenger who came to desire my presence to-morrow at the funeral of our brother Vanostrand : I have known him about fifteen years, and had great confidence in the man. He hath laboured as a local preacher, and three years as a travelling one ; he had his seals, and I know one. Some will complain of his negligence in Elizabeth circuit ; but what could the man do? He gave his life, and perhaps caught the cause of his death by bad lodging, and riding in cold weather. He told a friend he had settled his temporal and spiritual business ; he then slept in peace. Brother Vanostrand was a native of Long-Island. He followed the fortune of king George in the revolutionary war, but soon after peace he joined himself under king Jesus, and fought till he died 'in a good cause, as a Christian and a minister. I had some unpleasing symptoms, and am ready to conclude I shall linger into death, or at least never be restored to perfect health : my soul continually cries out, Thy will be done, O Lord!

Thursday 21. I attended the funeral, and gave an exhortation. I have rode twenty miles this day, with little rest and no food.

Friday 22. I rode eight or ten miles, I was touched with the fever.

Saturday 23. I slept well last night, but waked with a slight fever. I received a letter from Dr. Coke ; as I thought, so it is—he is gone from Ireland to England, and will have work enough when he cometh there. The three grand divisions of that connexion are alarming. It is a doubt if the Doctor cometh to America until spring, if at all until the general conference. I am more than ever convinced of the propriety of the attempts I have made to bring forward Episcopal men : First, from the uncertain state of my health ; Secondly, from a regard to the union and good order of the American body, and the state of the European connexion. I am sensibly assured the Americans ought to act as if they expected to lose me every day, and had no dependance upon Doctor Coke ; taking prudent care not to place themselves at all under the controling influence of British Methodists. I visited three families, talked, and prayed in each, but was rather outdone.

Sunday 24. At Sherwood's Valley : I had greatly desired to speak to these people, and was much assisted so to do ; my subject was 2 Cor. vi. 2. I considered, by way of introduction, what character of people they were who are to be the subjects of salvation—the lost, the enslaved, and those that cannot save themselves. First, Christ the author of this salvation ; the meritorious, efficient, and moving cause. Secondly, The nature of this salvation—to reach all the misery and guilt of sinners ; to save, redeem, and liberate. Thirdly, What bespeaks an accepted time and a day of salvation ; to have God, Christ, the Spirit, ministers, means, and people that have religion, Say, behold—now is the day of salvation ! I was able to speak fervently and regularly for an hour with great affection. I rejoiced to find that God had raised me up to call poor mourning souls to Christ, and to warn careless sinners. After twenty-six years the Gospel is established in this neighbourhood, at a small distance from this house. I preached at Peter Bonnett's before the war ; and after peace was restored, the blessing returned to his widow's house ; two of his daughters are in fellowship with us. The widow Sherwood's was the substitute house, after the widow Bonnett went to live at New-York : now they are about building a church for the word and worship of God. I am happy to hear, by letters, of a revival of the work in several places in Virginia, as also in North and South Carolina.

Monday 25. The day was clear, and very warm. I rode up to the Plains, and stopped at Elijah Crawford's. God hath honoured this house. Two young men are gone into the ministry out of it. I have rode nearly twenty miles, and had it not been for the heat, I should have done well.

Tuesday 26. I wrote a letter to ——, he was under grief and trouble. This day Joshua Wells returned from Wilbraham conference. Matters were conducted well.

Wednesday 27. The preachers came up ; and Thursday 28, we had a sermon, and ordination of deacons. I was employed about three hours, and faint indeed. I rode four miles, and lodged at Morgan's, East Chester : this was an excessively warm day.

Saturday 30. We rode to New-York ; a very warm day. I found myself much injured, but was well nursed at the north side of the city. They have a touch of the fever here in George-street.

Sabbath, October 1. We had much rain. Live or die, I preached at the old and new church on Isai. xxxiii. 20. and Deut. xxviii. 9. I had some disagreeable things, and was but ill fitted in body to bear them.

Monday 2. We rode about twenty-seven miles to Hammond's. My fever rises every night.

NEW-JERSEY.—Tuesday 3. We rode thirty miles to Joseph Hutchinson's. I lament most of all that I have not lived in a constant state of prayer. I have had most deep and sore temptations of many kinds, such as I could have hardly thought of in health. I must be tried so as by fire. By reason of the fever in Philadelphia our conference is moved to Duck-Creek, in the state of Delaware.

Wednesday 4. After the storm was over we moved on as far as Crossweeks, and lodged at father Lovell's. I was weak in body but comfortable in mind. I visited three families ; called at Hancock's, and saw my old friend of twenty-six years membership. I came on to Burlington. Serious times still in Philadelphia. I was very unwell ; I had an awful night.

Friday 6. We crossed Dunkes's ferry, and came a rough, crooked way to Germantown. We had a meeting at Dr. Lusby's.

Saturday 7. We rode over the rocks, after crossing Schuylkill at a ferry, to Chester, and thence to Aaron Mattson's. There is a new house and mill built since I was here ; but there is room enough for Christ yet. We rode to Wilmington, where I preached on Psalms xlvi. 1—5.

DELAWARE.—Monday 9. We came thirty-eight miles to Duck-Creek.

Tuesday 10. We began conference. I appointed the president elders to take my seat, and I sat alone, because the hand of the Lord was upon me. I was resolved to put out my strength to the last in preaching. My first subject was Isaiah i. 26—28. ; my second was on Luke xvii. 12. ; my third 2 Cor. xiii. 11. Great times : preaching almost night and day ; some souls converted, and Christians were like a flame of fire. Eleven persons were set apart for elders' and three for deacons' orders.

Friday 13. We rose. I was much outdone, yet happy. We appointed a standing committee to inspect and direct the press. We read some passages of the notes on the Discipline, and left the remnant to this committee.

MARYLAND.—Monday 16. We rode to Bohemia-Ferry, twenty miles. Dr. Ridgely has sent me a plenty of Columbo magnesia, soluble tartar, and bark. I am much grieved that I do not con-

verse more abundantly with God in my own heart and soul. We
had great peace. I have not of late, if at any time in these parts,
heard such an awful account of fever as we now hear rages in
Baltimore city and Point. It is reported that our conference was
first moved to Evans's meeting-house. I spent the evening at Mr.
Bassett's, and lectured upon a chapter.

Tuesday 17, was a very warm day. We rode from Duck-
Creek to North-East. They had managed the matter so as to
appoint for me and brother Lee to preach. I gave them a short
sermon on Gal. v. 7. "Ye did run well; who did hinder you that
ye should not obey the truth?" I lodged at Mr. Sheridine's.

Wednesday 18. We came to Josiah Dallam's.

Thursday 19. Reached Mr. Gough's. I was comforted in
seeing a few of my age who were my spiritual children.

Friday 20. After all the alarm we came to Baltimore ; a blessed
rain settled the amazing dust and purified the air.

Saturday 21. I opened conference, and gave up the presidency
to the presiding elders. Returned unwell. Very uncomfortable
easterly winds and rainy weather. I mentioned in my speech to
the conference the weakness of the episcopacy.

The conference rose on Friday 26. There was great peace,
and all the preachers, but myself, satisfied with their stations.

Sabbath day 22. I preached at Dr. Allan's church the funeral
sermon of Martha F. Allison, a Methodist for about twenty-seven
years—a class leader—a woman of sense and piety : the subject
was John xi. 24—27. We had a crowded house.

Sunday 29. I opened the new church in Light-street with reading 2 Chron. vii. 12. Psalm cxxxii. Haggai xi. Mark xi. The elders
read and prayed. My subject was Eph. ii. 19, 20, 22.; and at Old
Town I preached on 2 Samuel xvi. 17. I had to preach the funeral sermon of father Gatch on 1 Thess. iv. 13, 14. I observed
the pleasing, cheering, and charming manner in which the apostle
described the death of the righteous. Sleep—sleep in Jesus—a
rest from labour, sorrow, affliction, and pain ; happy opening vi-
sions of God ! Secondly—the hope the pious who are alive have for
their pious dead who have had experience, and long continuance
in religion, and a comfortable dying in the Lord. Those who
have no hope for themselves nor their dead, how awful their sorrow ! I feel myself very weak. I dined at Mr. Rogers's.

Tuesday 31. I went to see the poor orphans—to weep with sister Fonerdon's children, and dear Nelly Owens, her daughter also. They had a Nelly Owens baptised for the dead brother

and sister Reed, my dear nursing friends : my aged friends brought me their beneficence and tears.

Wednesday, November 1. We came off and preached at the widow Dorsey's on "If in this life only we have hope in Christ, we are of all men most miserable." We had a solemn assembly. I made a few observations on the hope Christians have of Christ only in this life ; if in this life only Christians could have hope in Christ, they would be most miserable. They are denied the sinful pleasures, profits, and honours of the world ; subject to great afflictions and persecutions ; often deprived of life in ages past : no mercy, no justice, no truth, no love ; lastly, that they could never be borne up under such principles and persecutions if it were not for the hope of future rewards : they which have no hope in this or the future world in Christ, are of all men the most wretched and miserable. My horse is a little ungovernable, the weather warm, and myself unwell.

Thursday 2. I did not preach, but exhorted at Shadrach Turner's : here are five children and a mother for Christ, and for usefulness.

Friday 3. We came to Georgetown. I felt very feeble in body, almost ready to faint before we reached Col. Bell's : I was glad through my weakness to be excused from preaching : brother Lee supplied the place. I visited John Long's family ; I saw mother Moore after more than twenty years—she is going on to glory. A son of brother Long's was sick, and distressed about his soul, and resolved to seek redeeming grace. We must needs go and view the famous bridge—it is amazing to see the river so contracted that a stone could be pitched over where the bridge stands : this is three miles above Georgetown : from the bridge upwards, there is a good road cut out of the rocks. The rain came on, and we were glad we could find Samuel Adams's, three miles from the bridge : here we were happily sheltered from the weather, and comfortably accommodated. I sent for brother Waters and his wife, and we improved the evening in the way Christians should ; in prayer, singing, reading the word, and exhortations.

VIRGINIA.—Sunday 5. We rode ten miles to Alexandria, and had only time to reach town when the rain came on powerfully. I made a feeble discourse on Isaiah xxxiii. 20. I ordained Thomas Lyell deacon

Monday 6. Came out of town late, and judged it best to call at William Bushley's. We had a storm of snow. My mind is dull and my body languid ; my only hope is Christ and grace.

Tuesday 7. We thought it good, as the weather was fine, to stand our course southward : we fed at Colchester, at the new bridge : we were told it cost eighty thousand dollars. This is a great relief to hasty travellers. We dined on the road, in the woods, on what we brought with us. We got to Dumfries, where court was then sitting : we met several drunken men in the way. I have not seen such sights for many days. We slept at Captain Ward's : they expected us the evening before. I ordained brother Hopkinson deacon.

Wednesday 8. We came away at eight o'clock, making twelve miles to Stafford court-house, breakfasted and fed, and then drove twenty-five miles to the widow Bombry's, where we arrived about six o'clock. The hills were very bad to climb, being much washed and broken : I was ready to be cast away, or overset. My body is still weak, and my mind greatly affected.

Thursday 9. I had gloomy feelings last night. Riding in the night was very injurious. I feel no evil, unless something like murmuring. When I am so unable to travel and yet go on, probably I do more than God or man requires of me ; but the will of the Lord be done ! If I suffer or sin in this, he will pardon my weakness.

Friday 10. We rested at the widow Bombry's : this mother in Israel treated us with every necessary mark of attention. I had an interview with sister Forks and her daughter. I found them still walking in the narrow way.

Saturday 11. We rode ten miles to Port Royal, and then came on nearly twenty miles to the widow Rouse's, in Essex, where we were kindly and comfortably entertained. We then hastened on to Lersy Cole's ; he and his wife were gone to quarterly meeting eight miles down the river ; but a pious young sister and housekeeper made us comfortable. We had a storm of wind and rain : when it had blown over, we hasted to the meeting-house. I gave a short sermon on " No man speaking by the Spirit of God calleth Jesus accursed ;" and that " No man can say Jesus is Lord but by the Holy Ghost." What is to be understood by calling Jesus accursed ?—To put him wholly out of the question ; to expel him from being any thing in our salvation ; and to say all the unkind things that the Jews said of him. We had to ride five miles to the widow Humby's ; here all was kindness and love. We rejoiced to see our much esteemed brethren, Cole, M'Kendree, and Mead, and to hear of a great and gracious work of God.

Monday 13. We rode to Pace's chapel, where I preached on
John xiv. 6. after which we had several exhortations, and the sacrament. We lodged at widow Campbell's : we have been fed by
the widows more than Elijah.

Tuesday 14. We rode to Shackleford's chapel, and held meeting three hours: we had a large and solemn congregation. I
preached, although very unwell, on 1 Cor. ii. 12. In the month of
July last, the Lord visited this place in mercy, and it is judged thirty
souls not only professed to be, but were really converted to God.
In speaking to-day, I showed—Of whom, and of what the apostles
wrote : the things freely given them to know as apostles and Christians—redemption, salvation in all its degrees—conviction of sin,
repentance for sin, faith, justification, regeneration, sanctification,
the resurrection, and glorification—that these things are not communicated by the spirit of the world, but by the Spirit of God.
We had a very warm day: we fasted eight hours, and held meeting three, and then rode nearly twenty-four miles, and lodged
at ———.

Wednesday 15, was a snowy day, and very cold : I rode seven
miles, cased and curtained up in the carriage. I kept house at brother Bellamy's : it is seven years since I was here. My mind
enjoys peace, but my body is languid. I had a severe fever, and
found it time to rest. A society of nearly forty here is now increased to one hundred, and it is hoped that nearly five hundred
have joined this year in Gloucester circuit. I preached at Bellamy's chapel on Hebr. iii. 12, 13. it was an exceedingly cold day,
but clear. We rode ten miles to John Ellis's, where we were
comforted with kindness, and blessed for one short night. We
rose early to go on our way, and, behold, who should meet us but
Bishop Coke, with a borrowed horse, and a large white boy riding
behind him on the same horse. We halted, and then agreed he
should have brother M'Kendree's horse ; but up came John Ellis,
and took the Doctor home, and brought him in a carriage to quarterly meeting. We stood on our course, and by the time we came
to Gloucester ferry, it blew a storm of wind and rain : I had only
to turn the chair back to the wind and sit wrapped up. After two
hours we crossed the river and rode in haste to John Ellis's, seven
miles. We drank, ate, prayed, and came on our way : the day, to
one in my state, was very uncomfortable. We rode thirty-two
miles this day, and stopped at our dear brother Taylor's, in James-
City. There are two very good meeting-houses built here since

I visited these parts ; one in James-City, and the other in New-Kent county.

Saturday 18. I delivered a feeble discourse on 1 Peter ii. 1, 2. I observed on the *malice*, for some real or supposed injury done ; *guile* to hide malice until an opportunity for revenge offers. *Hypocrites*—going beyond our attainments, professing what we do not practise, or not practising what we profess : *envious* at the excellences or happiness of others ; *evil-speaking*—all these arising from the bad state of the heart : chiefly pride and self-love. *Babes ;* not giving them strong food or medicines ; *babes ;* strangers to malice by want of understanding—and not having a capacity for guile ; strangers to hypocrisy ; no ideas of envy, not having speech to speak evil. Dr. Coke preached on Luke xii. 14. " For where your treasure is, there your heart is also." We spent a night at the widow Cowley's.

Monday 20. We rode thirty-one miles to brother Mooring's ; I had a thought never more to cross at old James-Town. But we had a remarkable time after we had embarked : myself and Dr. Coke crossing in a skiff, the horses and carriage came in a large boat ; my bible, which was clothed and bound up in a handkerchief, was accidentally thrown into the river, but the black man snatched it up undamaged. The weather being damp, we rested.

Tuesday 21. I wrote a small epistle to the official members of Baltimore, and another to Philadelphia, as also a short pathetic letter to my parents. We have rode little less than four hundred miles in twenty days, and rested one. We had very damp weather.

Wednesday 22, at brother Bellamy's.

Thursday 23. I rode about thirty miles to Mr. Briggs's, to see how the preachers would be accommodated, and where the conference would be held : Mr. Briggs was willing to take eight or ten of the preachers, and gave the conference the offer of his hall to sit in.

Friday 24. I visited my old friends, and wrote to Alexander Mather. My route, which I only guessed at, is now fixed by Norfolk, Portsmouth, Newbern, Kingston, Georgetown, and Charleston. Between five and six hundred miles in little more than a month ; sick or well, living or dead, my appointments go on.

Saturday 25. The conference began their sitting at Lane's chapel. About sixty preachers were present : nine or ten had located ; and four or five were added. Sabbath day two hours were spent in speaking of the circuits, and for souls.

Wednesday 29. At noon the conference rose ; the business was conducted with despatch, and in much peace. I desired the advice of the conference concerning my health : the answer was, that I should rest until the session of the conference to be held in April, in Virginia.

Thursday 30. I travelled under much weakness of body to Stith Parham's, at the High-hill store.

Friday, December 1. I collected the small remains of strength I had, to read, and hear read my manuscript journal. It was written in such haste that it was very incorrect. I visited Robert Jones's family, and on

Sunday 3, we had a family meeting : brother M'Kendree preached on faith, hope, and charity : on faith to me, as I felt the need of its exercise.

Monday 4. We stopped one night at Matthew Davis's ; and the next at Ira Ellis's. Our time was taken up in journalizing ; I came off twenty-five miles to Edward Drumgold's : once or twice I felt on my way thither as if the blood would rise into my mouth. I resolved to give up travelling this winter. Dr. Sims bled me ; and there appeared an inflammatory buff on the top. Oh! to rest—to be idle and dependant—is painful : but if this is to make me perfect, the will of the Lord be done ! I sent my papers to brother Lee, who proceeds to Charleston ; also my plan and directions how to station the preachers, to brother Jackson. I believed that my going to Charleston this season, would end my life ; yet, could I be persuaded it was the will of the Lord, I would go and preach. I cannot bear the fatigue of riding thirty miles in a day. I am much pressed to make my will, lest I should be surprised by death ; my mind is greatly calmed and centred in God. I have well considered all the solemnities of death.

Saturday 9, and Sunday 10. We sat melancholy in the house— dumb Sabbaths ! Dr. Sims read me Mr. Wesley's sermon upon the depth of the riches of the wisdom and of the knowledge of God.

Monday 11. I was led to meditate on the same subject : " By whom shall Jacob rise ?" 1. Jacob, the church. 2. Rise to spiritual glory. 3. By whom Jacob hath risen. 4. By whom the Church shall rise—it is a prophetic character of the Church. Jacob—see that man loved by his mother, hated by his brethren after the flesh, guarded against unlawful marriages, yet had two wives, representing the Jewish and Gentile state of the Church. See his afflictions and persecutions ; the danger of being extinct in his family ; yet preserved, his children, his piety, his prayers. A type of

Christ, and his Church. Jacob rise! rise, increase in children, in faith, in love, in mercy, in justice, in truth, in zeal, in ministerial gifts, in faithful watchmen. By whom hath the church risen? By Abel, by Enoch, by Noah, by Abraham, Isaac, and Jacob, by Moses and Aaron, Joshua, and the elders that out lived Joshua, by Joel, by Ruth, by Obadiah, servant of Ahab, by Micah, by Joash, by Jothan, Hezekiah, and his grandson Josiah; and all the prophets; by the great wrestling Jacob; by Jesus and his apostles; by faithful ministers in all ages, nations, and societies. We want knowledge to know, and time to mention their names. By whom shall Jacob rise? God will pour out his Spirit in the last days on ministers and people, old men and maidens, young men and children; ministers and members of his Church, magistrates and masters, parents and guardians. He is small: see all the little flock, the holy seed. All the weaknesses, all the apostates and backsliders, all the want of justice, mercy, truth, and true religion; these shall be replaced with opposite characters and graces; all the vacancies of ministers and virtues shall be filled up, and more abundantly supplied in spiritual and heavenly glory. When all shall know the Lord, and be taught of the Lord, and all be righteous, and the knowledge of the Lord shall cover the earth, as the water doth all the deep places of the earth and seas. But by whom shall Jacob rise? I answer, by the wisdom, power, mercy, truth, love, and holiness of God, displayed in a glorious Gospel. I am sure Jacob shall rise by the merit, righteousness, and intercession of Jesus Christ. I answer again, by the operations of the eternal Spirit of God, in its convincing, converting, and sanctifying influences, manifested by the calling and qualifying ministers for the work; that thousands of ministers may go forth; and millions of souls may be brought home by their instrumentality.

Tuesday 12. Whilst taking a sober, contemplative ride for three hours, I conversed sweetly with God; my mind and body were refreshed with a clear and cold day. I read a few chapters in the book of God. In the evening Mr. James Green Martin came to receive deacon's orders; he brought letters of consolation from Richard Whatcoat and Jesse Lee. Also the wishes of my dear brethren and sisters that waited to see me.

Wednesday 13. I felt a little better; I rode out, but it was not as comfortable a day as yesterday. The smallest exercise or application to study is too great for me. The doctor pronounces my complaint to be debility. I have taken cider with *nails* put into it, and fever powders, and must take more of the barks.

Thursday 14. My mind is grieved with the *old sore* in Virginia; but I must bear it patiently. One of our sisters asked me if we would not rebaptise persons that desired it. This put me to thinking and revolving the subject in my mind. I considered that there was neither precept nor example in holy writ to justify our rebaptising one who had been baptised in the name and form which Christ commanded in Matt. xxviii. 19.

Friday 15. Was my well day; I took some of the powders, had good nursing, and got rest. I only read the Bible and the Form of Discipline. I write, ride, and talk a little with the women, children, and Africans. My thoughts were led to meditate upon Timothy iv. 16. " Take heed unto thyself, and unto thy doctrine; continue in them, for in doing this thou shalt both save thyself and them that hear thee."

I. " Take heed to thyself,"—in religion, as in nature, self-preservation is one of the first laws. Take heed that thy experience in religion and doctrine be sound; that thou hast a good heart, and a good head, and a good life, and a good conversation, ministerial diligence and fidelity, in every part of Christian and pastoral duty. Saved already by grace, thou shalt be preserved from all the snares set for thy feet, and not backslide as a Christian minister, but feel persevering, sanctifying, glorifying, and crowning grace.

II. Thou shalt " save them that hear thee," from lukewarmness and backsliding; legality on the one hand, and making void the law through faith on the other; that they profess and possess, live and walk as it becometh the Gospel of Christ.

III. " Continue in them;" in all the doctrines, ordinances, and duties of the Gospel; the same Gospel, the same ordinances, the same duties which are designed to complete the work in the souls of ministers as Christians, are as needful to continue the work of grace as to begin it; and not only continue, but to finish and bring on the headstone with shouting.

Saturday 16. I employed myself as much as my health would admit, in reading the Bible and writing such observations thereon as were suggested to my mind.

Sunday 17. I had to keep house; O dumb day! I am better, yet it is not safe for me to go out such very cold weather. I read the Word of God (for my comfort) and preached.

Monday 18. Very little done; I wrote to Dr. Coke, advising against the British brethren going to law with the contentious party about their houses.

Tuesday 19. I am in a more comfortable state of body and mind,' for which I feel thankful : I am taking the bark.

Wednesday 20. I felt much amended by the bark and rest. It appears to have been the mount Moriah where Abraham essayed to offer up his Isaac, on which the temple of God was built upwards of eight hundred years thereafter, and before the offering of Christ, nearly or upon the same spot, eight hundred and seventy-two : the types and prophecies are not small arguments for the truth of the Scriptures ; for fore-knowledge doth not belong to man ; he cannot tell, only by probable conjectures, any thing that will befall himself, unless revealed by the spirit of prophecy. The prophecy made by the man of God, 1 Kings xiii. ; fulfilled by Josiah, 2 Kings xxiii. : between the prophecy and fulfilment a probable space of time of about three hundred and fifty years, completely accomplished in every punctilio, and the prophet's tomb and sleeping ashes taken notice of, the prophet's memory kept, who died a witness to what he said, to seal the truth, and his sleeping bones lying there on the spot : what man, untaught by God, who knoweth all things, could come and foretell such events which should so surely come to pass, without being taught and sent of God ?

Thursday 21. Perhaps we may call this one of the coldest days of this winter ; I slept under two double-milled blankets, beside coverlids and sheets, but could not keep warm. This is the fifth season of cold weather we have had in Virginia since the first of November : we have had snow, but this is gone in a day ; this excepted, it is cold enough for the north. Strange life for me—to sit and burn myself by the fire, and to be nursed. I feel a small return of health. I have been reading David's Psalms in Hebrew, and the book of Genesis in the English Bible. I could not but admire the provision made for the heathen nations, civil and barbarous, by Abraham's second marriage, and by Ishmael and Esau's posterity : this attended to according to their names, as traced in the Universal History, we should not wondering ask, Where did this or that nation of people come from ? either Indians or Africans. I cannot preach now, only to the family, and when a stranger cometh in.

Friday 22. I rose in the morning in some fear lest I had or should say too much on slavery. I made choice of a verse, 1 Kings xxii. 16. "And the king said unto him, How many times shall I adjure thee that thou tell me nothing but that which is true in the name of the Lord" or Jehovah. I have found relief by taking barks, in strength, in feeling, in breath, and in my breast, and have a hope of being raised up once more.

Saturday 23. Extremely cold. I am closely confined in my room, but could neither read nor write.

Sunday 24. It is exceedingly cold still. The pain in my breast is returned; I fear it is immoveably fixed more or less until death. Lord, thy will be done! Wearisome days are appointed for me. Brother Drumgold came in the evening of Christmas day: I am cheered with company and with Christ also. I feel as if the coming year would be marked with displays of divine power upon the souls of men to whoever may live to see it.

Tuesday 26. We had open weather and rain. I am so much better in health that confinement is as trying to me as hard labour. I hope, if it pleaseth my God, I shall have health to be of some service to mankind yet. Ah! what is life and all this dull round, but for God and souls!

Wednesday 27. A falling of snow—very cold. I have taken the bark; this is the ninth day, and I am strengthened; but the wine in the smallest portions makes me feverish, and it is astringent. I feel need of great patience, prayer, and faith.

Thursday 28. We had hard frost and snow. I am thankful it is rest time with the poor blacks, or many might be frozen to death. Ungrateful man that I am, how am I favoured above millions!

Friday 29. Extremely cold. Mrs. Selby desired to see me, bad riding as it was through the snow and ice. I am mending. I prayed for health, and had faith to believe I should recover. I thought if God would spare me I was willing to labour and suffer out my days; but the thoughts of being useless is most distressing to an active, benevolent mind.

Saturday 29. I felt weakness of body and dejection of mind, and sometimes I am brought to think of requesting, as Elijah and Jonah did, that I may die. I cannot pray in the family without injury, wherefore should I request to live? Oh! my God, thy will be done in all things—mine in nothing, but as it pleaseth thee!

Sunday 30. We had a meeting at my lodging.

Monday, January 1, 1798. Several local brethren were present —Drumgold, Lane, Moore, Smith, and Phillips. The brethren were lively in religion. I am now taking an extraordinary diet— drink made of one quart of hard cider, one hundred nails, a handful of black snakeroot, one handful of fennel seed, and one handful of wormwood, boiled from a quart to a pint, taking one wine glass full every morning for nine or ten days, using no butter, or milk, or meat; it will make the stomach very sick, and in a few days purge the patient well. I was better in my feelings than I have been since I have been taken ill; but I must flee conversation, grief, and care, with deep and close thinking and composition. I made a small meditation on being free from the ceremonial law. Polygamy, slavery, and such like, were never commanded under this dispensation, but only tolerated; and accompanied by strict injunctions to prevent men from running to greater lengths in these practices, as may be seen in Exodus xxi. Leviticus xxv. Deuteronomy xxiv. Polygamy was allowed to prevent general whoredom. Servitude was regulated to prevent slavery and oppression, death, and loss of limbs. If any had asked the Lord on the subject of slavery, as on polygamy, he must have said, Moses, as a man, suffered this, a less evil, to prevent a greater; but it was not so from the beginning of the creation: it is the fall which hath done this, not a holy God. It is man's work, of two evils, to choose the least. But God is not tempted of us to evil, neither tempteth he any man. Christians, of two evils, should not choose or use either if they would be like God.

Tuesday 2. Now I am brought to the second day of the new year—the last hath been a year of great affliction. I may have travelled about three thousand miles, and have been confined with affliction and weakness six months, adding the single days I have stopped, as well as weeks. In April last I had very little expectation of living until this day. I am now under the exercise to desire life, that I may see the connexion better organized, and be more personally useful.

Wednesday 3. This is a cloudy day; it is probably snowing north or west. I have a better appetite for food: my mind is greatly agitated at times; but patience shall have its perfect work. I pray, and sometimes I wind and pick a little cotton, and read and write about one hour in the day; but Christ is all! I cannot be inactive: the hardest work I have to do, is to do nothing.

Thursday 4. A proper day for rain! Last evening I had a very high fever; but I am as usual to-day. I read my Bible, and selected those texts which struck my mind, that if ever I should preach again I may use. Joseph said, I fear God; Nehemiah said, he could not oppress the people as other governors had done, because of the fear of God. *Fear of God*, in seekers, in believers, and in those who are sanctified: and the motives to the fear of God. First, He is holy; Secondly, He is wise; Thirdly, He is just;

fourthly, He is powerful :—If holy, he hath no sin ; if wise, he knoweth when we sin ; if he is just, he must punish sin ; and he hath power to punish it :—a man may be *wise*, but not *all-wise ; a* man may be just, but not infinite in justice : thus man may be holy, but not holy as God : man may be wanting in wisdom, in power, in holiness, and in justice. In some cases it may not be man's duty to punish, nor in his power—not so with Jehovah. Who will not fear him according to his attributes, and according to his word of threatened vengeance ?

Friday 5. The rain is over ; the clouds scattered and gone ; and nature smileth again. I only mourn the oppression I cannot remove.

Saturday 6. We have open and pleasant weather. It may be that many have overlooked the prophecies of Jacob in Genesis xlix. We may look for the fulfilment nearly fourteen hundred years after, in the coming of Christ ; and about one thousand years after, we shall see in Jeremiah, and Daniel, what Jacob farther re- ferred to. It appears that it was the wish of Jacob, that his young- est but one, Joseph, should have the birthright, which Reuben, his first-born, had lost by his unnatural incest in defiling his father's bed. Simeon and Levi—we cannot tell whether they had a bless- ing or a curse for their zeal against folly in Israel ; they punished whoredom with cruel murder, and yet we see how Levi's zeal wrought in the case of Cozbi : and the Lord confirmed the priest- hood by special grant to him. Joseph's prophecy concerning the Israelites' *exodus* from Egypt was not fulfilled for upwards of three hundred years thereafter. It seemeth that Jacob wished (but Je- hovah willed not) that Joseph, and not Judah, should be the ruler, and from him should come the Shepherd, the Stone of Israel, the promised Messiah : see this 1 Chron. v.

Sabbath 7. My mind is serene and happy. I was comforted in seeing one of the travelling preachers. The physic I have been taking operateth well. O that I may not flatter or elate myself! I can only promise to be more faithful if I have more grace.

Monday 8. I wrote a long letter to John Dickens upon the man- ner of expediting his books to the distant parts, viz. the Journals, Sermons, Saints' Rests, Patterns, Hymn-Books ; and that the Maga- zine should be our grand circulating medium ; only let us have more American Lives and Letters.

Tuesday 9. The weather is temperate : my mind is much pained. Oh! to be dependant on slave-holders is in part to be a slave, and I was free born. I am brought to conclude that slavery

will exist in Virginia perhaps for ages ; there is not a sufficient
sense of religion nor of liberty to destroy it ; Methodists, Baptists,
Presbyterians, in the highest flights of rapturous piety, still maintain and defend it.   I judge in after ages it will be so that poor
men and free men will not live among slave-holders, but will go to
new lands : they only who are concerned in, and dependant on
them will stay in old Virginia.

Wednesday 10. I have some peace and some pain of heart.

Thursday 11. My mind is exceedingly agitated on my peculiar
situation : I feel each day, like a day or year to me, as it is well or
ill employed.   Ebenezer academy is under poor regulations ; and
what is more than all, some gentlemen of Brunswick county had
the confidence and want of propriety to wish to wrest it wholly
out of our hands, after we had collected so much money to
build it.

Friday 12. My mind still in pain.   I read a chapter each day,
and take down those verses that appear to me the most select, and
which I have never used before in preaching ; they may be of use
if ever I should serve the sanctuary again.   I have read Kempis
and Young.

Saturday 13. I finished three feeble letters, to Nelson Reed,
Henry Willis, and John Harper.   I cannot read or write long
together.   I wind broaches of cotton for diversion, and recreation ;
I will not be idle.   The class met at my lodging ; and I ventured
to give a small exhortation and a prayer.

Sunday 14. I am still confined ; I must try emetic tartar, kill or
cure.   There is preaching at the chapel, a mile and a half distant,
but the weather is such that I cannot go with safety.   The invete-
racy of my fever was such, that on Monday 15 I was fully resolved to take three grains of tartar emetic, which operated powerfully and brought off a proper portion of bile : in this I hope
for a cure.   I must commend the old practice after all ; no anti-
billious pill will answer as well in my case and many others.

Tuesday 16. I read a letter and wrote a letter.

Wednesday 17. I am weak in body, but some better ; I read,
wrote, and wrought in winding cotton, as I could not be idle and
wholly inactive.

Thursday 18. I went from the place where I had stayed six
weeks, and had received every mark of affection, to brother
Drumgoold's, ten miles.   I felt at home here also.

Friday 19. My fever was light last night ; but this day I am uncomfortable.

Saturday 20. Very unwell. I am strangely brought down; Lord, let me suffer with patience; thy will be done! I could not do any thing at my books; but that I might not be wholly idle, I wound cotton broaches among the children.

Sunday 21. I sat at home reading a little. Monday, I am better; my fever is greatly broken. I can only write, and meditate about an hour in a day. I must have some exercise, if it is only women's work.

Tuesday 22. We had news from the assembly, that the American ambassadors were rejected at Paris. A report prevails that the French were about to invade England with one hundred and fifty thousand men. The British can raise two hundred thousand militia, and two hundred thousand regulars; there may yet be most desperate times—worse than in Julius Cesar's day. My mind is in peace. We have *winterly* weather: more snow after much rain this day: thank God I have where to lay my head, a little reading and winding of cotton that I may not be quite idle.

Wednesday 23. Nothing of moment except a few thoughts for Ebenezer school.

Thursday 24. I employed myself in winding cotton; I cannot think long, read, or write. Rebecca Drumgoold reads for me out of Watts, Alleine, and Baxter's Works. I am much tried: the weather is so cold that I must keep in the house.

Friday 25. Was a gloomy morning to me: nothing but the thoughts of death agitated my mind. It oppresses my heart to think that I live upon others and am useless, and that I may die by inches.

Sunday 27. A solitary day to me, neither preaching, reading, writing, nor conversing.

Monday 28. I was employed in revising my journal. I am like Mr. Whitefield, who being presented with one of his extempore sermons taken in short hand, could not bear to see his own face. I doubt whether my journals yet remaining will appear until after my death; I could send them to England and get a price for them; but money is not my object.

Tuesday 29. I was employed in explaining my manuscript; but am afraid of intense application.

Wednesday 30. Still engaged in revising my journal.

Thursday 31. I rode to Owen's, seven miles, and heard brother Whatcoat on the "end of the commandment." I had been kept back so long that I was constrained to spend about forty minutes in glossing on the epistle to the angel of the church of Ephesus;

I then commented on what law Paul must have alluded to in 1 Tim. i. 9.

Monday 4. I took four grains of tartar emetic, and had a large, bitter return.

Tuesday 5. My fever was very light last night. I received a most loving letter from the Charleston conference; there is great peace and good prospects there. I hope to be able to move next week. I have well considered my journal—it is inelegant; yet it conveys much information of the state of religion and country. It is well suited to common readers; the wise need it not. I have a desire that my journals should be published, at least after my death, if not before. I make no doubt but others have *laboured:* but in England, Scotland, and Ireland, and those kingdoms which have been civilized and improved one thousand years, and which are under such improvements, no ministers could have *suffered* in those days, and in those countries, as in America, the most ancient parts of which have not been settled two hundred years. Some parts not forty, others not thirty, twenty, nor ten, and some not five years. I have frequently skimmed along the frontiers, for four and five hundred miles, from Kentucky to Green Brier, on the very edge of the wilderness; and thence along Tigers Valley, to Clarksburgh on the Ohio. These places, if not the haunts of savage men, yet abound with wild beasts. I am only known by name to many of our people, and some of our local preachers; and unless the people were all together, they could not tell what I have had to cope with. I make no doubt the Methodists are, and will be, a numerous, and wealthy people, and their preachers who follow us will not know our struggles but by comparing the present improved state of the country with what it was in our days, as exhibited in my journal and other records of that day.

Wednesday 6. Rain and snow; I am a poor prisoner. Thursday 7. We made a visit to Matthew Myreck's, and returned.

Friday 8. It is very cold weather: I was glad to keep close occupied in reviewing my journal, and writing a few letters. This is a sickly time.

Sabbath 10. I did not preach—I cannot attend these meeting-houses, they are only calculated for summer, or good health. I have hopes of being useful once more. My mind at times is under strong temptations: I cannot bear confinement. Mrs. —— hath told some persons that she is convinced, by my means, that slavery is sinful. I would say, if so, move heaven with your prayers, and

earth with your counsels and solicitations ; and never rest till slavery is expelled from the plantation.

Monday 11. I had appointed to meet the trustees of Ebenezer
academy, at brother Holb's, on the north side of the Meherrin.
After some conversation they willingly agreed to address the conference in behalf of Ebenezer academy for an annual subscription,
to make provision for a man at about one hundred pounds a year,
who shall keep an English school under our rules, with the worship
and the word of God.

Tuesday 12. I rode to brother Pelham's ; here I was at home.
I spent my time with the women and children, in winding cotton,
and hearing them read. My soul was much blessed.

Thursday 14. The weather is cool and changeable. By letters
from the north I find that the book-interest is upon a good footing,
the fund-interest well secured, and great peace reigns amongst the
preachers.

Friday 15. There fell a heavy snow from six to nine and twelve
inches deep. I had to keep house. I had but little to say but what
would call for weeping, lamentations, and wo. I was a little recre-
ated by hearing Betsy and Nancy Pelham read Doddridge's Sermons
to Young People.

Saturday 16, and Sabbath 17. Clear, but cold, and much snow.
When I get sick and dispirited, I think, was I not a bishop, and
required by duty, and necessity, and conscience, to do the best I can,
I would rather go into some line of business to get my own living,
and not lounge about. I feel for those who have had to groan out
a wretched life dependant on others—as Peddicord, Gill, Tunnell,
and others whose names I do not now recollect ; but their names
are written in the book of life, and their souls are in the glory of
God. I reflected with pain, that we had never reprinted, in America, the life, labours, travels, and sufferings of that great man of
God, David Brainard, of gracious memory ; it would be a book
well fitted for our poor, painful, and faithful missionaries—none
but God and themselves know what they suffer ; the minutes of
which for one week might fill a volume written by an ingenious
pen, and feeling heart. The last week I spent in some pain of
mind, patience and prayer. It being meeting day at my lodgings,
I gave an exhortation to the congregation, having three subjects in
view ; First, The excellency of the religion of Jesus : Secondly,
The way to come at the knowledge of the hearts of men and women
—namely, by their actions : Thirdly, To put no confidence in frames

and feelings, whilst people are living in wilful sin, or the neglect of plain, known duty.

Sabbath day 24. It is such cloudy weather I cannot go out : I wind cotton, hear the children read, and teach them a little grammar. I have, by the help of a scribe, marked the states I have travelled through for these twenty years ; but the movements are so quick (travelling night and day) it seems that the notes upon two or three hundred miles are only like a parish and a day—on paper. The understanding reader that could judge the distance, would see that I purpose to have the names of the people at whose houses I have preached, or the journal will appear utopian.

March 3. I can only make a few weak observations. What little pen-work I dare do has been in writing a letter to York. I shall only journalize a little, and never enter deeply into my other subjects. I scorn to be idle ; the past week hath been spent in the cotton work with my fingers, and in hearing the children read, and instructing them in the English grammar. I have thought, if we do wrong we rank among the vilest of the vile, as having been more favoured than any others. Many other churches go upon the paths already trodden two or three hundred years. We formed our own church, and claim the power of a reform every four years. We can make more extensive observations, because our preachers in six or seven years can go through the whole continent, and see the state of other churches in all parts of this new world. We, of the travelling ministers, who have nothing to mind but the Gospel and the church of God, may and ought to be very useful.

Monday 4, I class among my weeping days.

I have rested at the comfortable house of my dear friend, Peter Pelham, from February 9 till March 9, on which day we rode through the heat to Hubland Saunders's, and on Saturday 10, to Ebenezer meeting-house, formerly Merritt's chapel. I met a few local brethren ; the house was open, and the day warm. I was soon outdone, and sunk into dejection ; the pain returned in my breast, and a discharge of blood took place.

Sunday 11. I sat alone at brother Merritt's house. It was expected I should preach—but Ah, wo is me, to be cut off from the happy service of the sanctuary through weakness of body ! O Lord, show me wherefore thou contendest with me ! I was concerned to bring in better order among the local line of the ministry, by classing them together, and then, being thus classed, by making them take regular stations on Sabbath days. I also

appointed them a leader, to meet once in three or six months, to
discourse about their souls and families, and the congregation and
society they attend.

I am now alone with God the Lord, my only hope ! In consequence of riding twenty-five miles, a bad road, and sitting about
three hours in conference with the local brethren, in an open
house, I am quite overcome. It shows that the main spring in my
system is broken or much weakened, so that every feeble attempt
I make to do any small service to the church is very burdensome
to myself, and will always give grief and disappointment to my
friends, to my dearest and best brethren.

Sunday 18. I have visited four families in Brunswick, and three
in Dinwiddie counties. On Saturday I had a close conversation
with some of our local ministry : we had great union. I was led
to inquire of them the state of their own souls, and the standing of
the societies and congregations they attended, and advised them to
meet in a conference class once in three months, and deal faithfully with each other, and plan their work. We were happy to
find seven out of ten were not in the spirit or practice of slavery.
I have made out since Friday week to ride about sixty-five miles,
and to meet as many of the local brethren as I could call together
from Brunswick and Amelia counties. I have in general enjoyed
peace of mind, and better health of body, than heretofore. I received a letter from the African preacher and society in Philadelphia, giving me an account of the revival of the work of God in
the congregation of the Methodists in the city, amongst both white
and black.

Sunday 25. Since the last sacred day, I have visited seven families. A friend of mine was inquisitive of my trade and appren-
ticeship—as Mr. Glendenning had reported ; as he asked me so
plainly, I told him that I counted it no reproach to have been
taught to get my own living. My health is somewhat better. I
am yet unable to read or write largely ; I can pray and praise the
Lord a little. I assisted Philip Sands to draw up an agreement for
our officiary to sign against slavery : thus we may know the real
sentiments of our local preachers. It appears to me, that we can
never fully reform the people, until we reform the preachers ; and
that hitherto, except purging the travelling connexion, we have
been working at the wrong end. But if it be lawful for local
preachers to hold slaves, then it is lawful for travelling preachers
also ; and they may keep plantations and overseers upon their
quarters : but this reproach of inconsistency must be rolled away.

Some of our local preachers complain that they have not a seat in the general annual conference. We answer, if they will do the duty of a member of the yearly conference, they may have the seat and privilege of the travelling line. The travelling ministry may complain, We must go at a minute's warning to our circuits, far and near; and attend with the greatest strictness to our appointments and societies The local preachers go where and when they please; can preach any where and no where; they can keep plantations and slaves, and have them bought or given by their parents. The local preachers can receive fifty or a hundred dollars per year, for marriages; and we travellers, if we receive a few dollars for marriages, we must return them at the conference, or be called refractory or disobedient. Let us not have the grace of our Lord Jesus Christ with respect of persons in ministers, any more than in members—in local preachers, any more than travelling ones. I have done great things this week—I have rode nearly sixty miles. I heard brother Ira Ellis, on the second epistle of John, verse 8. "Look to yourselves, that ye lose not the things ye have wrought; but that ye receive a full reward." Great need there is, in this degenerate day and place, for ministers and people to look to themselves.

Monday, April 2. I visited a local preacher, and gave him a plain and patient talk upon slavery.

Tuesday 3. I attended a sermon and sacrament at brother Pelham's.

Wednesday 4. Rode fifteen miles to brother Saunders's.

Thursday 5. Attended a sermon and sacrament, and gave a short exhortation on the purity of the communion. We rode fifteen miles after meeting to brother Drumgoold's; rested Friday. Saturday we rode eight miles to brother Owens's: brother Whatcoat gave us an excellent discourse on "He shall feed his flock like a shepherd:" we had two exhortations; mine was feeble. We had a meeting with the local preachers. I returned to brother Drumgoold's the same day. I feel that a little application to thought and bodily exercise is too much for me.

Saturday 7. I was once more privileged to sit in a serious assembly, at Edward Drumgoold's chapel: I also ascended the sacred stand after brother Whatcoat had given us a very plain, valuable, and useful sermon, properly heard, upon Acts xiv. 38—41. I ventured to give a gloss upon Acts ii. 40.

Sabbath 8. The last week was memorable for a prodigious falling of rain from Monday to Saturday. I rode, with great weakness, to my dear brother Seward's, seventeen miles, and on Saturday to Salem, for conference. Sabbath we had an open time.

Monday 9. We began conference, and ended on Wednesday evening: we had three public days. The peace and union of the conference was apparently great: I was assisted to attend.

Thursday 13. Rode twenty-five miles; the roads very deep and much broken; we stopped at brother Paup's. I am but feeble still, and cannot stand labour as in past days. I have travelled since I left brother Drumgoold's sixty-five miles.

Friday 14. We came the road to Harper's bridge, over Nottaway-River, fifteen miles, to brother Robinson's, in Dinwiddie county: this being a by-way the path was smooth. I have entered upon a tour of two thousand miles before I may probably see this part of the land again. Oh! can I perform such a toil? Weakness of body maketh me feel great heaviness of mind. I must think, speak, write, and preach a little; or I may as well give up my station.

Saturday 15. We rode to Henry Reese's; we have *proper* March weather in April. .

Sabbath 16. I attempted a feeble discourse on 2 Peter iii. 11. "Seeing then that all these things shall be dissolved, what manner of persons ought ye to be in all holy conversation and godliness." We had a large congregation: our brethren, Dyer, White, and Roper, were ordained deacons. I appointed my dear aged, and faithful brother Whatcoat to visit the four districts belonging to the Virginia conference, and wrote my apology as not being able to ride on horseback as heretofore. Notwithstanding my bowels were afflicted and much affected we left brother Henry Reese's, and rode through dust and deep cut roads thirty miles to Petersburg. I endeavoured to commune with God, but I had great sinkings of heart.

Monday 17. I preached at Petersburg very feebly on 2 Peter iii. 17, 18.

Tuesday 18. There was a severe frost. We then rode to Richmond: I was very unwell. I went to the court-house and made my apology for inability.

Wednesday 19. Being so unwell and crowded with company, I found it best once more to try for Baltimore: we came only forty miles to Lyon's, in Caroline county.

Thursday 20. We had a gentle ride to Todd's tavern.

Friday 21. We crossed the new bridge at Falmouth, and came to Stafford court-house to dine, and thence to Ward's at night—thirty-five miles.

Saturday 22. We came to Colchester to dine, and to William
Adams's at night, thirty miles. The roads were nearly as bad as
in winter, and amazingly ploughed up with frost and using. The
prospects for small grain are bad. We met with a powerful storm,
but my carriage kept me dry, and my cloak defended brother
George from damage. This has been a changeable day; heat,
wind, rain, and the vast fatigue of bad roads, deep gullies, heavy
mire, roots, and hills, bore hard upon me. I heard of brother
Vatters's preaching at the Fall church, a faithful funeral sermon.

MARYLAND.—Monday 24. We reached Turner's, and made a
rapid ride to the city of Baltimore. I visited until the Sabbath.
April 29, they would publish for me at Old-Town meeting-house.
I made an attempt on Psalm cxxxii. 9. "Let thy priests be clothed
with righteousness, and let thy saints shout for joy." I went to
the Point and heard a sermon on "Speak evil of no man." I
gave a short exhortation, and came home much more comfortable
than I expected. Our beautiful house is not ready yet: I fear, I
tremble in imagination, lest it should have more temporal than spiritual glory.

Wednesday, May 2. Our conference began: it was *half-yearly*,
to bring on an equality by the change from fall to spring. We
had to correct the many offences given at many conferences to one
particular man! I pleased myself with the idea that I was out of
the quarrel: but no! I was deeper in than ever, and never was
wounded in so deep a manner; it was as much as I could bear: I
cannot stand such strokes.

Sabbath 9. We opened the new house: brothers Lee, Bruce,
and Forest preached. Monday and Tuesday I visited brother
Willis.

Wednesday 12. I attended the public fast: my subject was "So
the Lord was entreated for the land." I observed—1. That there
were special times and seasons in which it becomes our duty, in a
most special manner, to entreat the Lord for the church and the
land. 2. Who they are who ought to be assembled—every order,
the elders and people at large; sanctified—that is, set apart from
labour and common service—the bride and bridegroom, the children, the infant offspring. 3. Who shall intercede—the priests,
the ministers of the Lord: again, if my people which are called
by my name shall humble themselves. 4. The special seasons—
calamities threatened by God or man, feared or felt, such as
sword, famine, or pestilence. 5. How we should entreat the Lord—
with fasting, prayer, reading, and preaching the word of God;

confessing our sins and sorrows, and acknowledging his mercies. The calamities of the church : idolatry, division, superstition, and backsliding. 6. The happy consequences of God being entreated—, he heareth and answereth, in temporal, and spiritual, and in eternal blessings.

Sunday 16. I had to go upon my watch-tower. My subject in our temple was 1 Kings ix. 6—9. It was observed on the first head of the discourse, What the pious Israelites had professed, experienced, and practised, namely, the knowledge, worship, ordinances, and service of the true and glorious Jehovah—they and their godly children had an experience of convicting, converting, and sanctifying grace through a promised Messiah ; and had pardon of sin, and peace with God. Israelites indeed—enjoying the love of God, and walking in loving, living obedience to all the known commandments of God. Secondly, How they might partially return from following the Lord : and, again, how they might wholly depart from God. Thirdly, The dreadful consequences. In this discourse the parallel was drawn, and a close application made, to the rising generation : some sentiments were expressed upon the burning of the former house ; the probabilities of the latter house also being destroyed, unless defended by the Almighty. At the Point I spoke on the epistle to the angel of the church of Pergamos—I was thankful that my strength was so great. Our congregations were large and seriously attentive.

Saturday 22. We rode to Perry-Hall, and continued there until the twenty-sixth of the same month. I was not employed. Brothers Bruce and Harper attending me, we read over my transcribed numbers of the Journal. A situation so healthy and agreeable had a good influence upon my body and mind ; and the kindness and company of the elders of this house were charming and cheering.

Wednesday 26. We rode about twenty miles to Deer-Creek. I was pleased to find here mother Watters, aged ninety ; her son Henry, sixty ; and brother Billy Watters and his wife from Virginia. But, O, how many are dead ! And some have fled to the woods, and some gone back to the world. The society is all gone that we had formed here more than twenty years back. A most serious aspect in sight—the fly hath eaten up the grain of the fields. My vegetable diet hath its salutary influence upon my system, much more so than medicine. Could I rest this summer, there would be hope of my health ; but I must move and live upon mercy, providence, and grace. Poor Deer-Creek ! the preachers have

left the place for want of hearers ; but I had many—and an opening on Romans viii. 26.   I saw a few who had followed the Lord
more than twenty years ago ; they have halted—but I trust they
will set out anew.   I felt life, and some enlargement upon it ; it
was a comfortable day.

Monday 31.   I rested on account of rain.

Tuesday, June 1.   We came to North-East.   Wednesday, We
were at Hersay's.   Thursday, We came to Wilmington, Delaware.   Friday, I preached on Luke xxi. 34—36.   Saturday, We
rode to Philadelphia.

Pennsylvania.—Sunday.   I enlarged on Galatians ii. 20.   It
was observed, That Christ crucified was the grand subject : next,
in continuance, the being crucified with Christ.   Secondly, "I live ;
yet not I, but Christ liveth in me"—in communicated grace and
life, as ministers and Christians : *to live by faith*, as well as to be
saved by faith.   *Loved me*, is the feeling experience of gracious
souls.   I received the probable news of the near approach to, or
death of my father.   I wrote several letters ; and feel abundantly
better in my body.

Our conference began on Tuesday, and we were closely confined
until Saturday.

Sabbath 10.   I preached on Matt. xxiv. 45—47.

We had close work, but good tempers abounded, and just measures were pursued.   I made an attempt to ride to Germantown,
but returned ; and it was well I did, for I had no sooner discharged
the fragments of the conference business, and the stationing of the
preachers, than the affairs of the society came in sight respecting the city.   I have my difficulties with the government of the
preachers ; but I have some trouble with the city societies : they
wish to have the connexion drafted, and some of the most acceptable preachers to serve them.   I made all haste to leave the city,
but not until I had met the trustees of the church.

Monday 11.   Was not an agreeable morning : we had some
rain.

I had a meeting with the trustees.   It was granted we should
raise a fund, by subscription, to finish the meeting-house in Fourth-
street.

New-Jersey.—I then came on to Burlington, where preaching
being appointed for me, I ventured out at eight o'clock in the evening, that my commission might not totally expire in this place.
My subject was Psalm xxxvii. 3.   I had an opening on the text, and
some consolation in my own mind.

Tuesday 12. We came to Crosswicks: there were very few at four o'clock ; as it was thought it would be most agreeable for me to preach, I made choice of Psalm xxvii. 6, 7. my state of mind was serene. Universal nature is beautiful at this season. I feel the want of a fervent, constant, holy flame, such as has been found in the hearts of martyred saints, and favoured souls.

Wednesday 13. We came to Hutchinson's ; and on Thursday to Brunswick ; where I bore my feeble testimony, and drew up a subscription for the purchase of a house for divine worship. On Friday we came to Elizabethtown ; and on Saturday 16th to New-York : here I received the serious confirmation of the death of my father, aged eighty-four or eighty-five.

New-York.—Sunday 7. I preached in the new church on Eccles. i. 1. At the old church, in John-street, my text was 1 Pet. iv. 10. " As good stewards of the manifold grace of God." I now feel myself an orphan with respect to my father ; wounded memory recalls to mind what took place when I parted with him, nearly twenty-seven years next September—from a man that seldom, if ever, I saw weep, when I came to America, over-whelmed with tears, with grief, he cried out, " I shall never see him again !"—thus by prophecy or by Providence, he hath spoken what is fulfilled. For about thirty-nine years my father hath had the Gospel preached in his house. The particulars of his death are not yet come to hand. I employed the remaining part of this week in visiting, reading, writing, attending preaching and love-feast. Brothers Lee and Wells were officiating ministers—myself a hearer.

Sunday 24. I preached in John-street church, from Job xvii. 9. " The righteous also shall hold on his way : and he that hath clean hands shall be stronger and stronger." After tracing the origin of the land of *Uz*, as to be seen in the genealogy of *Nahor*, his son *Huz ;* taking H as a prefix in Hebrew—as an article, the uz. In the genealogy of Esau we find Job's friends as princes and pious philosophers. This is the presumption—Jobab the father of Job, or Job *ab*, i. e. father, or grief, according to the Hebrew word. It was observed, from whom these words came, and under what great afflictions—

I. The difficulties and doubts of the righteous as being against their holding on their way.

II. Their privileges and promises.

III. Clean hands, clean hearts ; by renouncing oppression of . all kinds, civil, sacred, and domestic ; every act of injustice, all

ibery, all sinful practices; these shall " add strength to strength:"
e may see this exemplified in the Old and New Testament saints.
At the Bowery church I preached on the epistle to the angel or
shop of Smyrna.   On Monday I met the married sisters in the
d church.

Tuesday 26. I heard brother Nicholls preach in the new
urch. I read a little, write a few letters, and visit daily: life
pears to be but poorly spent with me. I met the married women
the new church.

Sunday, July 1. At the old church I preached from Phil. iii.
, 19, 20. At the north church, in the afternoon, on 1 Cor. ix.
: I was much heated and rather hurried in preaching. The
eather is excessively warm—the children are dying, and proba-
y so will the parents unless God send rain. I live wholly upon
getables, and wear flannel.

Mr. O'Kelly hath now published to the world what he hath
en telling to his disciples for years. Mr. Hammett was mode-
te ; Glendenning not very severe ; but James hath turned the
tt end of his whip, and is unanswerably abusive : the Lord judge
tween us !—and he certainly will in that *day of days*.

Wednesday 4. This day we had sermons in all the churches of
e Methodists. I had a meeting with the officiary at the Bowery
urch in the afternoon, and gave them a sermon upon 1 Peter v.

Sunday I preached at Brooklyn on 1 Peter iv. 17. ; and in the
ternoon at the old church on Rev. iii. 1—5.

Monday 9. We came to Berian's, at Kingsbridge, and on Tuesday
my home at the widow Sherwood's. We have a very neatly
ilt house here ; but I was so ill that Jesse Lee and Joshua Wells
d to fill my place. Mr. Phillips, of Birmingham, writes thus of
y father—" He kept his room six weeks previous to his death ;
e first month of the time he ate nothing but a little biscuit, and
e last fortnight he took nothing but a little spirits and water—he
ed very happy." My subject at Brooklyn was, " The time is
me that judgment must begin at the house of God." In tempta-
n, persecution, discipline, heresy, and schism, the general judg-
ent will begin at the house of God. What shall the end be of
em that hear, but will not obey the Gospel of God ? They shall
e judged by the Gospel as having, in their disobedience, forfeited
very blessing, and as having brought upon themselves every curse
e Gospel threatens—they are as completely damned by this diso-
edience, as the obedient souls are everlastingly saved by the
ace of God.

Wednesday 11. We had to keep in doors on account of rain, and could not attend at the White Plains.

Thursday 12. We were at our kind brother Banks's, upon the banks of Byram-River, near the line between Connecticut and the state of New York : my congregation was large, and seriously attentive : my subject was Luke xix. 10.

Friday 13. We rode over the rocks and hills to Stamford. We had a comfortable rain that cooled the air. I find I cannot preach often—I must spare myself or destroy myself.

CONNECTICUT.—Saturday 14. We rode to Joseph Hall's, Poquonock, and made it twenty-eight or thirty miles.

Sunday 15. I attended the congregation at Wheeler's, and feebly administered the word from Acts iv. 12. I had a desire to hear brother Jocelin in the afternoon ; but he addressed me, after his reading, singing, and prayer, desiring me to preach : my subject was Phil. ii. 12, 13. I applied the text to believers, seekers, and sinners.

Monday 16. I rode sixteen miles to New-Haven.

Tuesday 17. We took our departure from New-Haven, and came through North Brandford to Durham, twenty miles. The day was gloomy, and excessively warm at times. We crossed the rocks and hills to Hadam, and rode after sunset, for nine or ten miles, a most desperate road : this put my strength, courage, and skill, to trial. with all my patience, and every spring, and every part of the frame of my carriage : but we came safe to father Wilcox's, where we had many tokens of love shown us, to make rest comfortable.

Wednesday 18. It rained.

Thursday 19. At four o'clock, brother Lee gave a warm, encouraging sermon from 1 Cor. xv. 58. At the new meeting-house, (properly West Hadam,) where the Methodists are upon free principles, I added a few words ; and then began our march to New-London. We crossed Connecticut river at Chapman's ferry : we came on without touching the ground sometimes, as the carriage would frequently jump from rock to rock. After riding about thirty-two miles, we reached New-London at eight o'clock. James O'Kelly hath told a tale of me which I think it my duty to tell better. He writes, " Francis ordered the preachers to entitle him bishop, in the directing their letters." The secret and truth of the matter was this : the preachers having had great difficulties about the appellation of the *Rev.* or *Mr.* i. e. to call a man by one of the divine appellations, supposing *Mr.* to be an abbreviation of Master, (" call no man master upon earth,") it was talked over in the yearly conference, for then we had no general conference established. So we concluded that it would be by far the best to give each man his official title ; as deacon, elder, and bishop : to this the majority agreed. James O'Kelly giveth all the good, the bad, and middling of all the order of our church to me. What can be the cause of all this ill treatment which I receive from him ? Was it because I did not, I could not settle him for life in the south district of Virginia? is this his gratitude? He was in this district for ten years, part of the time in the very best circuits in the district, and then in the district as presiding elder ; and there was no peace with James, until Doctor Coke took the matter out of my hands, after we had agreed to hold a general conference to settle the dispute : and behold when the general conference by a majority (which he called for,) went against him, he treated the general conference with as much contempt almost, as he had treated me ; only I am the grand butt of all his spleen.

Sunday 23. I made a feeble attempt at the court-house on 2 Peter iii. 17, 18. I was greatly assisted in mind and body. In the afternoon I preached on Matt. viii. 36—38.

At the foundation of the new meeting-house, the frame of which was raised on Monday, brother Lee preached. I was pleased by moving along on a good road, but through an exceedingly warm day, fifteen miles to Norwich. The loss of rest last evening made the heat of this day more burdensome to my poor body. There is a growth of religion in this circuit ; but it is ploughing among rocks and stone walls in a twofold sense. The society came together, and after myself and elder Lee had exhorted, we had a speaking and living time among the brethren and sisters.

Tuesday 25. We rode through heat and over rocks twelve miles to brother Lyon's, at Canterbury ; this made me feel like Jonah. I was much outdone, having slept but little for two nights : but I was compensated for all in finding the life of religion amongst this people. Brother Lyon is the son of a godly father, who was a Baptist minister ; he was imprisoned for truth and religious liberty ; the aged man lived until we came : his wife is yet living and loving God. The father was awakened by Mr. Whitefield's ministry : the son is a man of piety and property.

RHODE-ISLAND.—Wednesday 26. We passed Plainfield and Sterling, and came to Coventry, in the state of Rhode-Island. They have established turnpikes upon the way to Providence, and greatly reformed the road : but I had to turn out to search for my friends, and the souls of my charge : we computed it twenty-five miles to General Lippelt's—such work as I had is not easily told : we came in about eight o'clock. Thursday, at General Lippelt's, I preached on 1 John i. 7, 8. I rested on Friday and Saturday, and on Sabbath day my subject was Hebr. ii. 2. Monday rode twenty-two miles through heat to Warren : we lodged at father Martin Luther's. Here John Hills, from Lewistown, Delaware, liveth ; but he is no Methodist ; who would have thought this once ? Mr. Wilson's book was read to me by brother Lee, particularly those parts in which he finds fault with the Methodists. It appears to be the language of two or three men ; who they are I know not : but be they who they may, they are mild without merit ; and in some things are very simple, if not silly, about our drinking water. But why, Mr. *Age of Reason*, whoever you are, will you find fault with the question, " Have you always a Bible about you ?" Poor divinity, and yet poorer spite.

Tuesday 31. We came upon Rhode-Island ; stopped at Matthew Cook's, dined, and then came to our little meeting-house, and had a good season on Hebr. x. 38, 39. This island is most beautiful in its situation, and cultivation ; the neat stone square walls, level fields of grass, corn, and barley, sloping to the water, are very pleasing to the eye : salt water prospects are most delightful. Upon the summits of the island you may see from water to water. Here fruit trees, fish, and shellfish abound. The Friends' meeting-house is large, and the settlement extensive ; and if the Baptists, Moravians, Episcopalians, Friends, and Methodists have any religion, there must be some good people here. Rhode-Island is by far the most beautiful island I have seen. I have been very low, and weak, and feverish of late : I can hardly write, think, read, preach, ride, or talk to purpose. It is a little trying to be with people who are healthy, active, and talkative, when you cannot bear a cheerful part with them.

Thursday, August 2. I returned to the north-east end of the island, where we have a small meeting-house, and some gracious souls. Brother Lee preached last evening at Newport. As I was unwell, I gave my services to brother Hall's family, where I was entertained with every mark of affection : may they, their own, and adopted children, be numbered with the saints ! I came away in weakness of body but strength of soul, to the house at the ferry which we came to when we first entered upon the island.

Friday 3. We preached at Bristol ; my subject was Luke xviii. 7. It was to me a serious, comfortable time : what but the

mighty power of God and the unceasing cries of his people can
help us here?

Saturday 4. We came through Warren, Swansey, Somerset,
Dighton, and Taunton, thirty-two miles: the day was excessively
warm; and Oh! rocks, hills, and stones! I was greatly outdone:
no price can pay, there is no purchase for this day's hire but souls.
We frequently spend a dollar per day to feed ourselves and horses:
I never received, as I recollect, any personal beneficence, no not
a farthing, in New England; and perhaps never shall, unless I
should be totally out of cash.

MASSACHUSETTS.—Sunday 5. I was very unwell in my *viscera.* I
attempted to preach on Rom. x. 1—3. I am under deep dejection
of mind at times, and distressed above measure with the people—
they appear to have so little genuine religion. We hear of a
serious mortal fever prevailing in Boston: it is what I have feared
would be the visitation of this capital town as in other cities; here
also are theatres, sinners, blind priests, and backsliding, formal
people, and multitudes who are Gospel-hardened. We came to
Easton; here we have a new house built. I felt exceedingly weak
after riding ten miles; the evening was very warm; I however,
gave them a discourse on 2 Tim. ii. 19. and passed the night in
some bodily distress.

Tuesday 7. I rode twenty-two miles through heat and hunger to
Boston: here I spent one night, very unwell in body, and with
pains and pleasures of mind, upon account of the preachers and
people.

Wednesday 8. I was advised to retire a few days to Waltham.
There is affliction in Boston—the malignant fever. But who can
tell the sick that are in the second or third house from his own,
in a town or city where it is needful to observe secrecy lest people
should be frightened away from their homes, or the country people
from bringing food? How many may be buried in the night, without any tolling of bells or funeral solemnity, thrown into a coarse
coffin, or a tar sheet? Oh! a solitary house, and social family; a
comfortable table, pure air, and good water, are blessings at Waltham. There is a rumour of the blood-shedding in Ireland.—Oh!
the trade and plague of war! I pity the old world; I fear for the
new—shall we be altogether unpunished? My calculation is,
that we have rode three hundred and thirty miles since our departure from New-York.

Thursday, Friday, Saturday, and Sunday. At Waltham. I
ventured to ride four miles, and preach two sermons; the first

on Acts ii. 17, 18.; and the second from Rom. x. 1—3. I was much enlarged, and had clear views, and saw and felt for the people.

Monday 13. We began our march to Lynn, in weakness of body, and distress of mind. I gave a discourse late in the evening on Hebr. iv. 9. and that night I slept but little. On Tuesday we began our journey for the Province of Maine: we passed through Danvers, Salem, Beverly; thence to Hamilton; where we were kindly entertained by some aged people: dined and hasted along through Ipswich, and thence to Newburyport: here I passed in sight of the old prophet, dear Whitefield's tomb, under the Presbyterian meeting-house. His sermons established me in the doctrines of the Gospel more than any thing I ever heard or had read at that time; so that I was remarkably prepared to meet reproach and persecution. We crossed Merrimac-River and bridge: and came in late to Mr. Merrill's, where we were kindly entertained. Here we were let into the secret of a negociation with a congregation by Mr. Elias Hull, one of our wonder-workers—I told you so —farewell.

NEW-HAMPSHIRE.—Wednesday 15. We entered properly into New-Hampshire. We passed Hampton falls, where the people and priests were about installing a minister into the deceased Dr. Langdon's congregation. We had a dripping morning: we however set out and rode about twenty miles to Portsmouth: there is a fever somewhat malignant and mortal here. This is a well fortified town against the Methodists. Mr. Hutchinson and daughter received us with great Christian politeness: being exceedingly outdone with heat and labour, I was easily persuaded to tarry until morning. We crossed Piscataqua-River at the town of Portsmouth, in a flat-bottomed boat. I am so weak that the smallest shock shakes me. At Portsmouth there is a strong tide, and this morning we had a heavy fog, so that we could scarcely see the tops of the houses on the other side of the river. We came through Old-York, father Moodie's parish, of whom many tales are told; one of which is worth telling to posterity—it is, that the only salary he received was the prayers of his people. We came on to Wells, and were kindly entertained at Mr. Maxwell's. I was restless through the night, and sleepy and sick through the next day, yet we rode forty miles to Major Illsley's, near Portland.

DISTRICT OF MAINE.—Friday 17. We passed New Stroudwater, named probably after the old one in Gloucestershire, in *Old* England. We have rode since Monday morning about one hundred and forty miles ; the roads tolerable ; the weather extremely warm ; and we are amongst strangers.

Saturday 18. We rode five miles to Presumscut-River, and stopped at father Baker's. Sabbath day, I preached in the barn on " Now is the accepted time, and now is the day of salvation." Mother Baker was sick, but had a sure confidence in God. Here we have the frame of a good meeting-house erected upon a beautiful spot.

Monday 20. We rode to Grey, and were kindly entertained at Mr. Ramsdell's. I preached to a few in a school-house on Matt. xxiv. 12, 13.—the case with these people, if their love was ever warm.

Tuesday 21. We came through Gloucester to the widow Roe's. We sat under a shade by the road side and read ———'s acknowledgment of his fall, in an address to the conference—so candid and apparently contrite never did I hear. My subject at Roe's was Acts ii. 21. ; the people appeared careless and unfeeling. In the evening there came up a very heavy gust of rain, lightning, and thunder, and I feared for ourselves. Next morning a dead ox was found about one hundred yards from our horses in the same field, and the presumption was he was killed by lightning, as there appeared to be one particular shock directed to that place. Oh Lord, thou preservest man and beast! My soul was much engaged in prayer.

Wednesday 22. We rode through the woods to Amariscoggin River, thence to Lewistown, where our appointment for preaching had been made at two o'clock, and another at four o'clock : no one attending at two o'clock, we came on to Monmouth.

Thursday 23. I was at home at brother Fogg's : he and his wife are pious souls ; such, with an increase, may they live and die ! I had taken cold in crossing the mountain, which was rocky and uneven. I preached in the open meeting-house to a congregation of people that heard and felt the word. My subject was Eph. vi. 13—18. I was raised a small degree above my feeble self, and so were some of my hearers. We rode that evening to Hopkins's, in Winthrop, where meeting was appointed in the Congregational house : as the day was damp, and myself sick, I declined ; and brother Lee preached, and the people said it was a good time. I found father Bishop, at whose house we staid ; his son and wife exceedingly kind. We breakfasted at our brother Prescott's. This part of the District of Maine is settled with people from the south of Massachusetts, and some from New-Hampshire

Saturday 25. We had to beat through the woods between Winthrop and Redfield, which are as bad as the Alleghany mountain,
and the shades of death. We have now laid by our carriage and
saddle, to wait until Wednesday next for conference : the first of
the kind ever held in these parts, and it will probably draw the
people from far and near.

Wednesday 29. Ten of us sat in conference ; great was our union
and freedom of speech with each other.

Thursday 30. was our great day : it was computed that from one
thousand to eighteen hundred souls attended public preaching and
ordination. The unfinished temporary state of the gallery was
such, that the plank and other parts would crack and break : we
had one alarm while ordaining, owing to the people's wish to gratify
their curiosity ; but no person was killed or wounded. My subject was 2 Cor. iv. 1, 2. it was observed, " *this ministry*," by way
of eminence distinguished from the law—the ministry of the Spirit
and power, and the word and letter of the Gospel : Secondly, The
apostolical manner of using the ministry—renouncing the hidden
things of dishonesty, not walking in craftiness, nor handling the
word of God deceitfully : not seeking either worldly honour, ease,
or profit ; but by manifestation of the truth commending ourselves
to every man's conscience in the sight of God—to sinners of all
characters ; to seekers, believers, men of tender and scrupulous
consciences. Thirdly, The temptations, labours, and sufferings the
faithful ministers have to meet with in the discharge of their duties :
Fourthly, The support they shall have by the mercy and power
of God, and fruit of their labours ; Fifthly ; *We faint not*—a person
that fainteth loseth all action ; is pale and dispirited : it is a near
resemblance of death, and sometimes terminates in death. Unhappy the man who is dead and useless in the ministry !

Weary of being shut up in one house for some days, I came in
the afternoon through the *dreadful swamp* to Squire Prescott's, at
Winthrop : I found a Congregational priest there. Early in the
morning I came to Monmouth to breakfast ; dined at Lewistown,
and lodged at the widow Roe's : the next day (Saturday) I came to
Grey to dinner ; thence to Falmouth, and lodged at Major Illsley's.
I came chiefly alone ; I experienced much bodily weakness : my
trials are great ; the roads are bad, and I fear the families are little bettered by any thing I could say or do for them.

Sunday, September 1. I am surprisingly supported, and am gaining strength, notwithstanding the heat of the sun and most desperate roads and rocks ; we have come nearly sixty miles in two

days. I had it confirmed that the ox was killed by lightning, which was found dead within one hundred yards of our horses. I went to Portland, unexpectedly, upon the Sabbath-day : I preached in the widow Bynton's back room to about twenty-five persons, chiefly women, my subject was 2 Peter ii. 9. In the afternoon I preached to about double the number on Phil. iii. 8. I returned Sabbath evening, to my very kind friend's house, Major Illsley's.

Monday 2. We came off in haste, and rode thirty-five miles to Wells. We lodged with Deacon Clark ; a most complete house of entertainment.

Tuesday. We rode forty-seven miles to Salisbury, near New-buryport.

NEW-HAMPSHIRE.—I passed Hampton and Hampton-Falls ; at the latter Mr. Whitefield preached his last sermon, and probably caught the cause of his death. I came over Piscataqua bridge, a most admirable piece of architecture ; it is double, and the toll-gate and Tavern stand upon the Island : we dined at Greenland, and had great attention paid us. The fever is breaking out again in Portsmouth, and it is awful in Philadelphia ; it seemeth as if the Lord would humble or destroy that city, by stroke after stroke, until they acknowledge God. Very serious appearances of this fever are now in New-York.

Thursday 4. Came from Captain Patake's to Lynn ; where I preached on Friday from Galatians v. 6—8.

MASSACHUSETTS.—Saturday. We came off with a design to call at Boston : the heat was excessive, and the sun met me in the face, so that I was almost ready to faint in the carriage : I changed my mind, and concluded to come on to Waltham, and spend another Sabbath. I missed my way a little, but came in about seven o'clock, riding since two o'clock twenty miles.

Sunday 9. I attended the chapel in the morning ; my subject was 1 Peter ii. 9, 10. ; and in the afternoon, at five o'clock, from the 11th and 12th verses of the same chapter ; many attended.

Monday and Tuesday. We continued at Waltham.

Wednesday 12. We came on to Weston, where I preached in the new house, a well designed building, on 1 Cor. xv. 58.

Thursday 13. We rode twenty miles, the way stony and dusty, to Mr. Nicoll's, at Westborough : here five preachers came together. With hard sighs I attempted to preach, and was most remarkably assisted upon Titus ii. 11, 12.

Friday 14. We rode forty-one miles over very uneven roads ; my horse ran away with me, but did me no hurt. We lodged at

Mr. Hubbard's, at Broomfield : I was surprised to see the meeting and dwelling houses they have built in this place, and the reforms they have made in the roads, since I came up through this part of the state seven years ago.

Saturday 15. We came once more to Silas Bliss's, at Wilbraham. We have rode ninety miles in two days, and I would rather have rode two hundred in the low level lands of the south of this continent.

Sabbath day. I attended at Wilbraham ; my subject was 1 Peter ii. 1—4.

Monday 17. We came to Springfield to dine, and then rode on through excessive heat and bad roads, sixteen miles to-day.

Tuesday 18. We came up to Granville, sixteen miles : it was well that I had help over the rocks and mountains.

Wednesday, Thursday, and Friday. We sat in conference ; about fifty preachers of different descriptions present : ten were admitted on probation. We had many weighty and deliberate conversations on interesting subjects, in much plainness and mode- ration. Six of us lodged amongst deacon Loyd's kind Congrega- tional people.

CONNECTICUT.—Saturday 22. We began our flight to the White Plains, across the hills and along most dreadful roads for a carri- age : we came to Canaan, about thirty-six miles, and lodged by the falls of Housatonick river. Its source is in some ponds and springs N. and S. W. of Pittsfield, Massachusetts, and running through the heart of Connecticut, empties into Long-Island Sound at Stratford : it is the second in magnitude to that which gives a name to the state.

NEW-YORK.—Sabbath day 23. We came on, twelve in company, to Dover, in the state of New-York. I should have stopped at Sharon meeting-house had we not expected a meeting at four o'clock in Dover. We made this Sabbath day's journey twenty- five miles ; the weather was very warm, and we had nothing to eat from seven o'clock in the morning until four o'clock in the afternoon. My subject was Hebr. xii. 12, 13. 14.

Monday 24. We came through Dutchess county, near the line of the two states, and down the waters of Croton-River. We lodged at Webb's, near New-Salem. We reached the Plains in about thirty-six miles, and came in about sundown. Most awful times in Philadelphia and New-York—citizens flying before the fever as if it were the sword ! I now wait the providence of God to know which way to go.

Wednesday 26. Came to my former lodging, where I lay sick last year: it is still like a home.

Thursday 27. We attempted to cross North-River at Woolsey's ferry, but the wind blew too strong. We visited a kind family, and returned to the widow Sherwood's. We have spent a day, and rode sixteen miles, and are now where we began. Friday we rode twenty miles and crossed at Bulls-Ferry, six miles above New-York: we were about two hours and a half in getting over: after which we rode eighteen miles to Elizabethtown.

NEW-JERSEY.—Saturday 29. We rode on to Brunswick, twenty miles, dined, and then hasted to Milford, twenty-two miles: here we spent the Sabbath day. I preached in the Hutchinsonian chapel, my text was Matt. v. 8. Now we meet the tidings of doleful distress from poor Philadelphia—ninety dying in a day—surely God will plead with us! Monday I rested.

Tuesday, October 2. I stopped and dined, talked, and prayed with the Lovell family, at Crosswick's, and came that night to Hulet Hancock's, who is a kind and gracious man.

Wednesday 3. Called upon James Sterling. This morning the certainty of the death of John Dickens was made known to me: he was in person and affection another Thomas White to me for years past: I feared death would divide us soon: I cannot write his biography here. We came to Germantown: and Thursday, twenty-five miles to Daniel Meridith's; where we tarried for a night. Next day we reached Thomson's mill, upon Great Elk: within a mile of this place, while going over a desperate piece of road, my carriage turned bottom upwards; I was under, and thrown down a descent of five or six feet: I thought at first I was unhurt, but upon examination I found my ancle was skinned and a rib bone bruised. Oh, the heat, the fall, the toil, the hunger of the day!

MARYLAND.—On Saturday we rode six miles to North-East: my bruised side pained me much, my spirits were sad—dark clouds impend over Methodism here.

Sabbath day 7. I preached in the North-East church on Hebr. xii. 15, 16, 17. The substance of my sermon was—1. A caution against failing to obtain the repenting, converting, persevering, sanctifying grace of God. 2. How some bad principles, persons, and practices were like wormwood, gall, and poison to society. 3. How small the gain, and how great the loss of peace. 4. That some might apostatize beyond the possibility of being restored

and weep hopeless and unavailing tears : I enforced the caution—
looking diligently to avoid the greatest evil and danger on the one
hand, and to secure the greatest good, grace, and glory on the other.
Monday we rode to the Buck, and dined with a daughter of Sarah
Dallam's. We then came on to Perry-Hall : in consequence
of the drought this place does not appear a *universal green*, as
formerly.

Tuesday 9. We came to Baltimore : here they have little to
boast of but health and trade : the outward building of a society-
house is going on. I had John Dickens's son with me : we sketch-
ed out a few traits of his father's life. For piety, probity, profitable preaching, holy living, Christian education of his children,
secret, closet prayer, I doubt whether his superior is to be found
either in Europe or America.

Friday 12. I had an appointment in the new church at ten
o'clock. I endeavoured to suit my subject to the season, and
to the time of affliction in our towns and cities ; it was 2 Chron.
vii. 13, 14.

VIRGINIA.—Saturday 13. We rode thirty-two miles to Turner's.
Here man and beast beginning to fail, I rested on Sabbath day ; we
had a long ride to Fairfax chapel, where we came in about twelve
o'clock. In consequence of my affliction of body and mind I was
but poorly prepared to preach ; however, I attempted a gloss on 1
Peter ii. 1, 2, 3. Here I saw and conversed with my old friend
William Watters.

Monday 15. We came to Alexandria—I preached in the evening
on Col. iii. 15.

Tuesday 16. Brother Lee and John Harper accompanied me ;
we came through excessive heat and dust, thirty miles, to Ward's.

Wednesday 17. I came to the widow Conner's, who keeps a decent boarding-house : we rode this day about forty miles, having
nothing to eat but a little bread and cheese. On Thursday, twelve
miles to the widow Collin's, where we breakfasted between eleven
and twelve o'clock, and in our usual manner prayed, and addressed
the family about their souls ; and then rode on, ten miles, to brother
Lyon's. Whilst others leave us, and say much evil of us, these
people in Caroline county keep closely to us. I felt very unwell,
occasioned, I suppose, by riding so late and early through the excessive heat, dust, and dews.

Friday 19. We came through the dust, thirty-five miles, to Richmond : here I heard of the death of John Norman Jones, who departed in joy and peace in Charleston ; this is the second preacher

we have lost in about one year in that city. Likewise of Hickson
and Brush, in New-York; M'Gee and Dickens, in Philadelphia; and
Francis Spry in Baltimore. M'Gee, William Dougharty, J. Brush,
Stephen Davis, John Ragen, James King, and John Dickens, died
of the malignant fever.

Saturday 20. I rested in Richmond: I here must record my
thanks to my ancient and firm friend, Philip Rogers, for the loan of
a horse, when mine was fully worn down, and unable to stand my
long and rapid rides.

Sabbath 21. I preached in the court-house, at the east end of the
city, on 1 John i. 6, 7.; and in the afternoon on Rom. x. 13, 14,
15, 16. On Monday 22, I preached at Manchester, on Hebr. viii.
10, 11. and on Tuesday rode to Petersburg by three o'clock, and
preached on Hebr. iii. 16. I spent the evening with, and slept at
Joseph Harding's; it was a renewal of our former friendship. I
spent Wednesday at Wood Tucker's, in as sweet affection as in ancient times. I exhorted his children to come to Christ.

Thursday 25. In company with my never-failing friend (as far
as man can be so) Richard Whatcoat, I came to Roper's. My horse
was taken sick, which detained me a night. On Friday, at Henry
Reese's, my subject was Matt. vi. 16. I had the pleasure of seeing seven preachers present. On Saturday 27, we had what was
much wanted—rain.

Sunday 28. I rode sixteen miles and preached at Mayes's chapel, lodging at Peter Robinson's: here I left my carriage and sick
horse with brother Mansfield. Monday, at Trotter's. Tuesday I
met the local brethren; in speaking of our own souls, and the
work of God upon others, we were quickened.

Wednesday 31. At Paup's chapel I preached on Eph. v. 25—27.
Brothers Lee and Harper exhorted: the meeting continued until
three o'clock. It was a cold day, but a warm meeting; two or three
souls professed to find the Lord in his pardoning grace.

Thursday, November 1. It rained. On Friday we rode to Benjamin Johnson's: here we talked over ancient and present times,
and of our feelings: the work reviveth in this society, and it is as
we wish it to be, and should be: the young people are coming to
Christ, and will fill up the places of their parents, who must shortly
go to glory. In the evening we came to brother Meridith's: God
hath blessed his little son; but we found the father sick.

Saturday 3. Rode to brother Soward's, near Roanoak-River;
where we designed to keep the Sabbath. I felt the want of a
cloak or the carriage.

Sunday 4. I have peace in my soul, but feel uncomfortable in my body.

Monday 5. This was a great day: many preachers, travelling and local, were present; my subject was Eph. iv. 11, 12.; we had a melting time: brother Dromgoold and myself wept; his wife and others praised the Lord.

NORTH CAROLINA.—Tuesday 6. We crossed the Roanoak at Moseley's ferry, and stopped at M'Lane's; here God is working amongst the people. We came on Wednesday, by riding two hours in the night through the woods, to Harris's, where I preached on Thursday 8th from 2 Peter i. 4. On Friday we rode to Colonel Edmund Taylor's. Sabbath day, at Bank's church, I preached on Hebr. vi. 11, 12. and administered the supper of the Lord, and ordained John Whitefield deacon; the church was so very open that we could not be outwardly comfortable; we tried to remedy it in some measure by closing up some of the windows with blankets. I lodged at Nathan Norris's, one of my sons in Christ, now a father of children, and a very useful preacher.

Monday 13. We rode twenty miles to Charles Cannon's; and on Tuesday, twenty-five miles to Snipe's. Wednesday we forded How-River, and came through a curious path, for a carriage, to the new meeting-house on Hickory Mountain; we dined with Mr. Reeves, an ancient friend of mine, and thence proceeded on to brother M'Master's, a local preacher: we have rode this day thirty miles.

Thursday 16. We rode from the upper branches of Rocky-River, twenty miles, to Pleasant Garden: when I came to the meeting-house, I had little strength of mind or body; we lodged at Daniel Sherwood's; my aged brethren and sisters from Maryland and Deleware, rejoiced to see me, a poor, feeble man, as I was; they had seen me in better times.

Friday 17. We rode to Mr. Bell's, on Deep-River; thence thirty miles to Woods's, upon ———— River; this day was very warm, and we had exceedingly uncomfortable roads. Going at this rate is very trying; but it will make death welcome, and eternal rest desirable. Saturday and Sunday, at quarterly meeting, my subject was Acts iii. 26. We rode down twelve miles to D. West's, and were benighted, which ill suited me. As we had to travel an unknown road to Henry Ledbetter's, I wished to continue on our journey, and not stop at Hancock; but the people thought and said otherwise, so I stopped, and brother Lee preached; after which

I gave a discourse on Acts ii. 39. and came off in haste. D. West escorted me down to the ferry, where we called in vain for the flat : D. West went over, and it was with difficulty that he persuaded the ferryman to come with the boat and take me : it being dark, and the wind blowing very strong and cold, we had hard work in crossing : I told the company so in the morning, but stay I must and preach, or be accounted proud. At Henry Ledbetter's I preached on Hebr. x. 23, 24 and at John Randell's, 2 Cor. vi. 1. Brother Jackson had secured for me riding and preaching enough as far as Camden.

Thursday 24. We recrossed the Pee Dee River at C.'s ferry, and made it about eighteen miles to Mask's, where I preached on Hebr. iv. 1. On Friday, at Bethel on 2 Cor. vi. 11. Saturday and Sunday, at quarterly meeting, at Jesse's (a coloured man) meeting-house, near Webb's ferry. My subject on Saturday was Acts ii. 17, 18. and on Sabbath day 2 Tim. iv. 1, 2. We then rode seven miles to Isaac Jackson's. Monday rode.

Tuesday 29. Preached, and rode twenty-two miles to Mr. Blakeney's, on Thomson's Creek. Wednesday rode to Horton's, and preached on Gen. xxiii. 19. At Crul's meeting-house, on Thursday, on ———, and at Granney's Quarter on 2 Cor. xii. 9. and on Friday we came into Camden. Brother Lee had gone along on brother Blanton's district.

SOUTH CAROLINA.—We have rode since brother Jackson hath had the command of us nearly one hundred and fifty miles, from Montgomery, in North Carolina, to Camden, in South Carolina. If I attempt my appointments that brother Lee has gone upon, I must ride one hundred and fifty miles next week to Washington, in Georgia. I have made little or no observation on the way, I have been so unwell. The people are remarkably kind in this country. I preached in Camden on 1 Kings viii. 35, 36. Here we have a beautiful meeting-house. It was a time of very severe drought, but I hope this place will yet be visited in mercy. Monday we rode to brother James Rembart's, and on Tuesday I preached there on Hebr. vi. 18. Here we seated ourselves for writing until Saturday 10. On Sabbath day my subject was Acts iv. 20. Monday, we rode to brother Bradford's, and on Tuesday to Jack-Creek. The changes of weather and lodging affect me much. I called and preached at Robert Bowman's. On Friday we came to Monk's corner, and on Saturday to Charleston. Fasting, and riding through the heavy sands, cause me to feel unwell. I received a *cooling breeze* in a letter from the north. For the first

time I opened my mouth upon Psalm lxvi. 13, 14. We have peace
and good prospects in Charleston, very large congregations attend
the ministration of the word. Brother Harper opened his mission upon " Thy word have I hid in my heart that I might not sin
against thee." In the evening I spoke upon our Lord's lamenta-
tion over Jerusalem. On Christmas day I preached from St.
Luke ii. 14. and at the new church on Haggai ii. 7.

January 1, 1799. Our yearly conference assembled at Charleston. We kept our seats for four days ; thirty preachers present.
We had great harmony and good humour. I gave a short discourse, addressed to the conference, from Hebr. xiii. 17.

I. *Your guides*—consequently governors. These how needful
in the night, if there be ignorance in the traveller, and danger in
the way, deep pits, wild beasts, or bad men. If it be in the morning, or noon day, how natural it is to follow a guide ; how necessity
and fear, upon the part of the traveller, will make him obedient.

II. People are to be led into essential truth, duty, and experience.

III. Ministers are to watch for their souls as they that must
give an account—the general and special accountability to God,
Christ, and the Holy Spirit, to the ministry, and to the church,
and to all men ; they must give an account for the loss of the
Christian traveller, if that loss be a consequence of neglect in the
guide. The joy faithful ministers have in the prosperity, spirituality, and happiness of the church ; *their grief* or *groaning*,
when so far from gaining other souls, they lose some already partially gained ; how much the interest of souls is concerned in the
prosperity of the ministry. *Pray for us* : the great duty of the
flock. *The argument.*—We have a good conscience : that this
being the case, their prayers might be answered. Live honestly,
do our duty faithfully, and take what is allowed us as wages—
paying our just debts to souls.

I ordained three elders and seven deacons. The generosity of
the people in Charleston was great. After keeping our ministry
and their horses they gave us nearly one hundred dollars for the
benefit of those preachers who are in want.

Sabbath day 6. Very cold, sleet in the streets, and dangerous
walking. We had a solemn sacramental season ; and a goodly
number of " Ethiopians stretched out their hands to the Lord."

Saturday 12. My time has been chiefly taken up in composing
and selecting from Cave's Lives of the Fathers, showing the primitive episcopacy. We are laid up for winter, when it is like

summer. I hope to labour upon the Lord's-day in the churches, so called.

Sabbath day 20. I preached at Bethel : my subject was Mark xi. 17. ; " And he taught, saying unto them, Is it not written, My house shall be called of all nations the house of prayer? but ye have made it a den of thieves." At the old church my subject was 2 Peter i. 16. A group of sinners gathered around the door, and when I took the pulpit they went off with a shout : I felt what was coming. In the evening there was a proper uproar, like old times. I employed the last week in reading, writing, visiting, and attending feasts of charity ; one with the white society, and the other with the Africans.

Sabbath day 27. I preached in the morning at Bethel, from Hebr. xiii. 20, 21.

I. It was a prayer : as he, Paul, had asked their prayers, he gave them his.

II. " The God of peace :" the gracious relation of the Hebrews as reconciled to God.

III. " Brought again from the dead ;" when it might be thought, all was lost when Jesus was dead ; again he had brought the Hebrews from a state of death in trespasses and sins.

IV. This was more than bringing the apostle to them, although he might be given to them of God to their prayers.

V. " Great Shepherd of the sheep"—all the sheep, Jews and Gentiles. *The Shepherd of the shepherds ;* doing *really,* what they, *under shepherds,* do instrumentally : he seeketh, keepeth, feedeth, and watcheth his ordained flock against those who would steal or kill them, and alienate them from Jesus, or the true fold, and faithful pastors.

VI. " Through the blood of the everlasting covenant :" see Exodus xxiv. 3. Moses said, Behold the blood of the covenant, when he sprinkled the people ; it is this that meriteth, sealeth, and sanctifieth.

VII. " Make you perfect in every good work"—as to the quantity and quality of good works : and,

Lastly, " Pleasing to God"—in gracious affections, purity of intention, and uniformity of conduct ; and all by the merit and intercession of Jesus Christ. In the afternoon I preached in Cumberland-street meeting-house on Deut. iv. 9.

Wednesday 30. Once more, through divine assistance, we left Charleston, and came twelve miles to brother Jackson's ; where we rested one day.

Sunday, February 3. By riding until ten o'clock in the night, we came, fifty miles, to Mr. Boon's. On Saturday I rode alone to Georgetown : we have made it nearly eighty miles from Charleston to this place. I preached on Galatians v. 24—26. : First, They that are Christ's in a special spiritual sense ;—his sheep, redeemed, sought, and saved ; his children, bearing his image. Secondly, How they are to be distinguished :—they crucify the flesh with the passions and desires thereof ;—the sinful love of the world, with the sinful fear and joy also. Thirdly, Let us walk in the spirit, as an evidence that we live in the spirit. Fourthly, Let us not be " desirous of vain glory ;" in forms, ordinances, or any outward appearances of men and things. Fifthly, Let us not by such mean measures " provoke one another," or envy one another. In the afternoon, I preached on Isaiah lxvi. 5.

Monday 4. Was an uncomfortable day ; so we did not ride.

Tuesday 5. We crossed Black-River, at Gadsby's ferry : the bridge over one of the natural canals was broken ; we had presence of mind to loose the long reins of the bridle : brother Lee put the horse through the ford, and I met him on the other side, and guided him out safe. This day we made it nearly forty miles to Rogers's, near Kingston.

Wednesday 8. We rode in a cold day, thirty miles, to dear brother Hawkins's, upon Little River, crossing Wacawman at Star-Bluff.

NORTH-CAROLINA.—Thursday 9. I preached at the meeting-house, from Luke iv. 18, 19. ; and came the same evening to father William Gause's ; where I preached, on Friday 10, upon Rom. v. 1—5. we had a living season here. I paid a visit to the sea, and saw the breakers ;—awfully tremendous sight and sound !—but how curious to see the seagull take the clams out of the sand and bear them up into the air, and drop them down to break them, and then eat the flesh ! This I saw demonstrated ; and if they fail once in breaking the shell, they will take it up again, and bear it higher, and cast it down upon a hard spot of ground, until they effect their purpose

We are now in Bladen circuit, Brunswick county, North Carolina. I have travelled nearly four hundred miles in the southern states, and spent three months therein. We rested on Saturday 9, and on

Sunday 10. We attended at Shallot church ; my subject was Acts xiv. 22. I showed, First, That the souls of the disciples must

be confirmed in doctrine, experience, practice, and discipline of
the Gospel of Christ in the church of God. It was observed, how
plainly these were taught in the oracles of God. I offered some
arguments in favour of revelation, to induce a continuance in the
substance and exercise of faith through life : through much tribula-
tion entering the eternal kingdom of glory : an object so great is
not to be gained without great trials from every enemy, in doing
and suffering the whole will of God. The day was so excessively
cold, and the house so open, that I was chilled through my whole
system. After meeting we rode on to Lockwood's Folly : here
are several young converts.

Monday 11. We came by Town-Creek, where I stopt fourteen
years ago ; but what a change since then! Stephen Daniel and his
wife are no more ; but their dear children are coming to Christ, to
fill up their parent's places.

Sister Daniel was an excellent woman. It seems as though old
Brunswick in North Carolina, would be a Methodist county, and
that most of the rulers would believe in Christ.

Tuesday 12. I preached at Sullivan's, on Town-Creek, from Gal.
vi. 9. the house was crowded with people ; there were many children to baptise ; but my spirits were sunk, and I had no heart to
speak.

Wednesday 13. We came on to Wilmington ; here I was in low
spirits still. This town has suffered by two dreadful fires ; but the
people are rebuilding swiftly. I was so afflicted in body, that
brother Lee had to preach two sermons in the church : the people
were very attentive.

Thursday 14. We rode twenty miles to Nixon's ; where I preached a little to a little flock, as there was only a half-day's notice.
Through this day I have been amazingly dejected, although I am
abundantly more happy in constitution and feeling than formerly.

Friday 15. At Stone Bay : no preaching by the Methodists at this
place. We lodged at friend Johnson's : on my last visit I preached
here. We made it twenty-seven miles.

Saturday 16. We rode eighteen miles to Lot Ballard's : here we
were at home. It was an excessively cold day ; at noon it changed to hail, and terminated in rain. I housed myself: and brother
Lee went to the New-River chapel to preach to the people.

Sunday 17. Cold as the day was, and unwell as I felt myself, I
could not be absent from the house of God : my subject was Acts
iii. 19. The slaves were not permitted to come into the house.

We rode to William Bryan's, at Bryan Town, upon Cedar-Creek : and on Monday we held a meeting at Colonel Bryan's, the father of William.

Tuesday 19. We were at Trenton court-house ; and on Wednesday at Lee's chapel : my subject here was Micah vi. 6, 7, 8. I endeavoured to show, First, That it is still the voice of many, " Wherewith shall I come before the Lord, to enjoy his favour, and presence, and bow myself before the high God ?" that is, worship him acceptably, as though they would give all they have in the world, no sacrifice should be too great ; but men are often great in promise, but defective in performance ; they promise much and do little. He hath showed thee, O man ! what is good—that is, true religion ; the blessed effects and fruits of it ; do justly and walk humbly with thy God ; see Deut. x. 12. Hosea xii. 6. First, Do justly according to human laws, and the claims and rights of men with men, as it respects continents, kingdoms, or families. Second, Do justice as it concerns the laws of God—as the second table is a claim of justice to obey parents, and not to take mens' lives nor their wives—to bear a true witness. Third, Do justly, according to the commandment of Christ, Matt. vii. 12. " Love mercy," as it extends to the souls and bodies of men ; this requires more than to do justly to them : " walk humbly with thy God"—feel thy total poverty and universal dependance upon God for all things, spiritual and temporal.

We lodged at Mrs. Knight's, the mother of our dear deceased brother Ahairs, once a travelling preacher amongst us.

Thursday 21. We came to Newbern, originally settled by Germans, and called after *old Berne*, in Switzerland. For sixteen miles of this road we had heavy rain ; but I was well cased up, notwithstanding which I took cold. We have travelled from Charleston three hundred and thirty miles in this our retrograde journey, which we have made longer by frequently turning out of our way.

Saturday 23. My subjects at Newbern were 1 Peter ii. 11, 12. Hebr. vii. 25. 1 Tim. iv. 8. We had very uncomfortable weather. We made some spiritual and temporal regulations, in hopes that matters would work much better in future.

Monday 25. It was cold to purpose, and we had twenty-four miles to ride to William Cox's, on Neuse, near the mouth of Contentny : here my text was 1 John iv. 16, 17. We hence in a manner fled through the counties of Craven, Lenoir, Glasgow, and Edgecombe.

Tuesday 26. I did not attend at the Rainbow meeting-house in consequence of my illness, the effect of my riding in the cold the day before.

Wednesday 27. I was comforted in administering the sacrament; after which, as the day was damp, I left brother Lee to finish, and rode along sixteen miles to Seth Spaight's; a deeply distressed man for the loss of his dear wife, who lately departed this life.

Thursday 28. We rode thirty-four miles to brother Toole's; the rain poured down upon us on our way, and we had to feed under a pine-tree.

Friday, March 1. We made out to ride ten miles, to Mr. Hodges, near Sosson's bridge, upon Fishing-Creek; where we were kindly and comfortably entertained.

Saturday 2. We came to brother Bradford's quarterly meeting: I was glad, after riding sixteen miles through the damp and severe cold, to sit by the fire.

Sabbath-day 3. I preached a little on 2 Cor. iv. 16—18.

Monday 4. The generally excessive rains having made the Roanoke impassable at the nearest ferry, we had to ride a circuitous rout through Halifax, which made it about thirty miles to Richard Whittaker's in Northampton. We had a bad swamp to cross, but I kept out of the water. It was well for me my carriage did not upset in the water, which it was very near doing. To travel thirty miles in such a cold day without fire, and no food, except a bit of biscuit, is serious. We were received gladly by our waiting brethren, Whatcoat, Wanner, and Lambeth. I am of opinion that we have left five hundred miles on the other side of the Roanoke, in all the ground we have rode over from Charleston, in South, to Halifax, in North Carolina. I went to Rehoboth (a new meeting-house) and preached on 2 Cor. ii. 14.

Wednesday 6. The cold and frost was very severe, and it was with great difficulty we made our way through the swamp from Richard Whittaker's. We rode to St. John's chapel, where brother Lee preached upon Rom. v. 5. The house being open, I was most severely chilled, and unfit for any public service. We lodged at Williford Horton's.

Thursday 7. We rode to Winton court-house; where I preached on Hebr. iii. 7. Two-thirds of my congregation were women; perhaps there will be more men when I go there again.

Friday 8. We rode to Knotty-Pine.

Saturday 9. I preached at Knotty-Pine chapel on Gen. xxiv. 17—19.: I was elaborate upon personal and family piety. Here

I saw sister Baker; she standeth fast in the liberty wherewith Christ hath made her free, and I hope and believe God will save her children: our souls were mutually blessed.

Sabbath day 10. At Gates court-house many serious people attended: my subject was Hebr. vii. 26. I administered the sacrament; and had a solemn, feeling season.

Monday 11. We rode to Constants chapel, on one of the branches of Bennett's creek. The main creek affords a landing at Gates court-house, and communicates, after a few miles, with Chowan-River. I was made very comfortable in soul and body at Isaac Hunter's; and had a happy meeting with the poor Africans at night.

Tuesday 12. The coolness of the weather increases. We rode thirty miles to George Sutton's, in Perquimons county.

Wednesday 13. It both snowed and rained. We had a meeting at a house near Maggshead chapel; where I preached a short sermon from 1 Peter iv. 18. We lodged at J. W——'s, a comfortable house, after a very uncomfortable snowy day.

Thursday 14. At Nixonton I declined preaching and made an exhortation, after brother Lee had given them a long sermon. It is probably eight years since I came through this circuit, which caused the people to exert themselves in coming out, so that we had a very large congregation.

We have rode, since we came across Roanoak, one hundred and forty-three miles to John Russell's. We have moved rapidly through Gates, Chowan, Perquimons, and Pasquotank counties: as we pass we have lovely levels, fine white cedar on the rivers, creeks, and swamps, for between six or seven hundred miles: from the low lands in Georgia, to Black-water in Virginia; it is fine lumber land, but unhealthy in some places.

Friday 15. It began to rain heavily, but ceased about twelve o'clock; we then rode to a school-house, where many attended: my subject was 1 Peter v. 10. I had the company of several preachers. I then rode on eight miles to brother Probry's; it was good for me to be there. Saturday 16. I felt greatly depressed in spirit, owing, no doubt, in some measure, to the changeable state of the weather. We crossed the Pasquotank at Sawyer's ferry; here we were told that we had but seven miles to ride; but we wandered until we made it twelve. We learned that one of the widow Sawyer's daughters was lately committed to the dust; at the gate of the yard we found the mother in tears. As I was not able in body or mind to preach, I gave an exhortation; and after we had dined, we rode ten miles to Samuel Simmons's, across the North-River swamps, which affords as low and as good land as any part of the beech lands of Cumberland or Kentucky. We swiftly passed through Camden and Currituck counties.

Sunday 17. I made a feeble effort to preach at Williams's chapel on James i. 24, 25. our congregation was large. I returned and left brother Lee to finish. We lodged at brother Brunnell's. On Monday we had a violent storm of wind and snow, which lasted until ten o'clock, and we had a bitter ride of nineteen or twenty miles to James Wilson's, at Hickory-Ground, in Virginia. I was exceedingly chilled on the way, the snow being from six to seven inches deep, and it blew a heavy cold wind.

VIRGINIA.—Tuesday 19. I preached at brother Wilson's, from 1 Cor. xv. 58. I sent my carriage for James Morris, (formerly with us) afterward an Episcopal minister, and now near death: he expressed great consolation in God, and love to me. He hath a pious wife, who is the mother of nine children. We lodged with John Hodge, who joined the Methodists in early life. I was pleased to find that the elderly Methodists had put their children to trades to learn to work for themselves. I am in hopes the parents will not leave them their slaves, but manumit them—by *will* at least.

Wednesday 20. At Cutherall's, near the great bridge, and near Manning's, where we preached before the revolutionary war. On Thursday we rode through the rain to Norfolk, where I preached on Friday from Gal. ii. 20. "I am crucified with Christ."—Christ crucified: and Paul crucified after the likeness of Christ, and for *Jesus*—crucified to the world in afflictions, hopes, and desires; *I live*—I have had a spiritual birth, and live a spiritual life of faith, love, and holiness; yet not I, as the author of my own birth or life: "Christ liveth in me,"—by his Spirit; "and the life I now live is by faith of the Son of God;"—faith of, and faith in Christ —"who hath loved me, and given himself for me"—that is, I know and feel my personal and real interest in, and union with Him.

We had a comfortable sacramental season in Norfolk on Easter-day; and at Portsmouth, I spoke on James v. 20. Brother Lee preached on Romans ii. 14. 1 Cor. ix. 19—22. 1 Tim. iv. 16.

Monday 25. We rode eighteen miles to George Walker's, in Princess Ann county, where I, with great labour, preached on Luke xxiv. 46, 47, 48. We calculate that we have rode eight hundred and eighteen miles since we left Charleston.

Tuesday 26. We came to quarterly meeting at Dawley's meeting-house; the day was cloudy, and myself also: as there were four preachers to attend, I staid at home. On Wednesday there was a most awful storm of rain and wind, which caused us to keep within doors.

Thursday 28. I rode seven miles to Nimour's meeting-house, where I preached on Hebr. ii. 1. The day was excessively cold and the house too. After preaching I rode nineteen miles, having no refreshment for man or horse until we came to James Dawley's, within two miles of Norfolk, about seven o'clock at night. On Friday we came into town, and attended quarterly meeting on Saturday and Sunday. My subject on Saturday was Psalm cxxvii. 1. and on Sabbath day James i. 24, 25. I had a painful night after preaching on Saturday, having a small ulcer formed in my breast.

At Suffolk I was addressed by two grand daughters of my dear, aged friend, Benjamin Welden, of James-City. I dined with Mr. Whitlock, and after the rain was over rode to William Powell's, forty miles from Portsmouth.

Thursday, April 4. I must needs preach at Wells's, the *schism* house; the great were there; my subject was 2 Tim. ii. 19. We then rode to William Blunt's. On Friday we were at Moody's, and on Saturday we came to the house of the widow of Henry Davies. On Sunday I preached at Lane's chapel from 2 Tim. ii. 15. but it was the dividing of blood from my lungs. On the way I ordained two local deacons.

Monday 8. We rode thirty miles to Jones's chapel. Tuesday, Wednesday, and Thursday, conference sat in great peace and love. As the house was cold, and I was very unwell, I could not attend; I had about two pounds of blood drawn from me.

Friday 12. We rode to father Nathaniel Lee's, and on Saturday 13, to Frederick Bonner's, where I rested—a solemn Sabbath.

Monday 15. By ten o'clock we came to Petersburg; and then rode on and crossed James River, at Woodson's ferry. We lodged at Keezee's, having rode thirty-two miles.

Tuesday 16. We came to Philip Davis's, twenty miles, near Putney, New-Kent. I feel low in body, but serene in soul. The brethren in Virginia, in conference, gave it me in charge not to preach until the Baltimore conference: I was willing to obey, feeling myself utterly unable. The houses that we preach and lodge in, in this severe weather, are very open. My breast is inflamed, and I have a discharge of blood.

Wednesday 17. I rested at brother Davis's; and on

Thursday 18. Rode to Benjamin Pace's, in *King's and Queen's county:* these are gracious and kind souls—God is still working in this place ; they have one hundred members in society.

Friday 19. We rode twenty miles to our dear brother Cole's, in Essex county. We rested on Saturday.

Sunday 21. Attended a meeting at Shephard's ; and then rode to the widow Cox's.

Monday 22. We crossed the Rappahannock, at Layton's ferry, and came to the widow Bombry's, in King George county. We have rode upwards of sixty miles in two days, through excessively cold weather for the season.

Tuesday 23. We rode thirty-five miles to Ward's, near Dumfries.

Wednesday 24. This is the great day of election ; and there is no small stir in Virginia, about federal and anti-federal men. We rode thirty miles to William Adams's ; I was much chilled, and very weary.

Thursday 25. The general fast day—I attended at Fairfax chapel ; Philip Bruce gave a discourse upon those words of our Lord, " And then shall they fast in those days." As I was unable to preach, I gave an exhortation from the subject. I find that very small rest, when joined with comfortable accommodation, gives me great strength of body : by this means I might be restored ; but I must keep moving. I was caught in a heavy thunder storm, from which I took cold, and had a high fever and headach ; I rested on Friday at William Watters's. Saturday, rode to Alexandria.—Monday and Tuesday, rode to Baltimore.

MARYLAND.—Wednesday, May 1. We opened our conference, which sat four days. We had preaching morning and evening. I gave a short exhortation before the sacrament.

Monday 6. We rode out to Greenwood, Mr. Rogers's country seat, who told me that when I was past labour, there was his house as my own. We asked for new wine ; but find the old is better : the fermentation is done.

Tuesday 7. We rode to Gunpowder-Neck ; I only exhorted a little, then went on to the bay side.

Wednesday 8. The wind was high ; I declined, but brother Lee waited, and crossed in an hour. I rode round, and lodged at Josiah Dallam's : but dear Sally, his wife, is gone ! I walked to her grave.

Thursday 9. I had a disagreeable passage across the Susquehannah. At this ferry, recently, three poor blacks have been drowned. I cannot omit relating a circumstance which took place when I was here last. A very large negro man, an old ferryman, to whom I talked very faithfully, was drowned. I remember to have told him that if he did not take heed and repent, he might be drowned and damned! the former is certain; the latter is to be feared, as it is reported the negroes were intoxicated. Doctor William Dallam escaped; and what is remarkable, the boat that saved his life, was made of wood taken from his father's plantation. Thursday evening I came to Back-Creek well wearied.

Friday 10. We rode to Chester-Town—went to meeting; and I exhorted a little.

Saturday 11. At Churchill church brother Lee preached, and I exhorted. We dined at Mr. Cossey's, and rode in the evening to brother Chair's.

Whitsunday 12. At Centreville, after brother Lee had preached, I feebly exhorted upon " Grieve not the Holy Spirit of God." We administered the supper of the Lord : I was weary at the end. I lodged at Thomas Wright's.

Monday 13. At Tuckahoe a multitude attended; my services were very small.

Tuesday 14. At Easton, a crowd of people attended; here I could say but very little. We crossed Dover-Ferry, and rode to William Frazer's, in Caroline county; and on Wednesday 15, held meeting in his dwelling house.

Thursday 16. At Henry Ennell's I could only gloss upon those gracious words, " Casting all your care upon him, for he careth for you."

Friday 17. I attended Cambridge quarterly meeting; which was held in a barn: I commented a little upon, " We have not followed cunningly devised fables." Having had but little rest for two or three nights past, I retired with Bartholomew Ennell's, and went on the way to Vienna, to visit Somerset. I rejoiced that Doctor Edward White was standing firm in the grace of God; and that the Lord had blessed the souls of his children.

Saturday 19. It rained plentifully until ten o'clock. We crossed at Vienna: it was very bad ferrying; the wind being against the tide, it raised high swells in the river. I came that evening to Thomas Garrettson's; we had a very serious congregation at Quantico chapel; I had taken cold and was very unfit to speak at all. We came to Salisbury, where we rested on Monday. Brother Lee preached three times. Here I got bled.

Tuesday 21. We came to Annamessex. My horse began to sweat, swell, and tremble—and died upon the road. Brother

Levan Moore was with me : we put his horse in the sulky, and both of us rode to Samuel Smith's.

Wednesday 22. I borrowed a horse of Samuel Smith, and crossed Pocomoke, and rode to Littleton Long's, where I gave an exhortation to a few people. It was a very extraordinary legacy of a living friend that put forty-five dollars into my hands ; had I not bought a coat I might have had fifty dollars in my pocket ; it would have been a wonder for me to have as much money by me ; but one hundred or more might be needful to purchase another horse.

Thursday 23. We rode to Downing's, where I gave a short exhortation, and on Friday 24, we came to John Purnall's ; he is gone to his long home. Here I gave up my borrowed horse, and the only alternative was to put brother Hardesty's horse in the sulky, and wedge ourselves with all our baggage together. We rode by Frederick Conner's, and made it nearly thirty miles, through excessive heat, to the widow Bowen's.

DELAWARE.—Sabbath 26. I preached at the chapel, and rode home with brother Leister, living in the north end of Worcester county. This day we enter the state of Deleware. I have had great dejection of mind, and awful calculations of what may be and what may never be. I have now groaned along three hundred miles from Baltimore.

Monday 27. After preaching at Johnson's we rode to the Sound, and lodged at Arthur Williams's, an aged Methodist preacher. I passed the night in great affliction.

Tuesday 28. We came on to Dagsborough just as the stage was about to set off for Milford. I paid the fare, and sent brother Hardesty along. I called upon William Johnston, a gracious soul. We then came into Milford about eight o'clock, after riding forty-three miles. Here I rested a day.

Thursday 30. I must needs ride twenty miles back to Lewis, principally to see the people.

Friday 31. Returned back to Milford. I had taken cold. I ordained three deacons and exhorted a little.

Saturday, June 1, was a very cold day; we rode to Dover; the crowds of people were painful to me ; I ordained two deacons ; was confined in meeting four hours, and attempted to preach, but could not.

Sabbath day 2. After meeting, I rode to Duck-Creek Cross-Roads, and called at Doctor Cook's to see Thomas White's children. Doctor Anderson, Doctor Ridgely, and Doctor Neadham considered my case ; they advised a total suspension from preaching, fearing a consumption or a dropsy in the breast.

Monday 3. I ordained one person at the Cross-Roads, and another at Dickinson's meeting-house. I dined with Mr. Moore near the Appoquimamink bridge, and then rode on to Wilmington ; we have made forty miles this day. What with labour and fevers my rest is greatly interrupted.

PENNSYLVANIA.—Thursday 6. We held our conference in Philadelphia. I retired each night to *the Eagleworks, upon Schuylkill,* at Henry Foxall's solitary, social retreat. The conference was large, and the business very important. Ezekiel Cooper was confirmed in his appointment by me as our agent in the book concern.

NEW-JERSEY.—Wednesday 12. After the rising of the conference I rode to Burlington ; and on Thursday 13, to Milford : on Friday to Mr. Drake's, near Amboy ; and on Saturday to New-York.

NEW-YORK.—Sabbath-day 16. I gave a short exhortation in the John-street church; likewise in the North-River house. It is an unseasonable day for religion ; it is time the conference should come ; may Almighty God bless and own their labours to the people !

Wednesday 19. We opened our conference for New-York, and all the New-England states.

The conference was crowded with work ; consequently I had but little rest, and what added to my pain, was brother Bostick's laying sick in the next room—heat and haste !

Sunday 23. We had a charitable day at all the houses, and collected nearly three hundred dollars : but the deficiencies of the preachers were almost one thousand dollars. I attempted to preach a little on Phil. iv. 19. ; and gave an exhortation at the Bowery church. I met the society at the old church at night. The excessive heat made us wish, and haste to leave town.

Monday 24. Was exceedingly warm ; we rode to Sherwood's ; but did not get there in time to meet our appointment.

Tuesday 25. We came to the Plains.

Wednesday 26. We rode about thirty miles; and came in about ten o'clock at night to governor Van Courtlandt's, whose wife is a Shunamite indeed.

Thursday 27. We toiled through the rain over Peekskill mountains to Richard Jackson's, where we lodged, about eight miles from Poughkeepsie. In the night I was taken with a violent pain in my knee. We have travelled over rough roads, and through great heat, since we left New-York, about one hundred miles.

Feverish and full of pain as I was, I attended meeting and gave an exhortation.

Saturday 29. I rode through heat, twenty-five miles, to Rhinebeck ; the pain in my knee subsided. On Sabbath-day I preached at the school church upon " Grace be with all them that love our Lord Jesus Christ.^" Brother Lee gave a sermon on the fruits of the Spirit.

Monday, July 1. I rested. My health is somewhat better. I must confess I never felt so great a resolution to resign the general superintendancy as I do now ; and if matters do not work more to my mind, it is highly probable I shall : my prayers and council will be turned this way until next general conference.

Tuesday 2. I visited Mr. Sand's family ; and on Wednesday breakfasted with Mrs. Montgomery at her beautiful retreat. Dined at Mrs. Livingston's, on the manor ; an aged, respectable mother of many children. The house, the garden, the river view—all might afford much painting for the pen of a Hervy. Brother Garrettson and his agreeable wife attended us.

Thursday 4. We rode twenty miles to what is called Hudson-City ; a mere blank.

Friday 5. Excessively warm : we stopped at Kinderhook, and at Miller's, time enough to hide from a heavy gust ; we then came on to Albany : we have rode thirty-five miles this day. I received a healing letter from T. M. ; but matters will not easily be done away with me ; if it were one or two only that were concerned, it would be but little ; but it is hundreds, yea, thousands of travelling and local preachers and official men ; and thousands of people also.

Saturday 6. I was awaked at twelve o'clock exceedingly sick, and totally disabled for public service ; I was not able to sit up until six o'clock in the evening. I rode two miles out of the city, to Mr. Marks's.

Monday 8. Rode to Coeyman's landing ; and then to the stone chapel ; here we have the good news of souls converted at prayer meeting. Rode in the rain and damp six miles to brother Blodgett's, upon Hocketuck, in Albany county and circuit ; here also I found the labours of Anning Owens had been blest in the awakening of some young women. Our congregation was large : I gave an exhortation and a prayer in much weakness of body. We rode back the same evening a few miles to father Waldron's.

Wednesday 10. I rose at five o'clock, very unwell ; but must needs ride in the heat and dust, over hills and rocks, thirty-five miles, and came to Crawford's and Dillon's about four o'clock ;

weary as I was, I could not feel satisfied without prayer and exhortation. We have rode in three days, upwards of sixty miles,
and held a meeting each day.

Thursday 11. We rode nine miles to Cockburn's, in Ulster
county : here I gave a small exhortation to a small congregation ;
it was a day of small things ; but it may not be so always.

Friday 12. I rode fifteen miles to Hurley, and stopped at Cornelius Cole's ; no appointments had been made ; but we called
a meeting in the evening. I rested on Saturday 13 at Marble-
town.

Sabbath day 14. I was very unwell, and the day was very warm.
I made an attempt to preach on Matt. xxv. 34—46. ; a marble-
hearted congregation as well as Marble-town ; and probably will
remain so whilst the love of the world predominates : family
prayer, class meetings, and prayer meetings, are neglected. Brother Lee preached at Hurley in the evening, and I gave a closing
exhortation.

Monday 15. We rode through dust and heat, without refreshment, twenty-five miles to Degoes ; here the people of the house
seemed all *soul;* we could not leave the place until we had called
a meeting.

Tuesday 16. We rode fifteen miles to Samuel Fowler's, and
dined : we then rode on to meet my appointment at Mr. Ellison's.

Wednesday 17. Jesse Lee gave an awakening discourse from
1 Cor. xv. 58.

Thursday 18. We rode over hills and rocks, through heat, and
with hunger, twenty-eight miles, without stopping until we came to
Leizier's, near the Jersey line, Orange county. We have travelled
and toiled nearly four hundred miles through this state : weary as
I was, I must needs ride five miles farther to Nicholas Simonson's,
where I was comfortably entertained.

NEW-JERSEY.—Friday 19. We came on to Sussex court-house ;
dined, and pushed on to father Freeman's—no appointments. At
night I was taken with great distress in my bowels, which held me
two nights and a day.

Saturday 20. I rode in great pain and heat, hungry and sick,
twenty-five miles to Mr. M'Collock's : how welcome a good house,
kind friends, and a cold day ! What is the cause of my affliction ?
Is it the water, or the weather, or my bilious habit ? I am at a
loss to know.

Sabbath day 21. At Colonel M'Collock's. Having been so unwell for some days past, it was enough for me to exhort a little

after Jesse Lee had given them two sermons. I was visited in the evening by John Hannah, an aged, social Presbyterian minister.

Monday 22. I rose to ride to James Bryan's, Bucks county, Laycock township, Pennsylvania. We followed Miskineeco Creek to the mouth ; we had traced the head branches of it already ; it is a most beautiful, useful stream, running through a rich vale into Delaware River, at Hunt's ferry. The weather is warm, and the roads uneven ; we had a journey of about thirty miles. We have travelled about sixty-five miles through Jersey, and about five hundred in a month.

PENNSYLVANIA.—Wednesday 24. We rose at three o'clock in the morning, and began our journey at five, over ridges and rocks, twenty-eight miles to Pottsgrove. We did not eat until we came to Coventry.—Thirty-six miles is the amount of this day's journey. O heat, drought, and dust!

Thursday 25. We had a most dreadful time over the mountains to the forest chapel ; here we found the people much engaged in religion ; this was a balm for every sore. We dined at Kerbury's and lodged at Abraham Lewis's.

Friday 26. We rode twenty miles to New-Holland, and had a sample of bad roads for a sulky. Here some souls have been brought to Christ. I was exceedingly spent for want of sleep and rest. After five o'clock we rode with elder Ware towards Strasburg ; night came on and left me two miles from the place in the woods—in darkling shades, a new cut road, and stumpy path. We came in about nine o'clock, having rode twelve miles. Thank the Lord for whole bones !

Sabbath day 28. There was preaching in Thomas Ware's orchard, in Strasburg ; we had the respectables of the town, and a large assembly. This place contains, I judge, between sixty and seventy dwelling houses.

Monday 29. I visited Jacob Boehm's ; God hath begun to bless the children of this family. The parents have followed us nearly the space of twenty years.

Tuesday 30. We had a serious earthquake at five o'clock ; the earth is growing old ; it groans and trembles ; which is the necessary consequence of " palsied eld." I visited John Miller's : thence we rode six miles to Martin Boehm's.

Wednesday 31. We had a comfortable meeting at Boehm's church. Here lieth the dust of William Jessop and Michael R. Wilson. I feebly attempted a discourse upon Hebr. vi. 12. In the evening we rode to Abraham Cagy's, near the mouth of Pagan Creek.

Thursday, August 1. After a suspension of rain in some parts, for two, four, six, and eight weeks, we had a gracious, moderate rain : on Friday the rain continued quickening, and thus saving the latter fruits of the earth. I rode to Mrs. Elizabeth Wright's. We crossed Canastoga at the mouth of Little Canastoga ; we had a very uneven path. Mrs. Wright's family are blessed—all the children profess religion—a father and daughter have died in the Lord. Our friends followed us from Paqua. Martin Boehm is all upon wings and springs since the Lord hath blessed his grandchildren ; his son Henry is greatly led out in public exercises.

Saturday 3. We rode to Columbia, formerly called Wright Ferry. The excessive warmth of the sun in crossing the water made me sick. We stopped at Drinnon's ; here we met Seely Bunn ; he had very late notice of our coming on Sabbath day. Seely Bunn preached in Little York, and Jesse Lee in the evening. I gave a short exhortation. Twenty miles made our Saturday's ride.

Monday 5. We set off for Maryland : I rode thirteen miles, and had my horse fed and shod. We continued on and dined at Littlestown, twenty-five miles, well spent with heat, hunger, and thirst. We then rode on ten miles to Tauny-Town : the inhabitants here, and hereabouts, are chiefly Germans and Romans. We crossed the Maryland line, and lodged at Bentley's. Next morning we rode on to Jeremiah Browning's, seventeen miles, before we breakfasted.

MARYLAND.—It may suffice to say my mind hath been kept in great peace ; but I have been greatly afflicted and dejected with pain and labour. We have visited six districts since the sitting of the Baltimore conference ; and in four out of six there is a happy revival of religion ; on the eastern shore—in Jersey—Albany— and Pennsylvania : and we hear a rumour of a revival in the northern district of Virginia.

We attempted a meeting at Lewis Broning's, at his mill near Woodsbury. In the evening we rode to Liberty, and lodged at Daniel Dorsey's. Oh, heat! heat! We have rode twelve miles this day.

Thursday 8. We held a meeting in the woods near Liberty ; the houses were not large enough for our congregation. I visited Eli Dorsey, and saw the children of my dear nurse, Sarah Dorsey, and the place where her dust is deposited until the resurrection ; Oh, once lovely features of body and mind! but above all her triumphant death !

Friday 9. I came eight miles to Edward Owings's, where I received every mark of affection I could desire.

Saturday 10. We rode to Stephen Shermardine's : it was well we had a short ride of four miles. the weather being so excessively warm : here we were treated kindly.

Sabbath day 11. We had a meeting at Fredericktown. I exhorted a little at every one of the above places.

We rode over the Catoctin Mountain to Samuel Philips's, to see his dear wife, who was very low ; the people came together, and John Potts gave them a sermon ; it was but little I could give them.

Monday 12. We rode to Joseph Howard's, upon Carroll's manor, where we had a 'comfortable meeting.

VIRGINIA.—Tuesday 13. We crossed the Potomac at Noland's ferry : the river was so low that those on horseback forded it ; I came over with the carriage in the flat. I think of nothing less than the resignation of my office of superintendent at the general conference.

Wednesday 14. We had a full meeting at Leesburgh : many of the brethren and sisters from societies in the country attended ; it was the time of court. A company of soldiers collecting attended in good order.

Thursday 15. We rode twenty-eight miles to Charlestown. We had a very rocky, uneven rode. We stopped at Key's ferry, and were kindly entertained. Friday at eleven o'clock we held a meeting in Charlestown, and then rode on eighteen miles to Millborough.

Saturday 17. We had a comfortable rain ; after which we rode on four miles to Winchester. Sabbath day we held meeting, and were about five hours in love-feast, preaching, sacrament, and exhortation. I rode home with John B. Tilden, seven miles from town.

Monday 19. We rode to Stephensburgh : here we held meeting. Tuesday 20, and Wednesday 21, it rained—we could not be more welcome at any place, or more richly accommodated than we were at Elijah Phelps's.

Thursday 22. We rode fifteen miles to Lewistown, where we dined, and then rode on to Pinnell's. Oh, the rocks, ridges, and gutters we had to cross at Chesters-Gap ! I would prefer riding two hundred miles upon the lowlands than seventy to Henry Frye's, in Madison.

Friday 23. We rode twenty miles and dined. We passed Culpepper court-house, and came within four miles of Henry Frye's, and stopped at a tavern, after riding in great heat and haste. I was sick: from hard labour, want of rest, and want of coffee, my stomach and bowels were greatly agitated: I need much faith and good water.

Saturday 24. We landed at the mansion, upon the banks of Robertson. Henry Frye may console himself with the last words of David, 2 Sam. xxiii. 1—7. I obtained an extract from Whitby on the Episcopacy of the Early Ages of the Christian Church.

Sunday 25. We preached at the Springs to about one hundred attentive people. I took a bad cold, and was very unwell.

Monday 26. We rode between thirty and forty miles to John Lasley's.

Tuesday 27. We had a crowded audience at the chapel: likewise at M'Gee's on Wednesday; on which day I rode twenty miles, and lodged at Richard Ferguson's. Thursday, at a new house in the woods, I preached on Psalms lxxxiv. 8.: and on Friday 30 I rode eighteen miles to Hezekiah Arnold's.

Saturday 31, and Sunday, September 1. I attended quarterly meeting at Devenport's meeting-house; and we had large congregations each day;—there was a shouting among the people. I attempted to preach upon Hosea xiv. 4. After meeting I was invited to spend a night at Colonel Fountain's.

Monday 2. At Beaver Creek meeting-house we had a lively time. I have travelled, since I came into Virginia, through Louden, Berkley, Frederick, Shanandoah, Culpepper, Madison, Orange, Louisa, and Hanover counties.

Wednesday 4. We came to Richmond; since Friday week we have travelled two hundred miles; to which we may add the labour of our meetings; in common three hours long, and sometimes longer.

James O'Kelly hath sent out another pamphlet, and propounded terms of union himself; for the Presbyterians, Baptists, and Methodists. The Presbyterians must give up their confession of faith. The Baptists, if they open a more charitable door, adult dipping. The Methodists must give up the episcopacy, and form of discipline.; renounce the articles of their religion, and the doctrine of the Trinity. I ask in turn, what will James give up? His Unitarian errors? Did he think the Protestant Episcopalians beneath his notice? I am now more fully satisfied than ever that his book is not worthy of an answer.

Sunday 8. I left my retreat at John Ellis's ;—a most agreeable, social, solitary situation, within two miles of Richmond. I would have preached within the walls of our new house at Richmond, but the excessive rain we have had of late prevented ; I was closed up in an upper room. My subject at Manchester, was 2 Tim. ii. 19.

Monday 9. We rode twelve miles to Falling-Creek church, where I spoke from Rom. v. 12. There is some small stir about religion here.

Tuesday 10. We rode twelve miles to Godfrey's, an aged man that stood alone when Mr. O·Kelly made a rent in the society. God hath blessed our labours here ; several souls, with his own children, are now brought to God. My subject here was 1 John i. 6, 7.

Wednesday 11. At Maxey's, my foundation was Matt. vi. 6. I observed, First, What things we are directed to pray for: Secondly, The rules to be attended to in prayer—the precept and example of Christ and the saints : Thirdly, The promise ; " Your Father that seeth in secret, shall reward you openly."

I put a blister upon my breast. Brother Whatcoat preached at Charity chapel ; where we administered the sacrament. We went home with John Hobson, and were treated with every mark of kindness we could desire. On Friday I preached at Smith's church ; dined at Robert Smith's, and then rode on in a very warm and dry day, twenty-six miles, to Daniel Guerrant's, and came in a little after eight o'clock in the evening. I have stretched along through Chesterfield, Powhatan, Cumberland, Buckingham, into Prince Edward county ; and this whilst enduring a raw and running blister upon my breast, excessive heat, and with very little rest by night or by day : I would not live always : weary world ! when will it end ?

Saturday 14. At Lackland's meeting-house I preached on 2 Peter ii. 17, 18. And on Sabbath-day on Psalm cii. 11—14. I felt some special assistance. I lodged at mother Lackland's.—The weather was very close and warm. On Monday we had a curious ride about the hills of Appomatox river, to Robert Martin's, eight miles.

Tuesday 17. We rode twenty miles to Mount Pleasant. I put a blister in the morning to my breast ;—but I must go to meeting and preach. Why ? because the Presbyterian minister and some of his flock came to hear me : my subject was Zech. xii. 10.

Thursday 19. We rode twelve miles to William Spencer's; and had a comfortable meeting in his school-house; he keeps a Christian school.

Friday 20. We came fifteen miles to John Spencer's, near Charlotte court-house. We have felt great spiritual affection and fellowship in our meetings this week. Richard Whatcoat attended us through the district, with a very sore leg; and myself had a sore breast inside and out.

Saturday 21. I rested at my hospitable home, that hath been so these twenty years, in Colonel Bedford's day, and now in John Spencer's; these people have not turned me out of doors, by separation, defamation, or reproach; they have made no such return for my love and labours, although some have done it. I could not be quite idle : I read over one number of my journal, and wrote a few letters.

Sabbath day 22. I had thoughts of staying at home, as there were no less than eight preachers at the quarterly meeting at Taply's; however I concluded to go. I gave an exhortation, and returned the same evening : our meeting was held in a dead place; yet we had a lively time.

Monday 23. I crossed Stanton River, and rode into Halifax county; we made it thirty miles to Hawkins Landrum's. Tuesday we had a large congregation and an affecting time upon the banks of Banister River : here I saw only two persons that I was acquainted with twenty years ago—they were brother Baker and his wife. I lodged at Robert Chapel's.

Wednesday 25. We rode to Armistead Shelton's, in Pittsylvania, twenty miles : we stopped to dine, pray, and feed our horses, at Clement M'Daniel's; the roads were much broken in some places, and it was as much as we could perform to reach Shelton's by sunset. My mind is calm—my body in better health.

Thursday 26. A congregation of from three to five hundred attended Divine worship : religion declines in this society; we advised close class-meetings, weekday prayer meetings, with fasting or abstinence. On Friday we rode twelve miles to Carter's, where a large company attended; my subject was, " What shall the end be of them that obey not the Gospel of God? "

Saturday 28. We had to travel a most uneven path up Sandy-River to George Adam's, twenty miles. Sunday 29. I attended at Watson's meeting-house, and preached from Zephaniah iii. 12, 13. I was much assisted, and much wearied by the time I had baptised several children. I visited our brethren, Trahan and Church, from Maryland, who have been Methodists for twenty-five years, and still not weary in well-doing.

NORTH CAROLINA.—We crossed Dan-River at Perkin's ferry, entering North Carolina, and came to John Harris's in Rockingham county,—pious souls from Dorset in Maryland.

By resting at times in this solitary, country life, I have my health better; whilst I am, in some degree, free from the knowledge and care of the church at large. On Tuesday, at Smith's meeting-house, I gave a short discourse on Hebr. iii. 12, 13. We dined at Martin's, and then came on to father Low's : we have rode but eight miles this day.

At Low's meeting-house a large congregation attended ; I spoke upon Isai. xl. 1. The heat was very painful. I suppose we congregate from three to six thousand souls weekly ; thus, if no more, I can say that my travelling hath brought thousands to hear the Gospel, who, probably, would not otherwise have heard it.

Thursday, October 3. We rode twelve miles to Covey's in Guilford county ; I thought it best to decline preaching for a few days.

Friday 4. We rode twelve miles to Mrs. Campbell's, upon the south fork of Haw River. We had to work our way through the woods. Saturday and Sunday, I attended quarterly meeting at Bethel, upon Belew's Creek, where I ordained five deacons, and preached from 1 Tim. vi. 11, 12. : we had a gracious time. We have rode only twenty miles in two days. I lodged at M'Daniel's.

Monday 7. We rode through Stokes county, and attended meeting at Love's church, which has glass windows, and a yard fenced in. After Jesse Lee, I added a few words on Hebr. ii. 1. We then came up to William Jean's, near the Moravian Old-town. We have rode nearly twenty miles this day. Sitting in meeting so many hours among such a multitude of people, and frequently with a blister on my breast, with the difficulties of driving along broken paths, cause me to be variously tried and comforted.

Tuesday 8. We held meeting and had a multitude of Germans present. I improved a little upon 2 Cor. v. 13, 14.

Wednesday 9. We rode through Salem ; here they have lately built a very grand church. The day was cloudy ; the rain began to fall upon us about a mile from Captain Markland's, on Muddy Creek, where we came after riding seventeen miles.

Thursday 10. Close housed ; about twelve souls attended, notwithstanding it rained powerfully, to whom I lectured on Hebr. xii. 1—4. I had an interview with Samuel Kenmish, the Moravian

minister, and visited him. Friday 11. At M'Knight's ;—a very uncomfortable day : thence we rode on to Hardy Jones's, fifteen miles.

Saturday 12. I said but little at the Academical school-house,
now a house for God. I went to see Charles Clayton and wife,
who were sick.

Sabbath day 13. Rode thirteen miles to Whitaker's church,
where I gave a short sermon on " Casting all your care upon
Him, for he careth for you." I was both sick and tired.

Monday 14. We came to Shadrach Dial's, from Delaware, near
Choptank, who in his younger days attended my ministry to advantage. I feel, in general, great weakness of body, but great confidence in God, and constant and near access by prayer. We are
now upon Cedar and Dutchman's Creeks, in Rowan county.

Tuesday 15. It rained and we rested. On Wednesday we came,
twelve miles, to Beal's chapel, where, after Jesse Lee had discoursed upon the word of the Lord as *a fire* and *a hammer*, I added a
few words on " Take heed how ye hear," who ye hear, what
doctrine ye hear—hear in faith, with prayer, with application,
upon all the truths of God. We dined, and then hasted on eight
miles to Prather's, in Iredell county. Directly after crossing
Hunting Creek, a little circumstance took place, which, if it had
happened in the creek, might have been attended with some disagreeable consequences ; it was caused by one of the hooks of the
swingle tree giving way.

At Basil Prather's chapel, I gave my thoughts upon " Ever learning, and never able to come to the knowledge of the truth :" I fear
this will be the case with many souls.

Thursday 17. We came up the ridges, between Rocky and
Hunting Creeks, eight miles, to John Templeton's ; over a path
no sulky ever went before ; my testimony was founded upon
James iv. 2, 3.

Friday 18. We had a very uneasy ride of fifteen miles, on the
borders of Surry county, over to Doctor Brown's, in Wilkes
county. I feel my mind in great peace and resignation, both as it
respects the church of God, and my own soul. The Presbyterians
here are much more friendly with the Methodists now than formerly : I dare not say it is policy ; it may be piety.

Saturday 19. We rode through a damp, and in the end, a rainy
day, twenty miles to George Gordon's, near Wilkes court-house :
we crossed and recrossed the Yadkin River.

Sunday 20. This is my American birth-day ; I have now passed
twenty-eight years upon this continent. Do I wish to live them

over again? by no means; I doubt if I could mend it in my weakness and old age; I could not come up to what I have done: I should be dispirited at what would be presented before me.

Monday 21. We came eight miles to William Trible's; we had an open time at a barren place, and I felt divine aid in a short improvement on Gal. ii. 19, 20.

Tuesday 22. We had a serious, laborious ride of thirty miles, to William White's, Esquire, upon Johns River, Burke county. In this route we had to cross the Yadkin ten times; Elk and Buffalo, each twice: twenty miles of the path were good; ten miles uneven, with short hills, stumps, sideling banks, and deep ruts: I have renewed my acquaintance with these rivers; they afford valuable levels, with rising hills and high mountains on each side: the prospect is elegantly variegated; here are grand heights; and there Indian corn adorns the vales: the water flows admirably clear, murmuring through the rocks, and in the rich lands, gently gliding deep and silent between its verdant banks:—and to all this may be added pure air.

Wednesday 23, and Thursday 24. Our quarterly meeting was held at William White's, Esquire, and grand patriarch of this settlement, whose family of children, grandchildren, &c. are numerous and extensively established here. Jesse Lee sermonized each day. My discourse the first day was 1 Tim. iv. 12—16. *Let no man despise thy youth.* I. That Timothy should be exemplary to believers, in his words, which formed his conversation;—at all times, and upon all subjects:—he that offendeth not with his tongue, is a perfect man;—*in charity,* love, and beneficence: *in spirit,* the spirit of his mind and temper; purity of heart and intention: *in faith;* justifying, persevering faith; confidence in the sure promises and prophecies of God's word: *attendance to reading;* the word of God in the church, in families, in the closet: *exhortation;* as a gift of God, in which some excel: *doctrine;* the grand doctrines of the Gospel—man's original rectitude—his fall—the atonement—repentance—justification—sanctification—the resurrection—the last judgment, and final rewards and punishments. *The gift that is in thee by prophecy;* it is probable, some person seeing the piety and simplicity of Timothy, had been moved by the Holy Ghost to prophesy that he would be a faithful minister of Christ;—the laying on of the hands of the presbytery The eldership—here the apostle mentioneth the eldership; and in the first chapter of the second epistle, sixth verse, the laying on or putting on of his own hands upon Timothy. That Timothy and Titus were apostles, and exercised episcopal powers, is plain : they were in-structed concerning bishops, elders, and deacons, what characters they should be. Titus was left in Crete, and directed to ordain elders in every *city*. *Meditate upon these things :* ministers should be men of much meditation and prayer ; men of contemplative minds, and ready to give up their mental and bodily powers wholly to the work of the Lord : *That thy profiting may appear to all men ;* in all things belonging to thy ministerial and Christian calling. The second day of the quarterly meeting I exhorted.

Friday 25. We had to cross and recross the Johns River, and man it over the hills. I came to Connelly's, twenty-five miles, and dined about five o'clock. I saw a natural curiosity in the moun-tains ;—an old trunk of a poplar had fallen, and four limbs of it had taken root at proper distances from each other, and had grown to be large trees—from fifty to sixty feet high, and eighteen inches in diameter.

Saturday 26. I stayed at the house, to read, write, and plan a little. I tremble and faint under my burden ;—having to ride about six thousand miles annually ; to preach from three to five hundred sermons a year ; to write and read so many letters, and read many more :—all this and more, besides the stationing of three hundred preachers ; reading many hundred pages ; and spending many hours in conversation by day and by night, with preachers and people of various characters, among whom are many distressing cases.

Sunday 27. The morning was damp and cloudy, yet I must needs go to the quarterly meeting, which was held in a very open house : my improvement was the first epistle of John iii. 18—22. The meeting lasted five hours.

Monday 28. We rode about forty miles, and fed upon the path. We came to Daniel Asbury's, in Lincoln county. I crossed once more at the *Horse Ford,* where I was formerly in danger of being drowned : at that time the river was high, myself weak, the horse I rode, low, and young ; and we went in at an improper place upon the rocks, and amongst the falls of the river.

Daniel Asbury, an experienced guide, conducted me across this time ; but not without some difficulty : his horse stumbled and wet his feet ; and my head began to swim before we got through ; and my carriage to pitch over the large stones, and small rocks :—I think I bid a final adieu to this ford : if I must try this route again, I am inclined to go by Morgan-Town, the capital of Burke county.

The winter approacheth—we must hasten south.

Tuesday 29. In the morning I rested : in the evening I walked out and preached, that the people might both see and hear me ; my subject was 1 Thess. ii. 11, 12.

Wednesday 30. We rode to Williams's chapel; where Jesse Lee preached. I added a few words. We then hasted to the widow Featherston's, on Dutchman's Creek. We have rode thirty miles this day over very uneven roads. We soon called a meeting after our arrival.

Thursday 31. We crossed the south branch of Catabaw, and soon after passed the line between North and South Carolinas, into York county. In consequence of our wandering out of our way in the Hickory barrens, we made it thirty miles to Alexander Hill's; where we held a meeting. God hath blessed the son and daughter of our host, which is better to him than thousands of gold.

SOUTH CAROLINA.—Friday, November 1. We had a strange route of twenty miles to Josiah Smith's, on Broad-River, Union county. Here we held a meeting.

Saturday 2. We came to Woads-Ferry upon Broad, at the mouth of Pacolet River, near a small town called Pinkneyville : thence to Spray's, over Tyger and Hendricks bridge, on the Enoree : we were benighted among the woods. The wagons and waters had made such deep ruts and gullies, that I almost despaired of getting onward, until I thought of the expedient of leaving the carriage, and mounting the horse's back, by which means I was better able to guide him : we came into Colonel Benjamin Herndon's, about seven o'clock, where we met brothers Blanton, Black, Norman, and Smith.

On Sabbath day I commented upon Romans ii. 16. According to my enumeration I have travelled one hundred and sixty miles in four days.

Monday 4. I rested.

Tuesday 5. I rode eight miles to Odell's chapel, Laurens county : it was a damp day, and we had an open house. I lodged at Henry Davies's, a native of Annarundell county, Maryland.

Wednesday 6. We came to Zoar chapel ; a new, unfinished building; the morning was rainy, yet two or three dozen people attended : we lodged at William Holland's.

Thursday 7. We rode sixteen miles in haste to attend the funeral of Nehemiah Franks, an aged man, who, we hope, died in the Lord ; Jesse Lee preached the funeral sermon ; after which I made an improvement upon Joseph's prophecy Gen. xl. 24. " And Joseph said unto his brethren, I die ; and God will surely visit you." I made some observations on his typical and gracious character ; his early piety, his persecution from his brethren, his scenes of adversity, imprisonment, exposure to death, and slavery ; his piety in prosperity and worldly honour ; an example for us ; how God visited the Israelites, and how he hath visited the people of America.

Saturday and Sunday. Quarterly meeting at Bramlet's ; I made a discourse upon Titus ii. 3.; we had a good season. I only gave an exhortation on the Sabbath. We are now at the widow Bramblet's, ten miles from the widow Frank's.

Benjamin Blanton came up with us sick ; his famous horse died of the staggers ; he reported two hundred and sixty dollars ; and he had received from the connexion in four years two hundred and fifty dollars. If we do not benefit the people we have but little of their money : such is the ecclesiastical revenue of all our order.

Monday 11. We rode sick, weary, and hungry, through a most barren country. Jesse Lee stopped to preach at Colonel Wolfe's ; I rode on to the Tumbling Shoals Ford, upon Reedy-River ; thence on to William Powels's, upon the banks of Fair Seleuda ; I came in as usual, sick indeed, after riding thirty miles ; jolting over the roots, stumps, holes, and gullies.

Tuesday 12. Rode five miles to King's chapel ; there were six travelling preachers present : the house was very open, and the two sermons and love-feast held three hours ; I was chilled exceedingly ; my subject was Ephesians v. 1—3.

Wednesday 13. We rode westward sixteen miles, to Warwick Bristoe's, where we held meeting, and then rode to Berry's ford ; thence to Thomas Terry's, a Yorkshire Methodist, whom I married seven years ago to Ann W. Dowell, his present good wife, from a Methodist stock on the mother's side in Ireland.

Thursday 14. We rode ten miles to the Golden Grove, at Cox's meeting house ; my subject was 1 John ii. 20. It is agreed that this is the best society we have in South Carolina : the land here is rich. We lodged at deacon Tarrant's. On Friday we crossed Seleuda at Wilson's ferry, and rode fifteen miles to Thomas Willingham's, upon the Indian lands

Saturday 15. We rode ten miles to Nash's meeting-house, in Pendleton county ; where I glossed upon Colossians i. 27, 28. I was much affected with the faces and manners of this people. Mr. James Nash is not, nor any of his family, in fellowship with us, but are our most kind friends : we were used in the very best manner, and this was more abundantly acceptable : *friends in need are friends indeed.* We had to preach in an open house ; it was a summer's day ; we had a love feast and sacrament : my subject was 2 Peter ii. 9.—the congregation was very large.

GEORGIA.—Monday 17. We rode twenty-six miles into the state of Georgia, crossed Rocky-River, properly so called, likewise the Savannah at the Cherokee-Ford : it was wide, deep, and there were large rocks in it, and I had no guide ; however, we came safe to William Tait's in Elbert county. Little did I think I should ever visit Georgia again, much less the frontiers of it. It was a rainy day ; but I was kept dry in the *felicity;* not so with brothers Lee and Blanton.

Tuesday 18. We attended at Tait's chapel, in the Forks : it was a cold day. I gave a short exhortation on Rev. xxi. 7. I passed a night with Charles Tait, formerly of Cokesbury, and was made exceedingly welcome and comfortable.

Wednesday 19. Rode twenty miles to Coldwater, in a cold day, and held meeting in a cold meeting-house, but we had a warm-hearted people. I gave a brief sermon upon Ephes. v. 8. "Walk as children of light." We lodged at, and were comfortably entertained by Ralph Banks.

Thursday 20. We rode sixteen miles, sometimes through the naked woods, to Redwine's ; where we had an unexpected congregation in the solitary woods. I held forth on "The Son of Man is come to seek and to save that which was lost." The house was open, but the people were simple-hearted, and very kind.

Friday 21. We came, sixteen miles, to Carrol's meeting-house ; a new log cabin in the woods. Some of the people of the congregation are from the east and west parts of Maryland. I felt that the Lord was with them. We have the kitchen, house, and chamber all in one, and no closet but the woods.

Saturday 22. At Park's new cabin chapel, after riding eighteen miles, I exhorted. We lodged at Stephen West Brook's.

Sabbath day. Still at Park's chapel : I preached upon 2 Cor. vi. 1. I doubt if there were ever twice as many crowded in so small a house—some stood upon the benches, and others upon the floor : public and private meeting held five hours. We afterward had to ride ten or twelve miles to lodge at George Christian's. We travelled through Elbert, but mostly in Franklin county We have crossed about thirteen branches of Broad-River. Three of them which rise near the head branches of Oconee, are large.

The land is not very fertile, except what lieth upon the water-courses.

Monday 24. We were detained by rain in the morning, but set off at nine o'clock, and came in half past one, after riding twelve miles to Charles Wakefield's, in Oglethorpe county : so called after the first governor of the state or province. Benjamin Blanton could go no farther, but went to bed with a high fever. I desired Jesse Lee to attend the appointments over the Oconee. We had the appearance of the beginning of winter, and were in a cold cabin, but with kind people.

Tuesday 25. We came six miles to Cornelius M'Carty's. Here we had to drop anchor again : brother Blanton could go no further this day ; and as there were three of us in company, and one who was well able to do the work, I felt it my duty to do as I would be done by, and have been done by, i. e. *to stay and take care of the sick man.*

Wednesday 26. After brother Blanton had been very ill, and in bed most of his time, I housed him in my carriage, and we proceeded down the Oconee, twelve miles, to Burrel Pope's, after a heavy siege through the woods, from one plantation to another, on brother Blanton's stiff-jointed horse, that I would only ride to save souls, or the health of a brother. Our accommodations compensated for all. I admire the soft soil of Georgia, and it is pleasant to see the people ploughing on the last of November, as if it were the month of April. The weather was very cold on Thursday and Friday. Saturday I rode seven miles up to Hudson's ford, at the mouth of Trail-Creek, to have a sight of Oconee-River. Jesse Lee visited the forks of the river, and formed a circuit for one preacher. The land upon the river is good. I returned to Henry Pope's.

Sabbath day 30. The weather still continues cold. At the new meeting-house my subject was Hebr. iii. 12, 13, 14. There appears to be more wealth than religion here.

Monday, December 1. We rode twelve miles, in a very damp day, to the widow Steward's : we had a large congregation for the day and place. The widow's house stands upon a line between Green and Oglethorpe counties.

Tuesday 2. At Greenesborough, in a large meeting-house built by and for the Presbyterians, we held meeting. We lodged at William Ufton's. We have travelled in two days about thirty-two miles. The badness of the weather, and my constant uneasi-

ness have injured me much : I have spoken very little in public :—
I drag along exceedingly heavy. It is serious work to be driving
through the back settlements, and having open meeting and dwelling houses, in the winter season.

Wednesday 3. At Burke's meeting-house Jesse Lee preached,
and I exhorted upon the importance of the ministry, and ordained
brother Watts a local deacon. We lodged at John Crutchfield's ;
where we had a gracious family meeting.

Thursday 4. We moved along in a cloudy, damp, cold day, fourteen miles, to Little Britain, a log pen, open at the top, bottom, and
sides : a few people attended ; my subject was Matt. vii. 8.

Friday 5. We rode, fifteen miles, through a heavy rain to Hill's
meeting-house, upon Long-Creek, where six or seven preachers,
with a few people attended : my subject was Hebr. x. 32. Hope
Hull, Josias Randall, S. Cowles, and William Partridge came a long
way to see me ; we had a family meeting at mother Hill's. It is
about twenty years since I first visited this house.

Saturday 6, and Sabbath day 7. We held our quarterly meeting
at Mark's meeting-house : I had dreaded this appointment. I had
some pain and some pleasure. The state of religion is low here.
Hope Hull preached on Saturday upon Jer. x. 8. we had some
signs to show that life had not entirely departed, in the love-feast
and sacrament. Benjamin Blanton preached Sabbath day, from
Isai. xxviii. 8. and I gave a gloss upon Joshua xiv. 8. " Nevertheless, my brethren that went up with me made the heart of the people melt ; but I wholly followed the Lord my God." In the introduction peculiar attention was paid to the dealings of God with
Israel from the beginning to the end ; the influence pious characters had in the case before us—two prevailing against ten ; that
the well-being of future generations required that a decided tone
to the morals, manners, and religious opinions, should be given by
the first settlers of the country. The weight of the discourse was
opened in two divisions ; First, What God had done for many
Christians ; Secondly, Their unfaithfulness and complaints, (like
the Israelites) and their bad influence upon the camp of Israel, as
at the present day.

Monday 8. We rode twenty miles to Hope Hull's, near Washington, in Wilkes county.

Tuesday 9, we rested ; and on Wednesday 10. I gave a discourse
at Coke's chapel, upon Gal. vi. 9. The rain began as we closed
the meeting. I dined at D. Merriweather's, and rode home with

Thomas Grant that evening, and was detained on Thursday and Friday in consequence of a rain.

We have had an exceedingly heavy rain : the Little River was impassable ; but I was kindly and comfortably provided for. I lament the state of religion in these new settlements. New lands, new officers, and new objects, occupy the minds of the people. I invented a continental general plan of movement through the eastern and western states, not much short of seven thousand miles.

Saturday 13. I made an attempt to reach Philips's bridge : but was soon stopped by a creek. Thence we went to a milldam, full of holes and rolling stones. I did not choose to risk the overturning of the carriage into the millpond or the creek ; so I returned to D. Merriweather's, and appointed a meeting at Coke's chapel, and upon the Sabbath day gave them a long, weighty talk upon 1 Cor. vii. 29.

Monday 15. We had to take the rain and mud upon the Augusta road; the wagons had been detained by high water ; men and wagons were very heavily loaded with rum. We rode twenty-four miles, and were kindly entertained at William Shield's.

Tuesday 16. Rode ten miles to James Allen's, and behold, neither the man nor his wife were at home ; the day was far spent, and it was raining, so we stopped.

Wednesday 17. Before we could get ready to move, it began to rain powerfully. We came down the Augusta road, gouged up by wagons in a most dreadful manner, in consequence of which, we were five hours in going twelve miles to Thomas Haine's, upon Uchee. I had great *intestine* war, having eat but little ; but here we have all things comfortable. I doubt whether we shall be able to cross Savannah-River in five days from this time ; the former freshet being increased by latter rains.

Thursday and Friday we rested. Saturday 19. We rode to M'Gee's to attend an appointment ; but the rain prevented the people from coming.

Sabbath day 20. We came into Augusta town. I went in the morning to *hear* a sermon, and in the afternoon I *gave* one upon Hebr. ii. 1. We have preached several years in this town, but with little success : we want a house of our own here. On Monday 21 the waters were much assuaged. Augusta town is greatly improved in houses since I was here last. The boat trade from Savannah is very considerable. After waiting an hour on the banks of the river, we crossed, and came in about sunset, after riding twenty-two miles to Cooper's in the pines.

SOUTH CAROLINA.—Tuesday 22. We came twenty-three miles to Chester's, the best entertainment we could find : it was but for a night.

Christmas day 25. We rode twenty-three miles to a *pole* meeting-house, near Trotty's ; thence ten miles to Jacob Barr's : here I was once more at home.

Thursday 26. We rode down Edisto-River, which was much swelled by the late rains ; I dined at Murray's ; we then proceeded up the stream to Mr. Hall's : we have rode twenty-five miles this day.

Friday 27. We crossed at Fourhold's bridge, which was scarcely passable, the water being deep, and spread out upon the low land nearly three quarters of a mile.

I came accidentally to my appointment at the Cypress chapel. My text was 1 Tim. ii. 5. " For there is one God, and one Mediator between God and men, the man Christ Jesus." I. The great proportion there is between a holy God and fallen mankind. II. The absolute, indispensable necessity of a mediator in nature and office.

Saturday 28. I never knew worse roads. I needed one to hold on one side of my carriage to prevent my being overset in the mud. Sabbath day I preached in the old church upon Psalm cxviii. 24, 25. On Monday and Tuesday we had a little rest.

Wednesday, January 1, 1800. We began our conference in Charleston, twenty-three members present. I had select meetings with the preachers each evening, who gave an account of the dealings of God with their own souls, and of the circuits they supplied the past year.

Saturday 4. After determining by a large majority that our next meeting together (by divine permission) should be in Camden ; the conference rose.

Slow moved the northern post on the eve of new year's day, and brought the heart-distressing information of the death of Washington, who departed this life December 14, 1797.

Washington, the calm, intrepid chief, the disinterested friend, first father, and temporal saviour of his country under divine protection and direction. A universal cloud sat upon the faces of the citizens of Charleston ; the pulpits cloathed in black—the bells muffled—the paraded soldiery—a public oration decreed to be delivered on Friday 14th of this month—a marble statue to be placed in some proper situation. These were the expressions of sorrow, and these the marks of respect paid by his feeling fellow-citizens to the memory of this great man. I am disposed to loose sight of all but Washington : matchless man ! At all times he acknowledged the providence of God, and never was he ashamed of his Redeemer : we believe he died, not fearing death. In his will he ordered the manumission of his slaves—a true son of liberty in all points.

Sunday 5. After the burden of care was thrown off, I again resumed the pulpit ; and in order the better to suit my subject to meet the conference, the new year, ordination of elders and deacons, and the General's death, I made choice of Isai. lxi. 2. " To proclaim the acceptable year of the Lord ; and the day of vengeance of our God to, comfort all that mourn."—

I. The acceptable year of the Lord.

II. The day of vengeance of our God.

III. To comfort all that mourn.

The congregation was large, decent, and solemn ; the ordination was attended with unction from above, and the sacrament with tenderness of heart. At the new church, before the ordination of deacons, Jesse Lee discoursed upon " The harvest truly is great," &c. After encountering many difficulties, I was able to settle the plan of stations and to take in two new circuits.

Monday 6. The main body of the preachers left the city. I desired Jesse Lee, as my assistant, to take my horse and his own and visit between this and the 7th of February, Croosawhatchie, Savannah, and Saint Mary's, (a ride of about four hundred miles) and to take John Garven to his station : the time hath been when this journey would have been my delight ; but now I must lounge in Charleston.

Sunday 12. We have had a week of snow, which made the ways extremely mirey. I attended the church in Cumberland-street ; my subject was 1 Peter i. 17—19. I did not enter, as I wished, into the marrow of the subject.

Monday 13. Benjamin Blanton left me to attend his charge of preachers, circuits, and to promote the sale of our books, within the limits of the Charleston conference. I have kept no journal from Sabbath to Sabbath. I have been employed in reading and answering letters to different and distant parts of the continent.

Sunday 19. My subject was 1 Peter i. 6, 7. I have been very unwell since Friday, but as I only attempt to labour upon Sabbath days, I could not stand back from duty ; I was greatly assisted in the morning, but much outdone in the afternoon in body and mind.

At intervals Nicholas Snethen read to me those excellent sermons of Mr. James Saurin, a French Protestant minister at the Hague ; they are long, elaborate, learned, doctrinal, practical, historical, and explanatory.

No journal until Friday 24. I have been very unwell in my bowels ; C. Patton sent me a decoction of bark, rhubarb, and nutmeg, which helps me much. This week I employed in answering my correspondents in the District of Maine, Massachusetts, state of New-York, Jersey, Pennsylvania, and Virginia. On Thursday night departed this life Edward Rutledge, governor of South Carolina ; he was one of the tried patriots of 1775 and 1776. The Africans give him a good character for his humanity : on Saturday 25, his dust is to be committed to dust. " I have said ye are gods ; but ye shall die like men, and fall like one of the princes."

Sunday 26. I was under some weakness of body and mind. I attended at the old church, and preached on Romans xii. 9—11. January 30th we had another snow. February 3d, I have kept no journal for some days. Sabbath was a cloudy day with rain ; my sacramental subject was Rev. i. 5, 6. I have had a distressing cold in my head ; notwithstanding which I have read much in books, letters, and lives.

Wednesday 5. I began to relax my mind from writing long letters. I dined with Jesse Vaughan, and afterward visited Mr. Warnack's family, at the orphan house ; there is no institution in America equal to this ; two or three hundred orphans are taught, fed, and clothed, and then put apprentices to good trades.

Friday 7. Jesse Lee and George Dougharty came to town : the former hath been a route of about six hundred miles ; and my poor gray hath suffered for it.

Sunday 9. I gave my last charge at Cumberland-street church from Rom. xii. 14—18.

Monday 10. I left the city of Charleston ; the day was cold and the roads bad : we came through Broughton swamp ; in the evening my carriage got set fast ; the second draught, the hook upon the swingle tree gave way, and I had to take to the mud to fix the traces ; at half past eight o'clock we came to Monk's Corner.

Tuesday 11. It snowed ; I was distressed for a wagoner whose horses ran away at the sight of my carriage, and whirled the wagon among the stumps and trees, happily no considerable injury was suffered. We lodged at the widow Turk's, near Nelson's Ferry— an extremely cold night.

Wednesday 12. We wrought our passage over and through the river and swamp, and as long as we kept the public road it was all swamp: we at length came to Gibson's chapel; where I preached upon James i. 25. We dined at Bowman's, and in the evening held meeting at Mr. Gales's.

Thursday 13, was a very cold day: it terminated in rain: no meeting at Bradford's.

Friday 14. We came to Rembert's, where, at three o'clock I spoke upon Hebr. iii. 3. to a few people; brother Snethen also gave them a discourse.

Saturday 15. We came to Camden: the weather is still cold; we stopped to feed at Navy's. We have rode, since Monday last, one hundred and thirty miles, and my horse would not have been so outdone in two hundred, if three hundred miles, upon good roads. My soul hath been kept in patience, and much prayer; my body is in great weakness, undergoing disagreeable changes with the weather, and my constitutional maladies.

Sunday 16. At Camden I preached upon 1 Cor. vi. 19, 20. We administered the Lord's supper; the day was cold for this climate; and but few people attended.

Monday 17. We rode twenty miles to Horton's; and on Tuesday 18, held meeting there.

Wednesday 19. We rode forty miles through the sands, and roads made bad by snow and frost; we were travelling as late as eight o'clock in the evening, groping in the dark until a boy guided us along by the blaze of pine wood to brother Shaw's peaceable dwelling: he was gone to his circuit, but his gracious wife and children were at home.

Thursday 20. At Jackson's meeting-house, we had some gracious feelings. After an absence of ten years, I called once more at friend Pace's.

Friday 21. We attended a meeting at Anson court-house. We had no small congregation at Mr. Cashe's new house: I was kindly entertained at his father's when in Virginia and Tennessee, and now by him: they offered us money, food, lodging, or whatever we wanted. At Threadgill's meeting-house, N. Snethen preached; we then hasted to Mr. Atkin's: we were compelled to wade Rocky-River—the water came into my carriage box.

Sunday 23. At Randell's church, in Montgomery county, (N. C.) I gave a discourse after brother Snethen, upon 1 Sam. xii. 23.

Monday 24. We came to Ledbetter's.

NORTH CAROLINA.—Tuesday 25. Crossed Pee Dee at Tindelsville, and landed at Andersonsborough without any difficulties; but when we came to Williams-Ford, across the River, it was impassable;

we then changed our course, and took the ridge road, which was open to the Montgomery line, thence we had to guess our way, until we came to Edward Harris's, where we fed, dined, and prayed with the woman and children, and then came on we knew not where. As the sun began to decline, we thought it time to look out; to our surprise we saw a Friends' meeting-house, as we judged by its form; I then concluded we could not reach Deep-River, and we stopped at John Henley's—we had all we wanted but prayer.

Wednesday 26. I had to pass over heavy hills, rocks, and small runs, and through thick clay: we were concluding when in Charleston, and after we set out, by the excessive cold, that there was snow not far distant: when we came into North Carolina, we found that upon Pee Dee, and Yadkin, and Deep rivers, the snow had fallen fifteen and eighteen inches deep, and continued nearly a month upon the ground, and had swelled the rivers, and spoiled the public roads. We lodged at Mr. Bell's; having rode only fifty miles in two days. We left two appointments on the west side of Uwany: so much for that siege: my horse had hard work; my carriage was very loose in the joints by constant and long play; and myself much tired; but I revived when I saw the lawyers going to the western courts: I thought, if they toiled and suffered for justice and silver, how ought I to labour for truth, and gold that perisheth not, and thousands of people, and hundreds of preachers.

Thursday 27. I gained a day by the overflowing of Uwany, and came to Daniel Sherewood's, in Guilford county, within twenty miles of the track I went down last fall.

Friday 28. It rained and snowed. I gave an exhortation, and ordained two deacons. We got our horses shod, and then rode to aged William Field's.

Sunday, March 2. We set out early and hasted through deep roads to the Hickory-Mountain chapel; not less then twenty-eight or thirty miles; N. Snethen went along, and preached to the people, and brought a few to meet me at friend Reeve's, where we dined about six o'clock.

Monday 3. We had no small race through Chatham county to Snipe's; we were lost three times before we came to Clarke's ferry, on Haw-River, and had to send a boy a mile for the ferryman, and wait nearly an half hour.

Tuesday 4. A clear, but very cold day. We were treated with great respect at the University, by the president, Calwell, and the students, citizens, and many of the country people: brother Snethen preached on "God forbid that I should glory, save in the cross of our Lord Jesus Christ." When the University is finished, I shall take notice of it; I stopped to baptise some children, and then rode on to Massey's.

Wednesday 5. We rode to Sihon Smith's; and I gave a lecture in the evening.

Thursday 6. We came to Raleigh, the seat of government; I preached in the state house: notwithstanding this day was very cold and snowy, we had many people to hear; I baptised a child, and came that evening to Thomas Proctor's.

Friday 7. We came to the Union church; many attended, but the excessive cold penetrated my whole system: we lodged at John Whitefield's.

Saturday 8. I rode twelve miles through the snow to Edmund Taylor's, senr. This week, from Monday to Saturday at noon, I have rode one hundred and ten miles: my mind is kept in great serenity. I have spoken every day but this.

Sunday 9. We have a great sleet: the healthy and the young went to Bank's church. At four o'clock we had a sermon at father Taylor's on Eph. iv. 3. "Endeavouring to keep the unity of the Spirit, in the bond of peace."—

I. The end; the unity of the Spirit.

II. The means; there might be a union in interest, in opposition, in sentiment, in ordinances, but not in the Spirit; that this union is a union in experiences by the Spirit; and in the spirits or minds of Christians. The means are set forth in the first and second verses of the same chapter; to walk worthy of their Christian character and calling—disorderly walking breaketh union. "With all lowliness," or every mark of humility: pride is sure to break union: it hath done it in heaven and Paradise. "Meekness;" unlawful passion will break union. "Long suffering;" if men will not suffer long from saints and sinners, they will break union with the Church of God.

Monday 10. I rubbed along, some how, to Smith's church; the distress I suffered in my bowels was great; and had been so for three days; my misery was so exceedingly great that I set off to leave the place; but my way from the dwelling-house lay by the church, the people were collected, I felt better, stept in, and gave an exhortation. I took *Stoughton's bitters*, and got relief; and then rode on to friend Harris's.

Tuesday 11. I preached a short discourse on Joshua's resolution, and rode twelve miles to E. Taylor's, junior: I felt unwell.

Wednesday 12. I attended the funeral of sister Broadie; she professed religion three years, lived happy, and died in the Lord. N. Snethen preached the funeral sermon from " A good name is better than precious ointment; and the day of death better than the day of ones birth." I gave some sentiments on " God forbid that I should glory save in the cross of our Lord Jesus Christ."

Thursday 13. We crossed Roanoke at Taylor's ferry: the river was very full. Hail, ancient Virginia, once more! In little more than four weeks we have rode nearly two hundred miles in South, and three hundred in North Carolina. We came to Howell Taylor's. N. Snethen preached father Young's funeral, on Isai. lvii. 1. I could only exhort. We rode home with S. Holmes, fifteen miles, and it was well we did.

VIRGINIA.—Saturday 15, Was a stormy day. One of my friends wanted to borrow or beg £50 of me: he might as well have asked me for Peru. I showed him all the money I had in the world— about twelve dollars, and gave him five: strange, that neither my friends nor my enemies will believe that I neither have, nor seek bags of money: well, they shall believe by demonstration, what I have ever been striving to prove—that I will live and die a poor man. At Salem we had a good Sabbath; my subject was Rom. xii. 19—21. Our meeting held nearly three hours.

Tuesday 18. I preached at William Owens's on Psal. xxxvii. 39, 40. we had an open, living time.

Wednesday 19, at Myrick chapel. Thursday 20, at Dromgoold's chapel: Jesse Lee and N. Snethen did the preaching, and I rode home with Peter Pelham: this day's work was riding twenty-five miles. We crossed a bridge like a castle at the Westward-Ford.

Friday 21. We escaped another dreadful rainy day: a prodigious quantity of water fell: we were housed; not a single person came to meeting; but we had a sermon at noon, and one in the family at night.

Saturday 22. We set out for Sussex, but missed our way; we soon came to an impassable stream; I asked a poor, unintelligible negro, Who lived near? he said, Lewis *Gig*, I recollected Grigg, and we went straight to his house and dined. We then pushed on, and finding the Three-Run-Creek too deep to cross, took up our lodging at J. Fisher's.

Sunday 23. We rode fifteen miles to Jones's chapel: I was very unwell, but gave a sermon on Hebr. xii. 28, 29. we had three sermons, N. Snethen, and Jesse Lee having followed me.

Monday 24, at Pennington's I spoke on Hebr. xiii. 20, 21. As we had reason to believe the river Notaway was impassable at Allen's bridge, we rode back seven miles to Smith's. Tuesday morning we had to ride nearly one mile through the water, which was sometimes knee deep, and sometimes up to our horses sides : after riding seventeen miles, we came to Mr. Briggs's about twelve o'clock ; the day was extremely cold, and indicative of snow : we gave two sermons ; my subject was 1 Cor. vii. 29, 30.

Wednesday 26. We gave an exhortation at Lane's chapel ; lodged at Philip Davies's ; and on Thursday 27, we rode to J. Moody's, twenty-four miles : we crossed Black-water at Broad-water-bridge —it was very deep wading. Brother Snethen preached in the evening.

Friday 28. At Blunt's chapel : here I was unable to add many words. The probability is we shall hold conference in this neighbourhood, as the small-pox prevails in Norfolk and Portsmouth, and the people in this settlement have made most generous offers to the preachers, provided they choose to sit in conference here. ·

Saturday 29, was a day of settled rain, and we were kept in the house, myself being very unwell.

Sunday 30. We rode sixteen miles through damp, cold, and cloudy weather, to a meeting-house near Everitt's bridge, not fit for a horse to stay in : I could not refrain from speaking on Psalm xii. 1. " Help, Lord, for the godly man ceaseth, for the faithful fail from among the children of men." See Isaiah lvii. 1. Micah vii. 2. It was observed, First, What the remaining remnant had to do when the truly pious were taken from the earth :—to be godly ; truly gracious souls ; faithful—faithfulness the test, and continued proof of such souls : the loss the world and the church sustained : moral men were valuable ; temperate men a loss ; friends to liberty and religion a loss ;—much more men of sterling piety.

Monday, April 1. We passed through Suffolk, and called upon Mr. Cowlings, whose pious father is gone to rest since I was here last. After twenty years, I called at Mr. Yerbery's, and then came on to Isaac Lunsford's. I was very unwell : for some days I have had chills, headach, and bilious symptoms ; to this succeeded violent vomiting, and a desperate night.

Tuesday 2. We came to William Wright's, on Pig-Point, where I preached a little on Hebr. x. 29.

Wednesday 3. At Crany-Island chapel : here dreadful havoc hath been made by James O'Kelly ; a peaceable society of nearly

ifty souls are divided, and I fear in the end, some may be destroyed : how he hath done this work we may know by reading
his Apology. N. Snethen gave a great discourse on 2 Cor. xiii.
5, 6, 7. It is astonishing to hear the falsehoods published against
me. I lodged at James Carney's.

Thursday 4. At Jolliff's I read a most gracious account of the
work of God on the eastern shore—in Cecil county, Duck-Creek,
and Dover, in the state of Deleware. I published it in the congregation, reading the letter : my subjects on which I preached, were
Hebr. xii. 15. and Luke xvii. 5.

Friday 5. We rode to James Taylor's : I was deeply afflicted,
probably occasioned by my eating of fish : I exhorted a little, administered the Lord's supper, and then rode twenty miles to Portsmouth, and gave a brief exhortation in the neat, new house. Saturday I visited the brethren in Norfolk : they presented me with
a plan of a new house, fifty by seventy ; and, wonder of wonders !
it is to be built on the lot adjoining that on which the old Episcopal
church stands !

Sunday 7. My subject was 1 Cor. xi. 1—5. We administered
the sacrament. In the afternoon I exhorted in Portsmouth, but it
was an offence to some that I did not preach, weak as I was ;—and
we had to administer the sacrament here also.

Monday 8. We rode forty miles to William Powell's, in Isle of
Wight county : it caused tears and some disappointment, because
I did not stop at Suffolk.

Tuesday 9. We went on to William Blunt's. Wednesday,
Thursday, and Friday, we passed in close, comfortable conference.
We had great accounts of the work of God in the state of Delaware, and also Franklin circuit, in Virginia. We had grace, but no
gold, and we wanted one hundred and forty-three dollars of silver
to pay the just demands of the preachers to their sixty-four dollars
per year. Friday afternoon we rode fifteen miles to Mooring's.

Saturday 12. We rode twelve miles to old James-Town ferry :
we crossed, and had a very good passage, notwithstanding it was a
very stormy day at times, with heavy showers: we then rode
twelve miles to James-City, and lodged at Edmund Taylor's : my
company felt the effects of being exposed to the rain : I was safe
under a cover, but had as much as I could well bear.

Sabbath 13. I preached at James-City chapel, on Col. iii. 1, 2.
we concluded our meeting at two o'clock, dined, and rode sixteen
miles to the widow Kerby's. A great hail storm came on a few
minutes after we got in

Monday 13. After the rain was over, we stood our course to Hampton: we came in about two o'clock. Brother M'Kendree preached the funeral sermon of a little child at three o'clock, myself spoke at five, brother Snethen at seven o'clock. My subject was Phil. iii. 8, 9, 10.

Tuesday 14. We rode back to York. I saw the grave where was buried the effigy of General Washington, at the probable place where Lord Cornwallis delivered up his sword to him. We lodged at brother John Stubb's, in Gloucester.

Wednesday 16. At Mount-Zion, Jesse Lee came in before us, and had began to preach : I had a headach and fever, so said but little ; I had the pleasure of beholding with my eyes the excellent plantation of Mr. Tabb, and of receiving every favour the heart of love, and the hand of liberality could bestow.—I am *a stranger that tarried.*

Thursday 16. At Cheese-Cake I said a little upon James ii. 5. here is a new house and society. Since I was here ten years ago, my old friend Douglas is gone to his long home.

Friday 17. We came in haste to Urbanna, fifteen miles. There had been some notice given that there would be preaching here : the court-house doors were opened, but not one soul appeared ; we paraded upon the green awhile, and then went to the ferry ;—wind and tide both ahead—a leaky boat, weak hands and oars, heavily loaded in the bow with four horses, and one of them ready to leap out : they cried out to me to put back ; after some hesitation, I thought we must go back or to the bottom : after cruising two miles, brother M'Kendree and brother Snethen waited ; brother Andrews and myself covered our retreat by riding twenty miles into Essex, and about sunset stopped at the widow Hundley's.

Saturday 19. We rode fourteen miles to S. Coles's. I judge I have travelled little short of five hundred miles this route, over Virginia ; having been in nineteen counties.

Monday 21. We rode twenty-five miles through a storm of rain to the widow Bauzee's.

Tuesday 22. We crossed at Port-Royal, and came to the widow Bombry's : here we joined brothers M'Kendree and Snethen. Wednesday 23, we rode forty miles to Ward's, near Dumfries, and Thursday 24, to Alexandria, and gave a short discourse on James i. 12. I knew not which was best—to attend the quarterly meeting in Fairfax, or to go to Baltimore ; I at length concluded upon the latter. We came through the federal city, and were afterward lost an hour in the woods, and were benighted. We called at the widow of senior John Worthington, and saw the old mansion ; we were kindly entertained, and had a comfortable night's rest.

MARYLAND.—Saturday 27 We came to the city of Baltimore, where I found cause of joy and sorrow.

Sabbath day 28. I attempted a discourse on James v. 8, 9. Bishop Coke is on his way to this city.

Monday 29. I visited, and prepared for the arrangement of the preachers at the annual conference for another year. The great accounts of the work of God in various parts, are as cordials to my soul. I am persuaded that upon an exact measurement, I have travelled eleven hundred miles from the 10th of February, to the 27th of April : my horse is poor, and my carriage is greatly racked.

Thursday, May 1 We opened our conference, and in three days we concluded our work in peace.

Monday 5. We came to Baltimore, and Tuesday 6, we opened our general conference, which held until Tuesday 20. We had much talk, but little work : two days were spent in considering about Doctor Coke's return to Europe, part of two days on Richard Whatcoat for a bishop, and one day in raising the salary of the itinerant preachers from sixty-four to eighty dollars per year. We had one hundred and sixteen members present. It was still desired that I should continue in my station. On the 18th of May, 1800, elder Whatcoat was ordained to the office of a bishop, after being elected by a majority of four votes more than Jesse Lee. The unction that attended the word was great ; more than one hundred souls, at different times and places, professed conversion during the sitting of conference. I was weary, but sat very close in conference. My health is better than when we began.

Tuesday 20. I came to Greenwood, (Philip Rogers's,) and Wednesday 21, I preached at Patapsco-Neck chapel, on Psalm lxxx. 17, 18, 19. We called at Tobias Stansbury's, and dined, talked, and prayed with his afflicted wife, who felt her confidence in God. We then came on to Perry-Hall, and were received with great openness of heart. Mrs. Gough is, I hope, dying to the world, and living to Jesus. Mr. Gough is most affectionately kind.

Thursday 22. We came to Gunpowder-Neck : bishop Whatcoat preached and I exhorted : I trust the Lord will return to this house. I believe some felt the word this day. We went home with Stephen Watters, once more, after an absence of sixteen years.

Friday 23. We came to Abingdon; the bricks are fallen down; the probability is we shall not rebuild with hewn stones. My text was Isai. xl. 10. "Behold the Lord God will come with strong hand, and his arm shall rule for him; behold his reward is with him, and his work before him." This text was given me by opening my Bible at the sitting of the general conference, when I trembled a little for the ark. The people have improved the chapel here; it was not burnt with the college, although it was within twenty yards. We lodged at William Smith's; it is above twenty years since I lodged at his father's house.

Saturday 24. We were at Bush Forest chapel; the most ancient in this circuit: my subject was Isai. xxxv. 3—6.

Sabbath day. We were crowded, as it was quarterly meeting. I went home with J. W. Dallam: I walked to the grave of my once dear Sally, his former wife.

DELAWARE.—Monday 26. I crossed Susquehannah, and came to North-East, we stopped a night at Howell's; brother Whatcoat preached.

Tuesday 27. We rode up to Back Creek, (a Bethel indeed,) at four o'clock, I gave a brief discourse on 1 Cor. vii. 29—31. The people sang and leaped for joy of heart; they have beaten down strong drink, and the power of God is come. We lodged at John Caman's.

Wednesday 28. At the Manor chapel we had a great time; my soul was divinely refreshed. We lodged at Governor Bassett's.

Thursday 29. We came down to Bridgetown, at the head of Chester River. In the evening I lectured upon Luke xix. 44. "Because thou knewest not the time of thy visitation." I gave the people one caution; I observed, First, What always marked a time of visitation to a people collectively and individually. Secondly, What our Lord must mean by knowing or not knowing this time of visitation; that it was the improving the time for all the valuable purposes designed. Thirdly, The dreadful consequences which will undoubtedly follow the not knowing, not improving a time of visitation;—that we might fear that every calamity which might come on us in time was judicial;—and eternal torment. I have been led to meditate upon what are the happy consequences of a revival of religion—pure doctrine—strict discipline—great harmony—love and life.

Friday 30. We were at Blackstone's chapel : brother Whatcoat preached ; I gave a short exhortation ; and several of the preachers joined in prayer. I rode in the afternoon into Dover forest, and lodged at Cox's, formerly Lockwood's ; but he is gone hence : the people could remember that I had not been in this neighbourhood for fifteen years.

Saturday 31. I preached at the forest chapel, on Habakkuk iii. 2. and rode to Dover that evening.

Sunday, June 1. This was a day to be remembered : we began our love-feast at half past eight ; meeting was continued (except one hour's intermission) until four o'clock, and some people never left the house until nearly midnight : many souls professed to find the Lord. In the evening I rode up to Duck-Creek, to meet the conference.

Monday 2. We had sixty-six preachers, all connected with the business of conference : we sat closely six hours each day, until Friday 6, when about nine o'clock the conference rose. One hour was spent in public each day ; but the people would not leave the house, day nor night : in short, such a time hath been seldom known : the probability is, that above one hundred souls were converted to God. The stationing of the preachers was a subject that took my attention ; it was with the greatest difficulty I could unbend my mind from this one hour, yea, many minutes, by day or night, until I read the plan. I felt myself bound in spirit, and perhaps conscience also, to push on to hold the next Sabbath in Philadelphia. Bishop Whatcoat and myself hasted to Wilmington on Friday ; and on Saturday we dined with Mary Withy, now raised above her doubts, and rejoicing in God ; through her instrumentality, a small society is raised in Chester ; and she hath fed the Lord's prophets twenty-eight or twenty-nine years. We came on to Schuylkill ; and thence to Philadelphia.

PENNSYLVANIA.—Sunday 8. I preached morning and evening, at Fourth-street ; now making what it ought to be, and seated properly. I preached at the African church, on 2 Peter iii. 17, 18. and at St. George's, on 1 Peter. i. 5—7. I spoke only once at the conference ; my subject was Psalm xxix. 9. " And in his temple doth every one speak of his glory ;"—truly fulfilled at that time and place ; surely we may say, our Pentecost is fully come this year. When we recollect what God hath wrought in Edisto in South, and Guilford in North Carolinas ; in Franklin, Amelia, and Gloucester, in Virginia ; in Baltimore, and Cecil, in Maryland ; in Dover, Duck-Creek, and Milford, in Delaware ! My health is restored, to the astonishment of myself and friends. Monday and Tuesday in Philadelphia.

NEW-JERSEY.—We rode to Burlington, through excessive heat and dust, in company with Richard Whatcoat and Jesse Lee : the latter wished to preach in the evening, and go on in the morning. The Baptist minister had appointed a lecture, and invited brother Lee to take his place : he accepted, and preached an appropriate sermon on Acts x. 25.

Thursday 12. I gave a lecture in Burlington on 1 Cor. vii. 29—31. this is an awful place.

Friday 13. We came through heat and dust to New-Mills; we were comforted in God : brother Whatcoat preached ; I made a short discourse on Hebr. x. 32. I wished some to look back to former feelings, duties, experiences, and days. We have rode above one hundred miles since our departure from Duck-Creek.

Saturday 14. We had to stretch along through Julia, Job's, and Reckla's towns, to Cross-Creek. We stopped and fed at Mr. Lovell's ; where we refreshed ourselves an hour : we then came on to M. Moore's, where I preached on Rom. xii. 1, 2. We then took the road through Allentown, to Joseph Hutchinson's ; and came in, weak and wearied, about five o'clock.

Sunday 15. At Milford, I gave a brief discourse on Rom. xiii. 11. we attended at Mr. Ely's in the evening : a few souls there appeared to be deeply impressed with religious truth.

Monday 16. My horse drove heavily; and I did not get in to Brunswick until one o'clock. We had a meeting; and under exhortation many felt the word. We then hasted on to Mr. Drake's, near Amboy, where many were waiting : at five o'clock I gave an exhortation, and I believe it was felt.

NEW-YORK.—Tuesday 17. We were at Staten-Island ; where there is a neat meeting-house, and as genteel, well-dressed a people as in New-York. My subject was Hab. iii. 2. Appearances were rather unfavourable : I was very unwell, and came back to Mr. Drake's the same evening.

Wednesday 18. We rode in haste to New-York ; and on Thursday 19. we opened our conference ; about forty preachers present. We had some knotty subjects to talk over, which we did in great peace, plainness, and love. Friday and Saturday, we were closely confined to business. Sabbath. My subject at the old church was Romans xii. 19, 20, 21. In my introduction I observed that the text was quoted from Lev. xix. 18. and Proverbs xxv. 21, 22. that it might discover to us what veneration the New Testament wri-

ters had for the old ; and what was required in a believer, under
that dispensation. Vengeance is not in our province ; we cannot,
in civil, much less in sacred causes, be our own judges or jurors : if
we must feed an enemy, and not only forgive him an injury, but do
him a favour ; surely then we ought to love a friend, a Christian,
and more abundantly a minister of Christ. This day we made a
general collection for the support of the travelling ministry.

Monday 23. Our conference concluded its sitting. The defi-
ciences amount to six hundred and ninety dollars : the monies collected, and the draft on the chartered fund amounted to four hundred and five dollars. A motion was made to move the next yearly
conference more into the centre of the work, but it was lost.

Tuesday 24. I have now a little rest. We have had a mighty
stir in the Bowery church, for two nights past, until after midnight ;
perhaps twenty souls have found the Lord. Bishop Whatcoat
preached the ordination sermon in the afternoon at the Bowery
church. I have now a little time to unbend my mind from the stations ; but still my work is not done. Tuesday, Wednesday, Thursday and Friday, I employed myself in reading, writing, and visiting.

Saturday 28. We left the city ; and rode twenty-six miles through
heat, and plagued by the flies, to my old home at the widow Sherwood's : but my dear Betsy Sherwood, my nurse, is gone, I trust, to
glory.

Sabbath day 29. We had a remarkably cool day, after a great
storm of rain and hail. I attempted to preach at Sherwood chapel
on 1 Cor. xv. 34. "Awake to righteousness and sin not ; for some
have not the knowledge of God. I speak this to your shame." I
observed that the apostle in Rom. xiii. 11. Ephes. v. 14. 1 Thess.
v. 6. and in the text, had indicated a sleep which professional and
real Christians might fall into ; an awful insensibility and inactivity
to spiritual things, so as to bring an amazing stupor on all the powers of the soul ; so that it would be insensible to righteousness,
which is religion ; the justifying, and sanctifying, and practical
righteousness of a gracious, wakeful soul : "some have not the
knowledge of God ;" living in sin, neglecting duty, and without the
knowledge of God ; ignorant of the fear, favour, nature, and love
of God. Brother Whatcoat and John Wilson both spoke ; souls
were quickened. In the afternoon, at New-Rochelle, brother
Whatcoat preached, and I gave an exhortation ; many attended. I
feel as if there would be a revival of religion in this circuit this
year.

CONNECTICUT.—Monday 30. We came to Byram-Bridge, and at Banks's we had a crowded house, and a feeling time; the aged people were very attentive.

Tuesday, July 1. In consequence of our circumlocutory motions we have rode about fifty-five miles since we left the city of New-York. We came to Stamford, where brother Whatcoat gave a sermon on "The faith and choice of Moses." I had only time to speak a few words on Luke xix. 44.

Wednesday 2. We rode on to Norwalk; stopped an hour at brother Day's, and thence rode on to Fairfield. It was a cool day. We had an elegant view: the fields in full dress, laden with plenty; a distant view of Long-Island and the Sound; the spires of steeples seen from distant hills—this country is one continuity of landscape. My mind is comforted and drawn out in prayer. We had not time to feed nor rest. It was with some exertions we came in time to Joseph Hall's, at Poquonak. After we got a little refreshment and rest I gave them a short discourse on Luke x. 2. Strength and time failed me, and I could not finish and apply as I wished.

Thursday 3. We came to Stratford, and stopped at brother Wheeler's.

Friday 4. The weather is damp and very warm. We came on to New-Haven, where they were celebrating the Fourth of July. I fear some of them have broken good order, and became *independent* of strict sobriety. Bishop Whatcoat preached in the San-diminian meeting-house purchased by the Methodists.

Saturday 5. We rode through excessive heat, over rocks and hills, to North Bristol, twenty miles. I discoursed with some liberty on Acts xxvi. 18.

Sabbath day 6. We rode six miles to Punsit's new meeting-house. A revival of religion has begun here; a dozen souls have professed to find the Lord, and several young people are under gracious visitations, and the aged are exceedingly cheered at the prospect. Bishop Whatcoat preached in the morning, and in the evening I made some improvement from 1 Peter ii. 11, 12.; after which we administered the sacrament. We were engaged five hours in public exercises: the day was very warm. We have travelled since last Saturday week one hundred and forty miles.

Monday 7. We rode sixteen miles to Hadley. The day was awfully warm until one o'clock, when a gust came up of wind and rain; we ran from house to house, and escaped being *much wet:*

we stopped at Mr. Woods's. Tuesday we rode on to New-London; twenty miles of the way the roads were exceeding rocky. My soul was kept in peace, but under great temptations of various kinds. We crossed Connecticut-River at Chapman's ferry, near Old Haddam. Where the roads here are improved they are made for ages, and are much superior to those in the south or west.

Tuesday 8. Bishop Whatcoat held forth in the new house in New-London; his subject was "With him is plenteous redemption." I gave a discourse upon "Christ, the author of eternal salvation to all them that obey him."

Thursday 10. We came on to Norwich Landing. I preached in the neat, elegant Episcopal church on Acts iii. 26. I felt uncommonly set at liberty : we had a very decent, attentive, well-behaved congregation. From here we hasted on to Norwich-town. Bishop Whatcoat preached. We had a most agreeable ride on the turnpike road, upon each side beautifully smiling with variety and plenty ; the stage passed us like a whirlwind.

Friday 11. We came to Preston, and were kindly entertained at Isaac Herrick's. It was the very height of rye harvest, yet many came together. I was greatly led out on the *great salvation*. I was refreshed in soul and body, and rode on in the evening to Nathan Herrick's. The simplicity and frugality of New-England is desirable—you see the woman a mother, mistress, maid, and wife, and in all these characters a conversable woman ; she seeth to her own house, parlour, kitchen, and dairy ; here are no noisy negroes running and lounging. If you wish breakfast at six or seven o'clock there is no setting the table an hour before the provision can be produced.

Saturday 12. We took our departure for Rhode-Island through Plainfield. The weather is still excessively warm ; the roads sandy, stony, and rocky, notwithstanding the turnpike. We passed Sterling, the last town in Connecticut. We wandered a mile or two out of our way, and had to pay for it, by going a cross path : we made it twenty-six miles to General Lippelt's. The general hath built a neat chapel for the use of the Methodist Episcopal church near his house. I was taken with one of my bilious eruptions through the night.

RHODE-ISLAND.—Sunday 13. Richard Whatcoat preached in the morning. In the afternoon my subject was Exod. xx. 24. " In all places where I record my name I will come unto thee, and I will bless thee." It was a feeling time, although I was very unwell all the day, but I could not stand back from duty.

Monday 14. We came on our way to Boston, through Providence; here we did not stop; the time is not yet come. We stopped to feed at a house that was not very agreeable to me, and I was glad to come off without dining. We came to Deacon Stanley's, at Attleborough, where we took some refreshment, and reached Mr. Guild's, and took lodging.

MASSACHUSETTS.—Tuesday 15. We came through Wrentham, Walpole, Dedham, and Roxborough to Boston : it was a damp day, with an easterly wind, unfriendly to my breast. As they were about finishing our church we could not preach in it. The new state-house here is, perhaps, one of the most simply elegant in the United States. We made our home at Edward Haynes's, late from England, where we had most agreeable accommodations after our toil.

Thursday 17. We have dry weather. We came through much dust to Lynn.

Friday 18. We sat in conference ; there were twenty-one members present : we had great peace and union.

Saturday 19. The conference rose after voting the session of the next yearly conference to be held at Lynn. And now the toil of six conferences in seven months, and the riding of thirteen hundred miles, is over. I found some difficulty in stationing the married preachers.

Sabbath day 20. We had an elaborate ordination sermon from Matt. ix. 36—38. " But when he saw the multitudes, he was moved with compassion on them, because they fainted, and were scattered abroad, as sheep having no shepherd," &c. There had been a long drought here, and nature seemed as if she were about to droop and die. We addressed the Throne of Grace most fervently and solemnly, and had showers of blessings. Whilst I was preaching the wind came up and appeared to whirl round to every point, and most gracious rain came on : this I considered as a most signal instance of Divine goodness.

Monday 21. We came to Boston, and preached in the tabernacle, now nearly finished, on Hebr. iii. 12—14. We were generously entertained at Edward Haynes's.

Tuesday 22. Bishop Whatcoat preached in Boston from Psalm cxvi. 7. Wednesday we came thirteen miles to Waltham, where we had a meeting ; the subject was Rev. xxi. 6, 7.

Friday 25. We rode through Weston, where is a grand steeple, porches, and even stalls for the horses ; and it is well if they do not make the Methodists pay to support their pomp. Oh !

religion in New-England! We came through Needham, Sherburne, and Holliston, and made it thirty miles over Crook's Hills, through excessive heat. We had not time to stop to feed, as we had appointed meeting at Milford, where we arrived a little after one o'clock. I was obliged to let brother Whatcoat ride in the carriage, or I fear he would have fainted; this made me low spirited, and unfit to answer questions.

Saturday 26. We had to ride through excessive warmth thirty miles to Thompson's, but we took the day for it: we got to Capt. Nicholls's about six o'clock, where we have a house built, and some ground to set our feet upon. I have been of late powerfully tempted, and distressed in mind and body. We had a finely dressed congregation—a good name is a great matter with these people. O Baxter! are these thy apostate children? Will Methodism ever live in such whited walls and painted sepulchres as these people, who delight to dwell insensible to the life of religion, and closed up in their own formality and imaginary security? We have now returned to the first town in Connecticut.

CONNECTICUT.—Saturday 27. I preached at the new house in Thompson: my subject was Mark viii. 34.

I. I observed the harmony of the evangelists, Matthew and Luke with Mark.

II. That our Lord had given the clusters of the grapes of the Promised Land in blessings and promises.

III. He had given such demonstrations of his power upon the bodies of men; the dead were raised, the hungry fed, the lepers cleansed, the lame and the blind were restored, the wind and the sea were at his command.

IV. He opened the distinguishing conditions of discipleship; the denial of self in every temper and affection that is evil. They that seek to save their lives by denying Christ, shall loose soul and body; if it is through pride and shame, Christ will not dishonour himself by owning such in the day of judgment.

Bishop Whatcoat preached in the afternoon on "Acquaint now thyself with him, and be at peace," &c.

Monday 28. We rode sixteen miles to the north end of Eastford. We have travelled nearly one hundred miles since our departure from Lynn. My subject at Joseph Work's was Matt. v. 2. "Blessed are ye when men shall revile you and persecute you, and shall say all manner of evil of you falsely for my sake." We lodged at Nathan Palmer's. I stopped a few minutes at Mr. Woodard's, in Ashford. We came on to Coventry, twenty miles. We stopped at John Searles's, and were exceedingly well accommodated, both man and horse.

Wednesday 30. We rode to Mr. Spencer's in Hartford. My mind is in peace; but I have uncomfortable feelings in my body. Here I met brothers Bostwick and Borrough. We have a house built in Spencertown for the Lord, and now they are building one for the Lord's servants—for the married preachers to live in who are sent to the circuit.

Thursday 31. Was excessively warm; we made it little less than thirty miles to Bristol; we stopped to feed our horses, but neglected ourselves. When we came to Samuel Smith's we were nearly outdone by excessive heat and hunger. This day we crossed Connecticut River, and passed the cities of Hartford and Farmington.

Friday, August 1. Freeborn Garrettson came up with us: he attended the funeral of the venerable mother Livingston; who was suddenly, and safely called home, aged seventy-eight, removed by a paralytic, and probably it was apoplectick also: perhaps it was about thirty-four years ago that this godly woman was awakened under the first sermon the Rev. Dr. Sadly preached in the Reformed Low Dutch church in New-York, as she told me; nor she alone, but six or eight other respectable women. Madam Livingston was one that gave invitation to the Methodist preachers to come to Rhinebeck, and received them into her house; and would have given them more countenance had she been under no other influence than that of the Spirit of God and her own feelings. I visited her one year before her death, and spent a night at her mansion; she was sensible, conversable, and hospitable.

Saturday 2. We attended the quarterly meeting for Litchfield circuit: my subject was 2 Pet. iii. 17, 18. I had liberty in preaching, and some felt tenderness of heart, and evinced it with weeping eyes.

Sunday 3. We had a living love-feast; some from Waterbury were fervent in spirit, serving the Lord. We had a crowded congregation, a close day, and the house was shut up. In consequence of my breast being weak, I declined speaking in public. Bishop Whatcoat preached, and F. Garrettson exhorted. Our meeting began at eight o'clock in the morning, and continued, with a few minutes intermission, until two in the afternoon; after which we came off, over dreadful roads, twelve miles to Torringford. I was pleased to see a house bought and fixed for brothers Joclin and Batchelor, the stationed preachers of the circuit, and their wives.

These brethren we left behind to improve in the after part of the Sabbath, and quarterly-meeting.

New-York, Monday 4.—We came on and stopped at Goshen, at Captain Wright's : the people flocked together at a short warning, and I gave a discourse on Isai. xxxv. 3—6. after which we dined, and came on across the hills and over dreadful rocky roads to Cornwall ; where brother Whatcoat preached in the meeting-house on "We know that we are of God, and the whole world lieth in wickedness."

Tuesday 5. We had another tolerable siege over the Housatonnick River and hills to Sharon ; here brother Whatcoat preached on "The Lord knoweth how to deliver the godly out of temptation, and to reserve the unjust to the day of judgment to be punished." I gave an exhortation, and then we came rapidly, fifteen miles, to C. Levie's, in the Nine Partners.

Wednesday 6. We came to Row's : bishop Whatcoat preached on 1 John iv. 17. I gave an exhortation : we then came on to Robert Sands's, and lodged all night. We came on to Freeborn Garrettson's new design, upon the Rhinebeck flats ; he hath a beautiful land and water prospect, and a good, simply elegant, useful house for God, his people, and the family. We have rode between eighty and ninety miles since last Sabbath ; not less than five hundred and fifty since we departed from New-York ; and one third of the roads were rocky and very uneven. I read a book of about five hundred pages, the author of which is a curious writer.

Friday 8 and Saturday 9. We regaled ourselves and horses upon the pleasant banks of Hudson ; where the passing and repassing of boats and small craft, perhaps fifty in a day, is a pleasant sight.

Sunday 10. We had a sermon, and administered the sacrament at brother Garrettson's ; and notwithstanding public worship was held at the Dutch church at the same hour, we had a large congregation : bishop Whatcoat and myself filled up the service of the day.

Monday 11. I rested and visited Dr. Tillotson's, at his very elegant country seat, beautifully situated : the house is finely set round with trees ; and there is a charming view of the North-River. I was unwell internally. I must always take great heed to what I eat.

Tuesday 12. We came through Poughkeepsie—no place for Methodism. We stopped at Elijah Morgan's ; brother Thacher was preaching when we came in. We have rode twenty-five miles this day, and dined in the road upon a water-melon that Mrs.

Tillotson was kind enough to give us as we came by her house. I was so unwell that I had but little appetite for any thing else.

Wednesday 13. We came on twenty-five miles to Courtlandt-town, where we saw the aged, venerable pair, the Lieutenant Governor and his lady : he is in his eightieth, and she in her seventy-eighth year. I had a very rocky ride over the mountains of Peekskill. I have great and sore temptations at times, but God is with me : I trust through grace to overcome them all. We stopped at Warren's; fed, talked, prayed, and refreshed ourselves a little.

Thursday 14. This day is very warm. I preached at Peeks-kill-town, upon the great salvation. Brother Whatcoat preached at Croton. We lodged at General Van Courtlandt's.

Friday 15. At the Plains, Richard Whatcoat preached : I gave an exhortation. We then rode on in haste to the widow Sher-wood's.

Saturday 16. We pushed on with great courage, towards New-York, but when within six miles of the city, my horse blundered twice, and then came down with great force and broke the shaft : I got out, and my horse recovered from his fall; a smith's shop being at hand, the shaft was mended in an hour ; and we came into New-York and found our service was wanting in the city, there being here only two preachers, and one of them disabled.

Sunday 17. We had much rain ; the streets flowing with water like streams. I gave them a sermon at the Bowery church, on "Who gave himself for us that he might redeem us from all iniquity, and purify unto himself a peculiar people, zealous of good works :" and at the old church, John-street, I spoke on "But we are not of them who draw back unto perdition, but of them that believe to the saving of the soul." It appeared most advisable to stay awhile on Monday to have a new shaft put to the carriage. We landed at Powles-Hook about half past five o'clock, and pushed on to Newark.

NEW-JERSEY.—Tuesday 19. We came off at five o'clock, and reached Brunswick by twelve o'clock, where we dined and rested, and then continued on to Joseph Hutchinson's, at Milford, forty-six miles ; we had a pleasant and cool ride for the season.

Wednesday 20, we came on to Hulet Hancock's ; and on Thurs-day 21, reached Philadelphia. I preached at St. George's ; and Bishop Whatcoat at the African church.

PENNSYLVANIA.—Friday 22. We rode to the Valley ; it was warm enough. Bishop Whatcoat preached at Daniel Meridith's.

Saturday 23. We had a *proper* siege up to Sawders-town, and got in by four o'clock. I gave a discourse on Hebr. x. 38, 39.

Sabbath-day. Bishop Whatcoat preached at Martin Boehm's church on Psalm lxxii. 16—20. We have now rode, from Monday, one hundred and seventy miles. We lodged at Abraham Keaggay's. Our Dutch Methodists are as kind, and more lively than many of the American ones.

Monday 25. We crossed Susquehannah at M'Call's ferry ; it is narrow, but very deep and rocky. After feeding man and horse, we came on to Sittler's mill, on Muddy-Creek ; as we were ten miles from the place we intended to reach, well wearied, and having bad roads before us, we brought to an anchor here for a night. What time I have had to read, write, or journalize, those who know the distance and difficulties that must have attended me through the last week, may judge ; it would be impossible for me to relate all the workings of my heart ; but I trust my soul has been kept in patience and devotion.

MARYLAND.—Tuesday 27. We came into Maryland : sometimes we had no roads, and at other times old ones that the wagons had left : thus we bolted and blundered along the rocky rivulets until we came within sight of James Fisher's. The meeting had been appointed at the widow Jolly's : the house was large, and we had no small congregation : they came, some to see and some to hear. I had walked where I feared to ride, and it was exceedingly warm ; but I took courage when I saw the people : the portion which I gave them was 1 John ii. 24, 25. We had hardly time to eat and breathe, before we had to beat a march over the rocks, eight miles to Henry Watters's, upon Deer-Creek. Brother Whatcoat went ahead and preached, and I came on time enough to exhort a little.

Wednesday 28. I preached at the Forks meeting-house (fifteen miles on a carriage road) warm as it was. Brother Whatcoat gave us a good sermon upon " Return unto thy rest, O my soul !" and so on ; I exhorted very little. The heat continued. That evening we came with equal difficulties to *Perry-Hall;* but the greatest trouble of all was, that the elders of the house were not at home : the walls, the rooms no longer vocal, all to me appeared hung in sackcloth : I see not the pleasant countenances, nor hear the cheerful voices of Mr. and Mrs. Gough ! She is in ill health, and writes, " I have left home, perhaps, never to return :" this intelligence made me melancholy ; Mrs. Gough hath been my faithful daughter : she never offended me at any time.

Thursday 29. At *Perry-Hall.* I preached on Matt. xi. 28—30. I was visited by elders Bruce and Snethen. I heard the reply to Mr. O'Kelly's Apology; soft and defensive, and as little offensive as the nature of the case would admit. I was invited to town, with the assurance that there was no danger of the fever: but it was very bad at the Point.

Friday evening 29. I held forth in Light-street on Psalm cxv. 1. "Not unto us, O Lord, not unto us, but unto thy name give glory, for thy mercy and for thy truth's sake!" My improvement was the application to Christians; First, To contemplate mercy and truth in the dealings of God to them in the Gospel: Secondly, That they should disclaim all glory to themselves: Thirdly, How the Jehovah God giveth glory to himself; and how we should glorify him. Brother Roberts wrote that they were a thousand strong in Baltimore. That there hath been a work in Annapolis, is certain: indeed it begins to be more and more general in the towns, and in the country.

Saturday 30. We had a most severe ride, nearly twenty miles, to Daniel Elliott's. At St. James's chapel God hath begun to pour out his Spirit; and almost generally through Montgomery, and Frederick circuits.

Wilson Lee is all upon the wing in the work: glory! glory! glory! I will not speak of numbers or particular cases, without more accurate information, which in my haste I cannot now obtain; but without doubt, some hundreds in three months, have been under awakenings and conversions, upon the western shore, District of Maryland.

Sunday 31. At St. James's Chapel I preached on Psalm xxxvii. 39, 40. we had an attentive, solemn sitting; and powerful prayer closed the whole. We dined, and rode on five miles to Henry Hobbes's. The people heard of us, and ran together in the evening. Brother Whatcoat gave a lively discourse upon these words, "Thy children shall be all taught of God:" we had a very quickening season. Perhaps six hundred souls, in this district and in Baltimore, have been converted since the general conference. Hartford, Baltimore, Calvert, Federal, Montgomery, and Frederick, feel the flame. Monday we hobbled along to Clarkesburg, on the way dined at Joshua Pigman's: here I once more saw his brother Ignatius: art thou he? Ah! But Oh! how fallen! how changed from what I knew thee once!—Lord, what is man, if left to himself! Brother Whatcoat attended the meeting, and the people continued in meeting at Clarkesburg until the morning.

Tuesday, September 2. At the Sugar-Loaf, my subject was Luke x. 2, 3, 4. compared with Matthew xiii. 16, 17. and 1 Peter i. 10, 12. we were crowded : in the exhortations, prayers, and singing, the power came down, and the work went on until evening. I then rode to Mr. Morton's.

Virginia.—Wednesday 3. We came to Leesburgh : some said, go this, and another that way : we made it nearly twenty miles, and were riding six hours, and crossed the Potomac at Conrad's ferry. Brother George was preaching : bishop Whatcoat spoke upon " He that believeth shall not make haste ;" but we had to make haste, after I had ordained S. Welsh, and Eskridge Hall, to the deacon's office. After we had dined, we rode twelve, if not fifteen miles, to the widow Rozzell's : we came in about seven o'clock ; and I gave a discourse on 1 Tim. iv. 16. We have travelled about one hundred and fifty miles through Maryland ; and we have had bad roads, but have met with good people. My soul hath been agonizing for a revival upon the western shore of Maryland for many years : and now the Lord hath sent it.

Thursday 4. We came to Rector-Town : most distressing roads for eighteen miles. The gentry had made a dinner at a small distance from the town : a kind of green corn feast, with a roasted animal, cooked and eaten out of doors, under a booth. I was greatly wearied with the ride ; but was animated while explaining 2 Cor. vi. 1. I then came to Benjamin Hitt's. We have penetrated through Loudon and Fauquier counties in two days.

Friday 5. We stopped at the court-house, and were richly entertained with a breakfast, at Mr. Johnson's : then we rode on to Norman's bridge, and passed another *old field-feast*, with a race tacked to it. We came to Roger Abbott's, upon Mountain Creek, in the forks of the Rappahannock river ; and on

Saturday 5. To Kobler's ; where many attended from different and distant parts : my text was 2 Tim. ii. 15. We pursued our way six miles to the river, and lodged at a widow's house, whose husband died in the Lord a few years ago. We had an awful Sabbath day's journey, through part of Culpepper and Louisa ; we came to Ferguson's about half after one o'clock : the people were waiting in the warm sun : the house could not hold them : after a little rest, I cried *Now is the day of salvation.* We had a hungry ride for thirty miles.

Monday 6. We rode to Lastley's meeting-house, eighteen miles ; many people were gone to court, consequently, few at meeting ;

but the Lord was eminently present whilst I enforced Habakkuk
iii. 2.

Tuesday 7. We rode to Risanna in Fluvanna county : I have
seen the hot, warm, sweet, yellow, red, and now have passed the
green springs. When we came within six miles of Magruder's,
brother Whatcoat being in the carriage, the hindmost brace gave
way : I took hold of a sapling by the road side, and put it under
the body of the carriage, and brother Magruder mounted the
horse, and we soon came to his house : that evening the breach
was repaired. I took William M'Kendree's horse, and went on
fourteen miles, to Richard Davenport's, in Amherst ; where we
were kindly and comfortably entertained.

Wednesday 8. We rode twenty miles through heat and over
hills, to North Garden, *Tandy Kegs*, Albemarle county. I was
divinely assisted while I opened 2 Timothy iv. 2. 1. Preach the
word. 2. The application of it ; that is, reprove, rebuke, exhort ;
to time his work ; be instant, in season, out of season ;—in the
morning, noon, and evening of life :—when it is the winter, spring,
summer, and autumn of the church ;—in her pleasing and unpleasing prospects.

Thursday 9. We rode to New-Glasgow, thirty miles ; and were
entertained most hospitably at Colonel Merideth's.

Friday 10. We rode to Lynchburg, twenty miles. Samuel
Mitchell had dinner provided in town, at Mr. Miller's, for the
preachers. I preached in the Mason's Hall—a warm day and
place, on Titus ii. 12. We then beat along to Samuel Mitchell's,
three miles of rude roads.

Saturday 11. We rode to the New-London Academy, sixteen
miles, now under the direction of Samuel K. Jennings, a local
preacher of ours : the institution belongeth to the Presbyterians
and Episcopalians. R. Whatcoat preached : I was deprived of my
rest the last evening, and very unwell ; yet I gave a short discourse in exhortation. We have been going at such an unreasonable rate, that I have not had time to put pen to paper, for a week
together. Good news from the South District of Virginia : brother Jackson writes, " two hundred souls have been converted this
last quarter ; there is a revival in all the circuits but two ; and
great union among the preachers and people." I am kept in patience, faith and love.

Sunday 12. We rode sixteen miles to Liberty, and preached in
Bedford court-house : I was sick in earnest. When I came up

into the crowd, the people gathered around my carriage, as if I had had a cake and cider cart; this sight occasioned a kind of shock, that made me forget my sickness. After alighting, I went immediately to the throng in the court-house; and founded a discourse upon Matthew xxii. 5. What great things the Gospel revealeth to mankind; First, The love of God. Secondly, The sufferings, and death, and merits of Christ. Thirdly, The gifts, extraordinary and ordinary, of the Holy Ghost: men make light of all the blessings of God, and of all the miseries and consequences of sin: they not only think lightly of, but are opposed exceedingly to them; "for the carnal mind is enmity against God;" and the things of God. I admired the attention and solemnity of the people; many of the men standing in and out of the house the whole time. We rode two miles to brother Patterson's, and dined; and then came on to Blackwell's to lodge.

Monday 13. We had a heavy march to Fincastle: I rode nine miles to Mr. Ripley's; and then gave up the carriage to William M'Kendree, and took his horse, and came in about ten o'clock. My subject here was Isaiah lii. 7. First, The Gospel;—good tidings of God, of Christ, of the Spirit of grace, of glory:—by comparing temporal with spiritual things, to restore the dead, the blind, the lame, the dumb, the sick, the poor; publisheth peace with God; with conscience; with all men: good tidings of good; the spreading of the work of God: salvation;—from all our sin, misery, and death. Zion thy God reigneth;—the glory of Christ's kingdom. The feet of the messengers, *beautiful:*—because of their message. 2. Their holy walk: their treading the mountains, enduring hardship; their innocence.

We made it forty miles from Liberty to Edward Mitchell's; where we lodged on Monday.

Tuesday 14. We began our route for Holston, by English's ferry, through Montgomery county. The first day we came to Mrs. Dialley's, upon Roanoake, twenty-eight or thirty miles: the river ridges were very rough: Mrs. Dialley received us with great maternal attention and affection: here I was told of my appointment at Raboue's, ten miles west, over the mountains. It gave me some grief, but it was too late. I was advised not to go Pepper's ferry road.

Wednesday 15. We passed Montgomery-town and court-house among the mountain barrens; we pushed on to Christian's—they are British people; we had an acceptable rest for a very warm day. We came to the ferry, and lodged at Draper's (a very quiet house) that night.

Thursday 16. We came to Wythe court-house, a pleasant town of about twenty houses, some neat, and most of them new and painted. We had good accommodations at Mr. Johnson's—both man and horse needed it.

Friday 17. We began at 6 o'clock to bend for Holston : it was computed to be forty miles distant. We came in about the going down of the sun at father Carlock's, a German. For two days past we found we could not stop to dine ; we rested only to feed our horses. After we cleared the mountains we came upon the perpetual hills. I judge we may charge for one hundred and thirty miles from Edward Mitchell's, in Botteiourt, to Russel's old place upon Holston. We took Saturday to refit and write ; brother Whatcoat attended the meeting. My mind hath been kept in peace ; I had enough to do to drive ; I could think but little—only now and then sending up a message to heaven.

Sabbath day 19. We attended at Carlock's ; a very sultry day, and many people were present. My subject was 2 Tim. vi. 2—12. It was judged best we should ride ten miles to Scott's, in order to make Edward Cox's the next day, to attend at Acuff's.

Tuesday 21. As we came off it began to rain, and that rapidly, with little intermission for two hours ; the horsemen were dripping ; the roads were so bad that it was with some exertion that I could so shelter myself as not to get wet to the skin in the drowning rain. Monday, we passed Abingdon, which is greatly improved. Breakfasted at Craig's, and then had a pleasant ride to Cox's, but it is excessively warm for the country and season. At Acuff's I talked a little upon coming to the Throne of Grace. We hasted home with Charles Baker upon Holston. If we have a dry moon and month we may get through the wilderness.

Wednesday 22. We rested—man and beast. We have rode sixty miles since Sabbath evening. I am not as patient, dependent, and prayerful as I wish to be. Bluntsville looks very respectable, and they have built a needful and good bridge at the end of the town. We crossed at Charles Baker's by putting the chaise to two canoes and swimming the horses over Main Holston. The stubble fields were upon the north side, so that we were compelled to work through the woods into the road to Snipe's ferry. We came along eight or ten miles where they had made new cuttings ; at last we struck into a new road and strayed three miles out of our way, we then returned back two. Now it was that I felt *properly* content to leave my *felicity*, so called, before it came to the wilderness. We made it nearly thirty miles to Ball's mill; we had no time from six in the morning till seven at night to feed man or beast.

Friday 24. We rode twenty-one miles to Benjamin Van Pelt's, upon Licking-Creek; we fed our horses twice, the riders not once! Here I left the horse and carriage, and borrowed a horse to ride to Kentucky. Saturday, rode twenty miles across to Holston quarterly meeting at the Stubble Fields. I now rode upon horseback, and the rain came on powerfully until we were dripping. I had no cloak but the carriage covering, the rain took shoulders, elbows, and feet—for eight miles it was violent; I had not been so steeped for four years. I washed the wet parts with whiskey, and did not take the damage I feared. Oh thou of little faith, wherefore didst thou doubt? Bishop Whatcoat preached. Our local brethren were loving and lively—brothers Van Pelt, Wells, and Winton.

Sabbath day 26. We had a good sacramental and speaking time. I preached on Titus ii. 14. and brother M'Kendree from Psalm xi. 2—6. I was led to recollect the loss of time and difficulty met with from Bottetourt to Holston, one hundred miles—few friends, rough roads—one week lost in riding.

Monday 27. We began our grand route to Kentucky at eight o'clock. We had to climb the steeps of Clinch about the heat of the day; walk up I could not: I rode, and rested my horse by dismounting at times. We came to Hunt's for the first night. Such roads and entertainment I did not ever again expect to see— at least in so short a time.

KENTUCKY.—Tuesday 28. We came to Davis's to breakfast, and at night we slept at Ballinger's, upon Cumberland-River.

Wednesday 29. We came to Logan's and fed: this low and new land is scented; I was almost sickened with the smell. We came to the elder of the Panies's and lodged.

Thursday, October 1. We came rapidly to Job Johnson's, and reached it by riding in the night: now I began to fail.

Friday 2. We came on to our brother Howard's. We crossed Kentucky-River at the mouth of Hickman; it was so low that we forded it with ease. We have travelled in five days one hundred and forty-five miles. I have slept uncomfortably this week.

Saturday 3. I came to Bethel. Bishop Whatcoat and William M'Kendree preached: I was so dejected I could say little—but

weep. Sabbath day it rained, and I kept at home. Here is Bethel—Cokesbury in miniature, eighty by thirty feet, three stories,
with a high roof, and finished below. Now we want a fund and an
income of 300 per year to carry it on—without which it will be
useless. But it is too distant from public places, its being sur-
rounded by the river Kentucky in part, we now find to be no benefit: thus all our excellencies are turned into defects. Perhaps
brother Poythress and myself were as much overseen with this
place as Dr. Coke was with the seat of Cokesbury. But all is right
that works right, and all is wrong that works wrong, and we must
be blamed by men of slender sense for consequences impossible
to foresee—for other people's misconduct. Sabbath day, Monday
and Tuesday, we were shut up in Bethel with the travelling and
local ministry and the trustees that could be called together. We
ordained fourteen or fifteen local and travelling deacons. It was
thought expedient to carry the first design of education into exe-
cution, and that we should employ a man of sterling qualifications,
to be chosen by and under the direction of a select number of
trustees, and others who should obligate themselves to see him
paid, and take the profits, if any, arising from the establishment.
Dr. Jennings was thought of, talked of, and written to. I visited
John Lewis, who lately had his leg broken; I left him with good
resolutions to take care of his soul.

Wednesday 8. We rode fifteen miles to Shawnee-Run, and
crossed Kentucky-River at Curd's ferry; the river was as low as
a stream, and the streams are nearly dried up.

Thursday 9. I preached on Hebr. iii. 12—14. at the new house
at Shawnee-Run. We had rich entertainment for man and beast
at Robert Johnson's.

Friday 10. We rode to Pleasant-Run to John Springer's: it
was a very warm day for the season. I had a running blister at
my side, yet I rode and walked thirty-two miles. We refreshed
ourselves at Crawford's tavern upon the way. We have visited
Knox, Madison, Mercer, and Washington counties in this state. It
was strongly insisted upon by preachers and people that I should
say something before I left Bethel—able or unable, willing or unwilling; accordingly, on Tuesday, in the academical hall, I gave
a long, temperate talk upon Hebr. x. 38, 39.

Sabbath day 12. It rained excessively; we were shut up;
William M'Kendree met the people. We have had but two
Sabbaths to spend in Kentucky, and in both I was prevented by
rain.

Monday 13. We left John Springer's, and came to Lewis Thomas's, fifteen miles; a deep, damp, narrow path; the underwood very wet. Crossed Cartwright and Hardin's Creeks. I gave a short sermon on Rom. viii. 9. " If any man have not the Spirit of Christ he is none of his."—

I. How we are to know when we have the Spirit of Christ—by the operations, gifts, consolations, and fruits of the Spirit.

II. We are none of his if we are not interested in the offices, if not partakers of the redemption and privileges of Christ.

III. That none can be interested in Christ, who are not partakers of the Spirit of Jesus.

My system is greatly affected with the weather; but my soul hath abundant consolation in God. It is plain there are not many mighty among the Methodists in Kentucky. In travelling between two and three hundred miles, I have visited six dwellings besides the academy. At Pleasant Run, October 12, we ordained Joseph Ferguson, and Moses Crame, to the office of deacons.

Tuesday 14. We began our march for Cumberland. We were told by two persons, that we could not cross the Rolling Fork of Salt-River; I judged we could, and as I thought, so it was: we forded it with ease. We came up a solitary path east of the level woods, and struck into the road to Lee's ferry. For ten miles of the latter part of this day's journey, we rode through barrens of hickory, shrub-oak, and hazelnut; thirty miles, if not thirty-five, is the amount of this day's work; in the morning there was a very great damp, and in the afternoon it was, I thought, as warm as the west of Georgia.

Wednesday 15. We crossed Green River, the main branch of which riseth near the Crabb Orchard. We crossed at the mouth of Little Barren River. We then made a bold push for the great Barren's; dining at Mr. Morrison's; I could not eat wallet-provision, but happily for me I was provided with a little fresh mutton at the house, made warm in a small space. Now we had unfavourable appearances of rain; we had bleak, barren hills to ride; which, although beautiful to sight, were painful to sense. The rain came in large and rapid drops, for fourteen miles; we were well soaked on all sides. A little after dark we came to Mr. Hagin's, upon Big Barren River; a good house, an excellent fire to dry our clothing, good meat and milk for supper, and the cleanest beds, all this we had. I have paid for this route.

Tennessee.—Thursday 16. We came on to Lucas's: this poor woman was excessively displeased because I asked her if she

prayed with her children. Next day we made thirty-five miles to
Sharpe's. old place, where we had good entertainment ; they
charged twenty shillings for men and horses. We thence hasted
to Mr. Dickinson's, on White's creek. I waked at four o'clock ;
ate but little breakfast, and rode twenty-eight miles—the poor men
and horses were tired down ; we fed the horses upon the path, but
had no food for ourselves until we came in. I have thought, as I
rode along, that in travelling nearly six hundred measured miles,
we have had only six appointments ; and at these but small congregations : have we wearied ourselves in vain ? Our judgment is
with the Lord ; I can only say for myself, I have had the Lord's
presence, and great support in soul and body.

Saturday 18. At Parker's my subject was Col. ii. 6. Brothers
M'Gee, Lugg, Jones, and Spier, local preachers, came to meet
me : we had a small shout in the camp of Israel.

Sunday 19. I rode to Nashville, long heard of, but never seen
by me until now ; some thought the congregation would be small,
but I believed it would be large ; not less than one thousand people were in and out of the stone church ; which, if floored, ceiled,
and glazed, would be a grand house. We had three hours public
exercises. Mr. M'Kendree upon " the wages of sin is death." Myself on Rom. x. 14, 15. Brother Whatcoat on " When Christ, who
is our life, shall appear, then shall ye also appear with him in
glory." We returned the same evening, after dining with Mr.
M'Kain. I had a feeling sight of my dear old friend Greenhill
and his wife : who would have thought we should ever meet in
this distant land ? I had not time as formerly, to go to their house
to eat and sleep. We had a night meeting at Mr. Dickinson's.

Monday 20. We came by Manslick to Drake's creek meeting-
house, at the close of a sacramental solemnity, that had been held
four days by Craghead, Hodge, Rankin, M'Gee, and Mr. Adair,
Presbyterian officiating ministers ; we came in, and brother M'Kendree preached upon Jer. iv. 14. after him brother Whatcoat upon
" We know that we are of God :" I also spoke ; my subject was
the work of God. Last Sabbath was my birth-day. This will make
the thirtieth year of my labours in America. It is supposed there
are one thousand souls present, and double that number heard the
word of life on Sunday.

Tuesday 21. Yesterday, and especially during the night, were
witnessed scenes of deep interest. In the intervals between
preaching, the people refreshed themselves and horses, and returned upon the ground. The *stand* was in the open air, em-

bosomed in a wood of lofty beech trees. The ministers of God, Methodists and Presbyterians, united their labours, and mingled with the childlike simplicity of primitive times. Fires blazing here and there dispelled the darkness, and the shouts of the redeemed captives, and the cries of precious souls struggling into life, broke the silence of midnight. The weather was delightful; as if heaven smiled, whilst mercy flowed in abundant streams of salvation to perishing sinners. We suppose there were at least thirty souls converted at this meeting. I rejoice that God is visiting the sons of the Puritans, who are candid enough to acknowledge their obligations to the Methodists.

We have passed only two counties in the District of Mero: *quiet* Cumberland keeps " the noiseless tenor of his way" through the midst of the settlement; Nashville crowns its lofty bank.

Wednesday 22. We had a meeting at Richard Strother's, upon a branch of Station Creek, and there were great emotions of tenderness among the people.

Thursday 23. We came to Edward's. Brother Whatcoat began —I continued upon Matt. xi. 28—30. William M'Gee concluded. We lodged with James Douglass.

Friday 24. We came to Thomas Blackmore's. Brother Whatcoat, and brother M'Kendree sermonized; the people were not greatly moved; I concluded with prayer.

Saturday 25. We crossed Cumberland River at Bishop's ferry. What a long, solitary river is this! It is probably seven hundred miles upon a line; and near one thousand in its meanderings, before it empties its waters into the Ohio, twelve miles above the mouth of the Tennessee.

We began our quarterly meeting at Elmour Douglas's. Brother Whatcoat preached: brothers M'Kendree and M'Gee exhorted. At the evening meeting there were more shouters than converts; nevertheless the Lord was in the midst.

We have rode but about sixty-six or seventy miles this week. The country is greatly in want of rain: the large streams are much absorbed; and the people grind their grain with horse-mills.

I could not be content to leave the settlement without a circumstantial account of the work of God; and I therefore desired John M'Gee to give it me; and I purpose to select such accounts annually, and to read them in the large congregations, and then to have them published.

Sunday 26. I attempted but little this day in public, except a gloss on a portion of the word from 2 Peter i. 16. We forded

Cumberland River, and came to John M'Gee's. We now began to think seriously upon our march through the wilderness, and providing food and provisions for man and horse—we took our departure.

Monday 27. We travelled through rich forests of beech, with rank undergrowth of cane or reed, and arrived at Fort Blount: thence pursuing our way up Lynn-Creek, we took the ridge and reached Mrs. Blackburn's, where we lodged, and were well accommodated. This day we have rode thirty-five miles.

We urged on our way, expecting rain, which overtook us about two o'clock at Flat-Rock. We pressed on over Drowning-Creek, and the sleepy, discoloured waters of Obeys-River. About twilight in the barrens we met the Presbyterian ministers, Hall, Montgomery, and Bowman, with whom we rejoiced at the work of God in Cumberland, and then parted. We came on to a place where we found the woods were burning, and finding we had made about forty-five miles we encamped whilst the rain was falling upon us.

Wednesday 29. We came to the new station at the Crab-Orchard, where, although the station was not yet put in order, Mr. Sidnor received us politely, and treated us to tea. Here we found a cabin under the direction of the Cherokee nation, on land they claimed as theirs. We journeyed on to Spencer's Hill, so called because here a man of that name was killed by Indians. Thence we travelled forward to Prospect Hill and the descent to Cumberland Mountain. On our route we experienced a heavy rain. Through damps and mud we pushed forward to Clarke's ferry, upon Clinch, in sight of the fort at South-West Point, at the junction of Tennesse and Clinch rivers, one hundred miles below the mouth of Powels-River. We have travelled nearly seventy miles upon land belonging to the Cherokee nation: the soil is generally barren and broken, except where we enter on Cumberland Mountain and the neighbourhood of the new station. This Indian land cuts the state of Tennessee into two parts, passing nearly through the middle, making an indent upon the state of Kentucky on Yellow-Creek. We arrived at Mr. Clark's, where we received great entertainment: there was a good fire in the hall, and we were provided with a good dinner, and treated to tea: a fire was also kindled up stairs, at which we dried our clothes, to which may be added excellent lodging in two inner rooms: thus were we within, whilst our horses were feeding to fulness in a grassy valley without. Our kind host rents the land from the Indians at 600 per annum; himself making the improvements.

Thursday 30. We rode slowly on to Starr's, twenty-two miles, and had a heavy shower of rain on our way. From Monday morning to Thursday afternoon we have made one hundred and thirty miles ; we have experienced no stoppage by water-courses, and have found the roads of the wilderness, their unevenness excepted, pretty good. And here let me record the gracious dealings of God to my soul in this journey : I have had uncommon peace of mind, and spiritual consolations every day ; notwithstanding the long rides I have endured, and the frequent privations of good water and proper food to which I have been subjected ; to me the wilderness and the solitary places were made as the garden of God, and as the presence-chambers of the King of kings and Lord of lords.

Friday 31. I gave a long discourse upon the epistle in the office of ordination for deacons, and ordained John Winton in the congregation.

Saturday, November 1. Came twenty miles to Knoxville, of which I had often heard, and which mine eyes now saw. We visited my old friend Greer.

Sabbath-day 2. I preached in the state-house on Isai. lv. 6, 7. I was very unwell, but was enabled to bear the heavy cross of public speaking : we had about seven hundred people in and about the house. We came off in haste, intending to make twenty miles that evening ; but Francis Alexander Ramsay pursued us to the ferry, franked us over, and took us to his excellent mansion—a stone house : it may not be amiss to mention, that our host has built his house, and takes in his harvest without the aid of whiskey. We were kindly and comfortably entertained.

Monday 3. We rode up to M·Cleary's, fourteen miles, where we dined, and pursued our journey to William Blackburn's.

Tuesday 4. Rode twenty miles up Nolachucky to Benjamin Van Pelt's, where I had left my horse and chaise. In this neighbourhood the land, except a few spots, is little better than barren ; nevertheless, good cultivation will make it productive. From the twenty-seventh of last month, the day on which we left the pleasant mansion of our friend Van Pelt, to the day of our return, we rode, I presume, quite six hundred and sixty if not seven hundred miles. Hitherto the Lord hath helped us. We have had twelve proper appointments ; two of which (Sabbath days) were near failing because of rain.

Wednesday 5. At Van-Town I preached in the new chapel on Luke iv. 18.

Thursday 6. Crossed Nolachucky at Querton's ferry and came to Major Cragg's, eighteen miles. I next day pursued my journey and arrived at the Warm Springs, not however without an ugly accident. After we had crossed the Small and Great Paint mountain, and had passed about thirty yards beyond the Paint Rock, my roan horse, led by Mr. O'Haven, reeled and fell over, taking the chaise with him ; I was called back, when I beheld the poor beast and the carriage, *bottom up,* lodged and wedged against a sapling, which alone prevented them both being precipitated into the river. After a pretty heavy lift all was righted again, and we were pleased to find there was little damage done. Our feelings were excited more for others than ourselves. Not far off we saw clothing spread out, part of the loading of household furniture of a wagon which had overset and was thrown into the stream, and bedcloaths, bedding, &c. were so wet that the poor people found it necessary to dry them on the spot. We passed the side fords of French-Broad, and came to Mr. Nelson's ; our mountain march of twelve miles calmed us down for this day. My company was not agreeable here—there were two many subjects of the two great potentates of this western world—whiskey—brandy. My mind was greatly distressed.

END OF VOL. II.

CPSIA information can be obtained at www.ICGtesting.com
Printed in the USA
240714LV00002B/17/P